Social Work Administration and Development

Social Work Administration and Development

SANJAY BHATTACHARYA

RAWAT PUBLICATIONS
Jaipur • New Delhi • Bangalore • Guwahati • Kolkata

ISBN 978-81-7033-926-7

Reprinted, 2017

Published by
Prem Rawat for **Rawat Publications**
Satyam Apts., Sector 3, Jawahar Nagar, Jaipur 302 004 (India)
Phone: 0141 265 1748 / 7006 Fax: 0141 265 1748
E-mail: info@rawatbooks.com
Website: www.rawatbooks.com

New Delhi Office
4858/24, Ansari Road, Daryaganj, New Delhi 110 002
Phone: 011-23263290

Also at *Bangalore, Guwahati* and *Kolkata*

Typeset by Rawat Computers, Jaipur
Printed at Nice Printing Press, New Delhi

Dedicated to
my venerated father

Mr. Santosh Bhattacharya

the cascade of my brainwave

Contents

Contents

Foreword

Social welfare in general refers to the well-being of people, condition of having good health, comfortable living and working conditions, etc. The concept and the expression 'social welfare' in the sense of a scientific programme have developed in connection with the social problems of our industrial society. Poverty, sickness, suffering and social disorganization have existed throughout the history of mankind, but the industrial society of present century had to face so many social problems that the older human institutions – family, neighbourhood, church and local community could no longer sufficiently meet them. Thus, need for a broader system of social services resulted. Since that time voluntary, public and government agencies have taken a progressively greater responsibility for the well-being of the citizens.

Social welfare administration refers to those actions that are undertaken with regard to the systematic execution of social policy, in the organization and administration of public and private social services to an individual, group and community.

Social welfare administration is the integral part of development. In simple words development is a process of directed change towards some objectives that are accepted as desirable goals. It also implies progressive improvement in the living conditions and quality of life enjoyed by society and shared by its members.

It is very heartening to go through the contents of Dr. Sanjay Bhattacharya's book on *Social Work Administration and Development.* It is a very comprehensive book published on this subject matter. He has covered different aspects of social welfare administration and development in the Indian context. He has discussed various issues, procedures and functions in the perspectives of social welfare administration and development. The book thus is a thriving attempt in blending conceptual discussions with practical implications. The book is suitable for courses in developmental studies as well as for various organizations interested in improving their developmental work. Dr. Sanjay Bhattacharya deserves admiration for this monumental work.

K.M. Thomas
Assistant Development Commissioner (Rtd.)
Government of Kerala (India)

Preface

Any profession would necessarily have to be conscious of the context in which it is operating in order to be relevant in its functioning. Social work also has been constantly evolving and attempting to redefine its mandates as per the changing needs of society.

Professional 'social work' is focussed on facilitation of empowerment and change, and it is based on an interrelated system of values, theory and practices. It involves the conscious application of values, philosophy, principles, methods, and skills, in social work practice.

However, in spite of the appropriate changes, and evolving perspectives, the core values of social work remain unchanged, e.g., such as helping; belief in people and society; social – justice, economic, political and legal; and solidarity and partnership with the marginalized.

Today, the process of globalization and the ensuing problems have ensured that social work practice not only has to be 'native' but also needs to 'internationalize' strategies for practice. In India, one faces a duality of the phenomenon of technological changes and their impact, on the one hand along with the traditional feudal society and mind set on the other. One sees newer forms of slavery, through liberalization, privatization, and globalization through institutions such as the World Bank, IMF and its policies. The role of society in intensification of democracy is increasingly being highlighted and acknowledged.

All these changes are important to understand social work in India. Some of the aspects that do influence social work are political philosophy and policies, government policies, community's changing needs and administration need, economic changes and activities such as consumerism and feminism. Social work also faces the challenges of providing services at the local micro level, and in seeking macro level solutions dealing with structural causes, which are reinforced by globalization.

This book on *Social Work Administration and Development* emphasizes the need for developing strategies and approaches to suit the new socio-economic reality by linking and integrating social skills with technical skills. It also covers the issues that are undertaken with regard to an individual, group and community in the process of organization and direction of a social institution. There has been a definite relationship between social welfare administration and development and its various aspects have been discussed in this volume.

It is hoped that the reader will not only gain a perception of social welfare administration and development, but will also be able to approve and put into operation various practices in the organizations as well as institutional set-ups.

In other words, it is intended as an in-depth knowledge source for practitioners in the Social Welfare and Developmental fields. Therefore the book will be useful to the students taking cause in Social Work, Rural Development, Public Administration, and Economic Development, etc., as well as Development experts, practitioners of NGOs and government organizations.

Sanjay Bhattacharya

Acknowledgement

I would be failing in my duty, if I do not recognize the help rendered by several persons in completing this volume on *Social Work Administration and Development*.

First of all I heave my heart to the Almighty whose guidance is constantly a lamp of light for my pathway.

I am highly indebted to a large number of my acquaintances and well wishers who have offered me the benefit of their know-how in the present venture. In particular, I am grateful to Gracious Thomas, Director, School of Continuing Education, IGNOU, New Delhi, V.P. Singh, Director, Crescent Institute of Management, Bhopal, P.F. Abraham, Lecturer, Ambedkar College, New Delhi, Magi Maria, Director, CEROWC, Bhopal, S.R. Billora, Reader, Institute of Open and Distance Education, Barkatullah University, Bhopal, Late C.P. Mathew, Faculty of Social Work, and Sarvesh Agnihotri, Librarian, BSSS, Bhopal for their keen interest in my academic quest and who at different stages have made helpful annotations and invaluable assistance in completing this volume, and as such I express my thankfulness to them.

I owe a deep sense of gratitude to my family members especially my loving father, Mr. Santosh Bhattacharya for his constant support, encouragement and motivation that has been a source of inspiration to complete this volume with full enthusiasm. I am grateful to my wife Renu Sanjay for her practical cooperation in typing out my manuscript and it has been of great value to me.

I am grateful to Rawat Publications, Jaipur, for having taken interest in bringing out this publication.

I do wish that this book enriched the readers with comprehensive understanding and information about the subject matter. I would be grateful to those who come out with constructive suggestions that I shall duly acknowledge with my heart-felt thanks.

Sanjay Bhattacharya
E-mail: mail2drsanjay@yahoo.co.in

1

Indian Social Structure and Social Issues

Social structure is the very base for the proper understanding of society. Social structure is an abstract and intangible phenomenon. In a social structure, individuals are the units of associations and institutions. And these associations and institutions are the units of social structure and are interrelated in a particular arrangement. The ordered arrangement, seen between the units, creates the pattern of social structure. It refers to the external aspect of society which is relatively stable as compared to the functional or internal aspect of society. It is a "living" structure which is created and maintained for a time and changes.

Human beings have always regarded themselves as uniquely special and have a different order of intelligence than any other living being. Human being is a social animal and therefore civilized. The study of human society, therefore involves the study of culture. No matter what aspect or part of society is considered, the presence of a cultural mode of transmission is of paramount importance. The analysis of human society must certainly be carried out in the cultural base, and one important part of human sociology is the study of the cultural origin and significance of culture. But, on the other hand, social science is not, except in the broadest terms, concerned with the totality of culture. The content of culture is extremely diverse, and embraces much more than the society needs to encompass. It includes art, music, architecture, literature, science, technology, philosophy, religion and a million other things.

Human Society

The term 'human society' was coined by Auguste Comte, a French philosopher, in 1839. The teaching of sociology as a separate discipline started in 1876 in the United States, in 1889 in France, in 1907 in Great Britain, after World War I in Poland and India, in 1925 in Egypt and Mexico, and in 1947 in Sweden.

As we know that sociology is a social science. The word 'sociology' is derived from the Latin word 'societus' meaning society and Greek word 'logos' meaning study of science. The etymological meaning of sociology is thus the science of society. One professor says that "as the study of society is that of the web or tissue of human interaction and interrelation, in other words we can say that society is the study of man's behaviour in groups or of the interaction among human beings, of social relationship and the processes by which human group activity takes place".

Nature of Society

Human versus Animal Society

Human beings are not the only creatures who live in societies. Ants, termites, birds, monkeys and countless other animals do perform the same activity as human beings. It would be surprising then if human society bore no relation to some of the animal societies. It is discussed under following points:

(a) *Basic Features of Any Society*: All societies, whether animal or human, have certain things in common which lead to their being classed together. In the first place, they all involve a certain level, of association, a level closure and more intricate than aggregation but less complex than an organism. In the second place, the units they bring together on this level are not cells or organs but individuals. Before we can understand society, it is therefore necessary to know something about aggregation on the one hand, and organisms on the other.

(b) *Societal Necessities*: As growing, living systems all societies have certain common needs that must be met if they are to continue. At the most general level, these needs are independent of the particular kind of society and may therefore be regarded as primary needs. The primary societal needs may be classified under the major categories as follows:

(i) Those having to do with the individuals in society, figured as physical organisms.
(ii) Those having to do with the division of function as between different individuals.
(iii) Those having to do with the mutual conclusion of the individuals within the society.
(iv) Those having to do with the perpetuation of the society through many generations.

(c) *Social Norms*: In every society, there are certain ways of doing a thing. These ways are called norms and when these have the approval of the society, these are called social norms and these are very much deep rooted in the social system of the society. It is with the help of these norms that the society comes into action and behaviour of social beings is governed and regulated.

(i) *Classification of Norms*: One cannot discuss for long the general subject of norms without making some distinction between the different types. Yet there are so many distinctions, which cross one another that a systematic classification is difficult. One way is to differentiate norms on the basis of the kind of sanctions applied. Some rules are supported merely by mild disapproval of the violator, while others are supported by physical force. This distinctions is correlated to some extent with another one namely, the degree of importance attached to the rule in the society and with still another, the manner by which the rule comes into being.
(ii) *Folkways*: Most of the patterns applied in everyday behaviour consist of folkways. These are relatively durable, standardized practices regarded as obligatory in the proper situation but not absolutely obligatory, enforced by informed social controls rather than by formal complaint of coercion, and originating in an unplanned and obscure manner rather than by deliberate inauguration. Like the folkways, which they uphold, sanctions are limited to particular groups.

Status and Role

Status is used to refer to an individual's total standing in society. MacIver describes status as the social position that determines for its possessor, apart from his personal attribute or social services, a degree of respect, prestige, and influence.

The social system is based on a division of labour in which every person is assigned a special task to perform and the task performed by an individual makes up the role he is expected to play in the life of his community. A social role, as defined by Lundberg, is a pattern of behaviour expected of an individual in a certain group or situation.

Some of the important aspects of status and role are discussed as follows:

(i) *The Organization of Status*: An individual carries his social position around in his head, so to speak and puts it into action when the appropriate occasion arises. Basically the positions tend to remain the same; it is mainly the occupants of the positions who change.

(ii) *Status and Office*: We give a name to each of the continuum, calling one the status and the other office. The term 'status' would then designate a position in the general institutional system, recognized and supported by the entire society, spontaneously evolved rather than deliberately created and rooted in the folkways and mores.

(iii) *Position and Role*: A position, whether status or office, defines a minimum of obligatory behaviour for the incumbent, but it cannot ensure that the incumbent will carry out this behaviour perfectly. How an individual actually performs in a given position, as designated from how he is supposed to perform, we call is role. The role then is the manner in which a person actually carries out the requirement of his position.

(iv) *Status and Stratum*: Since any single individual occupies not one but many statuses and office and since for his personal and social efficiency he must find some coherence in the several position he fills, we could expect that in any society certain positions will tend to adhere together in different individuals. For a mass of persons in a given society who enjoy roughly the same station, we can use the word stratum.

Social Action

Social action is a way of meeting the needs of the mass. It is an effort to achieve social progress to modify social policies and to improve social legislation, health and welfare services.

Elements of Social Action

A single act, from the subjective or voluntaristic point of view can be analysed in terms of indispensable and inseparable factors, as follows:

(i) *An Actor*: When we speak of the agent of action, it is not the body of the actor we have in mind but the ego or self. It is the 'I' or the 'me' rather than the 'it'. The ego then is the subjective entity that possesses awareness and has experience, which makes decision and then reflects on the decisions it has made, which holds together past event and imagines those that are to be.

(ii) *An End*: When the end has been attained the act is finished, because by definition the act devotes on the end. An end once attained is displaced by another and which initiates a new line of action. In this way, from the subjective point of view, each person's, behaviour consists of an interrelated series of acts.

(iii) *Means*: To reach any end, some means must be employed. In some situations, the means may be something simple like speech, demonstrations, etc. In others, it may be an elaborate apparatus like a factory. Often the same end is attainable by more than one means, giving the actor considerable choice as to which he should utilize.

Role of Group in the Psychological and Social Development

Several groups are a collection of human beings in close proximity to one another. In the human field, by group, we mean, any collection of human beings who are brought into social relationships with one another.

According to Bogardus, "a social group is a given aggregate of people playing interrelated roles and recognized by themselves or other as a unit of interactions."

Williams says that "groups are aggregates or categories of people who have a consciousness of membership and of interaction."

Characteristics of Social Group

- *Reciprocal Relations*: Members of a group are interrelated to each other. A gathering of persons forms a social group only when they are interrelated. Reciprocal relations form an essential feature of group.
- *Sense of Unity*: The members of a group help each other and defend their interest collectively.
- *Common Interests*: The interests and ideas of a group are common. It is for the realization of common interests that they meet together.

- *Similar Behaviour*: The members of a group behave in a similar way for the pursuit of common interest.
- *Group Norms*: Every group has its own rules or norms that the members are supposed to follow.

Classification of Social Groups

Cooley has classified social groups as:

- Primary
- Secondary

Primary Group

Primary group is the nucleus of all social organizations. It is a small group in which a small number of persons come into direct contact with one another; they meet face to face for mutual help, companionship and discussion of common questions.

The most important sphere of the intimate association and cooperation – though by no means the only ones are the family, the playgroup of children, and the neighbourhood or community group of elders. These are practically universal belonging to all times and all stages of development and are accordingly a chief basis of what is universal in human nature and in human ideals.

Characteristics of Primary Group

(i) *Physical Proximity*: In order that relation of the people may be close, it is necessary that this contact also should be close. Seeing and talking with each other exchange of ideas and opinions is easy. It makes possible the conversation of gesture.

(ii) *Small Size*: Relationship can be intimate and personal only in a small group, the members can know one another personally and develop a group character and an intimacy more quickly.

(iii) *Stability*: To promote intimacy of relationship, the primary group should be stable to some extent.

(iv) *Similarly a Background*: Each member must have something to give as well as to take. This feature is clearly evident in a discussion group where each member presents his own viewpoint and takes the viewpoint of others.

(v) *Limited Self-interest*: Though members join the group with the motive of satisfying their own interests, yet they should subordinate their interests to the central interest of the group.

(vi) *Intensity of Shared Interests*: The common interest is shared by every member and by being shared in all the interest acquires a new significance, a new emphasis and a new valuation.

Importance of Primary Group for the Individual

The first thing to be impressed about group is that it is a medium through which we learn culture, use culture and change culture. The group is an important factor in shaping the personality of individuals to secure certain external advantages, e.g., better wages, production efficiency and workers' morale, service of a teacher who cannot be hired by a single student. But there are two other advantages of a different sort, which induce members in association together. There are realizations of the human need for spontaneous living and the provision of stimulus to each member in the pursuit of interest. Few of the importance of primary group for individual may be discussed as follows:

Spontaneous Living: In primary group members come freely together. A family, a playgroup, a group of friends, a study group, and a tribal council come into of its own initiatives. The members of these groups do not come as representatives or delegates allotted certain duties but meet spontaneously without any direction from any quarter.

Provisions of Stimulus: The primary groups not only satisfy the human need for the spontaneous living but also provides stimulus to each of its members in the pursuit of interest.

United in Process: The primary group not only affects the quality of out interest by enlarging and enriching them but also the method of the pursuit. The members directly cooperate and do the same together.

Secondary Group

A secondary group is one that is large in size such as city, nation, political parties, corporations, international centre, club and labour union. Here human contacts become superficial and undefined. The relations of members are limited in scope and arrived by much trial and error and in terms of self-interest calculations of members. In other words, the groups that provide experience of social life lacking in intimacy are called secondary groups.

Characteristics of Secondary Group

(i) *Formal and Impersonal Relations*: It does not exercise primary influence over its members. The members need not meet face to face. They perform their jobs, carry out the orders, pay their dues and still may never see each other.

(ii) *Large in Size*: They might be spread all over the world, e.g., Gideon International consists of thousands of members scattered all over the world.

(iii) *Option of Membership*: The membership of most of secondary groups is not compulsory. It is not essential to become the member of Rotary International or Red Cross society.

(iv) *Active and Inactive Member*: Due to the absence of intimate relations, some members of the group become inactive while some other are quite active. A large number of members of national political parties do not take any active interest in the party work.

(v) *Indirect Relationship*: The members are scattered through out the length and breadth of the country/world. They communicate with each other by indirect means.

(vi) *Status of Individual Depends on his Roles*: The status of the president in a Trade Union depends upon the role he plays in the union and not upon the personal qualities or birth.

(vii) *Goal-Oriented*: The main purpose of a secondary group is to fulfil a specific function, e.g., a trade union is formed for better working condition of its workers. A school is opened to provide education.

Importance of Secondary Group for the Individual

The primary groups have an important place in a simple and small society but in modern era the trend is towards secondary groups. Man now depends for his needs more on secondary group then primary group. While the growth to secondary groups has created numerous problems, it has also brought some benefits. These benefits are as follows:

(i) *Efficiency*: A formal authority is set up with the responsibility of managing the organization efficiently. The organization of a secondary group is carefully worked out. The emphasis is on getting the things done.

(ii) *Channels of Opportunity*: They provide a greater chance to develop individual talents. There are thousands of occupations that open the way for specialized careers. The talented individuals can now rise from an unknown background to the highest positions in business, industry, civil or technical service.

(iii) *Wider Outlook*: It broadens the outlook of its members. It consists of members who are widespread. Their boundary extends beyond the primary group. A secondary group has to accommodate a large number of individuals and localities that widens the outlook of its members. It is more universal in its judgement than the primary groups that are influenced by local customs and personal attitudes.

Social Institutions

In every society, there are certain well established institutions which help to achieve the objectives. They are collective modes of behaviour that prescribe a way of doing things. The common practice is to refer to family, school, church, state and many others as the institutions of the society.

Family

At the outset, it is important to explain the sense in which the term 'family' is used. The word family has been taken out from the Roman word 'famulus' meaning a servant. In Roman law, the word denoted the group of producers and slaves and other servants as well as members connected by common descent or marriage.

Definitions

- Family is a system of relationship existing between parent and children.
- Family is the biological social unit composed of husband, wife and children.
- Family is a socially recognized social group charged with duty of population replacement.

Nature of Family

(i) *Universality*: Family is the most universal group. It is the first institution in the history of man. It has existed in every age and in every society and is found in all parts of the world.

(ii) *Emotional Basis*: The family is a fundamental unit of human society. It is based on our impulses of mating, procreation and parental care. It is a close-knit group, which fortifies these emotions.

(iii) *Formative Influence*: The family exercises the most profound influence over its members. It moulds the character of individuals.

Its influence in infancy determines the personality structures of the individual.

(iv) *Limited Size*: The size of a family is of necessity limited, for it is defined by biological conditions which it cannot transcend. Other groups may be smaller than a family, but they are not so because of biological conditions.

(v) *Responsibility of the Members*: In the family, the child learns the meaning of social responsibility and the necessity for cooperation.

(vi) *Social Regulation*: The family is peculiarly guarded by social customs and legal regulations. It is not easy to violate them. Family is the group in which the consenting parties may freely enter but which they cannot easily leave or dissolve; marriages are not trivially taken.

(vii) *Permanent and Temporary*: Family or an institution is permanent and universal, while as association, it is temporary and transitional. When the son marries, he goes out of the family and starts another family, which again may give rise to more families.

Forms of Family

(i) *The Patriarchal Family*: The patriarchal family was prevalent not only in the civilized society of antiquity but also in the feudal society. This type of family has became world famous. The Old Testament affords many descriptions of patriarchal families, such as those of Abraham, Jacob and Isaac.

Chief Characteristics of Patriarchal Family

- The wife after marriage comes to live in the home of the husband.
- The father is the supreme lord of the family property.
- Descent is reckoned through the father. The children are known by the home of the family of their father.
- The children can inherit the property of their father only and they have no right over the property of the mother's family.

(ii) *The Matriarchal Family*: In a matriarchal family, the authority vests in the woman head of the family with the males being subordinate. She is the owner of property and rules over the family.

Chief Characteristics of Matriarchal Family

- Descent is reckoned through the mother, not the father because maternity is a fact while paternity is only an opinion.

- Marriage relations are transient. The husband is sometimes merely a casual visitor.
- The authority in the family rests in the hands of wife or in some representative of the wife's kin.
- Property is transferred through the mother and only females succeed to it.

Functions of the Family

The major functions of the family are:

- The regulations of sexual behaviour and reproduction,
- Care and training of children,
- Cooperation and division of labour, and
- Primary group satisfactions.

Classification of Functions of Family

The functions of the family can be broadly classified as essential and non-essential.

Essential Functions

The essential functions of the family include:

- Satisfaction of sex need,
- Production and rearing of children, and
- Provision of a home.

Non-essential Functions

The non-essential functions of the family include:

- Economic security,
- Religious identity,
- Educational need,
- Health care,
- Recreational need,
- Civic virtues, and
- Socialization.

(iii) *Modern Family*: The modern family is democratic based on equality between husband and wife, with consensus in making decision and with increasing participation by children as they grow older. In the present modern scenario, some of the important features of family can be mentioned as follows:

- Decreased control of the marriage contract.
- Changes in the relationship of man and woman.
- Laxity in sex relationship.

- Economic independence.
- Smaller family.
- Decline of religious control.
- Separation of non-essential functions.

Marriage

Marriage is an institution, which admits men and women to family life. It is a stable relationship in which a man and a woman are socially permitted to have children implying in a right to sexual relations. Edward Westermark define marriage as the "more or less durable connection between male and female, lasting beyond the mere act of propagation till after the birth of offspring". Earnest K. Groves defines it as "a public confession and legal registration of an adventure in fellowship".

Forms of Marriage

(1) *One Wife Many Husbands (Polyandry):* In certain parts of the earth, polyandry long existed. It is a form of marriage wherein one woman marries more than one man at a given time. It is thought to be widespread in Tibet where the conditions of social life are harsh and where perhaps the efforts of two or more men are needed in order to support a family.

(2) *One Husband Many Wives (Polygamy):* Under this system, one man has two or more wives at a time. Polygamy is generally called polygying but strictly speaking the latter is a general term including both polyandry and polygamy. Polygying is found among Eskimo tribes, Crow and Hidatsa of North America and African Negroes. Westermark has mentioned the following causes of polygying:

  (i) *Enforced Celibacy*: Men do not approach the women during the period of pregnancy and while the child is being breast-fed. Due to this long period of enforced celibacy, a second marriage was contracted.

  (ii) *Earlier Aging of the Female*: In the uncivilized tribes, men remarried a number of times because the women aged earlier.

  (iii) *Variety*: The desire for variety is also the cause of polygying.

  (iv) *Social Prestige*: In some tribes, the leaders have more wives in order to prove their superiority. A single marriage is considered a sign of poverty.

The advantages/disadvantages of polygyny are:

(i) It checks prostitution because man can satisfy his sex desire in a better way by keeping himself within the confines of marriage.
(ii) The women possess lower position.
(iii) It destroys family happiness.
(iv) It creates jealousy among the wives and their children.
(v) The children cannot be looked after properly because too many of them are to be looked after.

(3) *One Man One Wife (Monogamy):* Under monogamy one man marries one woman at a time. This is the leading form of marriage. Its advantages are now well recognized. It produces the highest types of affection and sincere devotion. The children are well looked after. Both father and mother give earnest attention to the upbringing of their offspring. Under monogamy, the old parents receive favouring care by their children. Under polygyny, their days end in bitterness. According to Malinowski, "monogamy is, has been and will remain the only true type of marriage. It is probably on account of great advantages of monogamy that the public offices in India have been legally forbidden to practice polygyny."

(4) *Companionate Marriage:* This is the marriage of two persons on the understanding that if there is no child, the marriage may be dissolved simply by mutual consent. Judge Ben B. Lindsey was of the opinion that this system is much better than free love or trial marriage because the knowledge that in case there are no children, divorce may be obtained and will provide wholesome attitudes toward marriage. The opponents of the system, however point out that it leads to quick-marriage and quick-divorce trends and makes it easy for persons to marry on the basis of sex alone.

Kinship

Man does not live alone in society. From birth till death he is surrounded by a number of people - some of these people are his relatives, some are friends, some are neighbours while all others are strangers and unknown to him. He is bound to all those people who are related to him either on the basis of blood or marriage. The relations based on blood or marriage may be close or distant. The bond of blood or marriage which binds people together into a group is called kinship. Kinship is of two types: (i) affinal, and (ii) consanguineous.

(i) *Affinal Kinship*: The bond of marriage is called affinal kinship. When a person marries, he establishes relationship not only with the girl whom he marries but also with a number of other people in the girl's family. Moreover, it is not only the person marrying who gets bound to the family members of the girl but a host of relations are created as soon as a marriage takes place. Marriage creates a host of relationship, which are called affinal kinship.

(ii) *Consanguineous Kinship*: The bond of blood is called consanguineous kinship. The consanguineous kin are related through blood whereas the affinal kinship is related through marriage. The bond between parents and their children and that between siblings is consanguineous kinship. Siblings are the children of the same parents, thus, son, brother, sister, uncle, nephew and cousin are consanguineous kinship.

Education

Education is one of the basic activities in all human societies. The word 'education' is derived from the Latin word 'educare', which means to bring up. The idea of education is not merely to impart instruction to the pupil in certain subjects but also and principally to bring him up or develop in him those habits and attitudes, which may enable him to face the future well.

Development of Education

The development of education can be discussed as follows:

(i) *Education in Preliterate Societies*: In preliterate societies, education was usually informal. Brothers and sisters and adult kinsmen took part in transmitting social values regarded as essential. Through observation and direct contact the child acquired the knowledge of folkways and mores of the group as well as the training in practical techniques and skills. Though mostly informal, it was not entirely devoid of formal elements.

(ii) *Middle Ages*: It is only in civilized societies that education adopts institutionalized forms. Its degree of formality contents and objectives vary with the type of civilization. In Greece, the curriculum was based on literature, music and gymnastics to which mathematics and historical subjects were added. During the middle ages, seven liberal arts including grammar, rhetoric, classics, arithmetic, geometry, music and astronomy were taught mostly in the monasteries, abbeys and cathedral schools.

(iii) *Secular Education*: With the growth of science, commerce and industry and with the birth of Renaissance and the Protestant reformation, there came about secularization of education. However, it was not until nineteenth century that secular education became widely accepted. Democracy widened the objectives of education. Popular education was regarded essential to the very existence of democracy.

Religion

Religion is very old institution. Durkhiem says, "Religion is a unified system of beliefs and practices, relative to sacred things, that is to say, things set apart and forbidden." MacIver and Page say, "Religion, as we understand the term implies a relationship not merely between man and man, but also man and some higher power." Religion is even today interpreted and understood differently by different people.

Effects of Religion on Rural Life

(i) *Social Life*: Social life of the rural folk is very much influenced by religion. Every villager must perform every social function, which has the approval of religion. Unless he performs these functions, he will be considered socially outcaste. He cannot go socially against well-established religious practices, no matter whether he has money for the same or not. In fact, social life and religion are very well knit in rural life.

(ii) *Economic Life*: Economic life is also controlled by religion. Every economic activity is undertaken after taking religious consideration. Whether it is soiling or cutting of harvest, some religious function must be performed for that. Similarly, whether one starts a new business, purchases a new house or even equipment, some religious function must be there.

(iii) *Family Life*: Family life is very much influenced by religion in the rural areas. All functions connected with marriage must be keeping in view the auspicious time to be told by the priest. Every family tries that marriage ceremony should take place at the time as allowed by the priest or religion.

(iv) *Political Life*: Since religion has a deep hold over religious people, it is very difficult to separate religious life from political life.

Inspite of the fact that there is a conscientious political awakening in the rural areas, yet the voting pattern and political behaviour of each and every individual in the village is decided by the religion to which he or she belongs.

(v) *Individual Life*: Religious influences affects individual life of each and every person in the village. It is religion which makes them God fearing and as such they hesitate to commit any crime. This is the reason that the crime rate is much less in the rural areas as compared with the urban areas.

(vi) *Caste System*: Villages are still strongholds of caste system and religion is one important factor in this regard. Religious leaders in the villages make the people believe that caste system is not man made, but a God sent institution. It is, therefore, playing against the wishes of God to change the system.

Social System

The concept of social system is closely related to the concept of social structure. Social system refers to the functional aspect of social structure. Social structure is the means through which social system functions.

Elements of Social System

The main elements of social system are:

(1) *Belief and Knowledge*: Any proposition about any aspect of the universe that is accepted as such may be called a belief. According to D. Krech and R.S. Crutehfiled, "A belief is an enduring organization of perception and cognition about some aspect of individual world."

(2) *Sentiment*: Closely related to belief is the element of sentiment. Sentiments represent "What we feel" about the world. Sentiment is the chief element articulated in the internal pattern of a social system. The sentiments may be of various kinds, intellectual ethical, aesthetic, religious, etc.

(3) *End Goal or Objective*: The end goal or objective creates a social system. The members of a social system expect to accomplish a particular end or objective through appropriate interaction – had there been no human needs, goals of ends, there would have been no society.

(4) *Norms*: Norms are the standards for determining what is right and wrong, appropriate and inappropriate, just and unjust, good and bad in social relationship. Every social system is possessed of its norms, which the individuals are obliged to observe. Some norms are general and may not be violated by anyone.

(5) *Status-Role*: Status is the position, which an individual has in society. In a social system, each individual has a status. The place in a particular system, which a certain individual occupies at a particular time is his status with reference to that system.

(6) *Rank*: Rank as used here is equivalent to standing. It includes the importance an individual has for the system in which the rank is accorded. It is determined by the evaluation placed upon the individual and his acts in accordance with the norms and standards of the system.

(7) *Power*: Power refers to the capacity to control others, when there may take place any conflict among the different parts of the social system. Such conflict is harmful for the social system. Thus, there may arise a dispute between the students and teachers, which is harmful for the institution. There should exist some power with the capacity to control both.

(8) *Facility*: A facility has been defined as a means used to attain ends within the system. It is necessary that the individuals in a social system should be enabling them to perform their roles efficiently. Facilities should not only exist but should also be utilized.

Social Process

Social process may be described as the fundamental ways in which people interact and establish relationship. They refer to the repetitive forms of behaviour which are commonly found in social life.

The Development of Self

(i) *Cooley's Theory*: Cooley's concept of self-development has been termed as looking glass self-concept. According to him, man develops the concept of self with the help of others. Man does not come to form opinions about himself unless and until he comes into contact with other people and knows their opinions about himself. This forms the concept of himself on the basis of opinions held by others about him.

(ii) *Meads's Theory*: G.H. Mead has given a sociological analysis of the process of socialization. According to him the self develops out of the child's communicative contact with others. The new-born infant has needs like those for food and clothing that press for satisfaction. Mother satisfies these needs and child depends upon her.

(iii) *Freud's Theory*: The theories of Cooley and Mead presume a basic harmony between the self and society. According to Cooley, society and individuals are not separate phenomena but are simply collective and distributive aspects of the same thing. Sigmund Freud, the father of psychoanalysis does not agree with this concept of self and society. The function of the ego is that of the rider guiding the house, which is id.

Cooperation

The word 'cooperation' is derived from two Latin words, 'co' means together and 'operari' meaning to work. It is, thus, joint activity in pursuit of common goals or shared reward. It is goal-oriented and conscious form of social interaction. We may define cooperation as a process by which individuals and groups combine their efforts more or less in an organized way for the attainment of common objectives. Thus, it involves two elements: (i) common end, and (ii) organized effort.

Types of Cooperation

Principal types of cooperation are as follows:

(i) *Direct Cooperation:* Under this category are included those activities in which cooperating individuals do like things together, that is, perform identical functions like moving a pile of stones or pushing a motor car out the mud. Playing together, worshipping together, tilling the fields together are other instances of direct cooperation.

(ii) *Indirect Cooperation*: Under this category are included those activities in which people do unlike tasks toward a similar end. In other words in this type of cooperation individuals work towards common ends but each has his own specialized functions too as the case, for example, when carpenters, plumbers and masons cooperate to build a house.

(iii) *Primary Cooperation*: It is the cooperation, which is found in primary groups such as the family. In this form of cooperation there is identity of interests between the individual and the group.

(iv) *Secondary Cooperation*: This type of cooperation is found in the secondary group, such as – government, industry, church, and trade union, etc.

(v) *Tertiary Cooperation*: This cooperation is found in the interaction between the various big and small groups to meet a particular situation.

Conflict

Conflict is a conscious action and ever present process in human relations. According to Mazumdar, "Conflict is opposition or struggle involving an emotional attitude of hostility as well as violent interference with one's autonomous choice."

Types of Conflicts

Conflicts can be of following types:

(i) *Latent and Overt Conflict*: Conflict is usually described as latent or overt. In most cases, for a long time, it has existed in latent form such as social tension and dissatisfaction. Latent conflict becomes overt conflict when an issue is declared and when hostile action is taken.

(ii) *Corporate and Personal Conflict*: Conflicts are also classified as corporate and personal – corporate conflict occurs among the groups within a society or between two societies. Race, riots conflict upheaval, religious persecution, labour-management conflict and war between nations are the examples of corporate conflict.

Positive Functions of Conflict

The positive functions of conflict are as follows:

(i) Conflict tends to stiffen the morale and promote the solidarity of the in-group.

(ii) Conflict, conducted with victory, leads to the enlargement of the victor group.

(iii) Conflict leads to redefinition of value systems.

(iv) Conflict may lead to the working out of non-violent techniques for resolving crises.

(v) Conflict may lead to change in the relative status of the conflicting parties.
(vi) Conflict may lead to consensus.

Assimilation

Each and every society has culture and traditions of its own. These are very clear to the society and it wants to preserve them at all costs. But no society can live in isolation with the result that it is influencing and is being influenced by culture and traditions of other societies. Very slowly and gradually, a stage comes when cultures of two societies completely merge with each other. Such a stage is called assimilation. It is not confined to culture alone but to other fields as well. A boy and a girl, after marriage, get more or less completely assimilated.

(i) *Assimilation is not limited to single field only*: The best example of assimilation is that of the foreigners being assimilated in the host culture, i.e., abandoning their own culture and taking on that of the host country. But it would be wrong to limit the process of assimilation to this single field. Assimilation takes place in other cases also.
(ii) *Stages in the Process of Assimilation*: Assimilation is a slow and gradual process. It takes quite sometime before individuals or groups once dissimilar became similar, that is, become identified in their interests and outlook. The social contacts thus established finally result in assimilation. The speed of the process of assimilation naturally depends on the nature of the contacts. If the contacts are primary, assimilation occurs naturally and rapidly than if they are secondary.

Social Structure

Meaning of Social Structure: According to S.F. Nadel's view: "We arrive at the structure of society through abstracting from the concrete population and its behaviour pattern or network of relationships obtaining between actors in their capacity of playing roles relative to one another."

Elements of Social Structure

(1) *Normative System*: Normative system presents the society with the ideal and values. The people attach emotional importance to these norms.

(2) *Position System*: Position system refers to the statuses and roles of the individuals.
(3) *Sanction System*: For the proper enforcement of norms, every society has a sanction system.
(4) *Action System*: It is the object or goal to be arrived at by the social structure. The whole structure revolves around it.

Types of Social Structure

(1) The universalistic-achievement pattern.
(2) The universalistic-ascription pattern.
(3) The particularistic-achievement pattern.
(4) The particularistic-ascription pattern.

Social Institutions

We may also devote some attention to the concept of social institutions in this chapter because social institutions are essential to maintain the ordered arrangement of social structure.

Kinds of Institutions

(i) Family
(ii) Economics
(iii) Religion
(iv) Education
(v) State

Functions of Institutions

(i) Manifest
(ii) Latent

Role and Status

(i) *Nature of Role*: If we cast our glance at society, we find that individuals differ not only in such attributes as sex, colour, height, age, etc., but also differ in respect of their occupations.
(ii) *Nature of Status*: In its meaning, status is a term used to designate the comparative amounts of prestige difference or respect accorded to persons who have been assigned different roles in a group or community. Sometimes the word 'status' is used to refer to an individual's total standing in society. Status, which a social class or an individual enjoys, depends upon the social evaluations

whereby the community regards certain attributes or characteristics more or less valuable than the other ones.

Political System

A political party shall be treated as a recognized political party in a state if, and only if, the conditions specified below are fulfilled:

(i) That such party has been engaged in political activity for a continuous period of five years and at least one member to the house of people for every twenty-five members of that house or any fraction of that number is selected from that state.

(ii) That the total number of valid votes polled by all the contesting candidates set up by such party at the general election in the state to the house of people, or as the case may be to the legislative assembly for the time being in existence and functioning is not less than four per cent of the total number of valid votes polled by the contesting candidates at such general elections in the state.

(iii) Voting behaviour is affected by the following factors:

   (a) *Religion*: India, since ancient days has been predominantly a country inhabited by different religions. Votes are attracted towards the candidates belonging to their own religion.

   (b) *Caste*: Elections in India are contested very much on the basis of casteism. The voters are asked to vote for their caste candidate and casteism is maintained by the elected leaders after the elections are over.

   (c) *Community*: Community feeling is another factor influencing the voters. Community feelings had led the Telugu people to demand a separate state of Andhra.

   (d) *Class*: It is one of the factors influencing voting behaviour in the regions where the electorate is mostly composed of voters belonging to working class.

   (e) *Money*: Money perhaps plays the greatest role during elections; crore of rupees are spent in their bid to capture political power.

Economic System

(i) *Economic Development*: The twentieth century has brought about a rise in mass production of many near-monopolies and a high degree of division of labour. This description of economic development gives an idea of the differences between the economic systems of simple and complex societies as follows:

(a) Undifferentiated patterns of economic activity.
(b) Integrated system of living.
(c) Production is need-oriented and not for marketing.
(d) Primary techniques of control.
(e) Barter system of exchange.
(f) Non-existence of monetary and credit system.
(g) Informal structure of economic relations.

(ii) *Capitalism*: The following are the economic bases of capitalism:

(a) The institution of private property lies as the basis of modern economic life. It is the *terra firma* of capitalism.

(b) *Large Scale Production*: It is another important feature of capitalism which arose as a result of industrial revolution and made large-scale production possible.

(c) *Profit Institution*: According to Marx, capitalism cannot exist in the absence of institution of profit. The capitalists invest money and out of investment earn profit.

(d) *Market Economy*: Under capitalism there is no government control over the forces of production, distribution and exchanges.

(e) *Business Organization*: Capitalism is marked by vast business structures.

(iii) *Property*: Property is an important institution in the economy of societies. The advantages of private property are:

(a) *Incentive to Work*: It is said that man in general needs an incentive to work. The right to private property provides such an incentive. It makes people work and work hard.

(b) *Satisfaction of Natural Instinct*: Man has an acquisitive instinct. He wants to acquire something, which he can call his own.

(c) *Security Against Future*: A man of property has security against starvation. He can afford to pursue intellectual tastes.

(d) *Ethically Sound*: Private property is justified on the ground that it is the reward to an individual for his labour.

(e) *Economic Progress*: This incentive to private property leads people to exert themselves utmost for earning money.

(iv) *The Occupational Groups: The Trade Unions*

(a) *Growth of Trade Union*: The trade union is a phenomenon of the modern industrialized society. It is a group of workers engaged in a particular trade for the purposes of securing better wages, shorter hours of work and improved conditions of labour. The early trade union where small organizations of working men seeking some means of mitigating their weakness against the employer.

(b) *Aims of a Trade Union*: The trade in India is primarily an economic organization organized for economic struggle. Its essential function is to strengthen the economic status of its members and improve their working conditions. It is primarily concerned to promote the economic interest of the workers.

(c) *Methods of a Trade Union*: The methods which the trade union adopts, for getting its demands accepted are various and varied. The labour problems will never develop if capitalism has a social vision and the willingness to correct its own weaknesses.

Indian Social Structure

(1) *Caste System and its Origin*

(i) *Racial Theory*: One very old and important theory about the origin of caste system is the Racial Theory. Risely and Mazumdar are supporters of this theory. According to Risely, before Aryans came to India, they were divided into four classes, which came to be regarded as four different races after their settlement.

(ii) *Political Theory*: Some of our thinkers believe that not race but political convenience and manipulation by those who wanted to retain authority is the basis of the caste system. In India it is said that the Brahmins who wanted to hold authority devised this system.

(iii) *Occupational Theory*: Nesfield is of the view that occupation is the basis of caste system. In his opinion, function and function alone is responsible for the origin of caste structure in India. Thus, he and his supporters also do not believe that the system has any religious background.

(iv) *Traditional Theory*: This theory believes that caste system is not of human but of divine origin. They argue that the main four castes were created by God *Brahma*, whereas the sub-castes came into existence subsequently as a result of inter-cast marriages, etc.

(v) *Religious Theory*: Some of our thinkers believe that religion was responsible for the creation of castes. They also believe that those who had faith in the same gods came nearer to each other and formed one caste.

(vi) *Evolutionary Theory*: In this theory it is wrong to believe that castes came into being all of a sudden. They argue that gradually and slowly many factors contributed in bringing it into existence. Some of the factors, which contributed to it were desire for purity of blood and devotion to a particular profession.

(2) *Tribals and their Characteristics*

(i) A family has a limited size.

(ii) Member of family has relationship of permanent nature, either affinal or consanguineous supported by emotional attachments.

(iii) Husband and wife are permanent sexual partners.

(iv) At least one member of the family has to be a breadwinner for all the members.

(v) Members have a common habitation.

(vi) Members have a common nomenclature.

(vii) Family is the cradle of education for the children.

(viii) Family inculcates a sense of responsibility among its members.

Urban Growth in India

Gamut of Growth Rates

(i) It will be recalled that the growth rate for the total population of India for the 1951-61 decade was 21.5 per cent, if the rate of natural increase in population is taken as roughly 20 per cent for the decade both in the rural and the urban areas of India.

(ii) *Declining Towns*: An interesting aspect of urbanization revealed by our analysis is the phenomenon of declining towns by which we mean towns, which recorded a net decrease in population during 1951-61. This may not be a persistent trend over several decades but there are some towns for which we have observed such a trend throughout the period 1901-61.

(iii) *Declassified Towns*: The new definition adopted in the 1961 census was responsible for the declassification of 803 towns with a total population of 4.4 million. Except one town in Maharashtra all these towns had a population below 20,000. Fifty-four towns were merged with other cities and towns and as a result, they lost their identity in 1961. It may be noted that most of the declassified towns had a high population of workers engaged in agricultural activities, which militates against the concept of urban growth.

(iv) *New Towns*: There were as many as 497 places which were labelled 'towns' for the first time in 1961. Their aggregate population was 4.8 million. Of these 36 had a population of 20,000 or more. West Bengal had the largest share of new towns – 66, with a population of 7,15,000 while Rajasthan's share was the smallest – 3, with a population of 13,000.

(v) *Rapidly Growing Towns*: There were 278 towns in India which recorded an increase of 50 per cent or over in their population during the decade 1951-61. Their total population amounted to 13.3 million. West Bengal had the largest number of such towns – 37 in all, accounting for a population of 1.9 million, while Orissa had the smallest number of such towns – 8 in all, accounting for a total population of 1,75,000.

The Process of Urban Growth

(i) *Urban Economy*: There is hardly any study, which distinguishes between the economics of sale, the economics of location and the economics of agglomeration in India's cities and towns. In a study of the seven million-plus population cities of India (Mumbai, Delhi, Kolkata, Chennai), P.B. Desai observes: "Our million-plus population cities too have acute economic problems. Their income does not appear to yield surpluses that can be spent on programmes of housing and social overheads. It would appear that out of the sources of agglomeration economics, they can boast of only one factor, namely, the size of population."

(ii) *Urban Society*: From demographic and economic questions, we may now turn to some social and political questions, which are closely related to economic issues. The data regarding size, membership, composition and acceptance of familial obligations do not indicate any appreciable difference among the rural, fringe and urban nuclear families. The family of the urban immigrant group, however, shows certain special characteristics that sets it off both from the urban-local families and families in the rural and fringe groups.

(iii) *Urban Development with Social Justice*: There are today over 300 such colonies which house over 5,00,000 people who live under a constant threat of demolition of their houses by municipal squads. To make matters worse, the local politicians invariably make it a point to take up the cause of ejected persons and make it a big political issue. And, it is not that principles are always involved. All the political parties play this game.

(iv) *Urban Administration*: A major advance in local finance is possible through the intergovernmental cooperation and revenue devolution in a systematic manner. The integration of the urban local bodies with the state and national processes will substantially shift the responsibility of financing urban development to the upper-tier governments. However, the main initiative in this direction must lie in the state governments, although the passive role of the central government vis-à-vis urban development also needs to be changed.

Nature of Social Change

(1) Social change is a universal phenomenon and occurs in all societies. No society remains completely static. This is true of all societies, primitive as well as civilized.

(2) Social change is a community change and does not refer to the change in the life of an individual or the life patterns of several individuals. It is a change, which occurs in the life of the entire community.

(3) Nature and speed of social change is affected by and related to time factor – the speed of social change is not uniform in each change of period in the same society. In modern times the speed of social change is faster today than before 1947. Thus, the speed of social change differs from age to age.

Factors of Social Change

The factors of social change can be understood in terms of family, economic and social life as mentioned below:

(1) *Effects on Family life*
  (i) It has led to the disintegration of the joint family system.
  (ii) It has increased the number of divorces.
  (iii) It has led to the liberation of women. The "Lib movement" is the consequence of technology.

(iv) The invention of birth control measures has reduced the size of family.

(2) *Effects on Economic Life*

(i) It has given birth to capitalism and its attendant evils.
(ii) It has brought in higher standard of living.
(iii) It has given birth to trade union movement.

(3) *Effects on Social Life*

(i) It has led to the decline of community life.
(ii) It has grown the sense of individualism.
(iii) It has narrowed the gap of caste system.
(iv) Recreation has become commercialized.

Economic, Political and Social Change

Economic Change

Economic Development

In the primitive days, man satisfied his hunger by searching for food and living upon what he could raise. And, in this search for food, primitive people invented weapons and tools. The procuring of fruits, berries, greens and seeds was supplemented by some hunting. In places where animals were abundant, the technique of hunting became highly developed. The above description of economic development gives an idea of the differences between the economic systems of simple and complex societies, which are as follows:

(i) Undifferentiated patterns of economic activity.
(ii) Integrated system of living.
(iii) Production need-oriented and not for marketing.
(iv) Informal structure of economic relations.
(v) Primary techniques of control.
(vi) Barter system of exchange.

Capitalism

The features of capitalism are:

(i) *Private Property*: The institution of private property lies as the basis of modern economics life; it is the *terra firma* capitalism. The right to property is considered an inviolable right.
(ii) *Large-Scale Production*: It is another important feature of capitalism. Capitalism arose as a result of industrial revolution, which made large-scale production possible.

(iii) *Money and Credit*: In capitalism the institution of credit has become important. The capitalists got money on loan and developed their business.
(iv) *Business Organization*: Capitalism is marked by vast business structures. The capital of numerous shareholders is polled and an industrial house is set up.
(v) *Market Money*: Under this there is no governmental control over the forces of production, distribution and exchanges. It is controlled by the forces operating in the market.

Property

The Nature of Property Right

(i) *Transferability*: Property can be transferred by its owner by way of sale, exchange or gift. A landowner can transfer his land.
(ii) Property rights do not necessarily imply actual use and enjoyment of objects by the owner. One may own property without actually using it. In other words, possession of property may be in the hands of persons who is not its owner.
(iii) *Power Aspect*: Property can exercise control over those persons who do not have it. The extent of power which property gives to the owner depends not only upon the definition of his rights but also on the intensity of others, need and scarcity of the thing.
(iv) *Property is Usually Non-Human*: The object of property has no rights of its own but is simply the passive object of such rights. The land has no right of its own; it only serves the landowner. In other words, human being cannot be the object of property.

Political Change

The Origin of the State

There are different theories in regard to the origin of the state. They are:

(i) The Divine Origin Theory.
(ii) The Social Contract Theory.
(iii) The Force Theory.
(iv) The Patriarchal Theory.
(v) The Matriarchal Theory.

The Functions of the State

(i) *The State is a limited agency*: The state has limitation on the functions of the very nature of the state. The state has limits to what it can do. The state, as stated above, though universal yet it is a limited agency. It is limited by the means at its disposal.
(ii) *Maintenance of order*: The state alone can perform the primary function that is the maintenance of order; the primary function is the maintenance of order in society. The state is possessed of peculiar attributes, which enable it to perform this function.
(iii) *The State should not control public opinion*: Taking up the functions, which the state should not undertake, MacIver says: "The state should not seek to control public opinion, no matter what the opinion may be."
(iv) *The State should not enforce morality*: Secondly, the state should not enforce morality. The sphere of morality is distinct from the sphere of political law. There is no such thing as state morality. There is no morality, save individual morality.

Government

Sometimes, confusion is made between state and government and the two words are used interchangeably. Government is an instrument of the state through which it carries out its purposes. A state, as we have seen, is a politically organized and geographically limited body of people that possesses the right to use force. Most states have no written constitution.

Power Structure

To summarize power it is:
(i) the capacity or capability of carrying out one's will despite resistance,
(ii) a relationship between holders of authority and followers of authority, and
(iii) a participant in decision-making.

Bureaucracy

The social consequences of bureaucracy are:
(i) It lays stress on technical knowledge.
(ii) It is dominated by the principles of appointment.
(iii) It is subject to strict discipline.

(iv) A bureaucratic administration is objective-oriented.
(v) There is impartiality and objectivity in administration.

Social Change

Darwinism

The element in Darwinism that especially influenced Veblen was its implication that individuals have little or no control over the forces of change. Veblen analyzed human behaviour primarily in terms of natural play. Among instincts which guides human action, are the parental bent, benevolent feeling towards kin, etc.

Cultural Lag

Veblen's concept of cultural lag has been widely used by American sociologists for both social change and science and technology. Social problems in nature are due to the failure of institutions and organizations to keep pace with the relevant change in technology. Cultural lag as a concept denoting the divergence between improvement in science and technology and the static social institutions is a germinal thought to all sociologists. Veblen has thus contributed to a theory of modern social change in an evolutionary content, stemming from growth of progress in science and technology.

Nature of Social Change

(i) *Social Change is a Universal Phenomenon*: Social change occurs in all societies, no society remains completely static. This is true of all societies, primitive as well as civilized. Society exists in a universe of dynamic influences.
(ii) *Social Change is Community Change*: Social change does not refer to the change in the life of an individual or the life patterns of several individuals. It is a change, which occurs in the life of the entire community.
(iii) *Speed of Social Change is not Uniform*: While social change occurs in all societies, its speed is not uniform in every society. In most societies it occurs so slowly that it is often not noticed by those who live in them.
(iv) *Social Change Occurs as an Essential Law*: Change is the law of nature. Social change also is natural. It may occur either in the natural course or as a result of planned efforts. By nature we desire

change. Our needs keep on changing. To satisfy our desire for change and for our changing needs social change becomes a necessity.

Factors of Social Change

(i) *Military Social Selection*: War is a great selecting force. Healthy and brave people are selected for war who get killed and thereby the society is deprived of its best people.
(ii) *Political Form*: In civil wars and independence movements, the intelligent and honest people are killed. As we know that many Indian leaders were killed.
(iii) *Religious Form*: Some religions lay emphasis on celibacy. The religious leaders remain unmarried, which affects the birth rate and also deprives the society of intelligent children being born.
(iv) *Legal Form*: The laws of the country also act as social selection. The murderers are hanged which again affects the birth rate.
(v) *Economic Form*: There are some economic pursuits, which increase the death rate. Thus, minors and other workers working in risky factories like those of explosives are open to death risk.

Social Problems

Poverty

Poverty is relative to richness. Poverty is one of the foremost social problems faced by India and other countries. Poverty exists when one is not able to get sufficient food and necessities of life. When trade expanded, some people began to amass wealth leading to its uneven distribution. They started living a luxurious life depriving others of comforts. The members of society began to compare the differences in economic status and look upon themselves as either poor or rich in accordance with the prevailing living standards. So, poverty is considered a problem only when obvious differences in economic status among members of a society are established and compassions and evaluations of those differences are made. In the absence of these differences, poverty does not exist, even though life may be most precarious. Thus, poverty was not a problem in the middle ages, even though by modern standards the level of living at that time was incredibly low. Poverty was simply accepted as inevitable and is relative to richness.

Caste System

The merits of caste system are:

(i) *Spirit of Cooperation*: It has fastened the spirit of cooperation and fellow-feeling among members of the some castes. By helping the poor and needy, it has avoided the necessity of the state supporting the poor.

(ii) *Defines Economic Pursuits*: It defines the economic pursuits of the individual. There is an occupation pertaining to every caste so that the child's future is not only carved out already but also a proper place of apprenticeship is provided.

(iii) *Racial Purity*: It has preserved the racial purity of the higher caste by forbidding indiscriminate inter-marriages and has greatly fostered the habits of cleanliness by insisting on ritual purity.

(iv) *Cultural Diffusion*: It helps in cultural diffusion within the group. The caste customs, belief, skill, behaviour and the trade secrets are passed on from generation to generation.

(v) *Integration of the Country*: It develops class-consciousness without breeding class struggle. It has created an efficient organization of Hindu society without giving any chance to class frictions and factions.

The demerits of caste system are:

(i) *Denies Mobility of Labour*: It has denied mobility of labour since the individual must follow the caste occupation and cannot change it according to his likes or dislikes. This leads to stagnation.

(ii) *Untouchability*: It leads to social discrimination and untouchability. Large sections of people are reduced to the state of virtual slavery. In addition, it has also created many other social evils like child marriage, dowry system and casteism.

(iii) *Obstacle to the Social Progress:* It is a great obstacle to the social and economic progress of the nation. Since the people believe in the theory of *karma* they become conservative.

(iv) *Obstacle to National Unity*: It has proved an obstacle to the growth of national unity in the country. The lower classes feel discontented at the behaviour meted out to them in society.

(v) *Wrong Man in Occupation*: It often results in putting man on a wrong occupation. There is no guarantee that a priest's son would also like to be a priest or would possess those qualities for a succession priest.

Crime

Crime is a great social problem faced by every society. The law may be written or unwritten. When the law is not written then crime is generally recognized as transgressions against the traditions or mores of the community. Crime, therefore, may be regarded as behaviour of individuals, which the group strongly disapproves and since societies do not have uniform standards of right and wrong and since these standards change in a society from time to time, criminal behaviour is relative and not absolute.

In India, there are no dependable figures on crime. The available statistics cover only those arrested and convicted or the crime known to the police, and even these figures are not reliable. What is more serious is the conventional type of crime. By white-collar crime, we mean the crimes committed by the upper strata of society in their business and professional practice. Black-marketing, tax evasion adulteration and corruption are some of the crime frequently committed by the white-collar men, which have assumed serious proportions threatening the racketeers, black-marketers, smugglers, tax evaders and bribe takers who exert considerable political influence and public seems willing to support their activities through extensive patronage.

Unemployment

Closely associated with the problem of poverty is the problem of unemployment because when people remain idle they become poor. If there are needs to be satisfied, then men must be employed in satisfying them. Unemployment leads not only to suffering and privation but also adversely affects the social organization, which is the main interest of sociologists.

According to Chapman, unemployment is of two kinds:

(i) Subjective unemployment.
(ii) Objective unemployment.

There are four types of objective unemployment:

- (i) Seasonal unemployment.
- (ii) Cyclical unemployment.
- (iii) Structural unemployment.
- (iv) Normal unemployment.

Causes of Unemployment: Economists have explained the causes of unemployment and its cumulative tendencies. There is fractional unemployment due to a change over from one job to another and the immobility of those who do not feel inclined to move away to a strange district to find work on the one hand and unemployment due to more profound economic dislocations on the other. New inventions take jobs away from men before new jobs are created.

Social Problems

Man has been since the dawn of civilization applying his mind to find out a solution to the problems, which he met in the company of his fellow men. The modern man does not deal with the social problems through magic or supernatural forces but instead undertakes a scientific analysis of social problems. The modern approach at present is more realistic and promises to be more effective. There are two current methods to deal with social problems: (i) remedial, and (ii) preventive. The remedial method treats the symptoms of consequences of a problem instead of the underlying causes. The preventive method makes painstaking research to find out all the facts underlying each problem before taking a preventive action. Undoubtedly, if the social problem can be checked at its source, it is the best cure, but the remedial method is now the more common method.

Social Planning

(i) *Unemployment*: To study and solve the problem of unemployment, a separate ministry called Ministry of Labour and Employment has been created. The employment service was started in 1945 consisting of a network of employment exchanges. It renders employment assistance to all the employment services.
(ii) *Harijan Welfare*: To promote the educational and economic interests of the people belonging to the Scheduled Castes and Scheduled Tribes and Other Backward Classes and to remove certain social disabilities, the Constitution of India has provided numerous safeguards.
(iii) *Prohibition*: The Constitution of India has enjoined on the state to endeavour to bring about prohibition of the consumption of intoxicating drinks and drugs throughout the country. The Planning Commission has left to each state to fix target date and to formulate its policy in accordance with local conditions and circumstances.

(iv) *After Care Homes*: On the basis of the recommendations of the advisory committee on after care programmes and of the social and moral advisory committee, after care homes have been started to provide appropriate training and meet other needs of persons discharged from correctional and non-correctional institutions and to rescued women and girls and render necessary assistance for their economic rehabilitation.

AIDS: A Global Epidemic

HIV/AIDS, which has become a pandemic, is thought to be the most recent global health problem facing people from all walks of life. The HIV infection is now found on every inhabited continent. It knows no social, economic, religious, cultural, political or geographical boundaries, and serologic surveys show that infection by the virus is present in all parts of the world and widespread in many. The current estimates by UNAIDS/WHO are that over 40 million people are infected with HIV across the globe. The actual magnitude is unknown but further global spread and increase in numbers of HIV infections are certain. It is therefore likely that the new millennium will see a large increase in the number of HIV-related illnesses, including AIDS in most parts of the world. The virus is transmitted in the same ways but in varying degrees throughout the world and the range of behaviours, which place people at risk of infection, is the same. In fact in all countries, the greatest numbers of those infected have been adults in their chronologically productive and reproductive age group. However, the current manifestations of the epidemic are not identical throughout the world.

HIV/AIDS in India

The National AIDS Control Organization (NACO), Ministry of Health and Family Welfare, Government of India and the WHO, estimate that we have over 4 million people living with HIV in India and over 1,00,000 AIDS cases.

The overwhelming majority of people with HIV – some 95 per cent of the global total – live in the developing world. Almost universally, however, the epidemic has disproportionately affected individuals and communities who are marginalized or discriminated against for reasons of sex, age, ethnicity, race, sexuality, economic status, and cultural, religious or political affiliation.

Poverty is also seen as enhancing vulnerability to HIV. The growing rates of HIV/AIDS in economically disadvantaged communities of the industrialized world and in developing countries emphasize the role played by poverty in fuelling the epidemic.

Although people from every walk of life is at risk of getting infected, trends available show that the most vulnerable are the socially and economically disadvantaged, hailing from developing countries, such as the sex workers, refugees, migrant labourers, truck drivers, substance abjurers, women, children and those requiring blood and blood products.

Problems Faced

Some of the major problems faced in containing HIV/AIDS are:

(1) AIDS is increasingly emerging as a problem for the developing countries. About 95 per cent of all infections are reported to be from the developing countries.
(2) AIDS is threatening the economic gains and continues to ruin fresh initiatives in all fronts.
(3) AIDS is threatening human reproduction and survival.
(4) Discrimination, disrespect, inhuman treatment and violence against those injected with AIDS continue across the globe.
(5) The socially excluded and the homeless require rehabilitative care and support initiatives.
(6) There is a dearth of trained professionals, teachers, health care providers and pastoral workers.
(7) There is dearth of resources to meet the health care needs and social economic support services of the HIV/AIDS infected.
(8) There is a need for adequate educational and awareness programmes in local languages and dialects to reach the last person in the far-flung areas.
(9) Care and rehabilitation of hundreds of thousands of orphans are new challenges.
(10) There is a need to open and maintain hospices of HIV/AIDS patients.
(11) The existing therapies are costly and the existing hospital beds are inadequate all over the country.
(12) Self-abusive behaviour through drug abuse and sexual promiscuity continues among people of all walks of life.

(13) Trafficking among women, young girls and boys is rampant in many societies; most of the public campaigns often promote solutions which are contrary to morality and against human dignity.

(14) The study of ethics is almost absent in school curricula. Family life education with emphasis on sex education has not yet found a place in school education.

Care Providers

(1) Pastoral health care providers as well as every person has to be oriented to stand in solidarity with the AIDS/HIV infected and their families.

(2) Health care workers should be provided with adequate orientation to enable them to respond with compassion, care and unconditional love to those affected by HIV/AIDS.

(3) Unlike other diseases, HIV/AIDS requires specialized counselling services for the patients, family members as well as caregivers.

(4) Adoption and/or foster care of the orphans may be encouraged rather than setting up orphanages. This may be done keeping in view the local culture and social norms.

(5) Keeping in view the sensitive nature of the disease, every one involved in HIV/AIDS work are called to adopt non-judgemental attitude towards the HIV infected.

(6) Hospitals, treatment and health care institutions are challenged to adopt non-discriminatory approach in providing for the HIV/AIDS patients.

Suggestions

The following suggestions may help the pastoral health care providers as well as the patients in addressing issues pertaining to HIV/AIDS to some extent:

(1) There is a need for international, inter-religious, inter-denominational and inter-episcopal collaboration to combat the onslaught of HIV/AIDS.

(2) Efforts must be made to provide sensitization programmes of HIV/AIDS to all the religions. HIV/AIDS education should also form part of the curricula in formation houses.

(3) Educational and awareness programmes with accurate and complete information should be provided, and it should be

extended to health care, educational and rehabilitative sectors as well.

(4) All must respond to HIV/AIDS in a manner consistent with the best medical and scientific information.

(5) Study of ethics and sex education programmes needs to be extended to educational institutions.

(6) Everyone involved in HIV/AIDS prevention are called upon to caution people about 'safe-sex' approach. 'Quick Fixes' compromise human sexuality and may lead to promiscuous sexual behaviour.

Social Work Intervention: HIV/AIDS and Human Rights

The advance of anti-retroviral drugs in industrialized countries has left some with the illusion that the worst of the AIDS epidemic has passed. Nothing could be further from reality in the developing world where the silent voracious epidemic is wiping out the little gains of the public health and economic development efforts of the past years.

There is absolutely no reason to treat HIV-infected patients as social outcasts or objects of hate. Stigma and discrimination towards the victim and the family are the major obstacles to effective HIV/AIDS prevention and care. Since there is no exact medication for AIDS, awareness among the people especially the marginalized sections of the society is the only way to prevent. The social degradation and the ban imposed on the victims and the families deprive of their human rights.

Discrimination and Stigmatization towards the Family and Victim

Discrimination, stigmatization and denial (DSD) are the expected outcome of such values affecting life in families, communities, workplaces, schools and health care settings. Because of HIV/AIDS-related discrimination, stigmatization and denial, appropriate policies and models of good practices remain underdeveloped. People living with HIV and AIDS continue to be burdened by poor care and inadequate services, while those with the power to help do little to make the situation better.

In a study by UNAIDS in India, it was found that there was uncertainty among health care staff about basic HIV-transmission information and about the need for and purpose of universal precautions. Also, the study revealed a depressing picture of widespread labelling stereotyping and lack of care throughout the health sector, with the possible exception of small number of hospital where good practice and policies have been established.

UNAIDS also found that HIV/AIDS-related discrimination, stigmatization and denial in India is in some respect gendered phenomena. Women are often blamed by their parents and in-laws for infecting their husbands, for not controlling their parents; urges to have sex with other women. Children of HIV-positive parents, whether positive or negative themselves, are often denied the right to go to school or are separated from other children. People in marginalized groups are often stigmatized in India on the grounds of not only HIV status but also being member of socially excluded group.

Darker Side of HIV/AIDS Victims

There are many ramification of testing the patient. People have lost job, been thrown out of residences and schools and been denied services they desperately needed.

Physicians and other health care professionals have refused to serve people with HIV/AIDS. Morticians have refused to prepare the bodies for burial. People with HIV/AIDS need to have their rights protected including their rights to free choice. Mandated testing does not guarantee protection from discrimination. The differential treatment would make one feel much like a leper as must have felt or Biblical times.

Human Rights Principles Relevant to HIV/AIDS

Human rights principles most relevant to HIV/AIDS include the right to:

1. Non-discrimination, equal protection and equality before the law.
2. Life.
3. The highest, attainable standard of physical and mental health.
4. Liberty and security of person.
5. Freedom of movement.
6. Seek and enjoy asylum.
7. Privacy.
8. Freedom of opinion and expression and the right to freely receive the impart information.
9. Work.

10. Marry (with similar infected person as spouse to have a better part of remaining life).
11. Equal access to education.
12. An adequate standard of living (social security, assistance and welfare).
13. Share in scientific advancement and its benefits.
14. Participate in public and cultural life.
15. Be free from torture and cruel, in human or degrading treatment or punishment.

UNAIDS Activities in HIV/AIDS and Human Rights

UNAIDS has incorporated a rights-based approach in its prices, programmes and activities and works to mainstream HIV/AIDS into human rights as well as *vice versa* through:

1. Standard setting.
2. Mainstreaming HIV/AIDS in human rights mechanism.
3. Conductions research in HIV/AIDS on human rights mechanism.
4. Strengthening networks on HIV/AIDS, human rights, ethics and law.
5. Engaging critical sectors such as parliamentarians, civil societies and young people.
6. Conducting training on HIV/AIDS and human rights.
7. Providing technical assistance and advice to states.
8. Producing policy and best practices publications.

Compassionate Fraternity of Social Work Profession

Solutions to the problems must involve educating people about HIV/AIDS and preparing them to work with the people who have HIV/AIDS. Health care professionals need to learn what is safe and what is not. They need to work on their own fears and personal conflicts. It is unlikely that making new laws and mandating to people how they must behave will be enough.

All of these matters mean serious attention and considerations, because people who contract their deadly disease deserve attention and compassion. The social work professionals can play following role towards compassionate fraternity of HIV/AIDS patients:

1. Make the family members, neighbours, educational institution authorities and the people at large aware about the disease.
2. Arranging awareness programmes in various villages, slums, etc.

3. Conduct counselling and give some grant where there is an urgent need.
4. Make treatment facilities and public health system accessible to the patients of HIV/AIDS.
5. To reduce the cost of vaccine and make it affordable to the victims.
6. Make the allotted money of the government available to the people who are in need.
7. Family counselling centres must be set up at local levels, so that families at risk may be identified and through counselling, support and help they may be able to accept the fact and realize the pain of others.
8. Apart from counselling, HIV/AIDS awareness workshops, seminars, discussions, home and community-based programmes must be arranged.
9. Home and community-based care being provided to people living with HIV/AIDS is to be done in collaboration with the public, private and voluntary sectors.
10. Consider the victims as a human being, and do not degrade their life.
11. Allow them to enjoy their human rights and fundamental rights, so that they can survive till the last day of life.
12. Encourage health seeking behaviour in general population for reproductive tract infections and HIV/AIDS.

Even as a nation, India is very diverse in cultural characteristics, influenced by the west, in pluralistic and democratic with several political ideologies and languages.

The gap between theory and practice of social work has been a source of discontent not only in India, but also over the world. In India, this is also related to the western and urban bias of social work education. The need for native and adapt of theories to the local context has to be acknowledged.

There are some that believe that social work can only be developed within the local and cultural context. There are some others who believe that both universal and context specific social work, values and knowledge can be transferred through a process of adaptation. In India, important ideas have been modified to make them relevant to local condition and occasionally to form a new structure of ideas.

2

Social Change and Development

Change is the law of nature. What is today, shall be different from what it would be tomorrow. The social structure is subject to incessant change. Fifty years hence, the government is bound to make important changes. Family and religion will not remain the same during this period because these institutions are changing. Individuals may strive for stability, societies may continue unabated, yet the fact remains that society is an ever-changing phenomenon, growing, decaying, renewing and accommodating itself to changing conditions and suffering vast modifications in the course of time.

The social welfare service also plays a very important role specially in the context of developing countries, where poverty, unemployment, illiteracy, high infant mortality, malnutrition and poor housing, afflict a very large segment of the population and are to a very large extent, responsible for the problems which required a welfare intervention, led to the evolution of the development approach, and a thrust to welfare to make it an integral part of the development process.

As we know, social work is the art of helping people to help themselves. If so, social development is a process that cuts at the root of helplessness, it seeks to recreate a new set of values, attitudes and practices, with different, more suitable and efficacious 'institutions', that is, structures and organizations to translate those values into practice. In simple words, development can be defined as a process of directed change towards some objectives which are accepted as desirable goals. It also implies progressive improvement in the living conditions and quality of life enjoyed by society and shared by its members. In fact, it is a multidimensional process.

Social Development

Social development is a broad concept encompassing improvement in the social status of the people. Social development lays stress on provision of health services, education, housing, cultural amenities, protection of children, a change in the status of women, regulation of labour and improved status for workers and reduction of disease, poverty and other illness. According to T.K.N. Unnithan, "Social development may be seen as a process of ushering in a new order of existence. The quality of life and the quality of social relations which exist would indicate the level of the order of existence."

It has been realized increasingly over the years that social development is necessary, not only to provide opportunities to individuals for self-development, but also as a vital contribution to economic development. The distinction between social and economic development is no longer tenable. Economic development is necessary to achieve most social goals and social development, which is in turn necessary to achieve most economic goals. The purpose of development is to permit people to lead economically productive and socially satisfying lives.

Concept of Social Development: Indicators, Goals, Objectives and Problems

The process of development is now adopted by the modern states to lift their people from deprivation, disease, disasters and disabilities. The concern for promoting individual happiness and an ardent desire for strengthening community welfare activities through a process of socio-economic development are being considered among the essential characteristics of the modern welfare states.

Meaning and Goals of Development

The word 'development' is so often used in our daily life that we hardly care to think of its real meaning. The meaning of the term 'develop' is to unfold itself or to grow into a fuller or mature condition, and 'ment' stands for instrument of action, an act or process. In simple words, development can be defined as a process of directed change towards some objectives, which are accepted as desirable goals. Development implies progressive improvements in the living conditions and quality of life enjoyed by society and shared by its members. It is a conditioning process that takes place in all societies.

The hierarchy of goals of development may be shown in the form of a pyramid, wherein at the base are basic minimum needs followed by economic and social necessities for bare subsistence. The fulfilment of these needs leads to a higher set of socio-political needs and ultimately to the goal of the full flowering of human personality or 'total development' and the release of the creative energies of every individual.

(iv) Culture	(iv) full development of human potentials and creativity.
(iii) Socio-political	(iii) equity of distributive justice, social equality, redistribution of assets democracy.
(ii) Socio-economic	(ii) higher growth with greater equity, mass consciousness.
(i) Basic minimum needs	(i) eradication of abject poverty and unemployment – access to minimum income and public services through employment with people's participation.

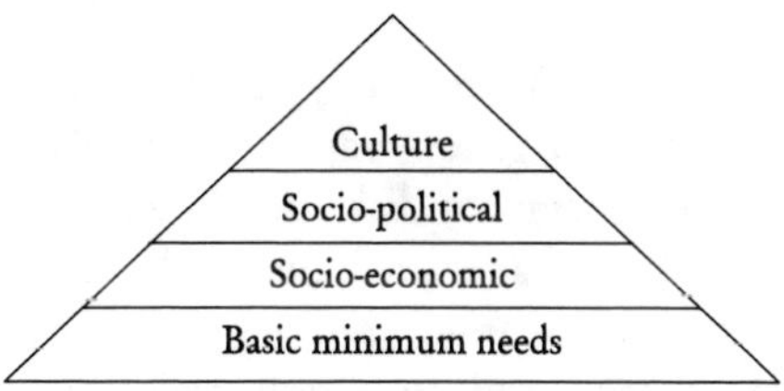

The final aim of development must be the constant increase of the well-being of the entire population on the basis of its full participation in the process of development and a fair distribution of benefits there from. Thus, the aim of development should be to enrich the quality of life.

Indicators

The literal meaning of the word 'indicator' is one that indicates, shows or points out. It thus reminds one of a pointed arrow which shows the direction and makes one think of an equally sharp, well defined measure or figure which can be plotted to show the trend of what is happening. It has a wider connotation than the 'index number', which has been defined in statistics as "a quantity, which shows, by its variations the changes over time or space of magnitude, which is not susceptible of direct measurement in itself or direct observation in practice".

(i) *Role in Development Planning*: According to Donald McGranahan, a former director of the UN Research Institute for Social Development, an economic or social indicator may be called a development indicator if "it represents some factor that is part of the process of development. This in turn implies a definition or theory as to what constitutes development. Since developing tends to be an interdependent process, a good indicator in fact reflects, in varying degrees, many more things than it directly measures."

The main functions of social indicators in development planning are: (a) quantification of the goals of development, and (b) measurement of progress towards those goals. They also provide the basis for the study and establishment of interrelationships between the different factors, which influence the development process, and for the projection of long-term trends. Key social indicators are sometimes used in the construction of development models.

Social indicators can further be used for the study and assessment of inter-regional, interclass and inter-group variations in social structure, social development and social conditions. They are also used for the identification of backward areas, backward classes and backward groups in order to formulate ameliorative programmes. Social indicators have often been used in combination with economic indicators in view of the inevitable interaction of social and economic phenomena.

Objectives and Problems

One of the major objectives of social development is to improve the well-being of the people. It is generally measured by the provision of social welfare services and the living levels. So, in order to achieve this social welfare objectives, it is necessary to attend to a wide variety or problems that the new industrializing countries are facing. These problems have been enlisted in Encyclopaedia of Social Work in India. These are as follows:

(1) Problems generated because of lack of industrial or economic development:
    (i) Poverty.

- (ii) Ill-health.
- (iii) Ignorance.

(2) Problems born out of industrialization and urbanization:
- (i) Bad housing, overcrowding and mushroom growth of slums.
- (ii) Family change, family breakdown, widowhood, orphanhood, old age, etc.
- (iii) Juvenile delinquency, crime and social defence.
- (iv) Psychological strains and breakdowns.

(3) Problems which crop up because of value change and readjustment of interests:
- (i) The lower status of women.
- (ii) The traditionally underprivileged groups and communities.

(4) Problems resulting from political reorganization:
- (i) Political minorities.
- (ii) Refugees.
- (iii) Corruption.

(5) Problem of individual handicaps:
- (i) The physically handicapped, blind, deaf, victims of accidents, prolonged illness, etc.
- (ii) The mentally deranged, the backward and retarded.
- (iii) The mentally ill.

The social development of services is to be improved, recognized and strengthened in these areas.

Areas of Development

In fact, there are three areas of development – economic, political and social. It is very difficult to isolate one from the other. Economic development in terms of an increase in national per capita income is no longer regarded as the only development objective. The same is true of the other two aspects.

Economic Development

Economic development – a high growth rate of the national product is a means to an end, i.e., it cannot in itself be the ultimate objective, the final goal of a dynamic society. Economic growth is never more than the method of obtaining the means through which a nation plans to achieve some form of social progress or social change. Developing nations have become increasingly conscious of the social aspects of economic planning. It is now generally realized that economic growth should be a means towards the eradication of hunger, illiteracy, disease, and reduction of existing social and economic inequalities. The consequences of growth without development are too painful to be ignored.

The attainment of ideals of modernization, rise in productivity, industrialization, social and economic equalization, development of modern knowledge, improved institutions and attitudes, and a rationally coordinated system of policy measures that may, on the one hand, remove the host of undesirable conditions in the social system that have perpetuated a state of underdevelopment, while on the other, promote better nourishment, better health, better education, better living conditions, etc.

Political Development

The Encyclopaedia of Social Work in India does give attention to the political aspect of international aid to less developed countries. Such help "would tend to allow countries recently on the way to development, someday to achieve by themselves their economic and social progress", a situation that will allow the formation of a true community of peoples. If the problems inside the underdeveloped countries have not been treated in the encyclopaedia, it is certainly in the spirit of its remark on international aid, that they need to be discussed. This involves respect for the personality and the independence of people on the one hand, and respect for the dignity and the freedom of persons on the other. Freedom is not the declaration of a moral or political system that has neither obligation nor sanction.

The people in countries that have just begun to develop, need a regime of law and system - regimes where there is freedom of each individual, where essential rights of the person are respected and where the possibilities of responsible participation are offered to the citizens. It is the progress in the direction of such participation that should be called political development. It is besides, in good measure, the need for political and civic dignity and in short the dignity of man himself, which generates the aspiration for economic development.

Social Development

Social development lays stress on provision of health services, education, housing, cultural amenities, protection of children, a change in the status of women, regulation of labour and improved status for workers and reduction of disease, poverty and other social illness.

Thus, social development is more concerned with the investment in human beings. It has been realized increasingly over the years, that social development is necessary not only to provide opportunities to individuals for self-development but also as a vital contribution to economic development.

Social development deals with the society and human resources, whereas economic development deals with economy and material resources. Social justice and human welfare are the key objectives of social development. Social development is considered as the development of society. Society is not just an assembly of people but it is a manifestation of human craving for reaching out to others. It is a web of human relations, conceiving society in this manner. Social development may be defined as development of the society from a less human to more human state of affairs. Social development comprises of four components, viz., material and social well-being of man, enlargement of human consciousness as reflected in the rise of a multinational human self, growth of humanitarian concern, i.e., concern for others, and strengthening of the sense of community life. The economic development, political development and social development are complimentary.

Social Problems and Its Impact on Social Work

Major Social Problems

There are some problems facing contemporary society and having far reaching effects on it. These are the problems of poverty, unemployment, crime and war.

(i) *Poverty*: Poverty is relative to richness. Poverty is one of the foremost social problems facing India and other countries. John L. Gillin asserted that poverty may be regarded as "that condition in which a person withers because of inadequate income or unwise expenditures, does not maintain a scale of living high enough to provide for his physical and mental efficiency and to enable him and his natural dependence to function usually according to the standards of society of which he is a member". Poverty exists when one is not able to get sufficient food and necessities of life.

When trade expanded, some people began to amass wealth leading to its uneven distribution. They started living a luxurious life depriving others of comforts. The members of society began to be compared with the differences in economic status and looked upon themselves as either poor or rich in accordance with the prevailing living standards. So, poverty is considered a problem only when obvious differences in economic status among members of a society are established and comparisons and evaluations of those differences are made. It is only when people feel resentment at their lot as compared with that of others that they feel the sting of poverty. In case of extreme privation too they may feel this sting without comparing their lot with that of others. They fail to achieve more than what they have and the awareness of this failure causes resentment of poverty among them. Therefore, it is the attitude of resentment, which brings the problem of poverty to the forefront. People are poor not because of an increase in misery but because of the attitude of resentment at what they do not possess and what others possess. They regard themselves as poor when they feel deprived of what others possess and enjoy. It is then that poverty becomes a social problem.

(ii) *Unemployment*: Closely associated with the problem of poverty is the problem of unemployment because for the poor, if there are needs to be satisfied, then men must be employed in satisfying them. Unemployment leads not only to suffering and privation but also affects adversely the social organization which is the main interest of sociologists. Defining unemployment, Karl Pribram has written that "unemployment is a condition of the labour market in which the supply of labour is greater than the number of available openings".

Though unemployment is universal but it is more marketed in India. The number of total unemployed youth with at least matriculation is just about at five million. This includes about 1.5 million unemployed graduates. Economists have explained the causes of unemployment and its cumulative tendencies. They have distinguished between the frictional unemployment due to a change over from one job to another, and the immobility of those who do not feel inclined to move away to a strange district to find work on the one hand, unemployment due to more profound economic dislocation on the other.

In India, the problem of unemployment among the educated youth is assuming serious proportions. The faulty system of our education has been responsible for it. We are admitting thousands of youth, boys and girls, to the institutions of higher learning without any prospects of employment for them. Even the technical people like engineers, doctors and those trained in specialized jobs are without employment. Unemployment is a great cause of social disorganization. The crisis in Indian society today is largely a crisis of finding suitable jobs for the millions who join institutions aimlessly and come out of them only to suffer frustration outside and become deviant. Unless and until employment opportunities increase fast enough, poverty cannot be removed.

(iii) *Crime*: Crime or delinquency is a great social problem facing every society. Crime is the price paid for the advantage of civilization. Crime is said to be a major social phenomenon of modern civilized and advanced societies. Though there was crime in primitive societies too, but then it was not a major social problem.

There are no dependable figures on crime in India. The available statistics cover only those arrested and convicted, or the crime known to the police, and even their figures are not reliable. What is more serious is the white-collar crime, which amounts to several times more than the conventional type of crime. By white-collar crimes we mean the crimes committed by the upper strata of society in their business and professional practices. The securities scam, the sugar, the telecom scam, stamp paper scam and the fodder scam are some examples. Racketeering, black-marketing, tax evasion, adulteration and corruption are some of the crimes committed by the white-collar men frequently, which have assumed serious proportions threatening the entire social fabric. What is a more sorry state of affairs is that the racketeers, black-marketers, smugglers, tax evaders and bribe takers exert considerable political influence and have entered the legislatures. The public seems willing to support their activities through extensive patronage. Our moral sense is at a low ebb. Moreover, the data from the penal institutions shows that a large percentage of inmates are repeaters, reflecting the failure of our society to rehabilitate the criminal. The country spends several crore of rupees in detecting, convicting and guarding the criminals, yet crime goes on increasing day by day. If we in India place high value on wealth, prestige and political power, regardless of the way in which they are acquired and if the leaders refuse to abide by laws which they wish to be enforced against other persons, then, of course, we cannot expect the incidence of crime to go down.

(iv) *War*: War causes mental derangement in the armed services by creating strains on the minds of the soldiers. During war, all the important social institutions such as family, school and church become subordinated to the state and the army. The traditional functions of these institutions are neglected. Family suffers a severe jolt; war separates many husbands and often ill-considered marriages prevents many parents from providing the parental supervision that they would otherwise give to their children. For many reasons, a relaxation of sex morality occurs in the minds of a nation at war. War propaganda distorts the mind of individuals and stirs up feelings of hatred, turning whole nations into mobs. The growth of war-occasioned political restrictions, places a great strain upon the citizen's respect for war. Many resent these restrictions and 'black-markets' flourish. The government becomes less efficient and there is popular revolution against government controls.

Solutions to Social Problems

Solution to social problems is beset with many hurdles. First, the problem should be accepted by the members of a society as a problem and as we know some die-hards may refuse to regard a particular situation as a problem. The existence of the social structure is supported by powerful sentiments and vested interests who deny the existence of the problem to safeguard the advantages according to them under the situation.

Second, some societies do not want to expose their ways of thinking, feeling and living to scientific inquiry. Third, finances may be hurdle; the necessary amount of money may not be available or some may object to expenditure for changing the established modes of living of the people. Finally, there is the problem of implementation; we may be possessed of sufficient knowledge of how to deal with a social problem, but that does not guarantee its implementation.

Social Change

The word 'change' denotes a difference in anything observed over some period of time. Social change, therefore, would mean observable differences in any social phenomena over any period of time. It may refer to the modifications, which take place in the life patterns of people. It does not refer to all the changes going on in the society. The changes in art, language, technology, philosophy, etc., may not be included in the term 'social change', which should be interpreted in a narrow sense to mean alterations in the field of social relationships. Social relationships are social processes, social patterns and social interactions. Thus social change will mean variations of any aspect of social processes, social patterns, social interactions or social organization. It is a change in the institutional and normative structure of society. According to Mazumdar, social change is a new fashion or mode, either modifying or replacing the old, in the life of a people or in the operation of a society.

Social Development as a Process of Social Change

The term 'social change' itself suggests nothing as far as its direction is concerned. It is a generic term describing one of the categorical processes. It only suggests a difference through time in the object to which it is applied. Social changes are of various types and can be explained by different terms such as growth, progress, evolution, revolution, adaptation and accommodation, etc.

Evolution

Evolution is a process of differentiation and integration. The term 'evolution' comes from the Latin word 'evolver' which means to develop or to unfold. The word 'growth' connotes a direction of change but only of a quantitative character, e.g., we say population growth. Evolution involves something more intrinsic change not merely inside but at least in structure also, for example when we speak of biological evolution, we refer to the emergence of certain organisms from others in a kind of succession. Evolution describes a series of related changes in a system of some kind. It is a process in which hidden or latent characters of a thing reveal themselves. It is an order of change, which unfolds the variety of aspects belonging to the nature of the changing object. We cannot speak of evolution when an object or system is changed by forces acting on it from without. The change must occur within the change unit as the manifestation of forces operative within it.

According to Herbert Spencer, there are four principles of evolution:

(i) Social evolution is one cultural or human aspect of the law of cosmic evolution.

(ii) Social evolution takes place in the same way in which cosmic evolution takes place.
(iii) Social evolution is gradual.
(iv) Social evolution is progressive.

Social evolution does not always proceed by differentiation. But the point at issue is whether this process of differentiation-cum-integration is sufficient to explain the general march of society, excluding thereby, any other kind of interpretation. In every field where we find the forces of differentiation at work, there the opposite trends are also manifested. Thus, in the development of languages where the process of differentiation has been stressed, we have many disconcerting facts. The modern language derived from Sanskrit like Bengali or Gujarati cannot be compared in their structure with the richness and diversity of their origin. Here, the process is not towards differentiation but towards simplification. On the whole, we find that social evolution does not always proceed by differentiation, but also by simplification and synthesis. To define, social evolution is the process by which individuals are detached from or fail to be attached to an old group norm, so that ultimately a new norm is achieved.

Progress

In the earlier theories of biological evolution, the idea of progress was closely associated with that of evolution. For the social evolutionists of the nineteenth century, social evolution was in effect with social progress. The technological advance of the same century led many philosophers and sociologists to conclude that the major trends of social phenomena are made for social progress.

Progress is a development or evolution in a direction, which satisfies rational criteria of value. According to Ogburn, progress "is a movement towards an objective, thought to be desirable by the general group, for the visible future". When we speak of progress we do not imply direction, but direction towards some final goal, some destination determined ideally. Progress means change for the better and hence implies a value judgement. It is not possible to speak of progress without reference to standards. Progress is achieved if, in a society, all aspects of social life move in a coordinated manner towards desired ends. Briefly to put the characteristics of progress are the following:
(i) Progress is change; a change in some direction.
(ii) Change can be called progress only when it fulfils the desired aim.

(iii) Progress is communal, i.e., related to social system.
(iv) Progress is volitional. It requires desire and volition.
(v) The concept of progress is variable. What is considered today the symbol of progress may tomorrow be regarded as sign of regress.
(vi) There are no limits of human progress.

Have we progressed? Standards of morality are no respecters of technical achievement. However, the answer to whether we have progressed or not depends upon our standards of moral value. We have invented aeroplanes and other fast-moving mobiles, but does it bring more security of our life? Our country is on the way to industrialization but does this bring health, happiness or peace of mind? There can be much difference of opinion about whether we have progressed or not. Progress in science is a good thing in itself. Evidence of progress in morality from preliterate society to modern civilization is simply lacking. In spite of the many technological achievements, big industries and imposing dams, the fact remains that in India the evils of unemployment, crime, violence and disease have not lessened. The family bonds have loosened. More marriages break down now than before. The social evils like drug-addiction, dowry system, prostitution, alcoholism, child exploitation and delinquency have increased manifold. We are politically hypocrites, economically corrupt, socially dishonest and morally unfaithful. In the face of these multitudinous defects in our social conduct, it would be hard to maintain that we have progressed. Thinkers like Mahatma Gandhi and Aurobindo Ghosh have warned mankind against moral degeneration.

Factors of Social Change

Social change has occurred in all societies and in all periods of time. But, the rate of social change differs from society to society. In one society, the rate is rapid while in another it is necessarily slow. There are various factors, which determine the rate and direction of social change. They are as follows:

Biological Factors

Under biological factors of social change, we include: (i) the plants and animals in the area, and (ii) human beings themselves. The non-human biological environment affects human, social and cultural life. Man utilizes the available plant and animal life in ways determined by his culture. For example cow is regarded sacred among Hindus. Many plants are used for medicinal purposes. Changes in geographic conditions such as change in climate, change in soil composition, drying up of lakes and streams kill some organisms and give birth to others. Changes affect the nature of man's struggle for existence.

The human biological environment includes the factors that determine the numbers, the composition, the selection and the hereditary quality of the successive generations. The human element in society is always changing. Every life has a different distribution of qualities and potentialities. If we compare ourselves with our parents, we will know that we are different from them in our make-up, in ideas and in most other things. No new generation is an exact replica of the old. Each new generation is a new beginning.

Moreover, if the growth of population is checked, it would mean a higher standard of living, the emancipation of woman from child-bearing drudgery, better care for the young and consequently a better society. The countries with growing population and relatively limited resources have an incentive to imperialism and to militarism. When the growth of population threatens the standard of living, it inspires a change of attitude. Thus, in the nineteenth century contraceptives were designated as immoral, but today they are not so regarded, rather their use is encouraged and patronized by the society. With the decrease of the size of the family, the facility of marriage and of divorce, the relations between husband and wife, the relations between children and parents, the mode of upbringing of children, the position of the mother in the house and the degree of economic self-sufficiency of the family have all been changing. Thus, it is evident that the changes in the numbers and composition of population are causing a number of changes in social relations.

Physical Factors

The surface of our planet is never at rest. There are slow geographical changes as well as the occasional convulsions of nature in the form of storm, earthquakes and floods. Besides the seasonal changes, there are sometimes epochal changes, which raise and submerge portions of the earth's surface. These changes in the physical environment sometimes bring about important changes in society. The floods in India may hasten the birth of model villages in place of those, which have been washed off, or they may lead to the construction of dams in order to prevent future floods. The leaders of the geographical school insist that only physical environment is alone responsible for the growth of human society.

It may also be remembered that physical environment governs the social condition. Every culture develops in some sort of physical setting. Environment, as we have seen earlier limits or permits the growth of civilization. At the poles and in the deserts, there can be no cities, for there is no economic surplus. Every civilization is exploitative. Its birth and continuance depends, among other things, on the presence of certain natural resources and the ability to conserve or find substitutions for them. At the poles and in the deserts, the available time is spent only in the business of keeping alive. Stability is maintained, and whenever any changes are made it is both slow and insignificant. In the more temperate climates, there are rapid changes in society. The absence of some factors can prevent the change in a certain direction. The non-availability of coal, iron and oil within the borders can prevent a large and populous nation from becoming a great military power. But, the physical habitat in no way 'causes' the culture. It only sets the stage for social life, a wide and elaborate stage or a small and barren one as the case may be. Davis says, "But the geographical environment, unaffected by man, changes very slowly and therefore, cannot explain most social changes". Nothing much happened to the climate of Europe during the last five centuries, yet the social system was tremendously transformed by industrial revolution. The same geographical environment may support extremely different civilizations, and similar civilizations can exist in quite different physical settings. In most cases, in which geographical change is alleged to produce social change, it will be found that the alleged geographical setting is in part man-made and therefore, itself socially determined.

Technological Factors

Technology affects society greatly, in that a variation in technology causes a variation in some institution or custom. The introduction of machine technology as a result of the discovery of the new sources of energy has had such far-reaching consequences, that it is often described as a 'revolution'. Invention and discovery are significant characteristics of our age. The present age is often called the 'age of power', the 'scientific age'. It has been well said that, "the most novel and pervasive phenomenon of our age is not capitalism but mechanization, of which modern capitalism may be merely a by-product". Mechanization has changed not only the economic structure of society but has also led to a steady devaluation of old forms of social organization and old ideologies. Ogburn says, "Technology changes society by changing our environments to which we in turn adapt. This change is usually in the material environment and the adjustment we make with changes often modifies customs and social institutions." The following are the effects of technology on different levels:

(i) *Changes in the Production Technology*: Industrialism has destroyed the domestic system of production, brought women from the home to the factory and the office, and distinguished their earnings. It has meant a new social life for women. The invention of gun powder changed the very technique of war. Standardization of goods, and evident consequence of modern technology, has made possible not only cheap production of goods but highly organized, efficient mass distribution of goods. Increased productive efficiency in industry released a considerable proportion of the population for service functions.

(ii) *Changes in the Agricultural Technology*: It has affected the rural community. With the invention of new agricultural tools and chemical manures, agricultural production has increased thereby raising the standard of living of the rural people. Fewer people are now needed to do agriculture. Consequently, many agricultural labourers have shifted to cities to find employment.

(iii) *Changes in the Means of Communication*: The changes in the means of communication also have affected social life greatly. Its techniques definitely limit the kind of organized life that people can have. The primary techniques of communication are speech and gesture since these techniques provide the base upon which all other modes of communication are built. The press has influenced entertainment, education, politics and trade. It has brought to the country dweller, knowledge of the urban life. The invention of radio, telegraph, telephone and Internet has influenced the business, recreation, public opinion and furthered the development of new modes of organization.

(iv) *Changes in the Means of Transportation*: The changes in the modes of transportation have variously affected our social relationships. Transportation is the physical conquest of space. The methods and means of transportation determine how easily men can move themselves and how easily they can meet people of other places or other societies to exchange goods or ideas. The importance of transportation in modern social life, can hardly be stressed. Modern man lives so much on wheels that he would not be able to live in suburbs and work in the city, were it not for the local transport, that he could not leave home for the station with only a few minutes to spare and were it not for the ships and trains that tie the many places of world together commercially. If the wheels of transportation were to stop for a single day, the life of the modern society would be put out of gear.

(v) *Effects of Technology on Major Social Institutions*: It may be summed up as follows:

(a) *Effects on Family Life*: Modern technology has changed the family organization and relations in general ways. It has led to the disintegration of joint family system. The employment of women in factories and offices has changed the forms of husband-wife relationship and affected the family structure and functions in several ways. It has led to the liberation of women. The 'Liberation Movement' is the consequence of technology. Love-marriage, late-marriage are the other effects of technology. The invention of birth control devices has reduced the size of the family.

(b) *Effects on Economic Life*: Industry has been taken from the household and new type of economic organizations like factories, agencies, stores and banks have come up. Economy has acquired a global character. It has given birth to capitalism and its attendant evils; it has brought in higher standard of living. Division of labour and specialization are the products of technology. It has caused economic depression, unemployment, industrial disputes, accidents and diseases. It has given birth to trade-union movement. It has created a middle class of white-collar employees.

(c) *Effects on Social Life*: It has led to decline of community life. It has brought about a sense of individualism. It has created the problem of houses and slums in the cities. It has changed the basis of social stratification with the birth of wealth. It has narrowed the gap of caste system. It has grown psychic conflicts and diseases. The modern man suffers from great mental strain, emotional instability and economic insecurity. It has also led to consumerism.

(d) *Effects on the State*: A large number of functions have been transferred from the family to the state. The idea of social welfare state is an offshoot of technology. The scope of state activity has been enlarged. The influence of pressure groups over the state has been increased. It has led to a shift of function from local government to the central government. Democracy has become the common form of government. It has made the state secular. It has increased the size and power of bureaucracy.

(e) *Effects on Religious Life*: With the growth of scientific knowledge, the role of superstition has decreased. There is now more of religious tolerance. The followers of different religions have shed off their orthodoxy and mix with each other. Religious fundamentalism is on the decline.

Cultural Factors: The Cultural Lag

Ogburn distinguishes between 'material' and 'non-material' culture. By material aspects of culture he means things like tools, utensils, machines, dwellings, the manufacture of goods and transportation. In the non-material aspects he includes family, religion, government and education. When changes occur in the material aspects, those in tune stimulate changes in the non-material aspects. The non-material culture, according to Ogburn, is often slow to respond to the rapid inventions in material culture. When non-material culture does not adjust itself readily to the material changes it falls behind the material culture, and the result is a lag between the two. This lag between non-material and material culture has been called 'Culture lag'.

In a sense, modern societies suffer from too little than too much change. People have changed their methods of cultivation of the soil, but not the methods of owning the land. They have changed their habitations but not the life they lead within them. They have changed their methods of warfare but not the forms of political organizations that make recurrent wars. The patriarchal type of family, adapted to agricultural conditions, is continued in a largely industrial urban society. During the late nineteenth and early twentieth centuries, industry changed first, and the family lagged behind in its change. Women are slow in following their jobs outside the home. Thus, after citing various examples Ogburn concluded that "the many and frequent technological innovations of our modern age by occurring prior to the social changes they precipitate, are the causes of many culture lags in society."

Problems of Social Development

There are number of reasons why people oppose social change and development. The following are the important reasons:

Desire for Stability

The first important reason is that people want stability. The individual must feel secure in his future expectations if he is to cooperate efficiently with others. Change disturbs the existing equilibrium and people are apprehensive of the future. There is always present a fear of the new, therefore, people are on their guards against change.

Inadequacy of Invention

Secondly, initially inventions are inadequate for one reason or the other. Some inventions have disadvantages, not compensated for sufficiently, by the advantages they possess. In some cases, the costs are prohibitive.

Ignorance

Ignorance is another reason for opposition. It usually takes a considerable time for a new discovery to be understood. The prevailing ignorance about the new germ theory of disease was not easy to dispel. It took many generations for the iron plough to be generally accepted. It was thought that the iron would somehow injure. This fear, however, could have been dispelled by showing positive experiments to the resisters about the new invention.

Habit and Tradition

Habit is another obstacle to social change. Individuals do things mostly by habit and custom. They dislike unfamiliarity. Adoption of an invention requires the substitution of new habits from those which are fixed. Traditional habits and reverence to the supernatural have made the people often opposed to birth control methods and such other countless innovations.

Economic Costs

Economic costs to create an invention may also prove an obstacle to its adoption in modern times; to launch an invention, mechanical or social, costs money. Thus, for the adoption of national compulsory health insurance, large sums of money may be needed. Hence, the mere cost of adopting inventions and reforms may prove to be an obstacle. Moreover, if the view in a previous trial proved to be expensive and socially disruptive, it would be greatly opposed now and in the future as well.

Vested Interests

The power of 'vested interests' constitutes an obstacle to innovation. The people who feel that social change endangers their interests fight every proposal when their rights are threatened. For instance, take the case of Zamindari system. Similarly, the construction of a railway line is often opposed by the people whose lands might be acquired for the purpose. Their opposition rests on their selfishness. The Indian Brahmins opposed reforms in Hindu code because it attacked their interest. So, it should be noted that such self-interest seeks change only when it brings power, wealth or reputation, for example, the political card played in the name of OBC's empowerment.

Intellectual Laziness

Finally, the fact of inertia and intellectual laziness leads man to oppose any change. He would much rather borrow than try a new path. Change cannot come unless there is a desire for change and a confidence that it will be helpful.

Strategy of Social Development

Strategy is one of the ways to proceed from the known to the unknown and from the simple to the sophisticated. It is a deliberate intervention with the instruments of policy and planning to bring about a non-random change towards the desired goals. It is, in other words, concerned with the micro-symptomatic treatment in social welfare.

Social Development as an Alternate Approach to Development

Balanced and Integrated Approach

As more and more of the social lags in development came to light in successive United Nations reports on the World Social Situations, there emerged an appeal for what was called a balance and integrated approach to development. It was argued to an extent, supported by empirical studies, that the social component of the national plans made a significant, although not always measurable or manifest contribution even to activating the fountain springs of economic advance. More and more progressive economists started emphasizing the non-economic determinants: for our purpose the social determinants of development, which made it appear as though the social sectors were ascending in prestige. However, doubts were expressed about the precise meaning of balance and the manner of integration.

Unified Approach to Development

The UN General Assembly endorsed the views of the experts regarding the need for a unified approach to development analysis and planning which will fully integrate the economic and social components. This unified approach was to include as components: "(i) to leave no section of the population outside the scope of change and development, (ii) to effect structural change which favours national development and activates all sectors of the population to participate in the development process, (iii) to aim at social equity, including the achievement of an equitable distribution of income and wealth in the nation, and (iv) to give high priority to the development of the human potentials, including vocational and technical training and the provision of employment opportunities and meeting the needs of children. The above criteria to be borne in mind in development analysis and planning processes, as well as in their implications, according to the particular development needs of each country."

Basic Needs Approach

Recently, another approach to social development has been formulated which is described, as the basic needs approach. It is gaining considerable popularity in national as well as international discussions on development. The background for this approach seems to be the realization that it is almost impossible to substantially reduce unemployment and poverty within the next two decades.

According to Streeten, there are two ways of defining a basic needs approach to development. The first definition embraces the components of previous strategies and approach such as rural development, urban poverty alleviation, employment creation through small scale industries, redistribution with growth, and other poverty, employment and equity oriented approaches. If there is anything new in this, it is a shift of emphasis towards social services and transfer payments, designed to help the poor, and an extension of 'new style' projects in nutrition, health and education. The second approach as one supplementing or complementing existing development strategies. This approach according to him, "focuses on the end, channelling particular resources to particular group, identified as deficient in these resources. It concentrates on the nature of what is provided rather than income". It does not replace the existing growth-related concepts, but is derived from the aim of meeting basic human need for changing composition of output, the rates of growth of its different components and the distribution of purchasing power.

Holistic Approach to Development

A holistic approach reveals the totality of the process of development, which in the past has been viewed fragmentarily and compartmentally based on the primary concern of the particular social science discipline such as economics, sociology, political science, etc. It is now realized that development as a concept is broader than economic growth or economic development and non-economic aspects of development do not follow as an inevitable by-development product of economic growth. A meeting of experts on social policy and social planning under UN auspices stressed that economic phenomena are, in fact, social phenomena: "They are social in nature, are socially conditioned and have social consequences, and any development planning limited to economic interrelationships and neglecting social conditions and social implications is bound to be misleading. It is most necessary to view the development process as a complex whole, comprising not only economic elements strictly, but also other social as well as political and administrative elements."

Rural Development, Urbanization, Transportation, Introspective Communication and Social Services like Education, Employment, Income, Health, Nutrition and Housing

The minimum needs programme is based on both productive and distributive strategies in the following manner. In so far as resources are directed towards raising education, employment, income, nutrition, health and housing, etc., there is production in each of these nation-building sectors. At the same time, since programmes and projects are focussed on the lower echelons of population, they ensure that benefits of development reach out to the larger masses.

Education

Thanks to the World Bank under the leadership of M.C. Namara, education has augured a respectable status in the developmental strategies around the world. It is, however, necessary to give much deeper thought to educational policies, quality and content of education beyond the well worn out cliché that education should be development-oriented.

The crux of successful educational planning lies in achieving balance or equilibrium between liberal and technical education, rural and urban education for boys and girls, lower and higher stages of education, etc. While revamping the entire education system, certain basic assumptions, which have guided educational planning, so far, also need to be reviewed thoroughly.

Employment

It is possible to increase the gross national product (GNP) and even the rate of growth of a country by capital-intensive method and automated technology without generating additional employment to any appreciable extent. As a corrective, national plans have now begun providing a few supplementary projects, which are regarded as labour intensive. It is not sufficiently realized though that employment generation cannot be just a patch on a development plan grossly oriented to GNP. In the first place, it presents a big, basic question of choice of a proper technology or at least a choice of a correct mix of technologies with optimum employment potential, consistent with the need of modernization of the economy.

Income

While the production of income is largely an economic process, its distribution is a matter of social concern and has political implications. As for more equitable distribution of income, social services have not received much attention as a national device to redistribute resources in favour of the lower income groups; taxation alone is an out dated and inadequate nexus to a more even spread of income and wealth. The main difference between taxation and social services in this respect is that the former can only level down, whereas the latter levels up the standard of living of the poorer sections of population.

Nutrition and Health

Much has been said and little done on the familiar fronts of nutrition and health in terms of need-based development. While the relationship between food and nutrition is a matter of common knowledge, considerable work remains to be done in terms of assessing and translating national requirements of nutrition into food policies and agricultural plans. The fluctuations of cash economy, state interventions in agricultural market, pressures of export promotion and dictates of foreign exchange earnings seem to be more important factors in determining crop patterns and food policies.

As for health, it is surprising that while universal primary education is one of the directive principle of state policy in most developing countries, universal primary health care or even immunization is considered a reasonable enough proposition to be aimed at, in any health plan for the development of societies.

Housing

Housing is one such sector on which there has been a deterioration, not only in terms of the shortages of the number of dwelling units, but in the standards of facilities available for decent family-living. Here again, the criteria of economic investment have led to the neglect of large scale public housing for the lower income groups, who cannot in the near foreseeable future afford to pay economic rent for their dwelling units. It is advisable that an innovative approach to low-income housing will have to be made if deterioration in the housing situation has to be contained before it explodes like a volcano.

Economic Growth of Social Change in the Context of National Development

What is more, with the adoption of national development planning as the official instrument of state policy, deliberately planned change in the predetermined direction is the order of the day. Economic growth is being planned and with it, what is called the infrastructure, be it physical, economic or social. In the process, it has been discovered that the social consequences of planned national development are not at all planned or are much less expected. This is what results in social dislocations and may even hold back or detract from the economic gains.

High rate of population growth on a large demographic base, increase in the proportion of dependent population, the runaway urbanization, the unabsorbed rural-urban migration, the atrophied functions of the family constrained by its abridged structure, the re-appraisal of traditional practices, values and institutions, emergence of counter-cultures or new styles of living, are all but examples on the broad spectrum of social change which our scientists can articulate as foreseeable, and therefore, forestallable.

To the extent social scientists can articulate the nature and scope of social change and to the extent social planners can advise adequate or near-adequate measures to either soften or harmonize the impact of such changes, it will fall upon the social welfare sector of national development plans to organize and maintain new kinds of social welfare services. The organization of a network of day-care services to take care of children outside of nuclear families in which both parents are working, provision of integrated services for school going children and the school dropouts in which health nutrition, education and recreation could be combined, re-organizing family services in anticipation of smaller families and the occupational cultural impact of Women's Liberation Movement, devising appropriate services for the growing proportion of the older people in the population, who cannot stay with families but cannot either be in situationalized modelling community services to match the expansion of high-rise, impersonal living, protecting against the inundation of the whole area of recreation by over-commercialized mass media are all clamouring for a whole new range of social welfare services. These would be the social services of the future. This pattern approximates with what Titmus calls "institutional redistribution model". "It sees social welfare as a basic integrated institution in society proving both universal and selective services outside the market on the principle of need."

Social Planning and Policy

A. Watenston defines social planning thus: "Social planning may be defined in terms of efforts to broaden the scope of development planning, through a better formulation of development objectives, the incorporation of new variables into the analysis of the social process and the design of new instruments of planning." In this context, the word 'social' is used primarily to mean conditions of well-being. It is also commonly used to refer to relationship between individuals. When the students of development refer to the social aspects as obstacles to development, it is very often the structural and institutional conditions that they have in mind.

According to Kulkarni, "Social policy is the strategy of action indicating the means and methods to be followed in successive phases to achieve the declared social objectives." He states that this definition is tenable because it is based on the common-sense meaning of the term used and for other good reasons. Elaborating it later, he mentions that the term 'social policy' has been used to refer to the social objectives of state policy and the policy regarding social services as a sector, and policy governing the promotion of social welfare services as part of development phase.

Social Policy and Development: Role of Social Service Sector in the Transformation of Less Developed Societies

In-depth analysis of this experience brought forth a clearer understanding of the inter-relationship of economic growth with social policy and development. This was reinforced by studies of experiments carried out, about the same time, in other developing countries. It helped to discover that social development was not confined only to the programme content of social services in the national development plan. Whether it was explicitly conceded or not, the relevance and immediacy of non-economic policy implications of economic growth were recognized as essential parts of the whole strategy of development planning. Most of these non-economic elements of the development policy had a direct bearing on social development. Broadly, there could be an underlying role of social service sector in the transformation of less developed societies. These are as follows:

Distributive Justice

Policy makers were sensitive to people's expectations from the development plans. They know that it was not enough to be able to show progress in terms of the GNP alone. In order to mobilize intelligent and wholehearted cooperation of the people in the implementation of development plans, it was vital to assure them in advance of a fair share in the benefits of development. This was all the more essential since development planning was launched within a democratic framework in

India. As it is, a developing country cannot afford to let the entire wealth and income produced by the development plans flow back into current consumption. It is necessary for it to plough back a substantial part of increased wealth and income into investments for further growth, thus leaving only a small balance for immediate improvement in the levels of living. If this small balance is not evenly spread out, there will be no incentive for the general mass of people to work or sacrifice for the distant and abstract gains of development.

Institutional Change

The other social policy implications of the technological change also become evident both on empirical grounds as well as on doctrinaire considerations. It was found that modern technology whether adopted wholesale from advanced countries or adopted to suit local conditions, was itself not enough for modernization of the economy. Modernization of the implements and inputs was a necessary condition for increased production; it was not a sufficient condition for sustaining it. This could be done only by brining about side by side a suitable institutional change, for instance, land reforms to match with the green revolution. This is another example of the relevance of social policy to economic growth and its impact on the social aspects of development.

Employment Promotion

In fact, by working out some kind of a ratio between investment and employment, the employment potential of each plan was announced at the beginning of each plan period. Very often, it was found that this employment potential failed to materialize to the extent estimated, because the actual extent of employment potential depended on several factors in addition to investment, e.g., the backlog of employment and underemployment, the rate of growth of population, the number of entrants into labour market year after year, the rural-urban migration and the choice of technology, all together have a vital impact on the employment potential of a project. It needed considerable modification in the strategy of development planning, the choice and adaptation of the technology and balancing claims of modernization and 'economics of scale' with human need. Concern for more and better employment became evident in the revised strategies of development. The co-equal importance of employment with the growth in the GNP has come to be regarded as much a concern of social policy as of sound economic growth.

People's Participation

If there is one principle, which has been recognized in Indian planning from its inception, it is the importance of people's participation. Sufficient time has elapsed since the introduction of Panchayati Raj and it has already been evaluated several times. In the light of these evaluative studies, the limitations and the potential of people's participation in development planning are quite well known. In any case, this is an aspect which emancipates exercises in economic growth from the exclusive hold of planning technocrats and gives it the necessary social orientation.

Human Resources

During the first one or two plans, some of the advanced agricultural or industrial projects remained unimplemented or under-implemented for want of manpower with the right kind of orientation/training or education. Thus, the importance of social services, particularly education and health was realized on the rebound. This fact came to be recognized as part of the social infrastructure required to promote economic growth. It was also referred to in the planning jargon as development of 'human resources'. In doing so, the priority accorded to education particularly vocational/technical training, was certainly raised but the approach still fell short of realizing the correct and complete significance of the human element in development. It is doing less than justice to look upon the people only as a resource for economic growth. In fact, they are ultimately the most important justification for economic growth itself.

Apart from directly improving the quality of human resources, social services also serve another purpose of social policy - fiscal measures, including the steeply graded structure of income and wealth taxes were gradually so directed as to narrow down the disparities of wealth and income. But these usually have the effect only of levelling down the higher income groups and to that extent may be regarded as serving the socialist purpose. But in the developing economy, some measures are also called for to 'level up' the standard of living of the lower income groups.

Planning Process at Union, State and Local Levels

Planning is a rational process, which involves a number of steps. We discuss here the important steps, which may be kept in mind while planning for social welfare at any level, i.e., union, state or local level. Whatsoever be the methodology of planning, there basic steps are essential.

Pre-Planning

The first important step of planning is the laying down of social policy. Policies may be thought of as the main system, which provides the framework for the accomplishment of intended objectives. Formulation of policies involves making explicit the various assumptions, which are made with respect to the basic premises and the priorities of needs and allocating finances accordingly.

The agencies responsible for policy formulation within the union and state governments are the legislature, cabinet and the concerned ministry. There are many other agencies, which guide the legislature and the executive in the formulation of policy, e.g., Planning Commission, National Development Council, Central Social Welfare Board, State Social Welfare Advisory Boards, etc. However, in practice, social welfare administrators have to play a key role in policy formulation in the form of advice to the political elite.

Analysis of Social Situation

This relates to a time from which the planning is to be done. It is nothing but setting up a baseline to help the planners to make projections for the planning period and to help in the evolution of plans. Generally speaking, the following data would be required to analysis the present social situation:

(a) Characteristic of population (age, sex), of the persons in need of social welfare services.
(b) Data on social welfare facilities such as public, private and voluntary agencies for social welfare, their geographical distribution and utilization by the community.
(c) Data on available resources, e.g., personnel, material and finance.
(d) Data on education and training institutions for social welfare.
(e) Data on nature and function of social welfare institutions.
(f) Data on the following indices:

(i) Population, area, density and percentage growth rate.
(ii) Sex ratio by age group.
(iii) Birth, death and natural growth rate.
(iv) Crude birth rate in rural and urban areas.
(v) Expectation of life at different age by sex.
(vi) Infant mortality rate by sex.
(vii) Fertility rate.
(viii) Per capita expenditure on health.
(ix) Literacy rate by sex.
(x) Work participation rate by sex, etc.

The data collected would serve as the base for planning. Social welfare statistics provide the key to a competent, sound and efficient planning. The data collected should be reliable and adequate.

Identifying Social Problems

On the basis of the statistics collected and processed, we may identify social problems at the union, state and local levels. We generally make a mistake in identifying social problems only at the macro-level. It is important, but we must also identify the problems area-wise as well, so as to ensure fruitful social action. In the present set-up, we provide the same social welfare programmes in all the areas without taking the facts of those areas into consideration. So, there is a need to work out statistics area-wise as well, to identify problems accordingly.

Selection of Priorities

Resources in the developing countries are limited and are insufficient to meet the needs of the people. Therefore, there is a need to select the pressing and urgent problems. There are a number of factors (economical, technical, financial, social, political, ethical, etc.), which must be taken into consideration while laying down the priorities. This can be decided with the help of techniques like cost-benefit analysis, cost effectiveness, etc. The rate of economic growth for many of the developing countries including India is very low and provide a sombre picture for their future. This indicates that now and in the foreseeable future resources will be desperately limited. Indeed these limitations necessitate the judicious use of resources through the fixation of right priorities.

Definition of Goals and Objectives

Goal is the direction in which the plan is to proceed and the term is used more in the case of long-term planning. Goals formulated are generally broad. A goal is usually described in terms of:

(a) what is to be attained?
(b) the extent to which it is to be attained,
(c) the population involved,
(d) the geographic areas in which the proposed programme will operate, and
(e) the length of time required for achieving these goals.

The objective is a precise statement of the ends intended to be achieved. We must build the hierarchy of objectives, i.e., ultimate, intermediate and immediate. Immediate objectives are further divided into effort objectives and performance objectives.

Write-up of Formulated Plan

After deciding the priorities, goals and objectives, the next major step is to prepare a write-up of the plan. This may contain a schedule (time sequence for the plan to be implemented) and procedures (a set of rules for implementing the plan) and other details so that evaluation becomes easy and meaningful.

Implementation

Plan implementation is an integral part of the planning process. It requires responsibility for translating the objectives of social policy into social action. Implementation is the real test of plan. In the foreword to the Fifth Five-Year Plan, Indira Gandhi wrote: "A plan is ultimately neither a mere catalogue of schemes nor a sophisticated exercise in numbers. It is a charter of the progress of a people who refuse to be overwhelmed by the magnitude and vast variety of their problems and difficulties but are courageously struggling to map out a programme of action which will, step by step and year by year, help to overcome them."

Evaluation

Evaluation is a built-in device to measure the effectiveness of planning. Evaluation measures the degree to which objectives and targets are fulfilled and the quality of the result obtained. It measures the productivity of available resources in achieving clearly defined objectives. It measures how much output or cost-effectiveness is achieved. It makes possible the re-allocation of priorities and resources on the basis of changing needs. The ultimate test of evaluation should be the perceptible change in the status of the people and improvement of the quality of life.

Administration of Social Welfare Organization

Organization is often observed to be the weakest element in the theory and practice of social welfare. Much of this is due to historical reasons. Social welfare programme emerged in the wake of rapid industrialization in the West as piecemeal corrective action.

According to Mooney, "Organization is the form of every human association for the attainment of a common purpose." And this is what Dimock and Dimock have to say of organization, "Organization is the systematic bringing together of interdependent parts to form a unified whole through which authority, coordination and control may be exercised to achieve a given purpose. Organization is both structure and human relations."

Organization affects the people who work for it in five different ways:

(i) The organization divides work among its members, by giving each employee a particular task; it limits and concentrates his attention of the task,

(ii) The organization establishes standard practices, by working out detailed procedures, it relieves employees of the need to determine such procedure, each time they use crossways,

(iii) The organization transmits authoritative decisions by dispatching such decisions downward, upward and crossways,

(iv) The organization provides a communication system, and

(v) The organization trains and indoctrinates its members by providing for the internalization of influence relating to knowledge, skills and loyalties; training enables employees to make decisions as the organization would like them to make.

It would, therefore, be of utmost significance to stress that organization is not merely a structure; in fact, it embraces a structure as well as the human beings who man and run it, in order to realize the pre-conceived objective.

Structure of Social Organization

Tribal Welfare

Development of welfare schemes for the tribal population must fulfil two essential conditions for their success, namely, conformity to the social values and patterns of life of the people for whom they are intended and even more so their psychological receptivity and ability to absorb. Theoretical perfection of a scheme or its applicability to people in general must not be regarded as the criterion for tribal people. Ignorance of these basic facts, and inability to appreciate them are responsible for the slow progress of many development schemes, which by themselves are unexceptionable. According to Jawaharlal Nehru, the first Prime Minister of India, we should keep in mind five fundamental principles of tribal welfare:

(i) Tribals should develop along the lines of their own genius and we should avoid imposing anything on them. We should try to encourage in every way their own traditional arts and culture.
(ii) Tribal rights on land and forests should be respected.
(iii) We should seek to raise a corps of tribal leaders who would look after their own administration and development.
(iv) Let us not over administer the tribal belt or overwhelm them with multiplicity of schemes.
(v) We should judge results not by statistics or by the amount of money spent but by the quality of human material that is involved.

Minorities Commission

The Minorities Commission was set up under the Government of India in 1978 to safeguard the interests of minorities, whether based on religion or language, with a view to preserving secular traditions and promoting national integration. The Commission consists of a chairman and other members belonging to the minority communities. The functions entrusted to the Commission are as follows:

(i) to evaluate the working of various safeguards provided in the constitution for the protection of minorities and in laws passed by the union and state governments.
(ii) to make recommendations with a view to ensuring effective implementation and enforcement of all the safeguards and laws.
(iii) to look into specific complaints regarding deprivation of rights and safeguards of the minorities.

(iv) to conduct studies, research and analysis on the question of avoidance of discrimination against minorities.
(v) to suggest appropriate legal and welfare measures in respect of any minority.
(vi) to make periodical reports at prescribed intervals to the government.

Scheduled Castes and Backward Class Welfare

Articles 341 and 342 of the Constitution of India specify that the Backward Classes comprise the Scheduled Castes and Scheduled Tribes. Besides these, the Government of India have also recognized as 'Other Backward Classes' the denotified nomadic and semi-nomadic tribes and also those who satisfy the economic criteria.

In consonance with the Article 46, the Directive Principles of the Constitution of India, various schemes through successive plans to raise the social, educational and economic standards of these classes to the level of those of the general population, have been undertaken by the Government of India. These schemes are intended to supplement the programmes undertaken for general sector for raising the standards of the population as a whole.

Handicapped Welfare

Handicapped persons with physical and mental impairment constitute the weakest segments of our population. Their disabilities are often compounded by prolonged social unconcern and traditional prejudices. Sustained and planned efforts are required to ensure their training, education and rehabilitation. Experience has shown that with proper education and training, the majority of handicapped persons can be enabled to live as self-reliant citizens and participate in the mainstream of national life. The following national institutes are functioning under the overall control of Ministry of Welfare in each major area of disability:

(i) National Institute for the Visually Handicapped, Dehradun.
(ii) National Institute for the Orthopaedically Handicapped, Kolkata.
(iii) Ali Yavar Jung National Institute for the Hearing Handicapped, Mumbai.
(iv) National Institute for the Mentally Handicapped, Hyderabad.

These institutes are apex organizations in the field of education, training, vocational guidance, counselling, research, rehabilitation and development of suitable service modules for the handicapped.

General Welfare and Social Defence

Development brings in its wake, problems of individual and social disorganization, some manifestations of which are juvenile vagrancy, delinquency and crime, drug addiction, alcoholism, immoral traffic in women and girls, etc. These are a cause for concern as the problem is not merely of suppressing deviant behaviour but tackling them through a range of preventive, corrective and rehabilitative measures. Social defence programmes are implemented by the governments. The ministry of welfare is primarily concerned with overall policy formulation, guidance, research and training. The National Institute of Social Defence, a subordinate office of the ministry of social welfare, looks after the work relating to prevention of crime and treatment of offenders.

Programme Implementation

Proper implementation of the social welfare programme is vital and great attention and energy are required to ensure this. The purpose of implementation is to ensure that the programme activity has been completed on schedule and within the budget, and that there are favourable conditions to maintain the desired changes generated by the programme, after the programme as such, is terminated. Programme implementation steps are repetitive ones and each programme manager will have to adopt the procedures to this own situation, depending upon the nature of the programme and the organizational structure. The steps in programme implementation are as follows:

Designing of Strategies

The key sub-steps involved are the establishment of explicit criteria for strategy design, the selection of flexible strategy, the assessment of their implications in costs and requirement, and their revision of the targets and strategies under consideration in the light of the assessment.

Planning the Programme

The team decides design for efficient performance. The thinking of the team shifts here from 'what is to be developed'.

Writing Programme Proposal

The products of earlier steps are re-examined synthesized, and documented in the form of a programme proposal.

Initiating the Programme

It involves obtaining approval for the programme proposal, appointing the programme manager, preparing the interim budget and beginning the recruitment of other programme staff.

Specifying and Scheduling the Work

It is projecting the details of work and deciding what tasks are to be done by whom, and when.

Clarifying Authority, Responsibility and Relationships

It means obtaining agreement as to who is responsible for ensuring that the work gets done, distributing decision-making authority among the programme team and the existing organizational units and establishing formal lines of communication.

Obtaining Resources

It includes obtaining the funds, manpower supplies, and equipment necessary for doing the programme activities.

Establishing the Control System

It is determining what information is necessary for programme control, identifying sources of such information and setting up reporting systems for the programme.

Directing and Controlling

It is motivating programme staff, executing programme activities, obtaining information for control and taking corrective action as necessary.

Terminating the Programme

It is handing over responsibilities to existing organization units, reassigning staff and preparing the final report. The implementation machinery can resort to modern methods of management to achieve desired results.

Participatory Rural Appraisal

We should encourage the active participation of citizens in the planning and implementation of social welfare and development programmes. Public cooperation is an active and living element in a dynamic democracy. The resources in the developing world are limited and we can serve more people in an efficient manner through their active involvement.

Responsibility for the administration of social welfare and development may be decentralized to a great extent to ensure close relationship with the beneficiaries and the communities to be served. This would also help in getting the feedback from the people, which would be useful in the planning and evaluation of social welfare services. Besides, we must provide these welfare services in the rural areas, urban slums, backward, hilly and tribal areas. Special efforts need to be made to extend social welfare services to the neglected rural areas on an adequate basis, taking into account the particular needs of these areas. Such services must be provided in these areas according to the needs of the areas.

Rapid Rural Appraisal Techniques

Technical standards for social welfare and development programmes may be developed by the government with the help of institutions engaged in the education and training of social workers. These standards may be adopted according to different situations to ensure implementation of the overall social policy. Technical standards should be simple and clear so that they are really understandable to all concerned with social welfare, and to the general public. Rapid Rural Appraisal Technique is also a way of community participation in programme administration.

In fact, social change and development is something more than socio-economic, political and environmental development. It is an integrative concept and this integration depends upon a clear enunciation of the values and the type of society towards which planning is to be undertaken.

3

Administration of Social Welfare

Administration is the core for the implementation of policies and requirements of the social welfare. The importance of the administration is very high, because it regulates the rules and regulations and the policies for social welfare. In every organization, not only in the field of social work but also in business and public services, it provides the base. With administration the organization is like a blooming flower, but without it becomes akin to a paralysed person.

After independence, from the year of 1947, the Indian government has taken great interest and initiatives to apply the administrative policies, and its needs were essential for the well-being and the betterment of the society as well as individuals. It is a legally binding document and its fundamental principles are non-negotiable. The government of the world has made these administrative policies for the better functioning of the organization. The administration gives guidelines for the social workers; keeps provisions for the people and the fundamental principles included in the Constitution acts as a safeguard for every citizen and also for all living beings.

Thus, we can say that the administration for any kind of organization requires the administrative policies for the better functioning in the process. Some more details of the administrative policies are given in succeeding paragraphs.

Social Administration

Social administration is described as the administration of the social welfare programmes. Social administration is an instrument or means of bringing social actions through implementation of the social policy. For this reason, the social policy must be studied in the socio-economic perspective of the country which is undergoing change and by implementation of social policy decisions for the welfare and the betterment of entire community. According to Forder, "Social administration is concerned with the study of the welfare system, and particularly the government-sponsored social services."

Social administration and the political development policies aims at producing maximum opportunities to the individuals, families and groups, for the self and the social development. Social administration is always in favour of the people and finds the means to give services and goals to the persons and families for making available such opportunities, which will help them to develop themselves and the society. We can also say that social administration is that part of the administration, which provides services to remove the existing disabilities and gives opportunities to all of them for the well-being of the families and the community at large. In fact, it plays an important role for the growth of the community.

Basic Concepts of Social Administration

Social administration implements social legislation, aims at private philanthropy and religious charities into the dynamics of services and benefits for the whole humanity. It means that the social administration is an art of implementing the social policy into social action. Social administration may be broadly defined as the study of social services whose object is the improvement of conditions of the life of the individual in the settling of family and group relations. It is concerned with the historical development of these services, both statutory and the voluntary, with the part they play in meeting certain needs in the social process. It is concerned with the machinery of administration which organizes and dispenses various forms of social assistance of the other, in the lives and needs, and the mutual relations of these member of the community for whom the services are provided by reason of their belonging to that community.

The aim of any state or country is to provide sound health and good life to the people. The well-being of the community depends upon the governmental management, how the government is able to handle the problems of individuals rather than the public. The administrative set-up must respond in the social direction and to the ideas, beliefs, expectations and the values of the people.

Social Welfare Administration

The administration of public and private social agencies is designed and organized to achieve the full effort of the services for which they have been established. The skills of administration have not been limited only to social welfare settings. They are derived from the public administration in general and from the techniques of business management. But the special objective of social services – to help human beings – is an element which distinguishes the management of social agencies from that of commercial and industrial enterprises and to a lesser degree, from other public services that do not directly deal with human beings.

Public welfare administration, like any government operation requires clear objectives, functional policies, an efficient organizational structure, coordinating services, precise staff organization of personnel, decent working conditions, sound methods of recruitment, selection and promotion of the personnel, and fiscal accounting and control as guarantees of the efficient and developed management. Social administration helps the agencies to organize the work in an effective way that results into a successful organization of an effective programme. Social welfare administration helps the agencies formulate effective project works, which in turn help the people of the society to develop themselves.

The administration of the social services and social welfare programmes legitimately should fall in the sub-area of social welfare administration. The main job of the social welfare administration is to identify and clarify the problems of particular territory and contribute possible solutions to the problems. But we must be aware of the fact that the success of social welfare ultimately depends on the adequacy to administrate or the administrative apparatus prevailing in the country. The guiding principle of any good system of administration is, having the sense of fellow feeling, belongingness and entire well-being of the citizens. Now let us examine some of the social welfare services.

Education

We know, education is an important means to make us into rational beings. Without it people are like animals. Aristotle says: "Man is a rational animal." Through education there is possibility of well-being of the society. When people are educated, it is very easy to make them understand what something really means. As we know, the work of social welfare administration is to identify and clarify the problems. Social welfare administration aims at the welfare of the entire community. Thus, we can say that education is the one primary element for the success of social administration.

Health

Earlier days people died of many kind of sicknesses due to their ignorance. Therefore, taking care of health can help the individuals lead to healthy and sound life. Now, it is the work of the social welfare agencies to make people aware of health so that they can look after themselves on their own. Here, the work of the social welfare administration can be to give education about the health care and motivate people to learn the art of cleanliness. We know that various social agencies of government as well as the NGOs provide lots of services in the form of materials and the facilities with regard to health. It is said: "Healthy mind resides in a healthy body." It means that if we have a healthy body, we have a healthy or a sound mind.

Housing

One of the welfare services of the social welfare administration is housing. The social agencies look at the condition and standard of the people and provide them with better housing. Housing is one of the basic requirements of the people. Along with bread and clothes, every human being needs a house to rest and to live in. It is the social welfare administration which looks after the needs of the people, finds out their problems and provides awareness and gives possible solutions to the problems. As we know that the Indian government has taken initiative to build houses for the people who are below poverty line. This programme has been started under the name of Indira Awas Yojana, which is the work of the social welfare administration. Today, many people have been benefited from this programme and are still continuing to do so in the process.

Welfare for the Backward Classes

Indian government as well as a number of NGOs are working all over the country for the betterment and the welfare of the backward classes. Today, the backward people are privileged everywhere to have their recognition with exceptional provisions, provided they are educated. It is also one of the means of social welfare administration to help the people to help themselves. For the welfare services, the social agencies put up lots of programme for the betterment and welfare of the individuals as well as the community.

There are other welfare services like, welfare for the handicapped, disabled, maladjusted and for the downtrodden ones. These services are implemented through the social actions. Social welfare administration works in such a way that it aims at the betterment of the individuals as well as the welfare and the development of entire society. These all are the characteristics of the social welfare administration.

Public Administration

Public welfare administration, like other government operations, requires clear objectives, policies, an efficient organizational structure, coordination of structure and services, precise staff organization, sound methods of selection, recruitment and promotion of personnel, decent working conditions and fiscal accounting and control as guarantees of the efficient management.

The organizational structure of the public social services and agencies is part of the central, state or local government set-up. The organization as a rule is determined by the law or statute and by the functions based on legal provisions, as well as upon the size of population and the territory served by the social agency. The legislative body influences the organization, personnel and content of services by appropriating or withholding funds for their operation. In private social agencies either the member or a board of directors exercise the power of ultimate control. Public administration is an essential part of the society. It is very important in the developing countries like, India, which are involving them to lift up the standards of their living. If there is no realization of public administration there will be no change in the society. Therefore, the progress of any state is determined by the quality of the public administration. It is said: "Administration is a moral act and administrator is a moral agent." The meaning of this statement is that the moral act of a society is determined by the administration and the one who administers this act is called the agent. Public administration is a machinery used by the service state to place itself in a position to make plans and programmes that can be carried out and formulated. Therefore, we can say that public administration makes plans and programmes that can be carried out for the betterment of individuals as well as for the development of the society.

Meaning

The word 'administration' has been derived from the Latin word 'ad+ministrate' which means 'to care for or to look after people, to manage affairs'. Therefore, public administration would mean to care for the public, to look after the public and to manage the affairs of the public. Public administration lends itself to two usages: it is an activity and it also refers to the discipline of intellectual enquiry and study. Maintaining law is part of public administration. But public administration is also a discipline like economics, sociology, history, etc., and is a subject of study; it studies these activities and functions and formulates concepts and builds models and theories. According to L.D. White: "Administration is the direction, coordination and control of many persons to achieve some purposes and objectives."

Scope of Public Administration

Having looked into the meaning of public administration, it is necessary to point out certain problematic areas of administration, in order to understand properly, the scope of the study of public administration. The problems of public administration can be divided into five clearly distinguishable categories. They are:

(i) *General Administration*: It is to ask who is to perform the function of direction, supervision and control over the administration?
(ii) *Organization*: How are the services to be organized for the actual and real performance of the administrative works?
(iii) *Personnel*: Who are to manage the different services and activities it has laid for the welfare purpose?
(iv) Material supply, plant and equipment to be provided to the personnel for the discharge of their duties.
(v) *Finance*: This is the prime cause of all above-mentioned problems.

Thus, the scope of public administration is to study the problems of men, money, machinery, materials and methods in administration. More concrete shape was given by Luther Gulick, to the above-mentioned problems of public administration in the letters called "POSDCORB". These letters stand for:

P – Planning
O – Organizing

S – Staffing
D – Directing
C – Coordinating
O – Operating
R – Reporting
B – Budgeting

These POSDCORB activities are common to all large-scale organizations. They are the common problems of management, which are found in different agencies, but study of public administration should not ignore the fact that the nature and character of various governmental agencies and services they perform, differ from one another. There are specific administrative problems involved in different organizations and the public agencies. Luther Gulick says: "Some may think that our greatest need in the cities, is water or sewers, or wide streets, or more schools, or housing. Fundamentally; they are wrong, the real things we need are brains, character, drive, organization and the quality of leadership."

History of Social Welfare in India

The history of social welfare in India can be traced back to the ancient times, when society had certain inbuilt organizations for the relief of those in need and distress. This was, however, based on the religious and socio-philosophical considerations, or acts of charity receiving social approbation. The responsibility of the society, towards individuals in distress and needy sections was shared equally by the community with the rules and regulation. Service to fellow men, love for charity and brotherhood existed even during the feudal times. The forms of charity were *Artha* or money, *Vidya* or education and *Abhaya* or freedom from fear.

The concern of Emperor Ashoka, one of the enlightened rulers of the Mauryan period (320-184 B.C.) for the welfare of the masses has been demonstrated. Welfare services for the handicapped persons were established during the Gupta period (320-425 A.D.). Thus, people's welfare was the highest priority of the state. Apart from the state and charitable societies, the three social institutions namely, the joint family, the caste and the community did a lot for the welfare of the members. The joint family was a large economic umbrella in which the responsibility for the care of the orphans, widows, the aged and the infirm was vested with the family. The caste system was another social institution that played its parts in helping the needy persons. The Village Panchayat served to meet the needs of sick, the handicapped, the aged and the destitute members of the community. The Hindu religion laid emphasis on charity and religious institutions such as temples – *Maths* and *Dharamshalas* were considered to be centres of social services on a large scale. The conspicuous example of the contributions made by the religious institutions is the great 'Buddhist Stupa' at Sanchi near Bhopal on which the names of hundreds of donors are engraved.

The Muslims, who ruled India in the thirteenth and fourteenth centuries, were also inspired by the same spirit of social services, particularly in the field of education. This was born out of *Zakat*, which implied a prescribed percentage of income to be given away by a Muslim for charitable purposes. An example of social work is illustrated in the activities of Feroze Dewaan-i-Khairat, for the assistance of the society and building hospitals for the sick and the downtrodden. With the beginning of subsequent expansion of the British rule in the country from the closing decades of the eighteenth century onwards, brought the country gradually to the western approach to social welfare and development. The Christian missionaries began to imitate gradually voluntary action programmes of the community to overcome their inabilities. Slowly, in the middle of the nineteenth century the government expanded the social services and promoted the welfare services among the people. The activities of Christian missionaries and the growing interests of the government with regard to social welfare and development also began to stimulate new thinking among some of the elites in the country.

Social Administration in India

Before India embarked upon planned development, social work was by and large, in the hands of the voluntary organizations. Lack of trained personnel, problem of financial resources and lack of leadership hampered their useful work. Planned development aimed at evolution of a national plan for government and for social welfare with coordination of the government and the voluntary efforts; and organization of a programme of financial and technical assistance to voluntary organizations. The state has, however, to undertake the responsibility of providing aid to the voluntary organizations for mechanical maintenance, expansion and development of welfare services. In 1953, the Central Social Welfare Board (CSWB), was established with an allocation of 40 million rupees for grants-in-aid to voluntary organizations, by a resolution of the Ministry of Education.

It was declared by Pandit Jawaharlal Nehru that "this attempt that we are making to encourage social welfare activities is in a sense rather unique. It was not some 'Central Authority' that is doing all by itself, nor does the burden of this fall on the social or to say the local social welfare organizations, it is certainly a combination of the two where the central social welfare board comes as a helper and adviser and at the same time the social welfare organizations which are best suited for it, undertake the work. In this case, we can utilize the energy, enthusiasm and initiative of vast number of persons all over the country."

Central Level

Here, we examine the organizational structure of the Central Social Welfare Board. At the top, there is the General Body. Next in hierarchy is the Executive Committee for decision-making. Next is the Chairman who administers the day-to-day affairs of the Board. The administrative structure has been broken into staff and line agencies, for the running of the administration of such a complex organization. This cannot be a single man's show. Immediately after the Chairman, there is an Executive Director, assisted by five Divisional Heads, namely, Joint Director, Planning Monitoring and Coordination, Joint Director, Industrial Programme Administration, Joint Director, Welfare Programmes Administration, Internal Financial Advisor-cum-chief Pay and Accounts Divisions, Joint Director, Administrative Division, etc.

The success and failure of an organization among other things depend upon the quality of participation, interest and responsiveness of its management. These members adopt the mechanism of institutional bodies to formulate policies because they cannot manage the affairs individually and in isolation from one another. The organizational set-up of Central Social Welfare Board in given in Figure 3.1.

State Level

The State Social Welfare Advisory Boards were set up in different states between April 1954 and August 1954. The State Social Welfare Advisory Boards are functioning in all states and union territories except Dadra Nagar Haveli. The Central and State Social Welfare Boards work on 50:50 basis. The main objectives laid down for a State

Figure 3.1
Organizational Set-up of Central Social Welfare Board (CSWB)

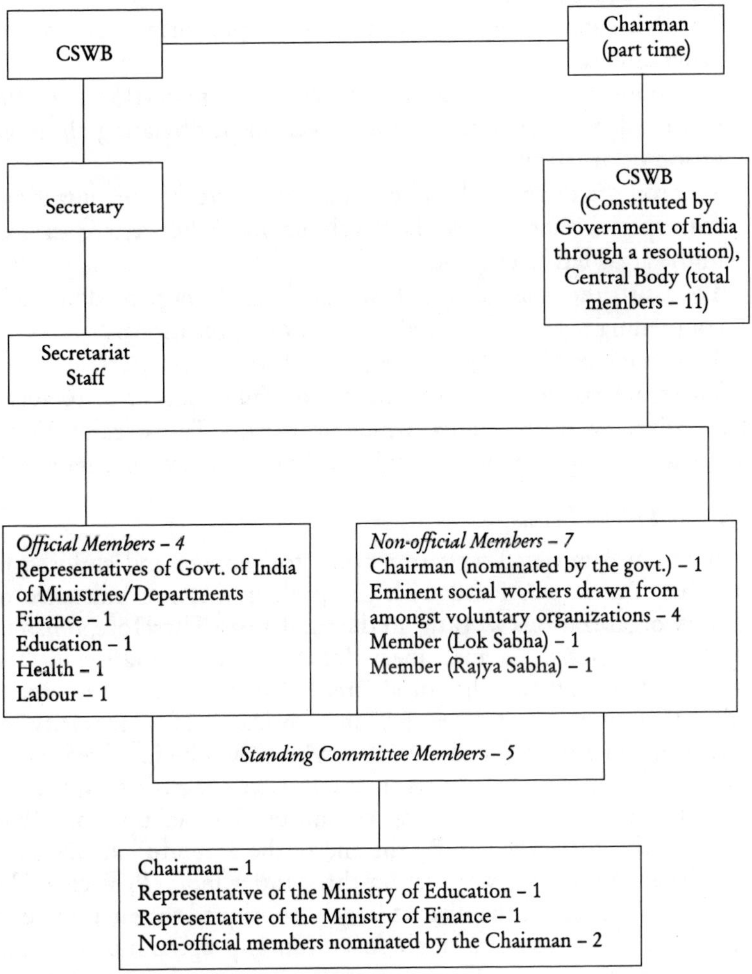

Social Welfare Advisory Board, is to work as an advisory board, as the name itself implies, to the ultimate achievements of objectives as earmarked for the central social welfare board. There are certain functions assigned to a State Social Welfare Board:

(i) To act as media for exchange of information between the field and the centre and vice versa.

(ii) To invite and examine application for grant-in-aid for voluntary welfare organizations and recommend the same to the central social welfare board.

(iii) To advice and assist the central board in sponsoring new welfare programmes and activities.

(iv) To coordinate the social welfare activities undertaken by the various departments of the state government obviating all duplication or overlapping.

(v) To promote the growth of voluntary social welfare organizations with special references to the development of the welfare services in the areas left uncovered.

(vi) To assist the central social welfare board in providing field counselling services for aided voluntary organizations.

(vii) To administer the programmes or rural welfare projects.

These are some of the objectives and functions of state social welfare advisory board under which it works. The organizational set-up of a State Social Welfare Advisory Board is shown in Figure 3.2.

District and Block Levels

In 1954, CSWB initiated welfare services for women and children in rural areas. But it was faced with the problems of non-existence of voluntary organizations working in the rural areas. Therefore, it had to take steps to sponsor a machinery for the implementation of the programmes meant for the rural areas. Consequently, the Board decided that a committee be set up consisting of a majority of non-official and a few official members who would be involved in the welfare or developmental efforts in the district for necessary coordination. The project implementing committee was set up from 1954 onwards at the district levels. By the end of the Second Plan, 324 such district level committees were set up throughout India. Project implementing committees in the district largely continued to remain bodies for the implementation of a single specification programme known as welfare extension project. These committees continued up to 1961, and thereafter, were wounded up and the work was given to *Mahila Mandals* to promote voluntary efforts. The Board, therefore, at present is not having any organizational set-up at district level. With the hoarding over of family and child welfare projects (281) from 1st April, 1982 to the state governments, the Board is not having any infrastructure at the block level as well. So the operating of programme of the board at present is done through the voluntary organization.

Figure 3.2
State Social Welfare Advisory Board (SSWAB)

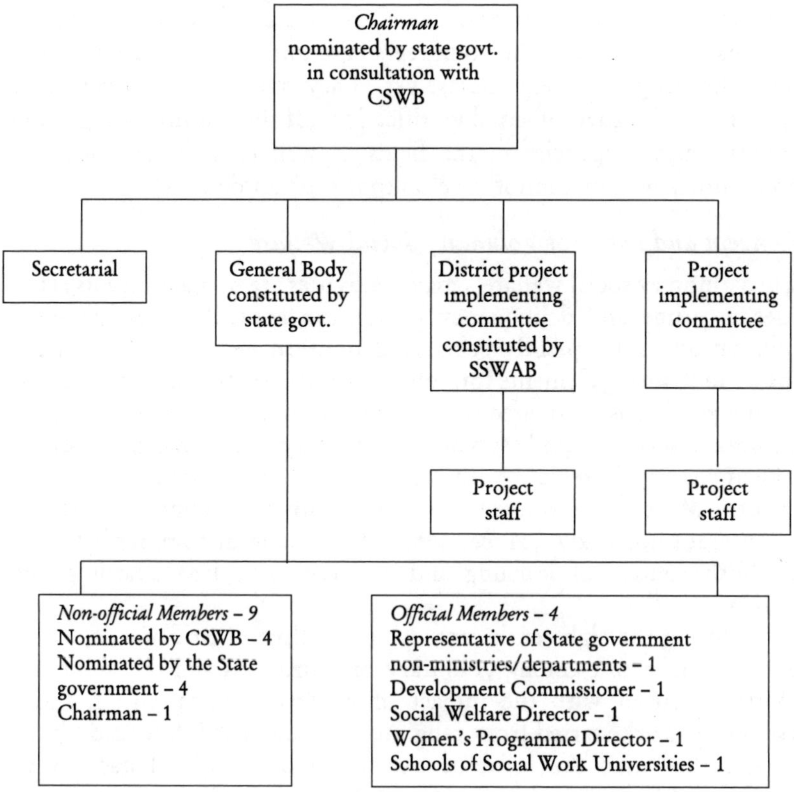

Voluntary Social Welfare

First and foremost, we have to understand the meaning of the 'voluntary'. The word 'voluntary' means to take up initiative with a greater purpose and to attain certain objectives. Voluntary welfare is a kind of self-help, meaning to give help to the needy and destitute by his or her own share. When we look back, in all the societies, at all times, people have been giving something in the form of cash or in kind and selfless services for the welfare of the needy, the destitute, the handicapped and the victims of natural calamities. We know that social work in the past was identified with the practice of charity, which was done through the basis of religions.

Today, the concept of charity has changed because of specific reasons. Social work has now become a profession. It is defined as: "social work is to help the people to help themselves". The voluntary welfare services exist all over the world but it has still to be improved in an organized manner. The volunteers take initiative as a profession to help the people to help themselves. They should keep away other agencies or the governmental gratifications. If there is no coordination among various agencies in the fields of welfare activities then this community welfare cannot develop to the extent desired.

Concept and Forms of Voluntary Social Welfare

The voluntary social welfare's major activities are to maximize its activities in crime and delinquency prevention control. In earlier days, religion and subsequently social and political factors have been the major motivating elements for voluntary services. Whenever, there has been a good cause and effective methods to motivate people to take to voluntary services, the reservoir of voluntary efforts has never dried. Indian history is replete with striking examples of noble voluntary efforts – *Madhukhan*, where the poor Brahmin boys support themselves in different households; *Adheenams*, where the joint community effort establish centres of learning and research with free boarding and lodging.

During the eighteenth century, at the time of British rule, a new era in social work among voluntary organizations and the voluntary workers started with the impact of western civilization. In India, voluntary work started from religious base and was influenced by the ideas rather than the form of western civilization and had for its watchword 'evaluation' and not as a revolution. Change was sought not as an individual but as return and restoration to the days of our past history.

When we speak about its forms, we come to know about its distinguishing factors under which it works for the betterment of the people to whom the services are rendered, for example, Indian Council of Child Welfare, the Children Aid Society, the Society for the Protection of Children in India, Association of Social Health in India, the All India Women's Conference and Council of Women in India, etc.

Importance of Voluntary Action in Social Welfare

Promotion of voluntary action is a time-honoured tradition of all democratic societies, which value citizen's participation. Importance of voluntary action in social welfare is very necessary because with the enactment of voluntary actions, social welfare can undertake any programme it wants to organize for the betterment and well-being of the society and individuals at large. All such societies have developed the mechanism of the voluntary association as a normal expression of democratic life and also a practical strategy of encouraging citizen's actions in combatting difficult social problems. The services which are being provided by such voluntary action groups are in tremendous boom, and in many cases a necessity. Orphanages started by the Christian missionaries encouraged a large number of individual philanthropists and voluntary organizations, both sectarian and secular, to work for setting up of home-like institutions for helpless women and children in various parts of the country.

Later, the organizations of these institutions, took active participation with the great interest in the reform and the rehabilitation of the victims. After care and follow-up services for the rehabilitation of juvenile and adult offenders were initiated after the Indian Jail Committee made a strong plea for the development of such services for ex-prisoners. The committee's recommendations stresses on the possibilities of the voluntary action in the field and provide a house for the setting up of the Discharged Prisoners' Aid Societies. They were inturn established in Madras (1921), Central Provinces (1925), Bengal (1928) Punjab (1929), Bombay (1933), Kerala (1956), etc.

Now, let us look at some of the voluntary action plans working for the welfare of the people:

(1) *Rehabilitation of Offenders*: Participation of the voluntary workers on the treatment of offenders in adult correctional institutions like prisons is effected through the system of non-official jail visitors. The Indian Jail Enquiry Committee of 1921 recommended the system for the purpose of ensuring prisoners' human treatment to which they were entitled under the Prison Act of 1894. The functions of these non-official jail visitors was to make surprise visits at regular intervals and to bring to the notice of the prison authorities the complaints of the prisoners regarding bad food, brutal and oppressive treatment, bribery, corruption and deliberate breach of the existing rules and regulations by the prison employees.

The Discharged Prisoners' Aid Societies, as non-official aided or say an non-governmental organizations, help the released prisoners in their social and economic rehabilitation in the community and thereby help in reducing the rate of relapse amongst the ex-offenders. These societies also provide legal and financial assistance to the released prisoners, arrange for their employment and maintaining after-care hostels. Most of the state governments, however, have not framed any rules for the purpose, and thus the scheme which has great promise has not been implemented in most part of the country.

(2) *Prevention of Juvenile Delinquency*: The field of prevention and control for juvenile delinquency has been and continued to be the mainstay of voluntary action in the country. A large number of institutions and agencies set up by the premier voluntary organizations like the Indian Council of Child Welfare, the Children Aid Society and the Society for the Protection of Children in India, provide for the care and protection of destitute, neglected, victimized and exploited children. These institutions have made a great contribution for eradication of juvenile delinquency in the country. Since 1974-75, the Government of India is running a scheme for assisting voluntary organizations for providing services to abandoned, neglected, orphaned and homeless children. The National Policy for Children and the National Children Board have reiterated the need and urgency of voluntary action in the field.

(3) *Supervision of Immoral Traffic*: The policy of encouraging voluntary action in the supervision of immoral traffic has found considerable governmental support ever since the enforcement of the Supervision of the Immoral Traffic in Women and Girls Act of 1956. There are some guidelines for the social workers. They are:

   (i) Constitution of a non-official advisory board consisting of not more than five leading social workers of the city to advise special police officers on the question of general importance regarding the Act.

   (ii) Requisition of the attendance of two more respectable inhabitants of the locality by police while conducting search without warrants of the premises where prostitution is carried out.

   (iii) Constitution of a managing committee of official and non-official workers for each protective home or similar institutions set up under the Act.

As few voluntary organizations, such as the Association of Social Health in India, the All India Women's Conference and the Council of Women in India, have been encouraged and assisted to undertake preventive programmes in the field. The Association of Social Health in India has a record of more than about fifty years of service in the field. The organization has around twenty-two states and hundred and forty district level branches in the country. The most important activities of the association at its state and district level branches are: Eradication of commercialized prostitution; running institutions for the shelter, training and rehabilitation of exploited women, and those in moral danger; organizing training programmes, seminars and conferences for voluntary workers in the field, to make aware of the problems; and, mobilizing public cooperation for the effective implementation of the SIT Act (Suppression of Immoral Traffic Act).

Administration of Voluntary Welfare Organizations in India

After independence, India came to realize the very importance of the administration of voluntary welfare for the betterment of the public services in the country. When we look at the history of voluntary welfare in India, we find its existence from the beginning of the World War I and II. From then onwards, the people started donating their money and things to the needy and the poor. Slowly, the individuals thought of organizing such committees to assist the needy. With the help of some of the foreign missionaries, these organizations tried to make some policies that would help them in their work at the time of services. After independence, the Government of India also took initiative to strengthen the organizations. It was the voluntary workers who thought of administering the social welfare services in the country.

Therefore, we cannot trace the exact timing of the beginning of the administration of social welfare in India. It has been in the process till now but it has advanced a lot at the moment.

Government and Voluntary Organizations

Voluntary Organizations

The working group on the administrative machinery for the welfare programmes set up by the Planning Commission in 1968, in its report about the present position of voluntary organizations, observes that the sphere of social welfare is still very largely the domain of voluntary workers and voluntary organizations. They constitute the kingpin of the machinery for the implementation of welfare programmes. Complete reliable data are not available about the total number of voluntary organizations in the country, but about 5,000 are known to be receiving grants from the Central Social Welfare Board and a much larger number is probably functioning with their own resources derived from religious and charitable organizations, private donations and the gifts, etc. In their aims and ideals, quality of personnel and standard of services, voluntary organizations are known to show wide variations, from some old well-established organizations with a distinguished record of dedicated service at the one end, to a few new organizations which have sprung up to take advantage of the government grants available for specific welfare activities at the other. The functioning these organizations and the range of their activities also vary.

Having discussed about the present position of voluntary organizations, let us analyse some of the problems that will be of help for the future set-up. The problems of voluntary agencies can be discussed under the following heads:

(i) *Programme Activities*: As we are aware that the scope of voluntary organizations is very wide; that it can organize all types of activities which are in the nature of palliative, rehabilitation or protective activities for all types of groups. Different people have different needs and wants, therefore, the voluntary organizations operate different activities for different people. These may be agencies for the welfare of children, young women, old persons, etc., or for the welfare of the philosophy of human problems or for the welfare of the physically, mentally or emotionally handicapped, for family welfare services or for the rural and urban communities.

The voluntary workers can assist the agencies in many ways. Some people may donate money, while others may give their free time for services whether as members of the managing committee as administrators, or may help in welfare, recreational, cultural, educational or other services to supplement the services of the paid staff.

(ii) *Financial Resources and Regulations*: Charity has always played a high and respected role in the cultural heritage of India. Charity was done, in order to help the poor and the donors believed that with the donations the poor are helped and in return the donors are believed to have personal salvation and satisfaction. But when we analyse the fact of charity giving, charity is affected by many factors. We know that in the past voluntary welfare agencies have been depending on the charity raised from a few wealthy people and the government assistance has been negligible, and also the donors, sometimes, dictated their own terms for using the money only for specific purposes or meeting the needs of a particular community. Inspire of all these difficulties, some of the funds had to be raised by the voluntary organizations so that they may keep up their voluntary character. It cannot be denied that the government grants have increased, yet some funds have still to be raised by the voluntary organizations.

(iii) *Personnel*: Proper staff is a very important tool of administration. This is particularly true about the social work which have been accepted as a profession. Since the agency needs technically trained personnel for running various welfare programmes on the proper basis, it needs to recruit trained staff with aptitude for social work. What happens in this process is that some of the agencies recruit the candidates who are not well trained in this field, resulting in a big chaos in the programmes. The staff should be recruited according to the personnel policy, already laid down by the agency. The idea is still prevalent that in order to serve one's fellow men, the qualifications necessary are a spirit of dedication, a large measure of goodwill and some leisure. But along with these qualities some training is also essential, as social work is a profession. Voluntary agencies being more specialists by nature and more easily recognized, there is need of special qualification and the training in their work. Training for the voluntary social workers administering such programmes need to be given in institutes or universities for a short-term or as per the requirement.

(iv) *Coordination*: Coordination can be defined as "a process of bringing into logical and organic relationship". It means adjustment, harmony and cooperation to achieve certain ends. There should be coordination and cooperation not only among various institutions within the agency but also between various agencies like public and private, which are providing social services to the community. Coordination within the agency means coordination between various departments of the agency, coordination between various staff members of the agency and coordination between sub-committees of the agency and of the board and also coordination between the board and the staff itself. Coordination between agencies, working in the community is of two types: financial and geographical.

In this case, one agency supervises and coordinates the work of other agencies in the same field like the Indian Council for Child Welfare and the All India Women's Conference. These agencies coordinate the work of the state branches who inturn coordinates the work of district units in any particular field (such as child welfare, women welfare, etc.). In India, where welfare services, both in private and public fields are developing rapidly, such kind of coordination is very necessary.

Government Organizations

The government organization is very important during these days, for the betterment and improvement of the people. Today, the government has started many organizations such as educational institutions, hospitals, prisons, after care homes, orphanage for the physically, mentally and emotionally handicapped, etc. Same activities are undertaken by the voluntary organizations also. But, it has been observed in the past that the voluntary organizations are much more effective than governmental organizations. There are certain reasons for this. It seems that the voluntary social workers come out of interest, emotions and kindness to serve others. On the other hand, in many cases, one can observe that government workers are only time and wage oriented. In spite of this, we still do find many government organizational institutions which are well maintained and equal to, if not more effective, than voluntary organization. Governmental organizations are self-dependent and have the ability to handle their organizations, whereas voluntary organizations have to raise the funds and have to depend on the agencies and government grants for the survival of their organizations.

Advantages and Respective Growth

Both, the voluntary social welfare organization and governmental social organization display lots of programmes for different people through different activities. When a voluntary organization does any remarkable and dedicated performance, governmental grants are provided to encourage the organization. On the other hand, voluntary organizations lighten the burden of the government because most of the welfare services are done by them and in return they get the appreciation from the government through assistance in the form of money and available services.

In this way, there is growth and development of the organizations as well as of the people. Many people who are in need, are benefited by these organizations. They get all the facilities to develop their living and economic condition through the voluntary as well as the governmental organizations.

Role of Institutional Organizations in Welfare and Development

Institutional social work is the youngest branch of social welfare activities. It is based upon the recognition that institutional cooperation in social work is needed in order to secure the well-being of humanity. It is also indispensable for securing world peace and stability. Assistance in the times of mass distress – famine, flood, earthquakes, fire and volcanic eruption – by one nation to another is a well known fact from time immemorial. But institutional activities in social welfare in a broader sense first began in the middle of the nineteenth century when the representatives of private and public charities began to organize international conferences in order to share their experiences and thereby to learn of effective methods in the field of social services.

There are both government international organizations and the private international organizations in this field. International social welfare organizations can be classified into five groups:

1. *Government Agencies of International Character:* The United Nations, World Health Organization, International Labour Organizations Act, etc., come under this category.
2. *Private International Organizations*: The organizations, which come under this category are: International Conference of Social Work, World Federation of Mental Health and International Union for Child Welfare, etc.
3. *Private International Organizations (Autonomous)*: They have an autonomous organization in each country, for example, International Red Cross Association, the Young Men Christian Association and the Young Women Christian Association.

4. *National Government Agencies:* These agencies extend their work to other countries, for example, the United States Technical Cooperation Programme properly known as Point Four Programme, etc.
5. *National Private Agencies:* National private agencies extending their social services to other countries, for example, the Ford Foundation and the Rockefeller Foundation in India.

Having discussed about different international organizations, let us analyze some of their characteristics:

(i) *The United Nations Children's Fund*: Its original title is United Nations International Children's Emergency Fund. It was established in the year of 1946 at the urgent request of UNRRA Council in order to carry out child feeding and child welfare services that could not be at any cost discontinued without grave damage to millions of the children, pregnant women and nurturing mothers. The UNICEF applies 'matching' principle. It requires that the government or voluntary organizations in the country where aid is given, provide indigenous supplies, such as flour, potatoes, vegetables, fruits, sugar or fats, transportation, as well as the staff for distributing of the UNICEF supplies of medical and child welfare services.

(ii) *International Labour Organization*: The International Labour Organization (ILO) was established in 1919, under part xiii of the Peace Treaty. It entered into the relationship with United Nations, as a specialized agency in 1946. The ILO works in the closest cooperation with Economic and Social Council for the protection of child and women labour, and the development of social insurance, public assistance of legislation and family allowances. ILO aims at promoting social justice and peace. It assists children through child welfare programmes, social security for mothers, anti-child labour measures, etc.

(iii) *The World Health Organization*: The World Health Organization assists number of developing countries to strengthen public health services, prevention of communal diseases, improvement of sanitation, child health services, maternal and infant hygiene, rural and urban health services, health education, etc. WHO had assisted India in establishing primary health centres and sub-centres in India. WHO's main objective is the attainment of the highest possible level of health for all the people of the world.

(iv) *Food and Agricultural Organization*: As a specialized agency of the United Nations the Food and Agricultural Organization (FAO) with headquarters in Rome, was established in 1945 with the purpose of abolishing famines and malnutrition, through increased food production and a better distribution of agricultural products. FAO plays an important role with other organizations. This is sought to be done through the People's Action for Development and World Food Programmes.

(v) *The United Nations Educational, Scientific and Cultural Organization*: UNESCO assists in universal and compulsory primary education, promotion of science and technology. It strives to promote mutual understanding among people by the distribution of cultural scientific and educational information through libraries, radio, movies, periodicals and newspapers.

Programme Planning, Budgeting and Accounts

For every distinguished programme, planning, budgeting and accounting are very essential. In the field of social welfare organization, all these planning, budgeting and accounting are to be taken into consideration. Without these elementary factors, no programme can be successful. Proper budgeting is needed for managing the programme with sufficient and available resources. First, planning is done according to the available budgeting and accounting capacity. Let us look at each of them in details.

Programme Planning and Development

Planning in India is considered as character of orderly progress. It provides a framework of time and space that binds sectors, regions and states together and relate each year's effort to the succeeding years. By strengthening the social and economic fabric of the country as a whole and of the different regions and states, it makes a powerful, contribution to the goal of national integration. Planning for social welfare is firmly based on the nature and extent of social problems pertaining to the society from which are derived priority goals. Planning is like a future picture wherein proximate events that are needed are outlined with some distinctiveness while remote and the events not designed appear progressively less distinct. In fact, planning may be defined as the process of deciding in advance the course of action to achieve the desired objectives.

Social welfare planning is the phase of the total process of social development which leads from policy statements to the concrete identification of the populations, whose social needs and demands are to be met, the indications of the types of social welfare activities that will be performed for these populations, with their general attributes that will be required to carry out the social activities. The trend of today is not to do planning in isolation but of total development. When we plan for development including social development, it is termed as development planning. It is a process of organizing national economic and social effort for the promotion of achievement of clearly defined national development goals. It is through development plans that social development and social welfare issues can be accorded their due place in the total process of development.

Planning Process in a Social Agency

Planning is rational process, which involves number of steps. The following are important steps, which may be kept in mind while planning for social welfare at any level, for union, state or local level. The methodology of the planning can differ from one to another but these basic steps are essential:

Pre-planning

The first important step of planning is the laying down of social policy. These policies are thought to be the main system, which provides the framework for the accomplishment of the intended objectives. Pre-planning for any programme of organization is very essential for the smooth conduct and for the success of the programme.

Analysis of Social Situation

This relates to a time from which the planning is to be done. It is nothing but setting up of baseline to the planners to make projections for the planning period and to help in the evaluation of plans. To analyse the social situation, one requires data such as characteristics of population, social welfare facilities, available resources, educational and training institutions, nature and functions of the social welfare institutions, etc.

Identifying Social Problems

One of the most significant factor of planning process is the identification of the problem. One may identify social problems at union, state and local level. One must identify the problems area-wise as well as ensure fruitful social action. In many cases, it is observed that social welfare programmes are provided without taking the facts into consideration. So, there is a need to word out statistics area-wise as well to identify problems area-wise.

Definition of Goals and Objectives

Goal is the direction in which the plan is to proceed and the term is used more in the case of long-term planning. A goal is usually described in the terms of:

(i) What is to be attained?
(ii) The extent to which it is to be attained.
(iii) The population involved.
(iv) The geographic areas in which the proposed programme will operate.
(v) The length of time required for achieving these goals.

Write-up of Formulated Plan

After deciding the priorities, goals and objectives, the next major step is to prepare a write-up of the plan. This may include schedule and the procedures for implementing the plan and other details so that evaluation becomes easy and meaningful.

Budgeting and Accounting in Social Welfare Agency

Importance

Financial administration in social welfare relates to the system concerned with raising, regulating and distributing resources needed for the substance and growth of the social welfare activities. As a tool of accountability, financial administration has few clearly identifiable operations, such as preparation of estimates, appropriation of funds, expenditure control, accounting, auditing, reporting, review and so on, which are integrated into a rational system. A good system of financial administration requires the dovetailing of all these basic processes in such a way that one supports the other. The effectiveness of social welfare largely depends on financial administration on the one hand, and decentralization of powers on the other. Social management includes those operations that are designed to ensure their lawful, purposeful and efficient use.

Budgeting

Budgeting is a system, which deals with inputs and outputs as well as the mechanics of processes behind the transformation of inputs into outputs. The financial system transforms financial resources into human purpose. Budget resources act as the balancing wheel of the financial system operating within the framework of a given socio-economic and political system. We know people have their aspirations and needs but they may not always be in a position to gratify their needs and interests in a concrete manner. Those who are in power, articulate the needs and aspirations of the people as they perceive them. Budget is a document, which reflects this process of articulation of objectives and concretization of programme. In this sense, budget is very much influenced by ecological factors, similarly, budget influences the economic and even social lives of the people directly or indirectly through the mobilization of resources and through the selection of programmes and projects for implementation.

Budget provides a framework for choices about ends and means which, in a fundamental sense, reflects the character of the social welfare activities of an organization, the ideologies and values that govern its operations and the interests of services.

Meaning of Performance Budgeting

According to the ARC (Administrative Reform Commission) study team, "Performance budgeting as is generally known is essentially a technique of presenting government operations in terms of functions, programmes, activities and projects. Through such a classification of transactions, government activities are sought to be identified in the budget in the financial and physical terms so that a proper relationship between inputs and outputs could be established and performance assessed in relation to costs." According to S.S. Visvanathan, "Performance budgeting is a comprehensive operational document conceived, presented and implemented in terms of programmes, projects and activities, with their financial and physical aspects closely interwoven."

Purposes

Performance budgeting is very useful for social welfare programmes. This facilitates better programming, decision-making, review and control for a more intelligible presentation of governmental activities to the public and the legislature.

The purposes are:

(a) to correlate the physical and financial aspects of every programme activity,

(b) to improve budget formulation, review and decision-making at all levels of management in the government machinery,

(c) to facilitate better appreciation and review by the legislative,

(d) to make possible more effective performance audit,

(e) to measure progress towards long-term objectives as envisaged in the plan, and

(f) to bring annual budget and development plans closely together through a common language.

Programme Formulation and Implementation

Programme Formulation

Programme formulation becomes a large and complex task after a positive decision has been taken on a programme idea. Nine steps are required for programme formulation:

(i) *Preparation of Programme Formulation*: The organization appoints a team to formulate a programme. A term of reference including time dimension, expected results, resources and problems are decided. The team obtains the necessary data required for the concerned programme.

(ii) *Analysis of Original Situation*: It is a clear picture of the organizational environment that is carried out, for example, description of the relevant organizations and agencies, their decision-making process and past experiences, relating to the success or failure of the programme, etc. The team should concentrate on producing reasonable and informative summaries.

(iii) *Analysing the Socio-economic and Demographic Situation*: The present and future analysis is done of the socio-economic situation, and the demographic situation.

(iv) *Analysis and Projection of the Problems*: We define the problems and the projection of the future situation which is worded out on the assumption that existing trends continue without change in the relevant system and their policies. However, we can change the projections based upon our assumption.

(v) *Achieving the Objectives and Targets*: It entails a statement of the problem reduction to be achieved through the programme and translating them into what would have to be provided at various future times in order to reach the objectives.

(vi) *Identification of Potential Obstacles*: It is an attempt made to predict the potential obstacles that might stand in the way of reaching the operational targets established in step (v).

(vii) *Design of Strategies*: These are those key sub-steps involved for the establishment of explicit criteria for strategy design, the selection of flexible strategies, the assessment of their implications in costs and requirements, and the revision of those targets and strategies under consideration in the light of the assessment.

(viii) *Planning the Programme*: Means, the team decides the design for efficient performance. The thinking of the team shifts from what is to be developed to how is it to be developed.

(ix) *Writing Programme Proposal*: The products of earlier steps are re-examined, synthesized and documented in the form of a programme proposal. These steps are very important for the places where the planning situation has not been implemented. It provides guidance for the programme implementation.

Programme Implementation

Proper implementation of the social welfare programme is vital and of great attention and energy are required to ensure this. In this context, India's Planning Commission said, "The success of the Third Plan will rest very largely on the efficiency with which it is implemented." The main purpose of implementation is to ensure that the programme activities have been completed as scheduled and within the budget, and that there are favourable conditions to maintain the designed changes generated by the programme after the programme as such is terminated. Programme implementation steps are repetitive ones and each programme manager will have to adopt the procedures to his own situation, depending upon the nature of the programme and the organizational structure through technical, economic, financial, commercial, organizational, managerial and social aspects and also through initiating the programme, specifying authority, responsibility and relationships, obtaining resources, establishing the control system, directing and terminating the programme, the derived results can be achieved.

Social Welfare and Social Legislation

We all are aware that our human motivation and social progress is limited. We cannot be sure that whatever we invest in this field will produce any measurable and remarkable results, but that is indispensable from any effort of promoting human motivation. This should not deter us from making the attempt. The laws by which we are governed is one such sphere. The entire field of legislation is to be reviewed and every statute, rule, custom or usage which forms our parts of body of law is to be tested in the light of the fundamental principles of our Constitution. Legislation design legal sanctions to minimize deviances and to maintain social stability. By means of new enactments, there will be institutionalization of a new pattern of behaviour manifesting new social values.

The Constitution has itself provided for making special provision for women and children. It has, likewise, indicated a priority of the interests of weaker sections of the people. The problems of immoral traffic is a part of the problem of traffic in human beings. Beggary is a part of the problem of undeserved want. There are several handicapped groups who are not at present covered by any protective law. The problem of juvenile delinquency is part of the children's problem. In our approach to the criminals, we have to pursue a positive and rehabilitative policy to reduce the penal approach to the minimum. The very fact that these have been long neglected is the most compelling reason for giving them a priority.

After the independence, there has been good progress in the enactment of social legislation in our Constitution. There are various provisions to which the state is committed under Fundamental Rights or Directive Principles and is passing legislation to implement them. The Indian Constitution has made provisions for these organizations, such as child welfare, youth welfare, prison reforms, women welfare, prostitution, labour welfare, social security and social assistance, welfare of backward classes, housing welfare, prohibition, beggary, gambling, etc. Thus, we can say the Constitution is very much alert and has taken major steps for the legislation of the society and grants the people a trust.

Social Welfare through Social Legislation

Legislation means to reinforce the existing modes and to provide a uniform procedure for the evaluation and punishment of deviance from the existing rules. Law is not something static and unchanging. It is a social instrument and it changes according to the changing social ideas. On the other hand, it must change too. It should be flexible and keep pace with the changing social needs.

Social welfare is concerned with the affairs and conditions of the people, which are equally the concern of the law. Law has to define its approach to social problems and ensure security of the society to improve its social and economic condition.

Aims of Social Legislation

Social legislation must incline towards realism and idealism to change and reorganize the society. Some of the aims of social legislation are discussed as follows:

1. To raise social status of the individual or groups who come from the societies of under privileged sectors.
2. To attempt to bring about the reforms in the working of social institution and structure of a given society.
3. To promote wider realization of fundamental rights and directive principles given in the constitution.
4. To prevent social ill-health and promote social health.

Role of Social Worker

We have seen that social legislation aims at the welfare of the weaker sections of the society. Since social work aims at the upliftment of the society, a social worker plays an important role for the framing, enacting and implementation of social legislation. The role of social worker in promoting social welfare through social legislation may be discussed as follows:

1. A social worker is in more contact with people. This enables him to identify various problems among them for with no legislations are available. A social worker can identify these needs and bring them to the notice of the concerned authority, analyse various aspects and suggest solution for them.
2. A social worker can build up public support in favour of social legislation to implement it successfully. He can make them aware of various problems and can suggest ways and means for them.
3. A social worker can see to it that the already existing legislations are being properly implemented or put into practice. He can also find out the shortcomings in the provision laid down in the existing social legislation and put forward further recommendations.

4. There are various loopholes in various legislation. As a result of which many culprits escape. Since social worker is a trained person, he can find out these shortcomings and recommend amendments to the concerned authorities.
5. A social worker can act as an instrument in creating awareness on social legislative issues.

Social Welfare Agency as an Organization

Social welfare agency works as an industry. An agency is that which provides some specific services. As in business organization, it can employ workers or resort to advertising or it can be called the secretariat agency. In the terms of social welfare agency, it would mean that it is a well-planned organization that provides specific services to the people who have social needs. Social welfare is exactly an agency because it covers the large area of human needs and problems. Social welfare agency helps the people to help themselves. Through various organized and well-planned services the agency motivates people to come out of their problems on their own; besides, the agency provides all possible means to satisfy the basic needs of the people. Today, social work has become a profession. Therefore, its need, in the development and betterment of society has greatly increased wherein a recognized agency is an organization that puts emphasis on the developmental activities of the needy, destitute, handicapped men, women and children, who are deprived of their social values and social acceptance. Thus, we can assert that social welfare agency is a well-planned and well-framed organization.

Organization: Meaning and Importance

Organization is the form of every human association for the attainment of a common purpose. Dimock says: "Organization is the systematic bringing together of interdependent parts to form a unified whole through which authority, coordination and control may be exercised to achieve a given purpose." It is often said that good people can make any organization pattern work. Some even assert that vagueness in an organization is a good thing in that it forces teamwork, since people know that they must cooperate to get anything done. However, there can be no doubt that good people and those who want to cooperate will work together most effectively if they know the parts they are to play in any team operation and the way their roles relate to one another.

This is as true in business or government as it is in football or in a symphony orchestra. Designing and maintaining these systems of role is basically the managerial functions of organizing. 'Organization' is a word many people use loosely. Some say, it includes all the behaviour of all participants. Others would equate it with the total system of social and cultural relationship. Organization implies a formalized intentional structure of roles of position. There are two kinds of organizations. They are formal and informal organization.

Formal Organization

Formal organization means the intentional structure of roles in a formally organized enterprise. Describing an organization as 'formal', however, does not mean there is anything inherently inflexible or unduly confining about it. If a manager has to organize well, the structure must furnish an environment in which individual performance, both present and future, contributes most effectively to group goals. Formal organization must be flexible. There should be room for recreation, for advantageous utilization of creative talents, and for recognition of individual likes and capacities in the most formal of organization. Yet, individual effort in group situation must be channelled towards group and organizational goals.

Informal Organization

Chester Barnard, author of management classic, *The Functions of the Executive*, described informal organization as a joint personal activity without conscious joint purpose, even though contributing to joint results. Thus, the informal relationships established in the group of people playing chess during lunch-time may aid in the achievement of organizational goals. It must be easier to ask for help on an organizational problem from someone you know personally, even if he or she may be in a different department, than from someone you know only as a name on an organization chart. Keith Davis described the informal organization as a network of personal and social relations not established or required by the formal organization but arising spontaneously as people associate with one another. Thus, the social welfare administrators and other top social welfare functionaries should strive as far as possible to create the atmosphere of an informal organization, which would develop the genuine feeling of good will and mutual trust among the social welfare workers. It should not be understood that social welfare functionaries should not follow the formal path. Both posses the good elements on their own.

Organizational Structure of a Social Welfare Agency

To put up any organization for a successful end, the structure of the organization is very important. However, the structure can vary in such parts as chief executive, departments, public undertakings, boards and commissions. Same is the case in the social work. The social welfare agency formulates certain organization structures. These organization structures are followed from the perspective of Indian policy on politics. The functions are the same in both agencies.

Structure in Chief Executive

(i) *Planning*: That is, working out in outline the things that need to be done and the methods for doing them to accomplish the purpose set for the enterprise.
(ii) *Organizing*: That is, the establishment of the structure of authority through which work sub-divisions are arranged, defined and coordinated for the definite objects.
(iii) *Staffing*: That is, the whole personnel functions of bringing in and training the staff and maintaining favourable conditions of work.
(iv) *Directing*: That is, the continuous task of making decision and embodying them in specific and general orders and instructions, or serving as the leader of the enterprise.
(v) *Coordinating*: That is, the all-important duty of interrelating the various parts of work.
(vi) *Reporting:* That is, keeping those, to whom the executive is responsible, informed as to what is going on, which thus, includes keeping himself or his subordinates informed through records, research or inspection.
(vii) *Budgeting*: With all that goes in the form of planning and accounting control.

Structure in Departments

For the departmental structure, a study on it reveals four different bases for the organization:

(i) *Purpose*: By purpose is meant the major objective to be aimed at or major service to be performed. Functional division of work is very common, and is regarded by many as the only efficient method. Ministries of Defence, Education, Transport or Communications and Railway in the Government of India have been formed on this basis.

(ii) *Process*: Process is identified with a technique, profession, or skill of a somewhat specialized type, though it is to be admitted that it is not quite easy to differentiate between process and function. Ministry of Law in India manifests this principle. Generally speaking, process or profession is found to be the basis of Staff organization, rather than of Line organization.

(iii) *Clientele*: Sometimes clientele too becomes the basis of organization. The Department of Rehabilitation at the Centre and the Department of Tribal Welfare in some states in India have been formed on this principle.

(iv) *Area/Territory*: It would mean that, the place where the job is done, may be the basis of organization. Underlying this principle is the belief that a region may have problems peculiar to itself, lending it a distinctive character, and thereby favouring separate handling or treatment. All these functions are prevailing in the social welfare agency for smooth operation.

Personnel Policies and Administration

Dictionary meaning of policy is plan of action. According to Edwin B. Flippo "Policy is a manmade owe of predetermined cause of action that is established to guide the performance of work towards the organizational objectives." It provides guidelines for maintaining consistency and continuity of plan, strategy and managerial decisions.

For the betterment of the organization the personnel policies and administration should be looked into with greater care. Recruitment and selection, training and promotion are the basic factors for the personnel policies and administration. Here, we deal with them in details.

Recruitment and Selection

According to D.E. Klinger, "Recruitment is the process of attracting qualified applicants for jobs." The need for a sound recruitment and selection policy is, thus, clearly indicated. "No element of the career service is more important than the recruitment policy." The need for a sound recruitment and selection policy was first realized by China centuries ago, and this recognition found reflection in the adoption of the merit principle, based on competitive examination. Russia was the first country in modern times to have evolved a sound recruitment system. In India, the merit principle has been in existence since 1853. Britain adopted it in 1857. The basic elements of such a policy include, or should include the following:

(i) discovery and cultivation of the employment market for posts in the public services,
(ii) use of attractive recruitment, literature and publicity,
(iii) use of scientific tests for determining abilities of the candidates,
(iv) tapping capable candidate from within the services,
(v) placement programme which assigns the right man to right job, and
(vi) a follow-up probationary programme as an integral of the recruitment process.

Problems of Recruitment

The problems of recruitment involves number of elements. We shall deal with them in brief.

(i) *Location of the Recruiting Authority*: The determination of the recruiting authority is one of the essential features of the personnel system. Indeed, this problem is of such general importance that the recruiting authority is determined by the Constitution of the country itself.
(ii) *Method of Recruitment*: Generally, there are two methods of recruitment, recruitment from within, and recruitment from outside the organization. The first method is, properly speaking, promotion, and the second one is recruitment in the true sense of the term. The best solution of the problem lies in a happy blend of the two in the light of administrative experience and the general political outlook. Direct recruitment should be the rule at lower levels; direct recruitment combined with a liberal system of promotions, recruitment from within, should be the policy for middle levels and positions should normally go by well designed system of promotion.
(iii) *Qualifications Required of the Employee*: The question of qualifications required of public employees is of enormous importance, as on it rests largely on the general efficiency of the public services. They can be divided into two parts – general and special qualifications. In general qualification, we have to look into such elements as citizenship, residence, sex, age, etc., and in the special

qualification, education, experience, personal qualification, technical experience, methods of determining qualifications, etc., are very important in the recruitment and selection.

Training

Training and education for the servants of public welfare services are very essential. Through training, persons can develop the quality and ability in themselves for the better tasks. According to William G. Torpey, "The training is the process of developing skills, habits, knowledge and aptitudes in employees for the purpose of increasing the effectiveness of employees in their present government positions as well as preparing employees for future government positions." The types of training can be divided into two parts namely – informal and formal training. The informal training is carried out by doing the work, and leaning from mistakes and implementing them through practice. On the other hand, the formal supports to inculcate administrative skills by well-defined courses at proper stage in the man's career.

Promotion

The word 'promote' is derived from the Latin expression 'promouere' meaning to move forward. The need for promotion arises from a variety of factors. An organization is enabled to retain the services of its personnel by the device of promotion. We know that man is a growing creature and if his need for recognition and advancement is not adequately satisfied by his organization, he is apt to seek change, thereby causing a large turnover of staff. A sound policy of promotion fosters a feeling of belongingness in personnel, contributes to a measure of community in policies and practices and leads to building up of traditions and conventions.

The principle for promotion is based on three important bases. They are:

(i) *Seniority*: The senior persons of the organization gets promotion to encourage and to appreciate his contributions to the organization. Thus, as a recognition he is given promotion.
(ii) *Merit Basis*: In promotion, especially in government organization, promotion is given to him/her who holds certain merits in his/her assigned jobs.
(iii) *Seniority-cum-Fitness*: Promotion also is made on the basis of seniority, subject to the rejection of the unfit.

Supervision of Staff Development

What is supervision? Supervision is a compound of two words 'super' and 'vision,' meaning superior power of perceiving. It means overseeing or superintending the work of others. It has been defined as "the direction, accompanied by authority, of the work of others". Supervision is more than inspection and investigation. Alas, it is more than superintendence as an administrative task. It has an education aspect too. A supervisor is supposed to teach the workers under him the best way of doing their work. Supervision is selecting the right person for each job; arousing in each person an interest in his work and teaching him how to do it. According to Halsey, "there are six qualities in a supervisor – thoroughness, fairness, initiative, fact, enthusiasm and emotional control".

The development of staff depends upon its methods and techniques of supervision. Millett suggests six techniques of the supervision – prior approval of individual's projects, the promulgation of service standard, budgetary limitation upon the magnitude of operations, the approval of key subordinate personal, a reporting system on the work progress and the inspection of results. When these techniques are used in any organization for supervision the development of staff will surely be an effective and developed one.

Management of a Social Welfare Agency

Management in a social welfare agency, works as the an important tool for the success of the organizations formulated by the agency. Every social welfare agency has its own managerial department to control and to maintain the work of the agency. Management is very much necessary for any organization.

Concept and Importance of Management

Policies provide an objective and management provides the action to get things done. 'Management' is the executive function that concerns itself with the carrying out of the administrative policies laid down by the administration. Management directs the active operations within the enterprises and combines the work of the employees with the available capital equipment and materials to produce an acceptable product. Management also makes the project or service according to the broad policies established by administration. The social welfare agency follows the same managerial procedure to maintain its stability.

The management is concerned with the implementation of the policy, and it is not directly concerned with goal or target fixation. The implementation of policies framed by administration is the main job of the management. Its functions are executive and largely governing. It is mainly concerned with the direction of human efforts in the execution of the plan and policy.

Motivating and controlling functions are involved in it. Management is the servant of administration; it gets salary or a part of the profit in lieu of its services. Management requires technical ability more than administrative ability. We are aware of the fact that the management is an executive function which is primarily concerned in getting things done with others. Planning, organization, staffing, motivation, direction, coordination and control are all functions of management. It is like the entire body of human being. Management uses the organization as determined by administration.

Manpower Planning

According to Edwin B. Flippo, "Manpower is an executive planning programme which can be defined as an appraisal of an organization's ability to perpetuate itself with respect to its management as a determination of measures necessary to provide the essential executive talent." There are two objectives of manpower planning:

(i) to utilize the present employees fully, and
(ii) to fill the future manpower needs.

James J. Lynch says, "Manpower planning is the integration of manpower policies, practices and procedures so as to achieve the right numbers of the right people in the right jobs at the right time."

Characteristics of Manpower Planning

The characteristics of manpower planning are as follows:

(i) Manpower planning includes an inventory of present manpower in order to determine the status of the present supply of available personnel and to discover undeveloped talent presently within the organization.
(ii) In manpower planning, the future manpower demand is estimated and for this, factors like retirement, death, dismissal, resignation, etc., are to be taken into account.
(iii) A plan is prepared to form an equilibrium between the demand and also pre-supply of manpower. Plans are also prepared for

matters like recruitment, selection, training, development, transfer and promotion.

(iv) Manpower planning benefits both the firm as well as the employees.

(v) To be effective, manpower planning must focus not only on the people involved, but also on the working candidates and the working conditions and relationships in which they work. It must plan for manpower management programmes.

There are five types of manpower planning. They are:

(a) Macro-level manpower planning.
(b) Micro-level manpower planning.
(c) Short-term manpower planning.
(d) Medium-term manpower planning.
(e) Long-term manpower planning.

Reporting and Public Relation

A report is an account or statement describing in detail an event, a happening, a situation, or evaluating an enterprise or a product that is happened frequently, both in qualitative and quantitative terms. It is generally written and submitted periodically and may include many statistical data.

For any organization or agency, reporting is one of the elements to run the job effectively. Reporting is necessary to evaluate the last programme for further development, the present functions whether it is going on smoothly, to plan for the future and to include what all are to be added or removed from the programme. According to the *Encyclopaedia America*, "Public relation is out of analysing, influencing and interpreting a person's idea, group, or business so that, he, or it, will be recognized as serving the public interests, and will benefit from so doing." According to Mittell, public relations of management have four primary aspects:

(1) Learning about public desires and aspirations,
(2) Advising the public about what it should desire,
(3) Ensuring satisfactory contact between public and the government officials, and
(4) Informing the public about what an agency is doing.

Bernays says, "Public relation is, information given to public, persuasion directed at the public to modify attitudes and actions and it efforts to integrate attitudes and action of an institution with its public and of its public with that situation." The main tool and technique of public relation is publicity. Publicity may be through, radio, television, Press Information Bureau, Publications Division, Directorate of Advertising and Visual Publicity, Films Division, Research and Reference Division, Directorate of Field Publicity, etc.

Coordination: Its Meaning and Importance

Meaning of Coordination

Coordination is the orderly synchronization of efforts to provide the proper amount, timing and directing of execution resulting in harmonious and unified actions to a stated objective. It is mainly concerned with synchronizing and certifying the actions of a group of people. Money and Railey define coordination as "the orderly arrangement of group effort to provide unity of action in pursuit of a common purpose". Coordination is a process of typing or integrating various factors of production and their functions in an enterprise so as to make a harmonious combination of the factors and synchronize the functions as to time, place and objective. It involves balancing and keeping together the different activities so as to maintain a well-knit aggregate function and ensure that the various activities are smoothly carried out. Coordination may be defined as the heart of management, which permeates the entire fabric of business management from the top executive to the workers down below.

Importance of Coordination

According to Chester I. Barnard, "the quality of coordination is the crucial factor in the survival of organization". The trained football team, the members of which willingly respond to their coach and captain, affords an excellent example of the highest form of coordinate effort. In short, we can say that smooth working of an enterprise and the definite achievements of its objectives depend on sound coordination. Effectiveness of coordination in an enterprise, can be brought through simplified organization, harmonized programmes and policies, well-designed system of communication and voluntary coordination through supervision.

Monitoring and Evaluation in Social Welfare Agency

Monitoring is the simplest method of knowing where we are in relation to the programme. It is normally used to send feedback information for initiating corrective action with a view to bring the lagging areas back on cause.

For any organization monitoring is very important. An organization to be on its right track has to depend on the act of monitoring. We can say that monitoring is a device used for observing, reporting and testing the organization. In a social welfare agency there are some groups of officials to monitor the works and the workers. Their work is to observe all the ongoing procedures; they are also to report the effectiveness and defects and drawbacks and also to test time and again whether the assigned work are on the right track and running smoothly. This is quite different from that of the evaluation.

All the programmes whether it is success or failure has to be evaluated. Evaluation is the assessment of progress of events. It is the appraisal and judgement of the work and its effectiveness. Evaluation in social welfare is very essential. Evaluation is a kind of collection of data to see whether their desired and expected needs are fulfilled, their success and failures. The evaluation is mainly done to know if the work is successful, then why it was possible, and if there is failure then the question arises why, where, when, etc., was the mistake. The collection of data is done through surveys. Evaluation helps an organization to take up major steps to improve the effectiveness of work that in the future they have organized or are to be organized. Ultimately, the social welfare agency depends upon the monitoring of works and the evaluation of the process. Therefore, we can confirm that an organization can be effective when there is the process of evaluation in the time process.

We have dealt with many aspects of administration of the social welfare so as to conclude the discussion on the topic we can say that it is a vast topic to be discussed. It covers mainly management, psychology, sociology, political science and the social work. Its importance has increased all over the world. Before independence, India was not aware of the methods and techniques of administration especially in the social welfare activities. But today, when we analyse deeply, we come to know that India has advanced very much in the field of administration.

As it is mentioned in the introduction that social welfare administration encompasses every act, every technique and every considerations in the process necessary to formulate social policy into social services, thus we can conclude saying that the "administration of any organization is very essential".

4

Economic Planning and Development

The first important task of a country is to maintain itself. There must be food, clothing and shelter for its countrymen. For that the country must have a properly planned economic stability then only we can say that the country is a developed country. Modern men spend most of their daytime making a living. It is not sufficient that there must be a system of production in society, equally important is its distribution system. In our country, one of the major causes of economic ills is improper planning. All people must plan for the development of the their society. Economic planning as an instrument of development was adopted in India in 1951, but its need was felt much earlier. During the pre-independence period, a few unofficial development plans were prepared at the initiative of both the nationalistic leaders and leading industrialists of the country. These plans, however, could not be put into practice. But the after independence, India formed a Planning Commission, which is doing great work for the development of the country. Of all the long-term objectives of economic planning in India, economic growth has always been given great attention by the government. The Indian Planning Commission has planned many plans like social development plan, social planning for welfare of society, etc. The government must make some programmes and plans for the development of society. If the economy of our country is high the standard of living of people will be better. For that the government needs proper planning and cooperation of people.

Experience in the field of community development was gained through the rural community development programmes which was begun in 1952. With this experience in the background, a number of pilot community projects were initiated in urban areas which included the projects in Delhi (1958), Ahmedabad (1962), and Calcutta (1966). In 1966, the Government of India decided to launch formally a national experiment in urban community development similar to that of rural community development.

What is Economic Planning?

The History of Economic Planning

The Indian National Congress, under the inspiration of Jawaharlal Nehru, set up the National Planning Committee towards the end of 1938. The Committee produced a series of studies on different subjects concerned with economic development. It laid down that the state should own or control all key industries and services, mineral resources and railways, waterways, shipping and other public utilities and in fact all those large scale industries which were likely to become monopolistic in character. Besides National Planning Committee, eight industries conceived "A plan of economy development", which was popularly known as the Bombay Plan. There was also a Gandhian plan, which was prepared by Shriram Narayan. The world famous revolutionary, M.N. Roy formulated the people's plan. All these plans are of historical importance only because they were paper plans, which were never implemented. Just after the attainment of independence, the Government of India set up the Planning Committee in 1950 to assess the country's needs of material capital and human resources so as to formulate plan for their more balanced and effective utilization. The first Five-Year Plan commenced in 1950-51 and it was followed by a series of Five-Year Plans.

Definitions of Economic Planning

(1) Lewis Lordwin says, "Economic planning is a scheme of economic organization in which individual and separate planned enterprises and industry, are treated as coordinate units of one single system for the purpose of utilizing available resources to achieve the maximum satisfaction of the people's needs within a given time."

(2) Dalton says, "Economic planning is the deliberate direction by persons in charge of large resources of economic activity towards chosen ends."

(3) Zweig says, "Economic planning consists in the extension of the functions of public authorities to organization and utilization of economic resources, planning implies and leads to centralization of the national economy."

Types of Economic Planning

Economic planning can be of two types – financial and physical.

Financial Planning

Financial planning is key of economic planning. If sufficient finances are available, it is not difficult to achieve a physical target. Financial planning is essential in order to remove maladjustments between supply and demand for calculation of costs and benefits of various projects. The Indian Planning Commission points out that "The essence of financial planning is to ensure that demands and supplies are matched in a manner which exploits physical potentiality as fully as possible, without major and unplanned changes in the prices structure." In the case of financial planning, the outlay is fixed in terms of money and the estimates are made on the basis of various hypotheses regarding the growth of national income, consumption, import, etc., to cover this out by taxation, saving and increase in the cash holding. It must establish equilibrium between the part incomes and the amount of investment, goods made available to private investors. In the public sector, a balance must be established between financial funds made available for investment purposes and the amount of investment goods which will be produced or imported. Financial planning is, thus, thought to secure a balance between the demands and supplies, avoid inflation and bring about economic stability.

Physical Planning

Physical planning is a development effort in terms of factor allocations and product yields so as to maximize income and underdevelopment. The physical balance consists of a proper evaluation of the relations between investment and output which are computed. These coefficients indicate the amount of investment and also the compositions of that investment in term of various kinds of goods needed in order to obtain an increase in output of a product by a given amount. Financial planning is only a means to achieve this end. Lack of financing to carry out an investment project in an underdeveloped country ordinarily does not reflect the lack of physical resources. Physical planning requires the fixation of physical targets with regards to agriculture and industrial production, social, cultural transformation service and income and investment levels of the economy. There must be proper balances in the various target set in the plan. Balogh says, "The only politically sound and morally responsible strategy involves steady pressure up to the limits of physical resources. It involves hair-sharp sectoral balance and concentration attention on the widening of supply bottlenecks as they arise."

Planning and Removal of Poverty

Rapid Economic Growth

The basic aim of economic planning in India is to bring about rapid economic growth through the development of agriculture, industry power, transport and communications and all other sectors of the economy. The basic measure of economic growth of the country is in the continuous expansion, year after year, of real national income and real per capita income. Economic growth, however, should also include improvements in physical quality of life consisting of life expectancy, infant morality and literacy, etc. Indian planning aims at increasing national and per capita incomes on the assumption that continuous increase in these incomes would remove poverty and misery and raise the standard of living of the masses. But when they found an increase in the degree of poverty in the country, the objectives of planning from the Fourth Plan onwards was not simply economic growth but raising the standard of living of those who have been living in abject poverty for generations and centuries. According to Fourth Five-Year Plan, "The basic goal is rapid increase in the standard of living of people", and emphasis is placed on the common man, the weaker sections and the less privileged. In fact, the slogan of "*garibi hatao*" (removal of poverty) and "growth with justice" were coined during the early 1970s to indicate clearly that emphasis would be on removal of poverty and not simply on increase in national income.

Increase in Employment

Unemployment and under-employment are important causes of poverty in India. Hence, from the very beginning, the removal of unemployment and under-employment have been important objectives of economic planning in the country. The Planning Commission has all along assumed that increase in investment would be accompanied by increase in employment as well as in the national income of the country. The Commission argued explicitly in the Third Plan that as the national income increased in response to investment and development outlay, the demand for labour would automatically rise and employment would expand. At the same time, the removal of unemployment would result in increase in gross national product and standard of living of people. Even though employment has been mentioned as one of the objectives of economic planning in all our Five-Year Plans, it has never been accorded a high priority. In no plan do we find separate employment plan framed for each one of the sectors and regions, as to boost employment on the one side and the national income on the other. This explains why unemployment has increased over the years. For the first time, the Planning Commission admitted in the Janata Party's Sixth Plan (1978-83) the possibilities of real conflict between employment and economic growth and accorded employment a pride of place in the plan. However, in the Sixth Plan, which was finally accepted and implemented by the Congress Party, the main focus reverted to the traditional growth approach, with the usual assumption that employment would increase with rise in investment, irrespective of choice of techniques.

Economic Planning and Social Change

In an unplanned society, various types of retrogressive forces operate, such as inequalities of income, poverty, absence of equal opportunities for progress etc. India's economic plans made conscious efforts to remove all these retrogressive forces and foster social as well as individual development. Reduction of inequalities of income and the establishment of socialist society create conditions in which everyone will have equal opportunities in the matter of education and employment.

Reduction of Inequality of Income

A very small group of people in India are better-off and have not experienced poverty and misery. These are the rich landlords in the countryside, the merchants, industrialists, bankers, top officers of the government, etc. The vast majority of people are, however, very poor because their income is very low. Such extremes in India have their roots in the traditional social formations and necessarily, therefore the reduction of inequalities of income and wealth would be possible only through destroying the semi-feudal relations of productions in our village. The Planning Commission outlines such measures as removal of all intermediaries and ceiling on landholding for the reduction of inequalities of wealth and income in rural areas. Another aspect of inequalities of income in India is the large disparities between rural and urban income which are bound to be accentuated over the years with industrialization and economic growth. The Planning Commission has suggested measures as the removal of poverty through raising agricultural productivity, development of agro-based industries, fair price to farmers for their products, etc. Even though reduction of income inequalities has always been mentioned as one of the objectives in all the plans, in terms of priority this objective invariably got a very low position. The Five-Year Plans never had a clear and positive strategy to redistribute wealth and income and wealth was the main criteria at that time. This could possibly be so because Nehru, the architect of Indian planning, did not believe that the problem of economic inequalities of income and wealth could ever be solved merely by redistribution. The Fourth Plan stated clearly, "In a rich country, greater equality could be achieved in part by transfer of income through fiscal, pricing and other policies. No significant results can be achieved through such measures in a poor country."

Establishment of a Socialist Society

Finally, the Indian planners visualized the establishment of a socialist society in which, everyone would have equal opportunities in the matter of education, occupation, etc. Wealth would be distributed equally and there would be no concentration of economic power in the hands of a few individuals or families. Above all, there would be no scope for exploitation of man by man. The first three plans talked of the setting up of socialist lines. The Fourth Plan talked about the "establishment of a social and economic democracy". The Fourth Plan stated, "The broad objectives of planning could thus be defined as rapid economic development accompanied by continuous progress towards equality and social justice and the establishment of a social and economic democracy." But the definition of economic democracy as given by the Indian planners is different from what is commonly understood elsewhere. In affluent economies where abysmal poverty has been eliminated, economic democracy is almost the same as a free market economy. In India, however, the broad definition of economic democracy is the availability of opportunities for education, public health and sanitation, drinking water supply, etc., for large masses of people, irrespective of whether they are rich or poor.

Need for Planning

Need for economic planning has been felt on account of the limitation of the market mechanism in the aspect of both efficiency and equality. According to Oshar Lange, "Economic planning or more precisely, the planning of economic development is an essential feature of socialism. It expresses the fact that socialist economic does not develop in an element way, but that its development is guided and directed by the conscious will of organized society. Planning is the means of the subjective operation of economic development of society to the directions of human beings." In market economics, both developed and underdeveloped planning has been adopted for overcoming the limitation of the market mechanism. Let us first consider the reasons for the introduction of planning in developed capitalist economy. The need for economic planning in the Third World countries has been felt particularly due to their economic background.

Planning Process

Planning Body

The first condition for economic planning is that a planning body is to be constituted by the government. In India and many other countries, this planning body is known as the Planning Commission. The main functions of this body are to survey the sources, spell out the broad objectives, lay down the priorities, formulate the strategy for realizing the objectives, determine the means of economic goals and targets for different sectors and units for the mobilization of various programmes.

Survey of Resources and Collection of Necessary Data

Survey of resources and availability of data on other aspects of economics are two important requisites of economic planning. The size of the plan is often limited by the availability of the resources. Therefore, the planning body must know the volume of material, human and capital resources which are at its disposal while formulating a plan. In developed countries, these resources have been properly surveyed and the reliability of data is high. In contrast, the position of Third World countries from this point of view is far from satisfactory. However, in whatever country the planning has been adopted techno-economic surveys are now being conducted on regular basis not only to assess the nations on a regular basis but also to study other aspects of economy. In the Third World countries, many data gaps exist, and even where data are available their reliability is questionable.

Planning Objectives

Economic planning implies certain goals. These goals are often clearly defined and the efforts are directed under the plan to realize them. If the plan is not consistent with the national goals, it is a useless exercise or even a deceit. In a number of developing countries though it is difficult to find any inconsistency between the objectives of the plans and the measures contemplated, yet planning is scuttled at the implementation level, because the rulers have no desire to realize the plan objectives. In fact, without commitment planning has little meaning.

Priorities

Economic planning requires spelling out of priorities for the public investment programmes. No country can ever meet all the investment requirements of its various sectors. We all know that a growing economy infrastructure should be developed, basic and more particularly the machine making industries are to be set up, agriculture should also be developed so that the supply of food does not become a constrain and finally no country can wait endlessly for the spread of education and medical facilities. But a developing country rarely has the resources to make massive investment in all the sectors.

Strategy and Development Policy

Economic planning implies a strategy for the realization of broader goals. In the absence of proper strategy, the planning might lack direction and the realization of the potential may always be in doubt. For example, a country desiring to attain a high level of development over the years must decide whether it can sustain its long-term development merely by giving a big push to the development of consumer goods industries, or there has to be a consistency between the development of both consumer and goods producer industries. It should also settle whether it prefers growth via export promotion or import substitute.

Objectives of Economic Planning

Economic Growth

Of all the long-term objectives of economic planning in India, economic growth has always been given greater attention by the government. The planners have often assumed that realization of other objectives is very much linked with the realization of growth objectives. This understanding is not altogether incorrect. Growth often enables a country to become self-reliant, creates more important employment opportunities, eliminates poverty and also reduces income inequalities. But this will not inevitably happen, because one cannot rule out the conflicts that might develop between growth and other objectives of planning. It has been observed in certain countries that economic growth has a tendency to benefit the cause of the relatively poor. Our own experience in this country over the past three-and-a-half decades has clearly shown that the gains of economic growth do not automatically percolate downwards and thus special measures are required to tackle unemployment and poverty problems.

Self-Reliance

There was not much emphasis on self-reliance when the first two Five-Year Plans were made. In the Third Plan, for the first time, the objectives of self-reliance was started. However, the concept of self-reliance adopted in this plan was rather nervous. It was defined merely as overcoming needs of external assistance. The Fourth Plan considered the goal of self-reliance and clearly determined the time phasing for its realization. The plan document stated, "Dependence of foreign aid will be greatly reduced in the course of Fourth Plan. It plans to do away with concessational imports of food grain under PL 480 by 1971. Foreign net of debt charges and interest payment will be reduced to half by the end of Fourth Plan compared to the current level." With the development of basic industries such as iron and steel, machine tools and heavy engineering, India's dependence on developed countries for capital equipment has considerably diminished. However, in totality the goal of self-reliance still remains unrealized. The prospects of the country on these fronts can brighten only if it can either discover domestic petroleum resources of considerable size or develop alternative sources of energy like coal and electricity.

Full Employment

Unemployment problem in a less developed country like India deserves particular attention, as its solution is directly linked with the amelioration in the condition of the poor. In recognition of this fact, full employment has always remained an objective of economic planning, though it never received the priority it deserved. According to Ashok Rudea, "In India, the government never formulated its employment policy in well defined terms. It also did not set a target data by which any able bodied person who wants to work and make an honest living can be assured of a job that would offer him at least a minimum subsistence." Low priority to employment under the various plans is clear from the fact that never in the history of economic planning in India was any plan framed keeping employment generation in focus. Over the past three-and-a-half decades the approach of the planners in India has been of linking employment programmes directly with investment targets. It was in fact always assumed that an increase in employment would automatically result in an increase in employment. Pramit Chaudhury has remarked "Although full employment was regarded as a desirable objective, its achievement was seen to depend on the fulfilment of achieving a capital stock objective and that in the long-term, there was no serious concern in the formulation of the strategy for the compatibility of employment targets with various output and investment targets."

Social Justice

(a) *Reduction in Income Inequalities*: For a considerable period, the philosophy of the plan in respect of income inequalities carried the imprint of Nehru's argument that in any poor country, this problem can be solved merely by redistributing income and wealth. Therefore, the plans without exception stressed the need for growth with a hope that in course of time, benefits of growth would trickle down and income inequalities would be reduced. Once it became obvious that nothing of the sort was happening in this country, the planners felt the compulsion of spelling out their approach towards income inequalities. This was actually done in the Fourth Plan. Prior to that in a passing reference the Planning

Commission had started in the Third Plan document, that income inequalities that are found in any country before modern growth takes place emanates in a feudal system. Inequalities in income and wealth resulting from modern income growth, particularly industrialization are far more complex. In the earlier phase of industrialization while the income of the common people remain low, a small minority managed to secure high income. In India, there are main sources of high receipts, viz., capital gain receipts, entrepreneurial and speculative profits, and salaries and perquisites of business executives. According to the Planning Commission for reduction of inequalities arising from the generation of these high incomes will require both restriction measures and fiscal efforts.

(b) *Removal of Poverty*: The tackling of poverty problem had first received the attention of planners under the First Plan. Until the completion of the Fourth Plan, the poor had received a raw deal at the hands of the government, which had expected them to benefit from growth efforts automatically. When in the world over it become clear that the benefits of modern growth did not reach the poor as was expected, there was a visible shift in the approach of planning. The needs for adopting the basic needs approach was felt in this period only. Reiterating this approach the Planning Commission in Sixth Plan document stated, "The incidence of the poverty in the country is still very high. Thus, determined measures are necessary to combat poverty, a substantial increase in the overall rate of growth of the economy will no doubt create favourable conditions for a country.

Economic Development

In the primitive days, man satisfied his hunger by searching for food and living upon what he could raise. As an aid in this search for food, primitive people invented weapons and tools. The procuring of fruits, berries, greens and seeds was supplemented by some hunting. In places where animals were abundant, the techniques of hunting highly developed. The hunting people did not go separately but rather lived in a small groups and moved in a group to hunt. Man moved forward again and he learned to domesticate animals, particularly the big animals such as cattle. Most of the hunting people had already domesticated the dogs which aided in the hunt and also helped somewhat in transportation. The domestication of animals became a group responsibility. The development of agriculture came next. When man turned to hoe-culture, he invented new tools to cultivate fields in a relatively larger scale. With the rise of agriculture man passed from flesh diet of nomads to a larger use of vegetable foods. With the cultivation of the soil, population multiplied. Agriculture made fixed abodes necessary and led to the establishment of village communities. The making of money became an occupation which besides adding to human welfare also created an unlimited amount of human ill will and misery. Down to the middle of the eighteenth century, agriculture was the leading occupational activity of mankind. With the Industrial Revolution and with the manufacture of tools on a large scale, there developed new types of agriculture. The Industrial Revolution furthered specialized. The city arose as a centre of trade and goods were assembled at certain places on certain days and sold. The city developed into a form of an economic group, besides being a social and political group. The use of the factory system in a large part of the world gave birth to capitalism. The twentieth century has brought about mass production and rise of many near monopoly and high degree of division of labour. The market situation has now been profoundly altered. The consumer has become more and more dependent upon the institutions of the market. Advertising profoundly influences consumer's wants and habits of buying. So, we can say that the economy has developed so much that today people are living a very good life, because of it. The development of economy, therefore, has brought a great change in the present society.

What is Economic Development?

Definitions

(a) Meier and Baldwin hold that "Economic development is a process whereby an economy's real national income increases over a long period of time."
(b) Robert Garner, "Economic development or its deficiency primarily results due to variations in tendencies, customs, traditions and their own political, social and religious institutes."
(c) Walter Krause, "Economic development refers to a process of economic growth within the economy, the central objective of the process being higher and raising real per capita income for the economy."

(d) Viner says, "The term economic development signify not merely economic growth, but economic development with which is associated either rising per capita levels of income or the maintenance of existing high levels of income."

(f) Nurkse puts, "Economic development of a country is related to large extent on any country's human qualities, social tendencies, political conditions and historical combinations."

Objectives of Economic Development

Development is both a physical reality and a state of mind in which society has, through some combination of social, economic and institutional processes, secured the means for obtaining better life. For a better life, development generally in all societies must have at least the following objectives:

(i) Increase the availability and widen distribution of basic life sustaining goods such as food, shelter, health, and protection.

(ii) Raise the level of living including addition of higher income, the provisions for more jobs, better education and greater attention to culture and humanistic values, all of which serve not only to enhance material well-being but also generate greater individual and national self-esteem.

(iii) Expand the range of economic and social choices available to individuals and nations by freeing them from servitude and dependence not only in relation to other people and nations, but also to the forces of ignorance and human misery.

Modern Concept of Development

In the context of the definition of development, it may be useful to refer to the new term - sustainable development, which is now in common use. This term was brought into vogue by the World Commission on Environment and Development in 1987 in its report titled, "Our Common Future." According to it, the term means: "Meeting the needs of the present generation without compromising the needs of future generation." In other words it envisages a "development that meets the needs of the present without compromising the ability of the future generations to meet their own needs". The ability to meet the needs is largely determined by the accumulation of human capital and man made physical capital depletion and changes of national resources. Hence, what matters is that the overall productivity of the accumulation capital including its impact on human health and aesthetic pleasure, as well as income, more than compensate for any loss from depletion of national capital. The need for keeping in view the interests of the future generations has arisen because in the past, while the benefits of development has often been exaggerated, the costs of development, in particular, the costs of environment loss have been ignored. It is, therefore, argued that their cost must be considered when development projects are decided upon.

Need for Economic Development

During the last few decades, the world has witnessed an increasing restlessness in underdeveloped countries to develop; this is possible due to two main reasons. In the first place, underdeveloped countries suffer from extreme poverty which makes it imperative for them to grow. Secondly, with the gap between developed and underdeveloped countries, they cannot ever dream of realizing this objective, unless there is some unexpected change in the world situation.

Appalling Poverty

Underdeveloped countries are extremely poor. Their per capita income is appallingly low which compel their vast populations to live under sub-human living conditions. Of course, with the setting up of certain modern industries some enclave type of development has taken place in the less developed countries, but it has failed to break what economists call low level equilibrium trap. Unemployment in these countries is mostly disguised and may be considered both as a cause and effect of widespread poverty. Due to abject poverty, when most people find it impossible to save, the rate of capital formation remains so low that the society cannot provide employment to the continuously increasing population. Hence, unemployment, particularly in a disguised form, steadily grows and in turn breeds further poverty. Moreover, poverty has resulted in subhuman living conditions in the Third World countries. The people in multitudes have been denied food, clothes, drinking water, shelter, medical facilities and education in countries of Asia, Africa and Latin America. People with conscience insist that no human society making a claim that is rational, can allow existence of poverty and destitution along with unbelievable affluence and luxury. They seem to believe that if these countries could be helped in coming out of the low level equilibrium trap and therefore in pursuing their development projects, the social tensions will be reduced and the threat to the existing system will be avoided.

International Inequality

A second compelling requirement of development in the countries of the Third World is international inequality. Having lagged far behind in the development race, these countries must now grow very fast, if the already wide gap between them and the developed West is to be reduced. Irrespective of their level of development, the Third World countries are now conscious of international inequalities and they all wish to realize their development potential so as to check further widening of gap between their living standards and those of the people in the developed West. The rich-poor countries divide is a modern phenomenon. All modern industrialized ones in the west, were once at subsistence level. In fact, until the advent of Industrial Revolution there were very little international inequalities. But, Industrial Revolution assisted by rapid technological development created wide international disparities.

Aspects of Development

Perspective of Economic Development

Economic development along with a high growth rate of the national product is a means to an end, i.e., content in itself by the ultimate objectives, the final goal of the society. Economic growth is never more than a method of obtaining the means through which a nation plans to achieve some form of social progress or social change. Developing nations have become increasingly conscious of the social aspect of economic planning. It is now generally realized that economic growth should be a means towards the eradication of hunger, illiteracy, disease and reduction of existing social and economic inequalities. The consequences of growth without development are too painful to be ignored. The correlation between economic growth and social development has tended to be low in the Asian, African and Latin American countries. Many writers have defined economic development in a broader sense. Myrdal has defined it as nothing less than the upward movement of the entire social system, such as, rise in productivity, industrialization, social and economic equalization, development of modern knowledge, institution improvement and rational coordination and a policy measure.

Perspective of Social Development

Social development is a broad concept encompassing improvement in the social status of the people. Social development lays stress on provision of health, services, education, housing, cultural, protection of children, a change in the status of woman, regulation of labour and improving the status of workers and reduction of diseases, poverty and other social illness. According to T.K.N. Unnithan, "Social development may be seen as a process of entering in a new order of existence. The quality of life and the quality of social relations which exist would indicate the level of the order of existence." Social development is more concerned with the investment in human beings. A unit of investment in education, health, social welfare, etc., is in the ultimate analysis, and as productive as a unit of investment in agriculture industry of trade. Social development deals with society and human resources whereas economic development deals with economic and industrial resources. Social justice and human welfare are key objectives of social development.

Social Development in India

As a matter of fact, social welfare envisages the provision of services intended to care for the special needs of persons and groups who by reason of some handicaps - social, economic, physical or mental are unable to avail themselves of such services and are traditionally denied the amenities and services provided by the community. For the fulfilment of these objectives it seems reasonably necessary that social development should proceed side by side with economic development. Social development is the process in pursuit of social objectives and this development is achieved through the plans prepared from time to time by the Planning Commission in India, which came into existence in 1950.

"The task before an underdeveloped country is not merely to get better result within the existing framework of economic and social institutions, but to mould and refreshing these so that they contribute effectively to the realization of wider and deeper social values." The above instance show that economic activity is a means to achieve the ends of social welfare activities. Jawaharlal Nehru, the first Prime

Minister of India, made this point even clearer by the statement of Third Five-Year Plan: "In the last analysis, economic development is but a means to an end in building up efforts for reduction in poverty and unemployment." However, in the light of past experience, it will not be realistic to rely solely on the growth process to find a solution to this problem. Specific policy measures will be needed not only to influence the composition of output in favour of mass consumption goods, but also to ensure a more regional and class distribution of output, giving a special attention to stimulate growth in more backward regions.

Social Planning

Social Planning in India

India's cultural nationalism has been a fact for the last two thousand years or more. What was imperfectly achieved was political nationalism, i.e., the identification of the people with the state. The contributions of the British rule lay mainly in activating this process. Small wonder that free India gave herself a Constitution formed by the ideals of liberty, equality and social justice. Fundamental rights relating to freedom of speech, association and vocation have been built into it and the direct principle of state policy entrusts it with forward-looking dynamics. In sum, the Constitution aims at the establishment of a welfare state. It accepts this particularly from the government with a federal set-up. Benefiting its own country from the experiences of other countries, it created a strong central government. The division of power between the centre and the state is embodied in the union, state and concurrent list but all the residuary power has been vested in Centre. The Constitution gives formal expression to the long standing aim of socio-economic revolution. It had been realized throughout the years of freedom struggle that without economic prosperity political independence would be an empty shell. To Gandhiji, Swaraj had always meant more than independence from the British.

According to Titmus, "Social policy represents a summation of acts of government deliberately designed to improve the welfare of the people." The first specific wider sense of deliberate design of a section of population was to be found in the Fourth Plan documents when it was observed: "In the concept of development, the centre of gravity has thus shifted from the economic to the social and we have reached to the points where this shift begins to approach the culture." Indian Planning Commission has done a very good job for the benefits of poor and the social planning did its work successfully.

The main objectives of social planning in India are:

(a) *Education*: As we know, education is what makes people human beings. Unless and until our own mind and heart are not moulded in particular way, our life is like darkness. One of the philosophers has said, "Your bright future lies in education." It means education is one of the means to inculcate the sense in our minds to develop ourselves. Today education is given much importance and lots of programmes have been made by the Government of India. The Indian government is trying its level best to educate people. Today, we find many schools, colleges and universities are opened to help the people to make their future.

(b) *Health*: In earlier days, people died of many sicknesses but they were not aware of them. They had a belief that sickness was caused by some evil spirits and they did not care about cleanliness and medicines. But now everything has changed. People have got awareness and now they do not believe in evil spirits. People became aware of the causes of their sickness and started taking care of their health on their own. Today, we find many hospitals have been built in all the parts of India. Earlier, people were dying because of lack of medicines, but today even a dying person also can be cured. The Government of India is spending huge amount of money on health. Many awareness programmes are being conducted in different parts of the country. The social planning is meant for welfare of the people and societies. Today, the civilized people have learnt the art of cleanliness and are leading a good and healthy life. For the uneducated people, government and NGOs are providing many programmes on health. It is said, "healthy body, healthy mind." Surely with a healthy body and healthy mind, we can work well.

(c) *Housing*: One of the major objectives of social planning is housing. The social agencies look at the standard of the people and provide housing specially to those who are not able to make or have no place to make houses on their own. Housing is one of the basic needs of the people, and the basic needs of human beings are food, clothing and house. Housing needs are fulfilled by the government. A person can work outside and earn food and clothing but it is very difficult to build a house. Today, the

Government of India has taken the initiative to build houses for the poor. The programme has been started under the name of Indira Awas Yojana. Today, many people have benefited from these programmes. In housing, the main objectives have been to direct the public housing programmes towards the construction of cheaper houses. The development also aims at the drinking water supply. Towns are constructed where the sufficient water is available.

(d) *Urban Development*: The concept of development is usually defined in terms of growth and directed changes. The population that is added to the town or city every year is not the population that is likely to add to the municipal revenues, though their need for services is the same as that of the other sections of the population. Development theory has long been popular among workers with children and families. it is only during the last two decades that the development concept has been applied to social welfare activity, even to whole nations. The recent analysis of the UN Commission on Welfare Administration carries the subtitle: The Place of Social Welfare in the Process of Development. In this report, the natural processes of urban growth is called 'urbanization', while urban development is reserved for formal processes and programmes of substantive services, that is, urban development is viewed as a type of directed social change that occurs in communities and urban areas.

(e) *Rural Development*: The earliest human communities were perhaps the loosely organized aggregations of a few families who carried on mutually interdependent activities in gathering food and defending themselves against their enemies. Gradually, man acquired skill and knowledge in agriculture. With the development of agriculture and the consequent stabilization of the sources of food, the people began to lead a settled life and human communities became more stationary. The major approach in rural development is extension education, i.e., to bring to the people information regarding the manner in which they can increase their output and other contributions using means suggested as a result of experimentation. Rabindranath Tagore was responsible for setting up the rural reconstruction programme at Shantiniketan in 1921. The basic idea was, to bring life in its completeness into the villages. This was accomplished by making the villagers self-reliant using modern methods for increasing production, making villagers aware of their cultural traditions and developing their physical and intellectual abilities. The rural population in India is very high. Their needs are manifold and with the resources of the country being limited, the government cannot meet the demanding challenges of rural development. The programmes act only as stimulants and demonstration. Ultimately, the community has to respond and organize itself to meet its needs.

Potent of Population

India is the world's second most populous country. According to the 1991 census, India's population was 83.39 crore which has by the end of 1996 increased to 93.4 crore. According to projections made in a World Bank Report, India's estimated population by 2150 will be over 1,756 million. India will thereby overtake China and become the most populous country in the world. The increase in world population, which started about the middle of the 17th century, was led by Europeans and until recently the Europeans continued to hold the lead. It was in Europe that the modern industrial civilization was born. Though the birth rate is decreasing all over the world, still the population is rapidly increasing. The population would thus grow very fast. But, the food growth in comparison would be very slow. The Industrial Revolution caused the first real burst of world population growth. Not only did it give an unprecedented impetus to population growth in Europe, but its rapid diffusion to other religions extended its influence around the globe. As the reader will realize, the downward trend of the birth rate is conspicuous. The decline is hardly due to lower fecundity of the people concerned. The delay in marriage can only account for a small variation in the birth rate, for the postponement of marriage has not been great. The fall in the birth rate has been mainly due to the desire to limit the size of the family.

Population and Economic Development

What is the role of population in economic development of a country? Is an increase of population an aid or an obstruction to the economic development of a country? To this, there cannot be a straight answer. It all depends upon circumstances prevailing in a country. In western countries, for example, the increase in population in the early 19th century served as a stimulant for economic growth. Now let us examine the effect of a fast expanding population on the economics of underdeveloped countries.

Population and Development of Agriculture

The underdeveloped countries of today are predominantly agricultural, with little or no industrial base. An overwhelming majority of the population of these countries derive their livelihood from agriculture. The pressures on the land is already very heavy, there being no other outlets for the people. If there is future expansion of population in such countries the additional numbers have no other alternative except to fall back on agriculture. But, the employment of additional number in agriculture may actually result in a deterioration of the productivity of existing land.

Population and Employment

Increase of population may not be much of a problem for an economically developed country, because in such a country the additional population can easily be put to production work with the availability of capital and other complimentary resources. But in an underdeveloped country, the increase of population creates the serious problem of unemployment and underemployment. Such a country is already labour surplus. Any increase in labour forces will surely aggravate the problems of unemployment, because additional population cannot be gainfully employed in the absence of capital.

Basic Needs and Population Growth

Housing

In so far as housing in the developing countries is concerned, majority of cities and towns have a variety of houses ranging between spacious dwellings of the rich and miserable houses of the poor. Housing is indeed, a global problem. Although the problem is very chronic in the developing countries, most of the advanced countries also face this problem though in varying degrees. Neither the capitalist, USA which is regarded as an affluent society nor the socialist super power like Russia is free from the housing problems. In the past few decades, many large cites of the developing countries have experienced an extremely high growth in their population. It is estimated that by the year 2000 more than one third of this increase is likely to occur in Asia. Two countries, India and China, between them will account for nearly 60 per cent.

Health

A good health is a basic need for most of the people of the developing nations. In addition to struggling on low income, many people in the developing countries fight a constant battle against malnutrition, disease and ill health. In the developing countries, the life expectancy average approximately is 49 years compared with 57 years among other nations. The Constitution lays down that the state, shall regard the raising of the level of nutrition and the standard of living of people. To give effect to this, health has been given priority in India. The population of India is very high. So, the main problems is that it is difficult to approach person to person for health. But, the government is doing its level best to give health facilities.

Culture

Culture is the soul of human civilization. Individual society and nations are symbolized by cultural heritage. India as well as the developing countries have their own culture and cultural heritage. This is regarded as the basic need of human beings. The preservation of cultural heritage of the country is very essential for the continuity of human race and civilization. Culture can be material when it deals with such objectives like income, clothing or housing. It is non-material when it deals with objects like worship, religion and God. For proper growth of culture, it is essential that the society must be prepared to take what is good in other cultures. Similarly, it should have the capacity of leading out to other cultures as well.

Communication

The history of modern means of communications in India may be traced back to mid-19th century, when postal services were thrown open to the public in 1837. The number of post offices in India was around fifteen thousand in urban and rural areas. India has direct postal communication with almost all countries. Radio broadcasts started in India in 1927. And television was started in India as an experiment on 15 September, 1959. We have today greater income from advertisement with television as the most expensive media. The media has changed the world and today in the absence of media the world will not move.

Elected Bodies and Development

Role of Elected Body

Sometimes, a confusion is made between state and government and the two words and are used interchangeably. The elected bodies which is elected by the people, work for the welfare of the people. A government includes only those officials and persons who are appointed or elected and who interpret and carry out the regulations of the state. Democracy is based upon two basic cultural values of equality and liberty. The elected bodies gather in the parliament and with other parties they discuss for the welfare of the country. They work for the development of villages and states. The elected body should work for the development of country. All ministers are responsible to the legislature for the acts of commission and omission of their own department. Each party has to put forward its programme before the people and ask the people to cooperate with them. They have to make a budget and put it before people. The elected body members must elect their leader who will lead and give them instructions.

Development of State

The origin of the state is an utter mystery. It is difficult to say when the concept of a state came into being. It is said that state was established and governed by God himself or some superhuman power. This power developed a variety of political organizations in their self-governing and self-sufficient state. State contained the citizens who shared in the governing process. Citizenship became an important function and almost a profession. The state performed multifarious functions and was in fact identical with the whole life of the society. The state is well adapted to regulate the exploitation of natural resources in the interest of present and of future generations of entire community. If the exploitation of natural resources is left in hands of private individuals then they will seek their own gains at the cost of communal gain. The state however, cannot create culture because culture is the expression of the spirit of people or an age. It may be emphasized here that in recent times, there has been a tendency towards the growth of state functions.

Today, there is no citizen and almost no organization which operate outside its orbit of power. The welfare of state is now a popular ideal.

The Planning Commission in India

After independence, the first task of the government was elimination of poverty and improvement for the teaming millions of the country who had been living in miserable conditions of poverty and starvation. For the welfare of people and development of the country, Indian government on 15 March, 1950 emphasized that "The need for comprehensive planning based on careful appraisal of resources and on an objective analysis of all the relevant economic factors has become imperative." It set a Planning Commission to formulate and secure the execution of plans for the most effective and balanced utilization of the country's resources. The Neogy Committee had recommended that the very nature of the task of economic planning requires that a single compact, organization authority directly responsible to the cabinet should be set up at the centre to devote itself continuously to the entire field of economic reconstruction in India. The Commission commenced work on 28 March, 1950. It has many functions which are helpful to our country:

(a) It makes assessment of the material, capital and human resources, technical personal and investigates the possibilities of augmenting such of these resources as are found to be deficient in relation to the nations' requirement.
(b) The Planning Commission formulates plans for the most effective and balanced utilization of the country's resources.
(c) The Planning Commission indicates the factors which are tending to retard economic, current social, and political situation and what should be done for the successful execution of the plan.
(d) The Commission, in framing its recommendation will act with close understanding and consultation with ministries of the central government and the governments of the state.
(e) The commission will make recommendations to the cabinet.

Social Welfare Administration and Social Development

The days are gone when the wheels of administration were set in motion simply to maintain law and order, primarily to safeguard the personal interest of the ruling class. Poverty, backwardness and inequalities are no longer regarded as inevitable evil. The process of development is now adopted by the modern state to uplift their people from deprivation, disease, disasters and disabilities. The concern for promoting individual's happiness and an ardent desire for strengthening community welfare activities through a process of economic development are being considered as among the essential characteristics of the modern welfare states.

Nature and Scope of Social Welfare and Social Development

In a developing society, the role of social welfare in ensuring growth with social justice needs no emphasis. But the determining of nature and scope of social welfare, however, is also by no means an easy task. There is considerable ambiguity in the meaning of various terms used in the literatures on welfare. In the past, welfare services were restricted to remedial and curative aspects only. Social administration is an instrument of bringing social action through implementation of social policy. Social policy must be studied in the socio-economic perspective of the country which is undergoing a constant change. The scope and content of social welfare services at any point of time would obviously be determined by the national perception of social issues and capacity to cope with them.

Major Social Problems of the Country

Poverty

Poverty is relative to richness. Poverty is one of the foremost social problems affecting India and other countries. John L. Gillin calls it: "That condition in which a person either because of inadequate income or useless expenditure does not maintain a scale of living high enough to provide for his physical and mental efficiency and to be enough for his natural dependency to function usually according to the standard of society of which he is member." Poverty is the insufficient supply of those things, which are required for an individual to maintain himself and those dependent upon him in health and vigour. The standards of poverty judgement are not uniform throughout. The members of society began to compare the differences in economic status and look upon themselves as either poor or rich in accordance with the prevailing living standard.

Unemployment

Closely associated with the problems of poverty are the problems of unemployment, because when people remain idle they become poor. If there are needs to be satisfied, then men must be employed in satisfying them. Unemployment leads not only to suffering and privation but also affects adversely the social organizations which is the main interest of sociologists. Though unemployment is universal, but in India, it is more marked. Karl Pribran says, "Unemployment is conditions of labour market in which the supply of labour is greater than the number of available openings."

Planning and Administration of Social Work

Central Social Welfare Board

The Central Social Welfare Board was set up in August 1953 with Durgabai Deshmukh as Chairperson on the recommendations of the National Planning Commission as a semi-autonomous body, but as a part of the administration set-up of the Ministry of Education. The major objectives of the board is to foster the healthy growth of voluntary social service agencies through well planned and directed financial aid. The board has specific groups of persons – women, children and the handicapped. It also coordinates the welfare schemes of various central ministries and state governments. Another function of it is to develop new programmes of welfare and organize pilot projects.

Administration of Social Welfare Agencies

The administration of public and private social agencies is designed and organized to achieve the full effect of the services for which they have been established. The skills of administration has not been limited to social welfare setting. They are derived from public administration in general and from techniques of business management. But special objectives of social services to help human beings is an element which distinguishes the management of social agencies from that of commercial and industrial enterprises and to a lesser degree, from other public services that do not directly deal with human beings. Public welfare administration, like other government operations, requires clear objectives, functions, policies and efficient organizational structure with coordination of services.

Problems of Social Welfare Agencies in India

Some of the problems of administration of social welfare agencies, both public and private, have been studied by the team on social welfare and welfare of backward classes. The team has pointed out the existing defects in the administration of these social welfare agencies and made certain suggestions for their improvement:

(a) *Central Public Agencies*: As recommended by the study of the team on social welfare, the various social welfare subjects dealt with by different department at the central level, now has been brought under one department – that of social welfare in the ministry of recreation and social welfare. However, in certain matters, the coordination of ministry of health and family planning, home affairs, community development, labour and employment will be essential.

(b) Social welfare includes policies and programmes relating to social welfare, central social welfare board, central institute of research and training in public cooperation, education training and rehabilitation. It may also be mentioned that only a part of the functions of the department listed above consists in direct implementation by the department, its main role being to provide the supporting financial assistance through grants. Largely programmes are implemented by either the state government or voluntary organization, or local organizations like Panchayati Raj Institution and Municipal body.

(c) *Child Welfare*: The nation's children are a supremely important asset. Their nurture and solicitude are our responsibility. Children's programme should find a prominent part in our national plans for the development of human resources, so that our children grow up into robust citizens who are physically fit, mentally alert and morally healthy, endowed with the skills and motivations needed by the society. This preamble of the national policy for children adopted by Government of India in August 1974 sums up the current national awareness and recognition of the paramount importance of investment in child welfare for ensuring proper environment and facilities for all the children in the country to grow and develop into useful citizens of tomorrow. When India attained independence, the founding fathers, realizing the need for protecting the rights of the children of the nation on whom the future of the country depends, had made certain constructive safeguards. The child's health is to be guard at two stages, i.e., at the pre-school stage and at school stage. But in our country, the main problem is that the child is being killed at the age of one or two or not taken care of at this stage. It is because of lack of awareness. For that the government has to plan for some kind of awareness programmes for people. The poor children must be taken care of by the government or NGOs. The social welfare agency is facing this problem the most. Assuming that about 49 per cent of Indian population is living below poverty line, a very large number of children are in varying degrees of deprivation and need social and welfare services very urgently.

Area Development

Indian programme combines the idea of community development and area development and the block organization is required to be responsible for the overall development of the area in its charge.

Development of Rural and Urban Areas

The concept of community development assumes the capacity of the people to solve their problems on their own. The earlier human communities were closely related and they used to help each other, which we do not find today. But, the Government of India is doing its level best to develop both rural and urban communities.

Topographical Factors

Among the topographical factors included are land, water, and climate. It is obvious that these factors influence the growth of village communities. Land is one of the most important topographical factor; people would like to settle at a place where land is fertile and plain. A temperate climate is a most favourable climate for the growth of village communities. The facilities of water also contributes to the development of rural and urban areas.

Economic Factors

Among the economic factors, we may include the condition of agriculture, rural economy and cottage industries. Agriculture is the mainstay of the village communities. The development of village communities is dependent on agriculture. If farming yields a good crop, the economic condition of the village people will be better. On the other hand, if they have to exert themselves to the point of exhaustion just to get enough for two meals a day, their economic and social condition will not be better. The village economy also is an important factor in the growth of village communities. The farmers must be in a position to produce good seeds, and should be given good breed, good manure and scientific implements. Cottage industries play an important role in the development of rural communities. It provides a means of livelihood to landless people; they also offer other means for utilization by the farmers.

Social Factors

Among the social factors, we include peace, security, cooperation and intelligence, etc. For development of rural areas, it is essential that there must be peace in the village. Besides peace, the village people must be guaranteed security, security from disease, and in agriculture. They also need security against natural calamites. Community development is not possible without cooperation. In the village there are many activities, for example, public health, peace and order, education and recreation, etc. Ultimately, the growth of the village community depends upon the intelligence of the villagers. With lack of intelligence, they will not be able to raise the agriculture output nor profit by the scientific discoveries.

Surplus Resources

Urban communities grow wherever a society or a group within it, gains control over resources of life. In ancient times, these resources were acquired through subjugation of man by man. Slavery, forced labour or taxation of ruling classes supplied the foundation for the growth of city life. In modern times, man has won over nature and extended his power. He has exploited the natural resources to such great extent through technological improvements that now relatively few can supply the basic needs of many.

Development of Transport and Communication

The development in methods of transportation and communication and facilities which cities offer for satisfying the desire for communication also explains urban growth. Industrialization also depends upon transportation so that raw material and manufactured goods can be carried in large volumes. In industrial cities the means of transport and communication are essentially developed. The city is concerned not only with other parts in and outside the country but also the means of local transportation by which different parts of the city are connected with each other. The city was divided into different areas: a market area, a developing area, a slum area, a factory area and so on, and only through proper transportation could these be connected.

Education and Recreational Facilities

Until recently, all high schools in India were in cities. Both communities, rural and urban need education. This element in a city is better equipped than in village, therefore, most of the schools, colleges and technical schools are found in urban areas and not in rural areas. There is a spread of education in the cities as compared to lack of it in rural areas. The government must now concentrate on rural areas on this aspect. People are migrating from rural areas to urban townships because of lack of educational facilities in rural areas. There are better recreational facilities in urban areas as compared to rural areas.

Urban-Rural Contrast

One of the most striking features of industrial age is the growth of city life. In ancient times, people mostly lived in villages, being engaged in agriculture. Cities areas have now developed as centres of trade or seats of government. There is a sharp difference between city and village life though with the expansion of urban influences on villages this difference has reduced to a considerable degree. However, in spite of recent trends of urbanization, the villages still retain many of their traditional features and present a sharp contrast to the urban life.

Primary Contacts

A village community is marked by immediate contacts between its members. There is a strong group feeling in the rural community. We find members in the village community helping each other and sharing their jobs along with joys and sorrows of each other. Their relations are personal. From such contacts, each person knows a great deal about his neighbours, their activities and attitudes. In the city life, on the other hand, nearness counts much less. The inhabitants of a city hardly know each other. Sometimes, they do not even know their next-door neighbours, nothing to speak of influencing their activities. In a big city like Mumbai, people living in lower storey do not know who lives in the third or fourth storey. These great differences, we find between rural and urban areas.

Areas of Specialization

Specialization is also seen in the physical structure of a city. Different areas are marked for different activities. Chandigarh, the capital of Punjab state, has been divided into two sectors, each sector marked by particular peculiarities. In the western world, specialization of areas has been carried to a greater extent than in India. The structures vary from city to city in accordance with size, site and needs of the city.

Social Mobility

The city promotes great social mobility. It lays emphasis on achievement rather than on the ascription of status. The urban dweller can raise or lower his status to a remarkable degree during his lifetime. The caste element in social stratification is minimized. Status centres on each others occupation, on the nature and competence of the activities and social climbing is most prevalent. The rural communities are similar to calm waters in a pool and urban community to boiling water in a kettle. Stability is the typical trait for one and mobility is the typical trait for the other.

Social Planning and Social Policy

"Making development plans seems to be the most popular activity of the government of underdeveloped countries since the war and nearly their biggest failure. An index of a failure one finds in an absence of correlation between developing planning and economic growth." Waterson defines social planning: "Social planning may be defined in terms of efforts to broaden the scope of development planning, through better formulation of development objectives, the incorporation of new variables into the analysis of social process and the design of new instruments of planning." One approach to social planning is to treat social development as a functional reflection of economic development. Social factors can be looked upon as requirement of economic growth or as contributing to economic growth.

Planning for Development

There is no doubt that generally the poor countries in their understandable eagerness to raise production levels in agriculture and industry rapidly, are putting too little emphasis on the need for production investments in human beings and directing too little attention to the need for raising labour efficiency. Nations took note of the interplay of economic and social factors in development in these words, "Negative social factors acting as obstacles of economic growth have necessary logical counterpart in positive or permissive social factors. If one kind of social condition holds back economic growth, another kind of social condition can facilitate it. Development is growth plus change, change in turn is social and cultural as well as economic, qualitative as well as quantitative."

Bureaucracy and Social Policy

Framing a policy is the domain of the politician - social policy is no exception. But, before any policy decision is taken by the cabinet, contours of a problem are drawn by top-echelon bureaucrats and alternative solutions with their merits and demerits are presented. Some remedial measures could be considered and planning may be decentralized. Today, it is only the bureaucrats in central ministries and in the Planning Commission in the centre, who move in the orbit of policy making. Popular support and participation can be decisive for the success of demarcating planning. Plans have laid repeated emphasis on involving the people. The communities' development programme is the largest single experiment in modernization aided to work with people and to mobilize them.

Development of Social Work Education

While social welfare was not unknown in India through the centuries, social work education is not indigenous in origin. It was greatly influenced by the pattern of development of social work education in the United States of America. Until the thirties, social welfare in USA was very much concerned with the provision of personal services, first through the Charity Organization Society and later through public aid. Clifford Manshardt, an American Protestant missionary, who had graduated in theology from the University of Chicago, came to India in 1925 through the American Marathi Mission, a present Christian organization. Manshardt mooted the idea of developing a school of social work to meet the need for trained manpower to work in Indian conditions.

Accreditation and Organization of Social Work Education

There is a tendency to set up institutions for social work education without proper planning and facilities at great cost to standards. Ultimately, the graduates from such institutions have difficulty in obtaining employment. Such institutions start without identifying the level at which the training is required and the type of syllabus, which will meet the local needs for manpower. In such a situation, there is need to establish an adequate accrediting organization at the national level. Social work education in India has now passed four decades. The profession is faced with many crucial issues related to organization structure and curriculum.

Economic planning and development is very essential for the welfare of people. India's independence in 1947, paved the way for the adoption of economic planning in India. Five-Year Plans have been very helpful to the country. During these years, not only the national income has increased, but considerable development has taken place in various economic sectors. The standard of living of people has improved. But still, there are also many areas of country which are still backward and government must take care of them. It will be successful if it makes proper plans for the development of these backward areas. The government planning mostly assumes that the realization of other objectives is very much linked with the realization of growth objectives. This understanding is not altogether incorrect. Growth often enables a country to become self-reliant, creates more employment opportunities and reduces income inequalities and communities will grow in a proper way. The Planning Commission is doing well in the development of the country. The government has to make some social work groups to make people aware of their rights so that they may feel secure, and they are not considered as backward people. The government and NGOs must take care of their needs, so that they may live a very happy and satisfying life.

5

Social Development Administration

Social development has its own impact on the society. As days and weeks, months and years passed, many aspects of human development is seen. The process of development is adopted by the modern states to lift their people from deprivation, diseases, disasters and disabilities. As rapid change is taking place in the society, there are many problems emerging in the urban as well as rural areas. So, social development is a constant process in the society.

The word 'development' is so often used in our daily life that we hardly care to think of its real meaning. The meaning of the term 'develop' is to unfold itself or to grow into fuller or mature condition, and 'ment' stands for instrument of action, an act or process. In simple words development can be defined as a process of direct change towards some objectives, which are accepted as desirable goals. Development implies progressive improvements in the living conditions and quality of life enjoyed by society and shared by its members. It is a continuing process that takes place in all societies.

Social development means something more than merely economic, political, social and environmental development. Development is a multi-dimensional process. It means improvement of the quality of human life, which is the change, and growth of human life.

Social administration is an instrument of bringing social action through implementation of social policy. Social administration may be understood as that part of administration, which provides and operates services leading to removal of prevailing disabilities and to the creation of opportunities for the well-being of individuals and families in the community. Thus, social administration in a broader sense regulates development.

Now, if we join development and administration together, then development administration is an action and goal oriented process. It is a coordinated effort encompassing a very wide range of activities of unfortunate, less privileged people leading a life of deprivations and dejection. Thus, the essence of development administration is to bring change and growth in the society.

Public Welfare Programme and Administration

The term 'public welfare' refers to the activities, which are carried out by tax-supported government and social work agencies. Government social services have become increasingly important in recent decades. The passage of the Social Security Act in 1935 drew the federal government deeper into the field of social welfare and aroused the hopeful attention of many people. There is little doubt among public welfare personnel that many improvements can be made in the organization of services of the local, state and federal governments. But any changes must be based on those which already exists. Thus, the public welfare programme depends on the government that exists in the country.

Public administration is a part of the wider field of administration. Administration is a process permeating all collective efforts, be it public or private, civil or military, large scale or otherwise, and is thus of universal nature. It is a cooperative effort, directed towards the realization of a consciously laid down objective. Pfeiffer and Presthus define administration as, "the organization and direction of human and material resources to achieve desired ends." According to L.D. White, "Administration is the direction, coordination and control of many persons to achieve some purpose or objective." And according to Herbert A. Simon, "administration can be defined as the activities of groups cooperating to accomplish common goals". So, the activities of public administration are expressed through organization and human beings. Public administration is a human activity. It is managed by human beings and it serves human beings. Thus, in the study of public welfare programme and public administration, the importance of 'human beings' and 'organization' should be kept uppermost in one's mind.

History of Government's Responsibility for the Welfare of the Disadvantaged

Public welfare administration as a discipline is not a very old one. It may thus be regarded as among the newest of the social sciences. Public welfare has had a link development. Historically, voluntary social work has been a feature of the general development of western individualism and democracy's stress on the prerogative of 'private enterprise', even in the social welfare field. This stress can be seen in the social work services of almost any American community with its usual array of voluntary casework agencies.

However, there has been another trend at work in western social welfare services, which has borne exceedingly important fruits in our time. This trend is the public welfare movement, which has sought to place responsibility for certain types of social well-being on the community as a whole, rather than on special groups within the community. Indeed, along with the voluntarily financed and managed social work agencies which carried heavy social welfare burdens for centuries, there has been the somewhat parallel growth of welfare services. Today, almost everyone feels that government must assume responsibility in the form of public welfare services. It has been made clear only recently however, that government should assume responsibility for more than a minimum of personal and social well-being. There was a time when it was popular to believe that the least assistance given to an indigent person was the most desirable. It was thought that this practice would encourage the person to seek employment on his own initiative. But, this outlook is seriously questioned at present. So, the object of public welfare is to assist threatened persons to live a normal existence in so far as is possible. Now let us examine public welfare organization on the basis of local welfare organization, state welfare organization and federal welfare organization.

Local Welfare Organization

The actual area of responsibility the local agency may cover, will vary according to the enabling legislation provided by the larger sanctioning body, as will be seen. Responsibility for government services varies considerably throughout the country. While there is but one federal government, there are fifty state governments and innumerable local units of governments. Each division of the government bears some relation to public welfare. In New England, in general, the local unit responsible for the government services is the city and town. But in the south and the west, the county is the local unit of responsibility. And in the Middle Atlantic States and the Midwest, a combination of county, city, town and township can be holding responsibility while in others, districts embracing several counties or towns. Thus, there is obviously much overlapping, variation, and competition in the division of local public welfare services.

The local public welfare agency may maintain only those activities which the state has delegated to it. Thus, a city or town, which derives its power from the state, will have the degree of its responsibility in local welfare activities defined for it. There may be a division of responsibility, which the state and the locality share. But, whatever the division of responsibility, the number and scope of activities, which a local department of welfare may maintain, are in large part determined by its legal relation to the state as defined in a city charter.

In most localities, the lower ranking positions in public welfare are regulated through civil services. The responsibility of political interference at this level is nonexistent. In some places, the lower staffs of local public welfare agencies are made up of people who have some professional education, but the specialization and skill of workers may vary throughout the country.

State Welfare Organization

The state organization of welfare services came rather late in the development of American social work. In many places, it has been built upon the already existing structure of the social services, which local communities provided. This type of growth often resulted in the states assuming primarily a coordinative function in relation to local agencies, especially in the earlier years. As a coordination agency, state welfare organization laid down the principles binding upon all local agencies and checked on local agencies for the purpose of increasing efficiency. Later on, communities often found it necessary to call upon the states for financial assistance in order to carry on a particular programme of activity. And thus, state came to have responsibility not only for coordination but for financing as well. In addition, state activity in public welfare has, on occasions, been even more direct.

(i) *Historical Growth of State Welfare Organization*: The first serious attempt to recognize public welfare on a state basis occurred in 1863 in Massachusetts when a state board of charity was constituted. The function of this board was primarily regulative or coordinative. It did little to disturb the relationships, which then existed among the local agencies and the direct service agencies managed by the state.

It was not until 1917, in Illinois that the first really integrative state department of welfare was initiated. This department effectually brought together the various government activities and agencies under the administrative direction of a single public welfare department at the state level. The state board of charity of Massachusetts and the first department of public welfare in Illinois were indications of an awareness of the need for more coordination in public welfare.

(ii) *Special Activities of State Welfare Organization*: From a relatively early time in American history, states have assumed responsibility for special groups of dependents. Criminals were among the first for whom the states provided. In time many other special groups were added – neglected children, the insane, the deaf, the dumb, the blind, the feeble-minded, the aged, the tubercular, the sick, dependent mothers and children, impotent poor, and able-bodied poor. Usually, each special activity had its appropriate administrative head and activities among the various departments of the state government were not coordinated.

Federal Welfare Organization

The traditional view of the function of the federal government did not ascribe any responsibility for extensive social services to the national community. Local responsibility was accepted everywhere, and not without considerable reason. Our social heritage made it exceedingly appropriate, even inevitable, that the emphasis in American public welfare should be on the local community.

(i) *Factors of Federal Welfare Organization*: A number of factors arose over a period of time in this country to modify the thinking and practice of 'individualism' and to affect, in turn the locus of responsibility for public welfare. Some of these factors were primarily technological. The inventions in communication and transportation helped shrink the size of the national community. The national community grew in size from a few million inhabitants in its earliest years to over a hundred and seventy-five million. Among other factors, which encouraged the rise of federal responsibility in public welfare, were certain philosophical or ideological ones. The older political theory, which made little room for government participation in social welfare, gave way, under the impact of many forces, to an outlook, which saw fewer problems in participation than it did in non-participation. Somewhat changed economic theories and practices contributed to this development too.

Federal government always has been responsible for the welfare of certain special groups within the population, such as the Indians and war veterans. The other reason is the significant rise of the depression of the 1930s. The depression taxed the financial resources of the voluntary agencies far beyond their limits. There were no practical means of assuming the burden of economic support for the many persons and families in need during that period, and there have been none since, aside from the federal government.

(ii) *Departmental Evolution*: The need for a federal department of welfare had been recognized for many years. Warren G. Harding, during his presidential campaign of 1920, advocated the establishment of a department of education and welfare. Soon afterwards a bill was introduced in Congress to set up a department of public welfare, but it failed to pass. In 1937, president Franklin D. Roosevelt's committee on administrative management advocated the creation of a department of social welfare. The need for such a department in the federal government was especially apparent as a result of the various social welfare organizations and activities introduced by the federal government during the period of the 1930s. In the year 1939, Federal Security Agency was established, and in 1946 the Children's Bureau was transferred from the Department of Labour to the Federal Security Agency, and the Social Security Board was abolished and its duties given to the Federal Security Administrator.

Further the long history of coordinative effort in the federal government among the social welfare functions led logically to the introduction in 1947 of a bill in Congress for the creation of a department of health, education and welfare. In 1953, president Eisenhower presented Congress with his Reorganization Plan Number One, which also provided for the establishment of Department of Health, Education and Welfare. And on April 11,

1953 the new department was set up and its establishment was an event of historical importance in American life.

Philosophical Functions and Practices in Welfare Programme

Functions of public welfare administration differs according to the level of government and the need of the people in a country. So, functions are not restricted to a particular way only. As we deal with the philosophical functions, we would make the division of public welfare organization functions according to the level of government.

Local Welfare Functions

First and foremost, the local public welfare agency may maintain only those activities, which the state has delegated to it. Functions depend on the needs of the people of a locality. So local government must be responsible for needs of children, unemployment relief, medical service and other welfare concerns. Local public welfare activities are not, however, always coordinated under the leadership of a single government agency, executive or board. Some services are organized under the direct legislative branch of a state government. Some services are more closely related to the judicial branch; still others are related to the executive. There is no easy way of deciding which government services should come under the jurisdiction of the legislature, the executive, and the judiciary. The local public welfare services are done more rationally and efficiently for the local community's development.

State Welfare Functions

At the present time, the states control various welfare functions. For purposes of classification, these functions may be grouped into three divisions:

(i) Supervision of locally administered welfare programmes;
(ii) State-operated welfare services and institutions; and
(iii) General activities of the state departments.

These will be analyzed briefly:

(i) *Supervision of Locally Administered Welfare Programmes*: State departments of welfare unusually have control over a multiplicity of welfare programmes, including many services which are not financed by the states, but over which the states have supervisory responsibility.

Basic to a state's supervision of local programmes is research. State departments regularly survey various forms of aid to persons in need in order to determine their effectiveness. When programmes are not found to be effective, recommendations are made for their improvement. Visitations are made to agencies and institutions to evaluate the quality of standards, which prevail. This form of supervision is important for agencies and institutions seeking state licenses for practice, and also for those which have been practising but may need the stimulus that come from on the spot estimate of strengths and weaknesses.

(ii) *State-operated Welfare Services and Institutions*: State departments also maintain such services as child welfare services, aid to the blind, services to Indians, general relief, and assistance to the aged. Many of these services are given directly to clients, but some are indirect. In some instances, the direct services are maintained by federal-state local arrangements in which the state has some responsibility for financing and supervision. Prominent among the services which state department offers clients directly are institutions for the sick, veterans, the aged, children, the mentally retarded and others. Other services are more indirect, for example, a state department may organize a training programme for the personnel of local departments or it may publish manuals to aid local departments in the administration of their services.

(iii) *General Activities of the State Departments*: State departments have responsibilities, which pertain to public welfare activities, but they also have responsibilities for establishing standards and for supervision on the voluntary welfare field as well. State departments are concerned with the matters, which affect all voluntarily financed institutions and agencies. They formulate policies, rules, and regulations, which are designed to fulfil these responsibilities. State departments of welfare act on applications of charitable institutions, health insurance, group, and others seeking incorporation, dissolutions of incorporation, or changes in their corporate powers and purposes. They license health dispensaries and issue permits for maternity care in public homes. They are responsible also for the visitation to voluntary institutions and agencies, as well as to those under government auspices. In these and other ways, state departments of welfare maintain functions which cover all social welfare activities within the states, whether government or voluntary.

Federal Welfare Functions

The Department of Health, Education and Welfare has a complex organization in order that all of its functions may have appropriate leadership and autonomy. However, within the department, the social security administration is in effect the chief social agency. The administration is headed by its executive officers, the commissioners of social security. The commissioner is charged with a variety of duties, including responsibility for the programmes under the Social Security Act and its amendments. In the maintenance of his responsibility, the commissioner has assigned certain duties to four programme bureaus:

(i) *Bureau of Old-Age and Survivors Insurance*: This bureau administers the federal government's old age and survivors insurance programme. It is responsible for assigning and identifying account numbers to individuals; maintaining records of earnings to be used in determining the rights of individuals, their dependents or survivors, to benefits or the preservation of benefit status during a period of disability; and for certifying to the treasury department the amount to pay on each claim. The purpose of this programme is to provide continuing income for individuals and their families as partial replacement of earnings lost through old age retirement, disability, or death.

(ii) *Bureau of Public Assistance*: The Social Security Act of 1935 made it possible for the federal government to help the state governments, provide monthly cash payment to aid persons who lack the means of self-support. The bureau is the agency by which the federal government's involvement in public assistance is organized and directed. Some of the programmes of this bureau are ment for:

  (a) Old people who lack means of support.
  (b) Blind people who need assistance.
  (c) Children who have been deprived of parental care or support.
  (d) Needy persons who are permanently and totally disabled.

(iii) *Children's Bureau*: It is responsible for the development of standards for the care and protection of children, for research and reporting on all conditions affecting the well-being of children, and for federal functions in connection with federal state programmes of maternal and child health, crippled children's services, and child-welfare services.

In detail, the bureau carries out the responsibilities; it conducts various studies pertaining to childhood; issues both technical and popular publications; cooperates with state and local organization in planning services for children; provides a clearing house of information on child life; offers technical assistance in the field of juvenile delinquency to states and communities planning the extension, improvement, and coordination of facilities; administers grants to state health agencies for extending and improving health services to mothers and children; administers grants to state crippled children's agencies for their improvement; administers grants to state public welfare agencies for the extension and improvement of services to homeless, dependent and neglected children and children in danger of becoming delinquents and provide information on services for children in the country.

(iv) *Bureau of Federal Credit Unions*: Federal Credit Union Act was passed in 1934 and aimed to create a federal credit union system, to establish a further market for securities of the United States, and to make more of it available to people of small means through a national system of cooperative credit. It provides convenient facilities for encouraging the development of habits of regular saving out of current earnings. They also make instalment loans of limited sizes to members at rates of interest, which must not exceed one per cent a month on the unpaid balance. In short, it is responsible for chartering, supervising, and examining federal credit unions.

People-State Relations, Structural Arrangement of Public Welfare System in India

When we think of people-state relationship, they are two parts or sides of the same coin. People are more important than the state but for the better development of people as a public in the society state comes to an existence. State serves as a symbol of unity of the people. The image of the state inspires unity among the people and provides them with an identity as a nation. It arouses national pride and a spirit of sacrifice among the people. However, the government represents only working arrangements to carry out the functions of the state. The government commands our obedience but the state commands our loyalty. Whether the government is good or bad, efficient or inefficient, the state continues to be a symbol of national greatness. It is matter of people who regulate all forms of social conduct in the state but the state can regulate only the external relationships of the people. The state derives its strength mainly from law, but society or the people of the country derive their strength from tradition, customs and conventions and more than that they have creative idea or solution for emerging problems in the society.

Public relation has existed in its present form for such a relatively short period that there is little general agreement on its precise definition or its proper scope, or its practical responsibilities. The term 'public relation' has been defined by the American Encyclopaedia as "the art of analysing, influencing and interpreting a person, idea, group or business so that he or it will be recognized as serving the public interest, and will benefit from so doing".

Structural Arrangement of Public Welfare System in India

Public welfare administration is structured on the basis of different levels of Government in India. So, the Indian public welfare system is arranged in the following ways: The Central Social Welfare Board; State Social Welfare Boards; Districts Social Welfare Officers; and Local Social Welfare Programme

(i) *The Central Social Welfare Board*: The central social welfare board was registered as a company on 1, April 1969 under Section 25 of the Indian Companies Act, 1956 in order to have greater autonomy and flexibility. The board is performing successfully most of the functions recommended by the study team on social welfare. However, it needs to be mentioned that:
    (a) There is no proper coordination between the state social welfare departments and the state social welfare advisory boards.
    (b) With the registration of the board as a society the staff working under the board is not given due protection.

(ii) *State Social Welfare Boards*: Public welfare programme is organized or administered by the state social welfare boards. At present, the welfare subjects at the state level are dealt with by various departments, which is not conducive to the efficient functioning of the programmes. For the success of public welfare programme, it is necessary to have a unified welfare department in each state dealing with social welfare, including welfare of backward classes. The functions of the state social welfare boards as recommended by the study team should be as follows:

(a) To promote the growth of voluntary social welfare agencies, with special reference to development of welfare services in areas not covered at present.
(b) To administer the grant-in-aid programmes:
    (1) On behalf of the central social welfare board for development and capital grants.
    (2) On behalf of the state governments for maintenance grants.
(c) To assist the central social welfare board in the provision of a field counselling service for aided agencies.
(d) To administer the programmes of rural welfare projects.
(e) To stimulate effective coordination among voluntary welfare agencies at the state and local levels.
(f) To assist the central social welfare board and the state government in the further development of welfare services.

(iii) *District Social Welfare Officers*: At the district level, at present, there are district welfare officers in some of the states but their duties and functions are different in different states. In some states, there are two welfare officers at the district level, one for social welfare and the other for the welfare of backward classes. The functions of the welfare officer should be to coordinate all welfare schemes in the district, supervision of schemes sponsored by the welfare department and assist the district level committees in implementing its programme and encourage it to originate schemes based on local needs. It deals with welfare services in the district.

(iv) *Local Level Social Welfare Programme*: At the local level, the agency for welfare programme in the rural areas is the Panchayat Samiti and its functional committees and in the urban areas, the Municipal Corporation or Board. The local institutions carry a load of multifarious duties and welfare activities. So, the activities for the welfare of the local people are organized on the basis of emerging of the current problems or according to the needs of the local people. This department is much more effective to bring changes in the society because it is the unit which directly deals with the problems of the people.

Modern Social Legislation

Legislation is the enactment of laws. Law is the body of rules, enacted or customary, recognized by a community as binding upon itself. The function of law is to provide, protect and promote a framework of social regulation with which the individual citizen can pursue his several notions of what makes for his happiness. This however, has to be consistent with the good of the community as whole. This is determined by the current social ideologies. The laws may be protective, regulative or of compulsive type. However, law often lags behind the needs of society. As Oliver Wendell Holmes said: "Legislation of today is to meet the social needs of yesterday."

Social legislation is that which services the present social and economic objectives of the nation and deals adequately with current social problems. It is meant for the development of the weak areas of the country, especially for the welfare of its public. Thus, social legislation has to concern itself with the promotion of the welfare of individuals and groups. Legislation should be so designed as to entrust the life of everyone with a purpose and with the means and opportunities for the fulfilment of the hopes and aspirations of the average citizens in the light of our Constitution. The Constitution which declares India to be a sovereign democratic republic, rests on four basic principles enunciated in its preamble and they read as follows: "Justice, social, economic and political; liberty of thought, expression, belief, faith and worship; equality of status and of opportunity; and promote among them all fraternity; assuring the dignity of the individual and unity of the Nation."

Social Legislation Before Independence

The social legislation passed before independence may be dealt under two heads, namely, central legislation and state legislation.

(i) *Central Legislation*: Social legislation of the earliest period was only concerned with checking certain evil socio-religious customs. Under the Act of 1829, *Sati* was prohibited. Next in order was the Indian Slavery Act of 1843, which prohibited the sale of any person on the ground that he was a slave. Next was the Caste Disabilities Removal Act, 1850, under which it was provided that no person shall be deprived of any right of property by person of his renouncing or excluded from the communion of religion or deprivation of caste. Next in succession were passed the Hindu Widow Remarriage Act, 1856 the Female Infanticide Prevention Act of 1870 and the Special Marriage Act, 1872 which was later amended in 1932. Persons marrying under this Special Marriage

Act were given protection from forfeiture of the rights of succession by extending to them the Caste Disabilities Removal Act.

During the 20th century were passed the Child Marriage Restraint Act, 1929, the Hindu Gains of Learning Act, 1930, The Hindu Women's Right to Property Act, 1937, the Hindu Married Women's Separate Maintenance Act, 1946 and the Hindu Marriage Disabilities Removal Act, 1946. Under Child Marriage Restraint Act the age of marriage for boys is 21 and for girls it is 18 years. The Hindu Gains of Learning Act rendered all gains acquired by any member of an undivided Hindu family by his own earning, the exclusive and separate property of the acquirer. Under the Hindu Women's Right to Property Act, the widow was given a share equal to that of a son in property of the husband. The Hindu Married Women's Separate Maintenance Act enabled a married woman to claim separate residence and maintenance from her husband on certain grounds. The Hindu Marriage Disabilities Removal Act validated all marriages between person belonging to same *gotra* or *Pravara*.

Similarly, for the welfare of children, youth and women workers certain Acts were passed. Among these the important one for children are, the Apprentices Act of 1850, the Guardian and Ward Act 1890, the Reformatory Schools Act 1897, the Children Act 1938. The Factories Act 1948, the Workmen's Compensation Act 1923, the Coal Mines Labour Welfare Fund Act 1947, the Mica Labour Welfare Fund Act 1946, etc. All these Acts were passed for the welfare of society – the public of the country.

(ii) *State Legislation*: State legislation's primary function is to realize an ever-ascending order of social rights for the citizens. It was required to promote the welfare of the community as a whole on indicated lines. Articles 1 to 48 deals with the human rights, which are observed by state legislation.

The state has to protect labour from exploitation, women from masculine domination, children from parental indifference and the poor from the dispensation of punitive relief. It has to guard against disease, disorder and immorality and also deal with those whose behaviour constitutes a threat to general welfare. The state has to provide certain tax-support services which are directed to the alleviation of distress, prevention of disablement and the rehabilitation of the disabled, and the self-maintenance of the individual. The state legislation has to promote the welfare of all, but with a declared bias in favour of the needy, neglected, and weaker sections of the people.

Social Legislation After Independence

After independence, there has been good progress in the enactment of social legislation. In our Constitution, there are various provisions to which the state is committed under the Fundamental Rights or Directive Principles and is passing legislation to implement them.

(i) *Child Welfare*: The Government of India formulated a bill after Independence to have a uniform and comprehensive children Act, but this could not be passed. A Children's Act was passed in 1960, which was applicable to Union Territories only.

(ii) *Youth Welfare*: The Suppression of Immoral Traffic Act was in force in various states before Independence which made provision for rescuing minor girls from brothels and from moral danger. There are also special Acts to prevent minor girls from exploitation such as U.P. Naik Girls Protection Act 1929, Bombay Devadasi Protection Act 1934 and Madras Devadasi Act 1947. There were also Borstal Schools Act in various states to accord special treatment to adolescent offenders. The first was the Madras Borstal Schools Act 1926.

(iii) *Prison Reforms:* The first Prisons Act was passed by the central government in 1894, which restricted and regulated the use of whipping, cellular confinement, and penal diet. After 1919, the jails became a state subject and the state governments tried to provide many amenities to the prisoners under the rules framed by them in consonance with the Prisons Act 1894.

(iv) *Women Welfare*: For the welfare and development of women many Acts are passed under the Constitution. Some of them are as follows: the Hindu Minority and Guardianship Act 1956 and the Hindu Adoption and Maintenance Act 1956; the Hindu Marriage Act 1955, prohibits polygamy and provides for divorce on certain grounds and minimum age has been fixed for the male and for the female. The Hindu Women's Right to Property Act 1956, which gives women equal powers in the family. Minority and Guardianship Act 1956, prohibits the child marriage and the Hindu Adoption Act 1956 provides for the adoption of boys as well as girls. A widow could now adopt a son or daughter in her own name.

(v) *Prostitution*: Besides certain provisions in the Indian Penal Code to protect the modesty and to protect women against illicit sexual intercourse and buying and selling of girls under 18 years, special legislation was passed by the states to check immoral traffic in women. Such Acts were the Bombay Devadasi Protection Act 1934, Madras Devadasi Protection Act 1947, etc. however, the most comprehensive Act to control prostitution was passed after Independence in 1956 by the Government of India.

(vi) *Labour Welfare*: The Factories Act was amended in 1948. Under the new Act, certain additional welfare measures are to be provided by the employers, such as washing facilities, canteens, rest shelters, creches, etc., on compulsory basis and appointment of welfare officers if the number of workers employed are 500 or more. Regarding this matter the Plantation Labour Act of 1952 was also passed.

(vii) *Social Security and Social Assistance*: The Employees State Insurance Act was passed in 1948, which is a pioneering attempt in social insurance. The important benefits provided under the Act are sickness benefit, maternity benefit, disablement benefit, dependent's benefit and medical benefit. The Coal Mines Provident Fund and Bonus Scheme Act was passed in 1948. And also to provide pension in old age an Act was passed in the year 1953.

(viii) *Welfare of Backward Classes*: Article 17 of the Indian Constitution abolishes untouchability and prohibits its practice in any form. The parliament passed a law defining offences arising from this practice and to prescribe penalties thereof. This is known as the Untouchability Offences Act 1955. The government, central as well as state have reservation of posts for the Scheduled Castes and Scheduled Tribes and there are specific funds allocated in the Five-Year Plans for the improvement of their social and economic life.

(ix) *Housing Welfare*: To provide houses to workers and low-income group people, the central government is giving loans and subsidies to state government, individuals and employees. Under the Coal Mines Labour Welfare Fund Act 1947 and the Mica Mines Labour Welfare Fund Act 1946, houses are being constructed for the workers in those mines. In the same way under the Plantation Labour Act of 1951, workers are provided housing accommodation by the employers.

Voluntary Action for Social Development

Social welfare has its origin in charity, philanthropy and poor-relief. It covers a very wide and broad spectrum of human activities. The term, however still remains unsatisfactorily defined. The common agreement on the term is that it denotes services meant to cater to the special needs of persons (and groups) who by reason of some handicaps - social, economic, physical or mental - are unable to avail themselves of or are traditionally denied the amenities, facilities and services provided by the community. Thus, welfare services are meant to benefit the weaker, dependent or underprivileged section of the population. The beneficiaries of these services may be physically handicapped persons, such as the blind, the deaf or the crippled; socially dependent individuals, like the orphan, the widow or the destitute; mentally retired persons; economically under privileged groups such as those living in slum areas; women handicapped by restrictive social traditions or practices.

Concept of Voluntary Action

Voluntary action is autonomous and flexible. It is initiated by a group of like-minded people to change and transform the socio-economic life of the people, specially the weaker sections, based on social justice and not merely for charity or relief. It is often used synonymously with voluntary effort, even though voluntary action and voluntary effort are not the same. While the former calls for planning and involvement of a group to deal with a problem the latter may not entail such steps.

The essential feature of voluntary action is that it is problem-oriented. It is initiated not only to solve the problems but also to prevent the occurrence of the problems. It takes problems into consideration and fixes up programmes to solve the problems without external control. Voluntary action ultimately aims at creating a situation conducive to the development of potentialities in individuals, groups and communities to find solutions to their problems, and ways and means to handling this to realize their ultimate goal. And, in fact, the basic task of any voluntary action group is to develop man and not just organize services for him.

Meaning of Voluntary Action

In general, the term 'voluntary' is understood as to denote that the work is done by the volunteers who are not paid for. Literally interpreted, it only means community action executed and regulated by the community itself. Very often voluntary action is equated with the work of non-official social service agencies operating in the community.

Lord Beveridge describes voluntary action as that action which is not directed or controlled by the state. He calls it a private enterprise for social progress. A voluntary organization or agency is one, which is initiated and governed by its own members without external control. Voluntary action presupposes the perception of need by the community or a section of the community, its assessment that the need can be met and its readiness to regard it a duty to mobilize itself to meet the need. Therefore, it is an indication of its continuing awareness of the changing needs of the community and of the desire to retain the principle of creativity in social life. The most important fact is that voluntary action keeps alive the spirit of voluntariness of working without being compelled or being required.

Characteristics of a Voluntary Organization

The group initiating the action may work informally or formally. When the group works formally, it comes to be known as a voluntary organization. So, the characteristics of a voluntary organization are the following:

(i) *Registration of Voluntary Organization*: A voluntary organization is registered under an appropriate name to give a corporate status to a group of individuals, so that they get a legal personality, and an individual's liability may give place to group liability. The Act under which the organizations can be registered, depends on Societies Registration Act 1860; The Indian Trusts Act 1882; The Cooperative Society Act 1904; and The Joint Stock Companies Act 1956.

(ii) *Structure of Voluntary Organization*: It has an administrative structure and a duly constituted managing or executive committee.

(iii) *Uniqueness of Voluntary Action*: It has definite aims and objectives and programmes for fulfilment of these actions.

(iv) *Self Organization*: Voluntary organization is an organization initiated and governed by its own members on democratic principles without any external control.
The basic commitment of the people engaged in voluntary action is to have planned change by organizing voluntary organizations for the development of economic and social life of the concerned community. The fundamental objective is to develop people's capacities and resources to enable them to take over and manage problems and tasks by establishing their own voluntary action groups and institutions.

History and Trend of Voluntary Action in India

Every event has its own explanation and history, so also voluntary action has its own history in the process of social development. It has grown gradually from its origin. Here, the history of voluntary action on the basis of age or century is put forward.

The Period of 17th Century

The Chinese traveller Hsuan-tsang observed in the 17th century that the Indian people were always in the habit of planting trees on the wayside to give shade to travellers. They voluntarily came together to dig tanks and wells for drinking water for the community. It seems that the community had its own indigenous organizations to provide such services on a collective basis.

The Medieval Period

In the medieval period in India, there was a system of *adheenams* prevalent in the southern part of the country. In this system, the community organized and established centres of learning and research, where free boarding and lodging were provided to students. A number of libraries were set up around such institutions of learning. Communities raised funds through their own organizations to distribute grants to hospitals, schools, colleges and poor homes. The practice during the medieval period of construction of *Dharamshalas* for travellers still continues.

The Period of Early-17th Century

The early-17th century saw the outbreak of severe famines, which swept across the countryside. These resulted in deaths of large numbers of people from starvation. The kings responded with royal charity doles. But there were no systematic efforts to meet the problem on a scientific basis.

The Period of 18th Century

The history of development of social welfare in India prior to independence is primarily the history of voluntary action. Before the 19th century, charity on a large scale on voluntary basis outside the religious channels took place mainly during emergencies, such as famines and floods. The rich and the ruling lot were enjoined to support the indigent. Further throughout the 18th century, the problems of individuals and groups were met by individual philanthropy and religious charity.

The Period of 19th Century

Voluntary action got a stimulus in the 19th century. It manifested itself in three directions: (i) religious reforms, (ii) social reforms, and (iii) voluntary social work. Raja Ram Mohan Roy had considerable influence not only in Bengal but also elsewhere in the field of social reform. His experiment of organizing vigilance committees of volunteers to fight *sati* yielded magnificent results. His voluntarism enveloped a variety of interests such as improving conditions of widows, education of women, removal of caste restrictions, etc. The Atmiya Society, the Unitarian Committee and the Brahmo Samaj were some of his creation in the eastern part of the country. Dadabhai Naoroji in the western part, played a pioneering role in the furtherance of education of girls, religious reforms and women's education. During the same period, primary schools in Marathawada were started on a voluntary basis and several teachers gave their services free, as such bodies lacked funds. Arya Samaj, Ramakrishna Mission, theosophical movement and Anjuman Himayat-I-Islam were some movements, which had a powerful impact in different parts of India. Christian missionaries did pioneering work in all fields of welfare whether it was the setting up of orphanages or institution for the handicapped, the old and the infirm. Later, philanthropic groups and other secular organizations also shared some responsibilities in this field.

The Period of 20th Century

In the early years of the 20th century, religious fervour gave way to rationalistic principles. The birth of the Servants of India Society in

1905, laid the foundation of secular voluntary action in India. A few years later, Mahatma Gandhi, with his high ideals and practical approach, inspired hundreds of sincere and conscientious workers to follow in his footsteps with a spirit of dedication. He provided a large number of constructive social welfare programmes designed to remove some of the evils that had crept into society. He was against untouchability and set up the Harijan Sevak Sangh in 1932, to improve the lot of Harijans.

Voluntary action got a big boost in the early-20th century. Actions, which had begun on an informal basis received formalized structure and got organized through registered bodies. The organizations engaged in voluntary action also underwent significant changes. A number of non-religious bodies started taking interest in the field of welfare. They attempted to change and transform the socio-economic life of the people. They laid greater emphasis on organizing the people either to adjust with the situation or to change the situation. In this period, there was spread of education, rising expectations, changes in aspirations of the weaker sections, especially women, Scheduled Castes and Scheduled Tribes. There was, however, a decline in the number of voluntary action groups that had been prominent in the earlier period.

Of the various forms of activity in the field of social welfare, the earliest were the welfare of women, children, the infirm and the destitute. This trend still continues.

Voluntary Sector in India

Voluntary sector would indicate different organizations whether they are governmental or non-governmental organizations. Voluntary organizations can be very important means for the upholding and promotion of democratic values and processes in a country like India. In any country whether developed, developing or newly independent, the mobilizing of a country's natural and human resources, stimulating the private sector institution, initiating the process of self-sustaining development, encouraging voluntary movement, helping the participation of people in the art of governance, working for ensuring human dignity, protecting fundamental rights, promoting awareness, arousing social consciousness, family or societal counselling and interaction with other international voluntary organizations can provide great motivation to the people of a country and that's why these are important for a healthy national life.

Since voluntary organizations serve a great deal, every nation needs them and they must evolve as democracy evolves. It is also inherent in the very nature of the voluntary organizations that they must come up on their voluntarism and there should be a very large network of them working in the service of the nation and its people in a number of fields. Voluntary sector can be grouped as follows:

Governmental Organizations

It is a programme organized for the development of individual, people as community or entire citizens of country as the development of the country organized by the government. So, the programmes organized for the betterment of the people by the government is known as governmental organization. In this system of organization, they are self-sufficient in the matter of resources. It is the government which makes the policy for the upliftment of the people who really need help or are to be developed.

Some of the governmental voluntary organizations are: Age Care India, All India Blind Relief Society, All India Crime Prevention Society, All India Deaf and Dumb Society, All India Federation of the Deaf, All India Panchayat Parishad, All India Seva Samiti, All India Women's Conference, Association of the Physically Handicapped, Association for Social Health in India, Bharatiya Adimjati Sevak Sangh, Bharatiya Grameen Mahila Sangh, etc.

Non-governmental Organizations

Non-governmental organizations are also known as private voluntary organizations. NGOs are aiming at helping the needy, handicapped and other destitute. NGOs basically are non-profit organizations providing material, technical, administrative and social services at nominal or no cost, to the very poor and needy. They should normally and theoretically have no official relationship with the government. This does not mean that they have nothing at all to do with the government. They certainly will have to have coordination with the government and its other wings which would give them access to such ways and means as should enable them to reach out to the needy people.

NGOs can play an important role in the domestic affairs of a country, and can also perform miracles in the promotion of world peace and social welfare activities. Thus, they can provide great motivation to the people of the country and that is why they are important for a healthy national life.

Network Organizations

Network voluntary organization is a system of developing and maintaining with the people in the same business. The techniques of network help the management to ensure effective planning implementation and review of projects. It focuses our attention on those activities, which need our top priority to accomplish results. It provides a standard method of documenting and communicating project plans, schedules and time and cost performance. Thus, it is complex in nature but effective in the development programme.

Development of Social Work Education

The word 'education' has been derived from the Latin 'educates' which means to lead out. That is to say the role of education should be growth and development of individual potentialities. With this view, social work was taken up as a subject for education, which means to make people aware of the social functions for the development of the individual, society and country.

While social welfare was not unknown in India through the centuries, social work education is not indigenous in origin. It was greatly influenced by the pattern of development of social work education in the USA, whose people were very much concerned with the provision of personal services, first through the charity organization society and later through public aid. It lead to the family and child welfare services. Family and child welfare as well as public aid resulted into the casework and gradually it took the form of group work and later on as a community organization.

In 1937, the American Association of School of Social Work laid down that all social work education must be offered at the graduate level by 1, October 1939. This curriculum lead to the establishment of Association of Schools of Social Administration and later the National Council of Social Work Education was established as the accrediting body for both the master's and the bachelor's level programmes as multiple accreditation by two separate associations was not favoured. These developments had influence on social work education in India.

Social Work Education in India

Clifford, an American protestant missionary came to India in 1925 through the American Marathi Mission, a Christian organization. This organization decided to undertake work in slums and, with that objective founded the Nagpada Neighbourhood House in 1926. Then the first school was founded in 1936 known as the Sir Dorabji Tata Graduate School of Social Work and later renamed as the Tata Institute of Social Sciences in 1944. Group work and community organization first appeared in the basic courses in 1948, twelve years after the introduction of casework in the curriculum.

Family and child welfare, medical schoolwork, psychiatric social work, and personnel management and labour welfare were included in the field of social work and in the year 1950 the public welfare administration was added.

Present Curricula of Social Work Education

The present curricula at the master's and the post-graduate diploma level show that out of thirty institutions, twenty-two offer specializations. Usually the first year is generic, and in the second year, courses in the specializations are offered. Fieldwork and research are also related to the area of specialization. In India, there are three major ways of viewing the term 'generic': (i) The course offers all the methods of social work, which are viewed in their application to all the settings; (ii) The course contains one paper on each field of social work; and (iii) The course offers core content and, in addition, has special interest papers or electives. In only one institution, the electives offered related to substantive areas of students' interest, social science content, or area of role.

In India, the new courses included the profile of poverty, problems of under-development and development approaches, social change, social action, communications, non-formal education, social education, population education and family planning, welfare of weaker sections, and social systems related courses including the economic, political and educational system. And thus at present society, social systems and social change receive greater emphasis in the curriculum of social work education.

Project Planning, Monitoring and Evaluation

Planning is nothing but anticipating and attempting to exercise some influence on the direction of the future event. It is an important human process. It is an outlook picture of future project programme. So project planning is very much needed to have a systematic and successful programme.

Monitoring is the continuous gathering of information on project inputs, outputs and effects, and on conditions that are critical to the success of the project. It provides project management with information on what is happening, comparison of actual achievements with original targets and objectives. So, it is the process of assessing whether and to what extent a course or action is being carried out as planned.

Project evaluation is a process determining systematically and objectively, the relevance, efficiency, effectiveness and impact of activities in the light of their objectives. It is also a method of measuring the outputs, effects and impacts of the project.

Concept of Planning and Project Planning

The planning of welfare services or organizations is relatively a dynamic concept. According to Dimock, planning is "the use of rational design as contrasted with chance, the reaching of a decision before a line of action is taken instead of improving after the action has started". Where as Seckler-Hudson would say planning is "the process of devising a basis for a course of future action". In the words of Millett, "Planning is the process of determining the objectives of administrative effort and of devising the means calculated to achieve them." In short, planning is the conscious process of selecting and developing the best course of action to accomplish a defined objective.

Planning for social welfare is firmly based on the nature and extent of social problems permeating in the society from which are derived priority goals. It is a kind of future picture wherein proximate events that are needed are outlined with some distinctness while remote events not desired appear progressively less distinct. Social welfare planning is the phase of the total process of social development which leads from the policy statements to the concrete identification of the populations whose social needs and demands are to be met, the indication of the types of social welfare activities that will be performed for these populations, with their general attributes, and the specification of the type of instruments that will be required to carry out the social activities.

Planning is necessary for providing effective services, constructing infrastructure, setting up an administrative structure, organizing conferences, raising funds or even arranging meetings with the committee. According to the draft of the First Five-Year Plan, "Planning is essentially a way of organizing and utilizing resources to the maximum advantage in terms of defined social ends." The two main attributes or constituents of the concept of planning are: (a) a system of ends to be pursued; and (b) knowledge of available resources and their optimum allocation. Unplanned administration is haphazard, scattered, disorderly and confusing. Planning is simply the introduction of orderly thinking into the areas of life, which have been ruled by unconsidered judgement. Planning is conscious and deliberate guidance of thinking so as to create logical means of achieving desired goals. Planning is a basic and fundamental approach or a way of dealing with the human problems, which beset us. Planning is a point of view, an attitude, an assumption that says it is possible for us to anticipate, predict, guide and control our own destiny.

Planning is fostering the thinking of a group of people, poised for development, and synchronizing their thoughts with their needs and abilities for an anticipated action, which will result in their welfare.

Planning is the blueprint of action, visualizing and foreseeing inherent bottlenecks in implementation as a result of the various system operations when physical inputs, will of the people and technology are harmonized for human welfare. The planning process brings forth a set of questions namely, the purpose, the methodology, the strategy, the beneficiaries, etc., of planning along with the what, whom, who and why of planning.

Principles of Planning

There are some basic principles, which must be kept in mind in any planning process.

(i) *Participation*: Planning should not just come from the top, it should be done at all levels. Discussions with concerned departments or a group of people or individuals will be helpful to make an effective plan, instead of one man at the top deciding everything on his own thinking. It should ensure participation of all levels in the picture.

(ii) *Continuous Process*: Planning is not an end, but it is a continuous process, because pitfalls in a plan are corrected and revised in the next, if the plan is not achieving the expected goals.

(iii) *Objectives*: Objectives of the planning must be laid down before-hand to make a plan effective. If objectives are not certain then the plans made out for them are definitely out of the mark.

(iv) *Need Basis*: Planning should grow out of the need of the people, so as to make it effective. Adequate factual data may be made in basic planning.

(v) *Requirement*: Planning requires professional skills, leadership and thinking of layperson. Planning constructed on the basic requirement is definitely effective with no doubt.

(vi) *Method of Evaluation*: Planning requires education of the people for proper thinking. The community needs and resources must be taken into consideration while planning. Effective evaluation method should be used to make sure the effectiveness of planning.

Steps in Continuous Planning

Planning is a rational process, which involves a number of steps. We discuss here the important steps, which may be kept in mind while planning for social welfare at any level, i.e., union, state or local level. Whatsoever be the methodology of planning, these following basic steps are essential:

(i) *Pre-Planning*: The first important step of planning is the laying down of social policy. Policy may be thought of as the main system, which provides the framework for the accomplishment of intended objectives. Formulation of policies involves making explicit the various assumptions, which are made with respect to the basic premises and the priorities of needs and allocating finances accordingly.

(ii) *Analysis of Social Situation*: This relates to a time from which the planning is to be done. It is nothing but setting up of a baseline to help the planners to make projections for the planning period and to help in the evaluation of plans.

(iii) *Identifying Social Problems*: On the basis of the statistics collected and processed, we may identify social problems at the union, state and local levels. We generally make a mistake in identifying social problems only at the macro-level. It is important but we must also identify the problems area-wise as well as to ensure fruitful social action. In the present set-up, we provide the same social welfare programmes in all the areas without taking the facts of those areas into consideration. So, there is a need to work out statistics area-wise as well as to identify problems area-wise.

(iv) *Selection of Priorities*: Resources in the developing countries are limited and are insufficient to meet the needs of the people. Therefore, there is a need to select the pressing and urgent problems. There are numbers of factors such as economical, technical, financial, social, political, administrative, ethical, etc., which must be taken into consideration while laying down the properties. This can be decided with the help of techniques like cost-benefit analysis, cost effectiveness, etc. The selection of priorities is needed in the planning process because the resources are limited.

(v) *Definition of Goals and Objectives*: Goal is the direction in which the plan is to proceed and the term is used more in the case of long-term planning. Goals formulated are generally broad. A goal is usually described in terms of:
   (a) What is to be attained?
   (b) The extent to which it is to be attained.
   (c) The population involved.
   (d) The geographic areas in which the proposed programme will operate.
   (e) The length of time required for achieving these goals.

(vi) *Write-up of Formulated Plan*: After deciding the priorities, goals and objectives, the next major step is to prepare a write-up of the plan. This may contain schedule time sequence for the plan to be implemented and procedures and other details so that evaluation becomes easy and meaningful.

(vii) *Implement the Plan*: Plan implementation is an integral part of the planning process. It requires responsibility for translating the objectives of social policy into social action. Implementation is the real test of the plan.

(viii) *Evaluate Achievements*: Evaluation is an important step in the process of planning. Because evaluation is a build up in device to measure the effectiveness of planning. It measures the degree to which objectives and targets are fulfilled and the quality of the result obtained. It is the process to check the achievement of the programme. So, evaluation should be an integral part of development process. It is not only to help to take decisions but also to identify alternatives which may facilitate better decision and help project holders to learn from their mistakes and shortcomings.

Community Participation

Development is a multi-dimensional phenomenon, which cannot be achieved unless the community itself is involved. Community participation is seen as a way to mobilize resources for social welfare that would otherwise not be available. Because communities, according to their capacity, need to mobilize human, financial, and material resources to supplement the resources provided by the national government and other extra-community sources, in order to effectively carry out local social welfare improvement efforts.

Community participation involves members of communities in planning, implementing and monitoring of social welfare activities. Thus, community is wholly involved in the programme rather than being asked to either contribute or to take advantage of the services offered under it. Community participation is the process in which individuals, families assume responsibility for their own welfare. They come to know their own situation better and are motivated to solve their common problems. This enables them to become agents of their own development instead of passive beneficiaries of development aid. They, therefore, need to realize that they are not obliged to accept conventional situations that are not suitable. They have to acquire the capacity to appraise a situation, weigh the various possibilities and estimate what their own contribution can be.

Purposes of People's Participation in Project Programme

The important purposes that can be served by encouraging people's participation are the following:

(i) Creating will and determination among the members of the community for improvement in their present and future life.
(ii) Identification and development of the local resources, thereby, generating self-reliance among the community.
(iii) Achieving integrated area coordination among various agencies interested in social welfare measures.
(iv) Mobilizing the available manpower for productive and useful activities for livelihood.
(v) Keeping the members of the community constantly informed about the development in the area.
(vi) Arranging functional literacy programmes which can help them in understanding new technology for sustainable development.
(vii) Organizing various clubs of youth, women, to serve as centres of discussion and development.
(viii) Providing an open forum for the community to discusses its problems and find indigenous solutions, which may be efficient and economical.

(ix) To develop local leaders who can further educate and mobilize the people in the area.
(x) Encouraging the people to adopt modern changes which can accelerate their socio-economic development.
(xi) Arranging extra-curricular activities to generate social awareness through well designed publicity.
(xii) Encouraging the people to develop themselves rather than depending upon the government for all activities, and thus, become self-reliant, which is the key to development.

Models of Community Participation

The following important models are available for community participation:

(i) *Bureaucratic*: In bureaucratic type of participation, the major inputs directives and resources come from the government, which is interested in accomplishing the goals. This model is rigid in nature and therefore it follows strictly the rules of the organization. Thus, this model effectively reduces opportunities for promoting public participation in spite of the desire to do so. But also it appears that some flexibility in specific areas of the programme seems to be reasonable precondition for effectively involving people in the programme. Such bureaucratic models sometimes retard the growth of the programme. Therefore, there is a need to use this model with caution and with proper training to the bureaucracy.
(ii) *Missionary*: In this model, some charismatic leaders create institutions which do useful social welfare programmes for the uplift of the poor masses. For example, Rama Krishna Mission founded by Rama Krishna and his disciples especially Swami Vivekananda did tremendous work in promoting the welfare of the people. The problem in such institutions is that these are mixed with different religious and sectoral feelings.
(iii) *Participative*: Community participation begins when the organizers start motivating, involving and mobilizing more and more individuals in the planned social welfare action and utilizing the local resources. After observing the activities of the programme, people come to take part and to work in the organization.

(iv) *Promotive*: In this model, the bureaucracy and the political elite may encourage the people to participate. This model in developing countries like India with rampant illiteracy, poverty, ignorance, etc., called for not only an active participation but also creates an awareness among the communities. So, the people are influenced to participate in the programme by publicizing the good points of a social change in view.

Essentials/Process of Community Participation in Social Welfare Programmes

The following ten steps are considered essential for community participation in social welfare programmes:

(i) Analysis of the needs and requirements of the people in the community.
(ii) Understanding the attitudes and practices of the people in the community – positive as well as negative.
(iii) Designing the social welfare programme to meet the needs of the people with the involvement of the people.
(iv) Educating the people through formal and informal channels to make them aware of the programme and utilizing the resources available with them.
(v) Kindling and generating interest among the people to keep up the momentum through the provision of resources not available locally.
(vi) Leaving the programme to the care of the people with aided guidance.
(vii) Removing aided guidance and handing over the programme to the people.
(viii) Occasional follow up to sort out any problem.
(ix) Birth of a permanent community managed social welfare programme.
(x) Birth of a welfare state.

Planning for Implementation and Monitoring System

Planning for social welfare or project work is the phase of the process of social development, which leads from the policy statements to the concrete identification of the population where social needs and demands are to be met. It is the indication of the types of social welfare activities that will be performed for the required people. But, social planning alone is not the complete element of the any programme. It has to be implemented or put into practice – then it can be an effective and meaningful one.

Implementation

Plan implementation is an integral part of the planning process. It requires responsibility for translating the objectives of social policy into social action. Implementation is the real test of planning. In the foreword to the Fifth Five-Year Plan, Prime Minister Indira Gandhi writes, "A plan is ultimately neither a mere catalogue of schemes nor a sophisticated exercise in numbers. It is charter of the progress of a people who refuse to be overwhelmed by the magnitude and vast variety of their problems and difficulties but are courageously struggling to map out a programme of action which will step by step and year by year help to overcome them." Planning and implementation are intimately connected. In this context, Geety says: "Plans alone cannot make an enterprise successful. Action is required, the enterprise must operate. Plans can however, focus action on purposes. They can forecast which actions will tend towards the ultimate objective, which tend away, which will likely offset one another, and which are merely irrelevant. Managerial planning seeks to achieve consistent coordinated structure of operations focussed on desired ends. Without plans, action must become merely a random activity, producing nothing but chaos."

Monitoring System

Monitoring is an important instrument in the implementation of a programme to ensure its completion within budgetary allocation and time schedule. It has to be built into a programme. Although actual monitoring begins with the initiation of the implementation of the programme, exercises for devising the monitoring system have to begin earlier. Monitoring not only includes the quantitative appraisal of the performances in relation to targets but qualitative assessment as to whether the objectives of the social welfare programmes are being fulfilled.

Monitoring is the simplest method of knowing where we are in relation to the programme. It is a process, which helps in detecting of flaws, assists in decision-making and in giving direction to the programmes. Monitoring is normally used to send feedback information for initiating corrective action with a view to bringing the lagging areas back on course. It may also include a review of the corrective action taken in response to feedback and flow of up-to-date information in various levels within the organizations and to the outside agencies. The main purpose of monitoring is directing and control over the programme's projects and to help future planning.

(i) *Factors of Monitoring System*: Monitoring is not just progress reporting at different intervals on physical and financial targets achieved or inputs provided for implementation of the programme. It is a system for the two way flow of information, both laterally and vertically, to aid in decision-making. Monitoring action of the social welfare programme would involve the following factors:

- (a) Identifying the different units involved in the planning and implementation of programme and establishing necessary linkages and commitments, both inter and intra departmental.
- (b) Identifying items on which feedback is required and the level at which the feedback on different items are to be given.
- (c) Identifying the personnel at different levels and defining their roles in monitoring.
- (d) Developing performa for reporting which may be simple, structured to the extent possible, carry complete instructions for filling them up and be capable of being handled by the field level staff.
- (e) Determining the periodicity of reporting which will depend upon the item, the need for information, stage of implementation, etc.
- (f) Processing the information received, analysing them in terms of projected progress, indicating the positive as well as negative elements, the nature and extent of shortfall, reasons thereof, and suggesting the corrective action that is needed.
- (g) Sending the relevant information to the decision-making points and transmitting the decision to different implementing levels.
- (h) Storing data and developing facilities for their retrieval when necessary, particularly when need for the evaluation of the programme.
- (i) Identifying the critical and vulnerable points in the implementation of the programme for obtaining feedback for immediate action.

(j) Determining the degree of precision expected in reporting information, since precision makes demands on time, costs and manpower.

For building up an efficient monitoring system provision of appropriate manpower, training of personnel, supervision, etc., are necessary with due importance given to the intermediate and apex level.

(ii) *Techniques of Monitoring*: The following techniques can help us in efficient monitoring:

(a) *Design of an Efficient Information System*: Modern technology has been able to make a major contribution towards improved management practice with respect to information system. Every management organization has an information system, which can be conceptualized as the link in collecting, processing and reporting the data necessary for planning and control. This system is capable of providing management with the information necessary for day-to-day management of the social welfare activities.

(b) *Use of Performance Budgeting*: The budget is a financial representation of the plan for purposes of accounting. For successful operation a programme budget system depends on having working cost accounting system. Cost accounting is a means of keeping the financial records of the organization in a manner which permits costs to be associated with the purpose for which they are incurred. It is used to determine the costs through services delivered for the activities performed.

(c) *Network Techniques*: Basically, PERT and CPM are techniques of project management used to ensure effective planning, scheduling and control. These techniques can be used for any project where the start and the finish of the project can be identified – installation of plant and equipment, construction of a building, town planning, etc.

(d) *Work Study*: Work study is really an effective service to management, because it pays dividends which are handsome, speedy, and beyond expectation. But it must have for its success, the unstinted support of the management. Regarding the matter of work study Pandit Nehru said, "work study, almost a new idea has now come to us in order to improve our administrative methods, to streamline them, and make them more efficient and effective".

(e) *Organizational Analysis*: Organizational analysis is a technique to ensure the achievement of maximum results with minimum costs in term of human and material resources by the organizations. The objective of organizational analysis is to improve pattern of relationships between persons in an organization and thus, create harmonious arrangement of work with reference to its main objectives. Organizational analysis is needed in all the organizations whether old, new or proposed. It should be a continuous activity and should be used at regular intervals of time to ensure that the structure and functions of the organizations are in tune with their objectives. Its purpose is to weed out those activities, which impede the performance of an organization.

(f) *Social Cost Benefit Analysis*: Socially profitable projects are those projects where discounted social benefits are greater than discounted social costs. In private profitability calculations, the earnings equal the actual output produced multiplied by their market price, and the costs equal the amount of inputs actually used, multiplied by their market price. Social cost benefit analysis rejects this notion of projects. Social cost benefit analysis measures the benefits in term of the positive effects of the project and costs in terms of the negative effects of the project.

(g) *Supply System*: Over the past several decades the techniques of industrial engineering and operations research have been able to make major improvements in the logistics system of all organizations with supply and distribution components. This functional area is particularly susceptible to significant improvement in technical service and to reduction in cost by the application of analytical techniques. Interviews with those responsible for a sample of supply systems gave no indication that the advances made in this fields are appreciated. There is probably no area where adoption of modern management techniques will have a quicker pay-off in improved services at reduced cost.

(h) *Systems Analysis and Operations Research*: The disciplines of systems analysis and operations research provide the logical approach, using mathematical and other empirical tools, to support the analysis. These disciplines, widely developed in the era following World War II, but deriving from previous work in statistics and industrial engineering, offer powerful techniques to be used for the improvement of management system. They provide an analytical approach, which supported by specific techniques, can have application to many of the management problems. The techniques of system analysis and operations research can be used by any decision-maker who is sufficiently alert to be able to recognize their potential contribution and who is capable of a dialogue with and providing direction to the systems analyst.

Evaluation of Programme, Project and Organization, Utilization of Evaluation for Promoting or Modifying Policies and Programmes

Evaluation of Programme, Project and Organization

Since the social welfare administration seeks to achieve social changes through planned efforts, the internal devices alone cannot be considered adequate. Evaluation must, therefore, ensure objective assessment of the performance. Careful evaluation is the backbone of all social welfare programmes. It is indispensable as a guarantee of effective use of resources and of accountability for their use. Evaluation would be futile unless it is carried out in a systematic and coordinated fashion with clearly defined objectives and consistent evaluations. There may be situations where there might be reluctance to disclose some known problems for fear of adverse public reaction. Such situations are inherent but not desirable in the field of developmental administration. To meet such a situation it is necessary to evolve methods and machinery by which objective assessment is undertaken by an agency external to the organization.

And here lies the importance for evaluation. Evaluation has been variously described by various authorities. Some look upon it as a process by which the values of an enterprise are ascertained, others regard it as an analysis by which one is able to understand and appreciate the relative merits or deficiencies of persons, programme situation, methods and process, though some authorities maintain that evaluation does not, and should not, concern itself with persons. According some authorities, evaluation is essentially an 'achievement audit' – a systematic and continuous enquiry to measure the efficiency of means to search their particular preconceived ends. It has also been called 'social audit'. Broadly-speaking, evaluation is a systematic assessment of progress on the role of the implementing machinery; and analysis of problems and difficulties arising in the effective implementation of a programme, and indication of the corrective measure necessary; all by an independent agency.

The role of evaluation in judging the effectiveness of social welfare programmes and the efficiency of its delivery system can hardly be over estimated. Thus, every programme has some objectives or goals to achieve. Evaluation helps to determine the growth of programmes as it relates the performance to the goals in view. In this process, evaluation covers aspects relating the services, their utilization, their relevance or appropriateness to local needs and expectations, viability of the programme, efficiency of the personnel, and the consequences or impact of the programme.

(i) *Purpose and Scope of Evaluation*: The purpose and scope of evaluation especially in the field of social welfare administration are implied in the definition of the term; more specifically they are:
   (a) To determine social change, growth and social progress.
   (b) To determine the physical and financial requirements in a given time towards the ultimate social welfare organizational goal in relation to the total time set for its achievements.
   (c) To determine the shortfalls and the reason therefore, i.e., to judge the efficacy of methods for social cost benefit analysis.
   (d) To provide guidance in the execution of social welfare programmes.
   (e) To provide satisfaction and a sense of security to personnel connected with the implementation of the social welfare programmes.
   (f) To provide a sense of satisfaction to the community by creating a responsible public.

(ii) *Aspects of Evaluation*: A comprehensive evaluation of the social welfare programme basically cover the following aspects:
   (a) The concept behind the programme, the assumptions underlying the same and the extent to which these are found to be relevant and valid.
   (b) The costs of implementing the programme and whether it is possible to get more results out of the funds available.

(c) The operations involved in the implementation of the programme. The extent to which it has been able to tackle the desired results.
(d) The impact of the programmes.

Utilization of Evaluation for Promoting or Modifying Policies and Programme

For effectiveness of programme to know the progressive success or failure in any programme whether it is governmental or non-governmental and to make decision for improvement, we need to evaluate the programme. It is the process of research in the programme. Evaluation is needed for the improvement of programme and for promoting or modifying policies in the programme. Evaluation of any programme is required for following reasons:

(1) For better utilization of economic resource.
(2) To provide better services to community.
(3) To obtain opinion of beneficiaries.
(4) To know the impact of development in the programme.
(5) To judge the effectiveness of group.
(6) It is useful for future plan and for decision-making.
(7) To avoid weaknesses and future mistakes and shortcomings.
(8) To know whether the policy laid down in the programme had been fulfilled.
(9) To see the effectiveness of techniques and skills.
(10) To understand the amount and degree of participation of the people.
(11) To help the agency in its organization for completion of programme.
(12) To help the agency to make comprehensive review.

Principles of Evaluation

Evaluation is the assessment of progress of events to know its success and failures. All the programmes whether it is successful or failure, has to be evaluated. It is applicable in both government as well as voluntary organizations. The guiding principles of evaluation can be as follows:

(i) The objective of programme must be clear.
(ii) Evaluation should involve minimum possible cost.
(iii) Evaluation should be done without prejudices of day-to-day work.
(iv) As far as possible, the agency must call outsider for evaluation.

(v) The overall examinations should reveal strength and weakness.

Limitations

Some of the limitations in evaluation may be as follows:

(i) Changes may come very slowly through the programme, e.g., impact of education programme, so going for evaluation just after launching the programme may not bring much change.

(ii) Sometimes changes may occur but may disappear after the agency has stopped implementing programme, e.g., as in adult literacy programme, if there is no follow up or reinforcement of programme the positive impact may be diminished.

(iii) All our ideas and thinking may be reflected in evaluation due to lack of objectivity.

Management of Social Welfare Organization

Organization and its Types

Organization is the important factor in social welfare activity. People are engaged in different activities. Human actions are sometimes planned and sometimes spontaneous, unplanned and sporadic. But human activity if consciously devised and carefully directed can be purposeful and result-oriented. All persons who involve in activities act in an organized fashion. An organized demonstration becomes purposeful and achievement-oriented, the moment people involved in it act in an organized or planned fashion. A planned human endeavour presupposes existence of an organization. An organization tries to establish an effective behavioural relationship among selected employees and in selected workplaces in order that a group may work together effectively.

What is an Organization?

Many scholars of an organization or public administration and management have tried to define the term 'organization'. A vivid definition of organization is given by two teachers of public administration; J.M. Pfiffner and F.P. Sherwood. According to them, "an organization is the pattern of ways in which large numbers of people, too many to have intimate face to face contact with all others, and engaged in a complexity of tasks, relate themselves to each other in the conscious, systematic establishment and accomplishment of mutually agreed purpose".

The effort of Pfiffner and Sherwood is undoubtedly creditable because of the presentation of a scientifically structured definition. The definition given by them highlights many aspects of an organization as given below:

(i) Organization is a 'pattern of ways'.
(ii) Large number of people in an organization do not have face-to-face contact.
(iii) People in organizations are involved in complex tasks.
(iv) People in organizations develop network of inter-relationships.
(v) Organizations and people involved in organization, consciously select, systematically choose, establish and cooperatively pursue and accomplish mutually acceptable and agreeable goals and purposes.

According to Mooney, "organization is the form of every human association for attainment of a common purpose" and according to Dimock "organization is the systematic bringing together of inter-dependent parts to form a unified whole through which authority, coordination and control may be exercised to achieve a given purpose – organization is both structure and human relations". Thus, organization considered in strictly limited sense may mean, men or people, assigned roles, duties or jobs, work relationships, interaction consciously devised with cooperate efforts of people involved in the organization.

Why an Organization at All?

The importance of organization is accepted by all. Even a noted economist admitted that organization is an important agent for development. "The agents of production are commonly classed as land and capital .... It seems best sometimes to reckon organization apart as a distinct agent of production." Thus, some people accept the importance of organizational structure for production.

Lepawsky highlights the 'graphic convenience' and 'teachable' quality of an organization. He says that "the real importance of organization falls between two extreme positions – one is 'the best' and the other is one which magnifies organizational form, making it a super subject either parallel with or inclusive of the whole subject of administration".

Without organization, human action cannot be planned, systematic and purpose-achievement-oriented. For every human activity, organization is a necessary precondition; without organization planned human actions are impossible. So, the purpose of public organization is the reduction of economic, social and psychic suffering and the enhancement of life opportunities for those inside and outside the organization. Organizations are important because a large number of people spend a big chunk of their time in organization.

Objectives of an Organization

The objective of an organization is that of a common purpose. It may be some product or service, which must be undertaken and attained, at least in part, before the individual interests of the participants may be realized. Within this definitional framework, profit cannot be considered as an organizational purpose. The objective of the organization is usually accomplished through the process of specialization of activity. The total purpose is subdivided into sub-objectives whose accomplishment will permit the organization to be effective. In the viewpoint of La Porte, "objective of organization is not only the common purpose but also the reduction of economic, social and psychic suffering, which should be of major importance while accepting the purpose of a public organization".

Elements of an Organization

For systematic and smooth functioning, there must be three basic elements in an organization:

(i) *Complexity*: In any organization, there is not only one category of people but different levels of people work for the common goal, because there are different parts or levels of functioning in an organization. And it is well known that it is impossible to work at every level with the same standard of people. So, complexity in the nature of an organization is important for better and successful functioning.

(ii) *Conscious Rationality*: Every individual of an organization should be conscious and rational enough for producing better work in his own department of the organization. This is an important element in an organization because many people systematically and consciously combine their individual efforts for the accomplishment of a common task.

(iii) *Presence of Purpose*: 'Purpose' is a prominent element of an organization in public welfare administration. Without a purpose, an organization is incomplete. Every individual's function in an organization is based on achieving the commonality of organizational purpose.

Characteristics of Organization

The basic characteristics of any organization are the following:

(i) *Structural-Oriented*: An organization is a structured collective or entity in which persons, consciously and deliberately organize their activities and efforts. It is a structured entity denoting human activity, i.e., persons. Persons are an important element of an organization.

(ii) *Process-Oriented*: The organized form of activities or efforts of individual in an organization are patterned actions which take the form of 'process'. These people are interacting in different organization processes.

(iii) *Specialization-Oriented*: The patterned actions in interacting processes get highly complicated and complex or these become specialized, resulting in complexity of tasks.

(iv) *Behaviour-Oriented*: An organization in essence, is a human system, an energic input-output system and also self-acknowledgement system of line and staff model where organizational roles to be performed by line or staff officers are determined on the basis of organization's problems, needs and capacities rather than on the basis of broad principles such as "staff advises and line decides".

Types of Organization

Organizations classified on the basis of relationship are called 'formal' and 'informal.' The classification is purely from the point of view of structural design. It is a complete impossibility to have a pure formal organization and also an informal one. Hicks says, "Formal and informal define the extremes of a continuum of organizational types."

(i) *Formal Organization*: Etymologically speaking, formal refers to something pertaining to the form or pattern, which is conventional, ceremonial, according to rule, explicit of form or of routine. Merton expresses his view on formal organization in these words: "A formal rationally organized social structure involves clearly defined patterns of activity in which, ideally, every series of actions is functionally related to the purpose of the organization – there is an integrated series of offices of hierarchies statuses in which where a number of obligations and privileges closely defined by limited and specific rules. Formal arrangement of functions usually called the formal organization – an interrelated pattern of jobs, which make up the structure of a system."

Formal organization is a planned organization. It corresponds to a certain design. The central to distinction between formal and informal organization is the difference between authority and influence. In the words of Simon, organization means "a planned system of cooperative effort in which each of the participants has to have a recognized role to play and duties and tasks to perform". The key to the whole process is effective cooperation among the persons engaged in the organization.

Formal organization generally refers to the organizational pattern designed by management; the blueprint of division of labour and power of control, the rules and regulations about the wages, fines and quality control, etc. Formal organization is characterized in the following ways:

(a) Formal organization is a well-defined structure, i.e., clear-cut description of authority, power, accountability and responsibility relationships.
(b) Formal structure defines channel of communication.
(c) Formal organization gives clearly specified jobs for every member.
(d) Explicitly stated hierarchy of objectives, role, prestige, rank, etc.
(e) Formal organization is well-ordered and controlled patterns of status, role, prestige, rank, etc.
(f) Formal organization has durability and planned nature, emphasis on order, therefore, inflexible.
(g) Membership of formal organization is gained consciously at a specific time and are usually open.

(ii) *Informal Organization*: Generally speaking, an informal organization is born as a consequence to the social needs – the desire of human groups to associate most conveniently without the restrictions imposed by formal organization. An informal organization is a natural result of man's social interaction with others. It is believed that whereas the formal organization is rationally created for technological purpose, the informal organization naturally arises from man's quest for social satisfaction.

The informal organization refers to people in group associations at work, but these associations are not specified in the blueprint of the formal organization. The informal organization means natural groupings of people in the work situation.

Informal organization is a need – fulfilment device generated from within and also from without when it is found that the exiting 'formal' communication arrangement is inadequate or insufficient. So, informal organization which is not recognized in the formal organization, plays vital role in determining the way work will be done. Thus, it is inevitably complementary and supplemental to the formal one. Informal organization is characterized in the following ways:

(a) It is not deliberately structured but an outcome of automatic growth and development of human and social relations – unofficial in character, emergent of social and personal needs.

(b) In informal organization, people are motivated and influenced in their cooperative efforts by status or recognition of desires, friendships, racial origins, cliques, sentiments and social customs.

(c) The motivating force is social and personal needs and demands.

(d) An informal organization is neither prescribed nor predetermined, it is spontaneous, transitory growing.

(e) Informal organization has a leadership structure, rules, standards, norms, way of rewarding compliance, but all are neither prescribed nor followed by any mandatory procedures for execution.

Now, it is clear that an informal organization is important and should ordinarily be encouraged to grow in order to supplement the formal one because the actual working of any organization is not always according to the formal plan. The informal relationship of the persons working in the organization may be different from the formal expected relationship. It is better to encourage informal relationship among social administrators to promote and ensure effective social action.

(iii) *Non-Formal Organization*: Organization existing within formal organization is non-formal organization that permits and sometimes encourages such behaviour by members. This non-formal behaviour is frequently desirable and also work-oriented and contributes significantly to efficiency. Behavioural factors such as unnecessary socializing on the job, group values and cultural likes and dislikes serve as basis for non-formal behaviour in formal organization.

Non-formal organization always exists along with formal organization. It serves as an adjunct, is intangible, and takes on different degrees of importance depending upon the activity and the persons involved. A manager should be aware of the presence and influence of non-formal organization.

(iv) *Line Organization*: The line type organization is commonly used for small enterprises, especially by retailers and manufactures having perhaps seven to eight employees. It has outstanding advantages – quick decision making is fostered; buck passing is eliminated; and excellent management training experience is provided. This type of organization has inherent disadvantages such as executives tend to become overloaded with too many duties; specialization is not practised; management members may be difficult to replace; and insufficient time and effort is given to activities such as managerial planning, research and development, and overall controlling measures as governing body. In this type of organization, the authority flows from top to bottom.

(v) *Staff Organization*: The use of the term 'staff' gives rise to many misunderstandings in management. Literally, the word means stick carried in the hand for support. Hence, staff authority relationships originally were thought of as those relationships used to support line authority relationships. This concept still exists today and is valid. Staff means a supporting role and functions; it is intended to help the 'order'. With the passing of time, additional meanings of staff authority, or what this help consists of, have developed the term 'support' instead of 'staff' which is currently in use. In most enterprises, use of staff in organization structure can be traced to the need for help in handling details, locating data required for decision, and offering counsel on specific managerial problems.

Most staff authority relationships are characteristically a manager-to-manager authority relationship and exist among any managerial level of an organization structure. The managerial recipient of staff authority is commonly called a staff executive or staff officer. He has the charge of this respective staff organizational unit. The concept of staff authority is quite old and staffs were employed by government and armies in ancient history too.

(vi) *Line and Staff Organization*: Most enterprises operate amid complexities and ever increasing advances in knowledge and technologies. These along with expansion of an enterprise makes it necessary eventually to relieve management members with line authority of certain duties. The need for certain specialists is recognized. For example, the expert in establishing work standards, the legal advisor, the researcher, and the tax expert are incorporated into the formal organization structure primarily so that the line manager is relieved of part of his duties and thus able to concentrate his efforts on the direct doing activities in keeping with the enterprises' objectives.

The line authority remains the avenue for command or performance of the work. It consists of the authority relationships between line managers. Generally speaking most staff managers do not exercise their staff authority along the channels of line authority. Staff managers exercise their proper staff authority to help line managers who command, to achieve work performance. What is a line manager? and, what is a staff manager? depends on the type of authority possessed.

(vii) *Committee Organization*: It can be defined as: "A body of persons elected or appointed to meet on an organized basis for the discussion and dealing of matters brought to it." Committees are common yet controversial in most organizations. They can and do exist at any organizational level, serve in various capacities and for different purposes, are known by many different names, and enjoy wide degrees of acceptance among management members. Extremely important work is accomplished via the committee route. Typically educational enterprises are loaded with committee, and they are common in government and in business. In trade associations and most professional societies, the major portion of the organization structure is made up of committees.

The committee usually has a formally recognized and permanent place in the organization structure. Its makeup, duties, membership, and decision-making power may be carefully spelled out. For example, some business enterprises have at the top level, a planning and policy committee, or a general management committee made up of selected company executives. The committee meets regularly, may be weekly, makes decisions, ensures that they are enforced, and participates in the management affairs of the company.

(viii) *Social Organization*: It is apparent that in a democratic society, the ultimate authority of a business enterprise rests with public or society. The professional privileges are derived and controlled through laws and marketing process. Then, beginning with the policies, a management system is organized to achieve the organizational objectives. Procedures and control mechanism is introduced by the management in a systematic way.

Different Types of Welfare Services

Before we deal with the social welfare services, we need to have clear understanding of welfare service. Welfare service means relief, curative and rehabilitative services for a target group, namely, the clients of welfare programme. It is concerned itself more with trying to solve the problems of the clients after they have arisen. Thus, its primary motivating forces is humanitarianism and development of the people. There are different types of welfare services, which are as follows:

(1) *Diagnostic Service*: Diagnostic service is a programme of identifying the nature of the problem of clients. In this process, social worker studies the nature and the essence of the problem, and accordingly plans an organization to solve the problem of clients.

(2) *Ameliorative Service*: In ameliorative programme, social worker or an organizer takes steps to make improvement in solving of problems of the clients. He makes aware of their problems and for the development and betterment of clients what action is to be taken.

(3) *Remedial Service*: In this process of welfare service a social worker tries to solve the problems of the clients, in other words he provides a remedy or cure for the weaker section of people or the client. Here, the financial resource plays an important role for the implementation of the programme for solving the problems of the clients.

(4) *Rehabilitative Service*: It is the important process of welfare service in which organizer or social work agency tries to bring back the normal life of the client. Rehabilitation programme should make

available to disabled persons on the basis of individual needs, a wide range of services including: (a) comprehensive medical, psycho-social, and vocational diagnosis and evaluation; (b) physical restoration, including medical, surgical, psychiatric and hospital services, medically related services; (c) social services in relation to physical, vocational, psychological, emotional, and social problems; and (d) vocational guidance, training and employment placement and evaluation.

Organizing Span of Control, Decentralization and Delegation

Organizing Span of Control

In an organization, a superior has to exercise control over the activities of his subordinates. He has to ensure that everything is being done, in accordance with the rules and instructions. But, there are physical and psychological limitations on the span of control that a superior can exercise over his subordinates. An important limitation on the span of control, is imposed by the human span of attention. For the sake of illustration, it can be observed that an individual can effectively supervise the activities of only a limited number of persons, say seven, nine or twelve.

If a superior is expected to control the activities of more persons than he can actually do, the result is delay and inefficiency. Many attempts have been made to search for an 'ideal number' of persons whose activities a superior can control. Such a search is useless. The fact is that how many persons can be effectively controlled by a superior, depends on the energy of the supervisor, the nature of work involved and the physical location of the employees. When a superior is exercising control over persons with homogeneous functions, he will be able to exercise control over a large number of people than a man who is to control persons with different kinds of functions. It can be said that an engineer supervising engineers may be able to control more people than an engineer having medical, educational, and social workers reporting to him. Further, if a superior has to exercise control over persons who are scattered geographically, he will be able to control less number of people. To sum up, the quality of work in an organization up to some extent depends on the effectiveness of control of the superior over the subordinates, but a superior cannot exercise control over unlimited number of persons, because the span of control is limited by the span of human attention.

In static sense, the control in social welfare administration implies measuring of social action against the standards set in social policy and plan and the correction of deviation through the process of feedback. According to Henry Fayol, "In an undertaking, control consist in verifying whether everything occurs in conformity with the plan adopted, the instructions issued and principles established. It has for its object to point out weaknesses and prevent recurrences. Control is that force which guides it to a predetermined objective by means of pre-determined policies and decisions. A good control system not only means seeing that people do, what they are supposed to do, but also indicates when there are deviations from plans and when it is advisable to change the means of gaining the objectives or even to change the objectives so that social welfare programmes remain relevant and purposeful and meet the growing unmet welfare needs of the people."

In the dynamic sense, control may be thought of as helping in setting new social welfare goals and measures to cope with changing socio-economic environment and needs of the people. So, control must by considered as a continuous and fundamental managerial function that usually follows other functions. And, therefore, control must be used to improve social welfare programme delivery system.

(i) *Aspects of Control in Organization*: Control is of inevitable significance in efficient administration especially in social welfare administration. So, control in social welfare can be viewed in the following from three aspects:
   (a) *Operational Control*: Whose purpose is to keep the social action in accordance with its norms to produce desired impact.
   (b) *Programme Control*: Whose purpose is to ensure that the social welfare programmes achieve the results as anticipated.
   (c) *Social Control*: The purpose of social control is two fold: to ensure the viability of social welfare measures in its larger social environment and to maximize the benefits the social welfare measures are producing for the community in relation to the inputs received from community.

(ii) *Controlling Process in Social Welfare Administration*: Controlling process entails a number of steps, which should be followed to ensure social welfare action. These are:
   (a) *Establishment of Control Standard*: The first important element of the control process is to determine the goals,

objectives or targets of each social programme, against which the actual performance is to be measured.

(b) *Measurement of Performance*: The second basic step in ascertaining social welfare is the evaluation of performance in terms of social welfare control standards. We must be clear that the measurement of performance must be in units similar to those in which standards were designed.

(c) *Comparison between Performance and Standards*: The third step is to compare the actual performance with the set standards of performance. It is in rare cases that performance achieved and the standards set coincided. It is, therefore, suggested to be realistic and accept a range of tolerance within which normal performance should have occurred.

(d) *Determining the Reasons for Deviation*: It is very important to find the cause of deviations to ensure fruitful social action. This is an intellectual exercise and it is based upon the case studies of programmes.

(e) *Correction of Deviation*: It is the final and important step of the controlling process. It is based upon the analysis of the reasons of deviation, when there is a prompt need of corrective action, through changes in social policy, performance standards, structure and contents. This is very important, otherwise we would be repeating the same mistakes resulting into poor performance. Thus, there is a constant need of administrative improvement and reform.

Delegation and Decentralization

Delegation is the process whereby a superior divides his total work assignment between himself and subordinates or operative personnel in order to achieve both operative and management specialization. It is the entrustment of responsibility and authority to others and the creation of accountability for performance. It is to be clearly understood that delegation is not a process of abdication. The person who delegates does not divorce himself from the responsibility and authority, which he entrusts.

Decentralization would mean the progress of transfer of administrative authority from a higher to lower level of government. The essential element in decentralization is a twin process of deconcentration and devaluation. In deconcentration, a superior officer, in order to make his department function effectively and efficiently, delegates to his subordinate field officials the power to act in his name without transferring to them the authority he enjoys. Devaluation, which also implies dispersal of authority is a process wherein power is transferred from one organ of government to another by means of a piece of legislation or constitution.

Thus, decentralization and delegation can lighten the burden of the social welfare administrator and enable him to devote attention to important aspects of planning, policy making and coordination. So, delegation and decentralization should be clearly made use of to achieve the objective of best social action.

(i) *Aspects of Delegation*: There are three aspects of delegation: the entrustment of work of responsibility to another for performance; the entrustment of power and right or authority to be exercised; and the creation of an obligation or accountability, on the part of the person accepting the delegation to perform in terms of the standards established.

(ii) *Importance of Delegation*: Delegation of responsibility and authority is an important aspect of successful administration to place the responsibility for decision at the lowest possible organizational level, in order to obtain decisions as speedily as possible. No administrator can do in detail all the work he is administrating, for by definition an administrator manages the work of others. Therefore, the principle of delegation of responsibility should be followed to the utmost extent, consistent with efficiency and coordination of policy. The responsibility and authority of individuals should be clearly defined in writing and the authority placed in each position must correspond to the responsibility, which the position carries.

Supervision

Supervision is considered to be an integral part of social welfare administration. Regardless of the degree to which field operations are deconcentrated geographically, the headquarters has to maintain continuous supervision over such operations. Supervision is a compound of two words 'super' and 'vision' meaning superior power of perceiving. Supervision means superintending or overseeing of the performance of a social welfare worker or a group of workers in order to ensure that proper procedures and standards of performance are observed, qualitatively and quantitatively to achieve the objectives of social welfare activity. Effective supervision becomes all the more important in social welfare administration and has the direct and immediate responsibilities for providing basic services and amenities at the grassroots level to all the beneficiaries. According to Williamson, 'supervision' is a process by which workers are helped by designated staff members to learn according to their needs to make the best use of their knowledge and skills, and to improve their abilities so that they do their jobs more effectively and with increasing satisfaction to themselves and agencies.

Who is a Supervisor?

America's Fort Hartly Labour Act of 1947, defines supervisors as "those having authority to exercise independent judgement in hiring, discharging, disciplining, recording and taking other actions of a similar nature with respect to employees". Therefore, supervisors are those persons in authority who have direct control over their working force. According to Allen a supervisor is an authority who is responsible to get the work done. He is to see that directions are being followed, instructions and orders are being carried out, the plans, polices and programmes are being executed and deviations, if any, are being corrected and reported on to the authority to whom one is answerable.

Role of Supervisor

A supervisor as an enabler has to perform multifaceted roles, while at supervision. As a guide, consultant, leader, counsellor and an adviser, his role broadly encompasses the following aspects:

(i) As a line supervisor, he has to exercise control in line of command.
(ii) As a functional supervisor, he has to work as a specialist to afford consultative and counselling service.

    For performing the role of a line and functional supervisor, a supervisor has to: (1) be attentive, receptive and a good listener; (2) create and stabilize a friendly interest and secure sympathetic and uncritical atmosphere; and (3) handle the situation with insight, imagination understanding and skill and to know what related services are available in locality, district, state and at national level.

Principles of Effective Supervision

For the effective function of social welfare organization, the following principles are suggested for good leadership:

(i) *Do not be an Autocrat*: Autocratic leadership is self-defeating, because the workers feel alienated and do not obey the leader willingly.

(ii) *Listen Carefully*: The leader should be a good listener. He must listen carefully to everything told to him by subordinates. He must accord full opportunity to the worker to present his case; only then it should the leader to express his opinion.

(iii) *Do not Decide Hurriedly:* It is rash to form an opinion about some person hurriedly after a casual glance or brief hearing as most of the complaint are not genuine. But some are certainly so and if these are not removed, the morale in the company or organization would suffer.

(iv) *Do not Argue With Subordinates*: Under no circumstances should supervisor indulge in arguments with his subordinate, because if he fails to persuade or convince by his arguments, he is liable to issue orders to vindicate his point of view. This creates frustration and a sense of insecurity among the workers. A good leader should not argue but listen carefully and issue orders only after careful listening.

(v) *Do not Criticize Publicly*: If a worker is rebuked publicly he feels insulted. The workers are usually rash and they tend to retaliate if they are wounded emotionally. Therefore, a good leader avoids discussing the faults of workers in public. He points them out to him in private and in a direct manner.

Methods of Supervision

There are broadly six methods of supervision. Supervision needs specialized knowledge and skills for utilizing it to achieve the intended results. So, supervisor has to possess certain qualities, while at supervision:

(i) *Prior Approval:* Prior approval means that prior approval of the competent authority has to be obtained before the work on a particular project is started. In this manner, the supervisor will be in a position to gather detailed information about the intentions of the operating organizations. Moreover, the supervisor will come to know about the details of work, which his organization, where he performs his work, is going to expect. Deviations, if any, would be corrected and controlled without any misunderstanding, wastage of time and energy in terms of money, manpower and material resources. This system is generally followed in most of the social services programmes.

(ii) *Service Standards*: Service standards means setting up norms of administrative output. Setting up of norms is not an easy process. Difficulties lie in striking a balance between quantity and quality, the achievement of targets and the way it has to be done. The supervisor has to work with thoughtfulness, fairness, tact, emotion, etc., for effectiveness and efficiency of service standards so laid down.

(iii) *Budgetary Limitations*: Budgetary limitations means that the operating units work within the budgetary allocations and have to carry out the work within the limited budget provisions. This method is being followed in day-to-day financial administration of the organization.

(iv) *Approval of Personnel*: This means to reserve the right of approval of personnel in key positions in the organization to the chief executive, while leaving the initiative of selection in the hands of the operating head. This method helps in exercising control over the personnel in a manner stipulated for achieving the objectives of an organization.

(v) *Reporting System*: Reporting holds a key position for assessing day-to-day performance of an organization. It helps in identifying shortcomings and bottlenecks in execution of the programmes and projects and in turn, ways and means for corrective action. Reporting system works as one of the means for effective monitoring of the progress of an organization.

(vi) *Inspection*: Inspection is a very effective instrument of supervision. The supervisor has to ensure that the inspection is timely, result-oriented, humanistic and problem solving. It helps in bridging the role conflicts and establishing harmonious contacts between the supervisor and the subordinates in the performance of their work.

Inspection has to see that the existing rules and regulations are observed. It is a sort of performance audit. The inspection is related to instructing and guiding the persons working in the organization as well as improvement of efficiency. Besides all these methods or techniques, the techniques of drawing work plans, written procedures on manuals, written and oral instructions, staff meetings, and administrative follow up, i.e., the methods adopted for proper duration may also be adopted at supervision.

Team Work, Working with Volunteer Para-Professionals and Other Professionals

When people perform task together, it is called a team or they act as a team. It is one way of interaction of people and when groups seek to develop a cooperative state it is called teamwork. Team is a group of persons irrespective of their number. A team may consist of thousands of workers engaged in an organization or a few say five or ten. But here, we use the term to a limited definition, i.e., a small group of members interacting regularly.

A group can work together as a team only when each one knows the role of the other persons with whom he has to interact in the group and each one must be qualified in performing his job effectively. It will promote cooperation among the members of the team. The team members work with cooperation in each operating situation without waiting for someone to give an order. In other words, team members work voluntarily to the job situation and take necessary action to further the team goals.

Team work needs a supportive environment from the management that helps the group task the necessary steps towards team work and these steps lay the foundation stone of the very basis of cooperation, trust and compatibility. Studies show that greater the trust and compatibility in a team, the greater their effectiveness tends to be. So, it is the responsibility of the management to provide supportive climate within the organization. The supportive environment includes the way in which reports and records are maintained. It may encourage or discourage the teamwork, although they are not directly involved in performance of the job.

Some of the essential elements for successful team work would be that there has to be an understanding between the members of the team and the leaders, understanding of the interaction among the people; team building is need of the individual to build and secure a special status or position; and they should involve themselves together to take decisions. Following these essential elements team members can work effectively in the organization.

Hence, from the above discussions, it is clear about the different dimensions of social welfare administration and the intervention of social work in welfare administration and development.

6

Voluntary Action, Voluntary Organization and Management

Voluntary action, voluntary organization and management have played tremendous role in the life of people as well as society. Each has its purposes and principles to solve the problems of situations. Voluntary action is autonomous and flexible. It is initiated by group of like-minded people to change and transform the socio-economic life of the people, specially the weaker section, based on social justice and not merely for charity or relief. Voluntary action and voluntary effort are not the same.

Voluntary action may include a wide range of activities like construction and maintenance of educational institutions, hospitals, inns, roads, etc. Voluntary organization along with management also has contributed a lot to the society, too. Voluntary organizations deal with some certain programmes and make people aware of their problems to be solved by themselves, because it gives them confidence to stand on their own feet and face the problems. Management too is essential to give assistance in economical problems. Management deals with budgeting, planning, administration in social welfare, along with project planning.

In all societies, at all times, people have been giving their best in the form of cash and service for the welfare of the needy. These, all show that in the life of human beings voluntary action, voluntary organization as well as management take them towards a developed situation. These programmes are not just enough to help the people but they stimulate them to do things by themselves.

Voluntary Action

Voluntary action is autonomous and flexible. It is initiated by a group of like-minded people to change and transform the socio-economic life of the people, specially the weaker sections, based on social justice and not merely for charity or relief. It is often used synonymously with voluntary effort, even though voluntary action and voluntary effort are not the same. While the former calls for planning and involvement of a group to deal with a problem the latter may not entail such steps.

The essential feature of voluntary action is that it is problem-oriented. It is initiated not only to solve the problem but also to prevent the occurrence of the problem. It calls for understanding and identification of the problem, fixing up of priorities, formulation of programmes taking into consideration the problem and available resources and, finally, carrying out the programmes by a group of individuals working independently without external control or coercion. Voluntary action ultimately aims at creating a situation conducive to the development of potentialities in individuals, groups and communities to find solutions to their problems, and ways and means to handling these to realize their ultimate goal.

The basic tenet of an external voluntary action group is to act as a catalyst, and pull out of the community or the area of work by developing people's institutions and organizations as early as possible.

Voluntary Action: Individual and Collective

The voluntary action for social advancement is generally inspired by two main motives – mutual aid and philanthropic. The first motive has its origin in a sense of one's own need for security against misfortune, and realization that, since one's fellow men have the same need and by undertaking to help one another all may help themselves. This motive may give rise to organizations in the form of friendly societies, cooperative societies, housing societies, etc. The philanthropic motive is the desire by one's personal action to make life happier for others and has led to the development of an immense variety of institutions and societies.

The pioneers of voluntary action may be either politicians or non-politicians or they may be both. The non-political figures are pioneers of direct voluntary action rather than of action designed to influence parliaments and governments. It is common to all these men and women that they set out to do things without asking what they would get thereby for themselves.

Lord Beveridge, discussing the background of pioneers in the field of voluntary action, points out three other significant things. First, they mostly come from the middle class; that is to say, people who have to work for a living but do not as a rule work under direction of another or to fixed hours. Second, there is the religious motive, which urges them to undertake such tasks. As he remarks: most of the pioneers, so far as anything is known of their opinions, were moved by a religious motive or came from a home where religion was a reality. Third, they have the need for material resources to put new ideas into practice; some of the pioneers had fortunes of their own, others had the fortunes of their friends at call.

Voluntary Organizations

As already stated more than 120,000 voluntary organizations are working which are directly or indirectly engaged in the promotion of social welfare. The activities carried out by them are not met purely by their internal resources as most of them are funded by the Unions, State or other statutory organizations created for the purpose. So, their main job is to channelize the resources given to them through grants-in-aid along with their internal mobilization.

A study of four voluntary institutions (two from each district) operating in Punjab indicates that 47.15 per cent resources were raised from non-statutory sources, 27.02 per cent from state government, 12.07 per cent from local bodies, 11.08 per cent from Central Social Welfare Board, and 2.68 from central government.

However, in quantitative terms the resources with the voluntary organizations were not adequate. Many voluntary agencies were finding it difficult to raise adequate funds to run the programmes and promote good standard in services. These institutions were experiencing the following problems in raising the adequate resources:

(1) With the high cost of living, people have little money to donate. Besides, there appears to be no coordination between the agencies located in an area. Majority of agencies of the area sometimes have been noticed approaching the same person for collecting money one after the other. Often, their purpose also have been noticed to be the same.

(2) Industrialists and businessmen find it more profitable to invest money in political fields, with their own axe to grind, rather than donating money to charitable institutions.
(3) The various agencies engaged in providing grants-in-aid programmes appear to be gaining more and more hold on the institutions through its rules and regulations for utilization of grants.

Management of Organization

Leonard D. White says that from one point of view, organization is a formal declared pattern of relations established in government by law and by top management. He further says that an organization is the set of work relationship that grow out of the mutual interactions of persons working together over long period of time. White suggested three weaknesses of the above definition.

Without organization, human actions cannot be planned, be systematic and purpose-achievement-oriented. For every human activity, organization is a necessary pre-condition. Without organization, planned human actions are impossible. In order to answer the questions – what is the need of an organization or why an organization at all – organization is the reduction of economic, social and psychic suffering and the enhancement of life opportunities for those inside and outside the organization.

New Fields of Voluntary Action

We have seen above that voluntary action sprang up in the fields of education, social security in the form of friendly societies, homes for the destitute, the disabled, etc. Some of these function have been taken up by the state for their heavy financial responsibility and other reasons, but new needs have grown up with industrialization and urbanization and some of these can be better met by the voluntary organizations for certain reasons. For example, even if we give sufficient income to an old man he will need proper medical care, leisure, proper housing, special occupation and company.

Similarly, in the case of children who are parentless or who cannot be protected by their parents because of uncongenial environments, protection in foster homes, children's homes or some advice through family welfare services will be essential. Some of this work can be done by public agencies but it is often asserted that the services offered by public agencies are inferior, less efficient, and lack the human touch. The voluntary organizations generally represent the sincere and general desire of their founders, to do good to those in special need. In many children's homes, as reported by the Curtis Committee (1945) in England: "There was lack of understanding of children's needs which led to a dreary uninteresting life in many of the homes, and that this showed itself in a lack of liveliness and vigour in the children."

Historical Development of Voluntary Action

Origin

Social welfare has its origin in charity, philanthropy and poor-relief. Presently, it covers a very wide and broad spectrum of human activities. It denotes services meant to cater to the special needs of persons who by reason of some handicap – social, economic, physical or mental – are unable to avail themselves of or are meant to benefit the weaker, dependent or underprivileged sections of the population. The beneficiaries of these services may be physically handicapped persons, such as the blind, the deaf or the crippled; socially dependent individuals, like the orphan, the widow or the destitute; mentally retarded persons; economically under privileged group such as those living in slum areas; and women handicapped by restrictive social traditions or practices.

History

The history of development of social welfare in India prior to independence is primarily the history of voluntary action. Before the nineteenth century, charity in a large scale on voluntary basis outside the religious channels took place mainly during emergencies, such as famine and floods. The rich and ruling were enjoined to support the indigent. A system of *madhukari*, was prevalent in some parts of the county. Under the custom, poor Brahmin boys supported themselves during their studentship by taking meals once a week by turn in one of the households with whom they had prior arrangements and who had volunteered to provide such a service to their students. The Chinese traveller Hsuan-tsang observed in the seventh century that the Indian people were always in the habit of planting trees on the wayside to give shade to travellers. They voluntarily come together to dig tanks and wells for drinking water, for the community had its own indigenous organizations to provide such services on a collective basis.

In the medieval period in India, there was a system of *adheenamo* prevalent in the southern part of the country. In this system, the community organized and established centres of learning and research where free boarding and lodging were provided to students. A number of libraries were set up around such institutions of learning. Communities raised funds through their own organization to distribute grants to hospitals, schools, colleges and poor homes. Voluntary action in social welfare in India in earlier times had, however, a rather restrictive and sectarian bias, based on caste and religion.

Voluntary action got a stimulus in the nineteenth century. It manifested itself in three directions, namely: (i) religious reforms, (ii) social reforms, and (iii) voluntary social work. Raja Ram Mohan Roy had considerable influence not only in Bengal but also elsewhere the field of social reform. This experiment of organizing vigilance committees of volunteers to fight *Sati* (1815-1820) yielded magnificent results. This voluntarism enveloped a variety of interests such as improving conditions of widows, education of women, removal of caste restrictions, etc. The Almiya Society (1815), the Unitarian Community (1822), and the Brahmo Samaj (1826), were some of his creations in the eastern part of the country. Dadabhai Naoroji in the western part, specially Bombay and Maharashtra, played a pioneering role from 1849 to 1865 in the furtherance of education of girls, religious reforms and women's education. During the same period, primary schools in Marathwada were started on a voluntary basis, and several teachers gave their services free since such bodies lacked funds. During the latter part of the century, leaders of public opinion, influenced by western liberal thought but retaining at the same time their strength of conviction in India's ancient culture and thought, organized voluntary movements. These were Arya Samaj (1875), Rama Krishna Mission (1897), Theosophical Movement (1893) and Anjuman-Himayat-I-Islam (1898). The argument of the leaders of these movements was that all religions were fundamentally right, but the shedding of welfare extraneous impurities was required. These were of the nature of protestant movements against the existing state of affairs.

Christian missionaries did pioneering work in all fields of welfare whether it was the setting up of orphanages or institutes for the handicapped, the old and the infirm. For instance, up to 1895, only Christian missionaries had set up orphanages. Later, philanthropic groups and other secular organizations also shared some responsibilities in this field. However, a large part of the appeal was denominational.

The formalization of voluntary action may be traced to several circumstances: social awareness on the part of national leaders and absence of welfare services for the deserving and the needy; rehabilitation of refugees from Pakistan after the partition of the country; breakdown of traditional institutions such as the joint family and the village community which had provided basic security; spread of education; rising expectations; changes in aspirations of the weaker section, specially women, Scheduled Castes and Scheduled Tribes; and promotional efforts of the government. There was, however, a decline in groups that had been prominent in the earlier period.

Of the various forms of activities in the field of social welfare, the earliest were the welfare of women, children, the infirm and the destitute. This trend still continues.

Voluntary Action in Different Stages of Development of Society

Rural development is a perennial subject in India. Gandhiji's name is almost synonymous with it. Right from the days when Spencer Hatch and F.L. Brayne, I.C.S., pioneered early experiments in rural development in Marthandam (Tamil Nadu) and Gurgaon (old Punjab), several approaches and strategies of rural development have been tried out in India. Likewise, there is the outstanding contribution of Rabindranath Tagore through his Sriniketan experiments. Although, as a nation, we have been paying lip service to Gandhian thought on Gram Swarajya, the nature and extent of its adoption in practice have varied considerably during the last decades.

Community Dethroned

Earlier, during the 1950s, we had the world famous programme of community development, which was launched and implemented with great zest and high hopes. At one time, it was considered to be the panacea of all our rural problems and it was described as a silent revolution sweeping through the countryside. Considering that the programme, and even the phrase 'community development' is no longer in vogue, it seems to have been abandoned with a harsh judgement that it is "incapable of delivering the goods". But it is forgotten that there was the 'community' in community development. Since then we have tried several other approaches in terms of Integrated Agricultural Development Projects (IADP), new strategy of agriculture, the 'Green Revolution' and the application of science and technology in the latest programme of Integrated Rural Development (IRD) and now, since we miss the 'community' in all of these we try to bring it in as an afterthought, as it were, under various names like voluntary action, people's participation, etc.

Macro Orientation

Apparently, there are various interpretations of the term 'Integrated Rural Development'. It is, however, presumed that in most interpretations, social development, is regarded as a vital constituent of IRD, the other two being 'economic growth and physical (area) improvement'. In making that assumption, however, we still learn the concept of social development as unwrapped. In the rural context, it is essential to distinguish between the previously popular concept of 'community development' and the more recent use of the term 'social development' For purposes of this understanding, two distinctions are suggested: (i) The concept of community development is applicable more appropriately at the micro-level whereas the notion of social development connotes the macro dimension; (ii) The process of institutional, structural or systemic change is fundamentally inherent to social development. It may not be an equally essential ingredient of the process of community development.

Wheel Within Wheel

There is, however, more to social development than mere institutional change. One could, under it, consider it to mean transformation in values, institutions and practices, brought about by the deliberate use of the instruments of policy and planning with the active involvement of concerned people in order to raise their levels of living and quality of life. One can identify and discuss the rule of voluntary action in the context of this meaning of social development as a component of IRD.

Native Institutions

Further, the term 'voluntary action' itself calls for some amplification and clarification. Literally interpreted, it only means community action willed and regulated by the community itself. In this interpretation, the identity of the community is distinguished from that of any public authority set-up, statute or state directive. Very often voluntary action is equated with the work of non-official social service agencies operating in the community. This is only the conventional usage of the term 'voluntary action'. It is common knowledge that many of the unofficial agencies, particularly those operating in the village originate outside in the urban areas and are run by non-residents, in other words for all practical purposes, they represent a third party alien to the local community. For a proper meaning of the term 'voluntary action', the fountain springs must be located in the community itself. The question then arises whether the representative organizations such as those established under the Panchayati Raj can be considered voluntary. Strictly speaking, it will not be correct to refer to them as voluntary for a couple of reasons. In the first place, the Panchayati Raj Institutions now operating in the states are set up and governed by statutes and to that extent cease to be voluntary. Secondly, for all practical purposes, they function as local self-governments. Then, there are the people's institutions, e.g., the *Mahila Mandals*, youth organizations or such other non-statutory indigenous organizations. It may be recalled that the official programme of community development and welfare extension projects sponsored by the social welfare board had provided for such people's institutions and for their participation in the programme of local development.

Involuntary Shramdan

In the 1950s, there was a wave of the so-called Shramdan project in which the local people participated in a 'voluntary' manner and the term 'voluntary' was used only or mainly to denote that the work done by those volunteers was not paid for. Although, spectacular results have been claimed for the movement of Shramdan, its evaluation has brought forth rather mixed reports.

According to one assessment, in a country where there is chronic mass unemployment, such non-paid labour is less than fair to the daily wage earners, considering that most of them participated in the Shramdan projects at the cost of sacrifice of their wages. Besides, if such non-remunerative work was done because of compulsive persuasion or persuasive compulsion of the officials in charge, it could not be rightfully called voluntary.

Gandhian Constructive Programme Organization

When Gandhiji took the reigns of Congress in 1920 after the death of Gokhale, Phirozeshah Mehta and Tilak, he declared himself keenly interested in removal of untouchability without which he proclaimed

Swaraj would be meaningless. In 1920, the Congress passing under the leadership of Gandhiji, adopted a distinctly political resolution for the admission of the depressed classes to Hindu temples. He also took up other constructive programmes and temperance cause. When he was charged with under emphasis on social reforms, he said, in the Congress president address in 1924, "Everything that is absolutely essential for Swaraj, is more than merely social work and must be taken up by the Congress." The decision to take up the cause of untouchability gained added strength in 1922 when Gandhiji after the first civil disobedience movement gave the country the *Bardoli* programme, in which the first programme was the removal of untouchability. His special contribution in the organizational field was to set up the appropriate national organization with dedicated persons to solve specific problems, e.g., the *Harijan Sevak Sangh*, the All India Village Industries Association, the *Nai Talim Sangh*, etc. The Swaraj Party which came into existence in 1923 gave full support for carrying out the Congress constructive programme in relation to *Swadeshi*, temperance, inter-communal unity and the promotion of national education.

The new social workers were reformers not from independent conviction but in submission to Gandhiji's leadership and they drew their strength from the organization and funds, but political agitation often affected their work.

Professionalization in Organization

For any discussion on social work as a profession, it will be expedient to examine some of the definitions of profession. Carr-saunder and Wilson observed that "The possession of an intellectual technique acquired by special training, which can be applied to some sphere of every day life, that forms the distinguishing mark of a profession."

The profession is also conceived as a medium of delivering services. Hughes is of the opinion that a profession delivers services-advice or action or both to individuals, organizations or governments, to whole classes or groups of people or to the public at large. Denzin, however, viewed professions as social movements in the sense that they recruit only certain types of persons, develop high elaborate ideologies and supra-individual values, own mechanism of socialization and often attempt at proselytization to bring new persons in the field.

Goals, Structure and Functioning of Voluntary Organizations

Functions of Voluntary Organizations

Voluntary organizations are indispensable and they perform a number of functions for the welfare of its members, the development of the country and integration and solidarity of the society and nation. Some of these objectives and functions may be discussed as follows:

(1) Man is by nature gregarious. The urge to act in groups is fundamental in him. People therefore, form groups and associations voluntarily for their own benefit as also for others with a view to leading a full and richer life, as is reflected in voluntary associations formed for promotion of recreational and cultural activities, social services, professional interests, etc.

(2) A pluralistic society with a democratic system requires a multitude of independent, voluntary non-government associations as buffer between the individual and the state, preventing the government from developing monopoly in various fields. Voluntary organizations involve citizens in noble affairs and avoid concentration of powers in the hands of government and thus serve as power breakers. Sharing of power by voluntary groups restrain governments from developing monopolistic approach to organization of services.

(3) They enable the individuals to learn the fundamentals of group and political action through participation in the governing of their private organizations.

(4) Organized voluntary action helps groups and individuals with diverse political and other interests and contributes to strengthening of feeling of national solidarity that promotes a participative character of democracy.

(5) The state does not have the requisite financial resources and manpower to meet all the needs of its citizens. It can therefore, only take the responsibility of providing them minimum needs. The voluntary organizations by raising additional resources locally can meet the uncovered needs and enrich local life.

(6) Voluntary organizations also help the state in the areas which are its exclusive responsibility but for which it has limited sources and perform such functions in much better way as compared to the state organizations. Education, for example, is the responsibility

of the state but the educational institutions being run and managed by voluntary organizations far outnumber the government institutions and excel the latter in quality of service also in view of the flexibility, ability at experimentation, pioneering spirit and other virtues. Same is the case in respect of the provision of health services, which is again the responsibility of the state. But the hospitals sponsored by philanthropic and charitable institutions are well known for better care and concern in comparison to government owned hospitals.

(7) Voluntary organizations thus, have not only a role to play in the field of accepted state responsibilities but they can also venture into new needs, work in new areas, unveil social evils and give attention to hitherto unattended and unmet needs. They can act as sappers and miners of unfolding developing revolution. They can function as reconnaissance squads. They can be forerunners of change and anticipate and take action to make it less painful. They can work for progress, development and consequently in course of time they can help the state in extending its activities over wider areas, thus raising the national minimum.

(8) They act as a stabilizing force by welding together people with such groups as are not politically motivated and are not concerned about the fortunes of one or the other political party in capturing government power, but are above party politics and are interested in other areas of nation building and thus contribute to national integration and concentration on non-political issues.

In sum, voluntary organizations' main functions comprise giving concrete expression to the fundamental right of freedom of association, identifying the needs of individuals, groups and communities and initiating projects and programmes to meet them on their own or with the grant-in-aid of the government, sharing the responsibility of the state in providing minimum needs of the citizens, covering the areas of uncovered and unmet needs, providing opportunities to people imbued with the spirit of service and dedication to organize themselves to promote public welfare, mobilizing public support through publicity campaigns raising functional resources through contributions and donations and finally organizing activities of non-partisan and non-political nature for well-being of the society, enriching the likes of citizens and progress of the nation.

Goals of Voluntary Organizations

Organizations, being a deliberate and purposive creation, have some goals. The ends for which they strive are variously referred to as 'purpose', 'mission,' 'goal', 'target', or 'objective'. Though there is some difference in these terms, they are used interchangeably in practice. This goal-oriented aspect of organizations indicates that organizations have goals, though some people assert that organizations do not have goals, rather individuals engaged in them have goals.

There is another viewpoint in this regard. Parsons has pointed out that organizational goals are intimately intertwined with important and basic societal functions, such as integration, pattern maintenance, and so on. From this point of view, organizational goals are really an extension of what the society needs for its own survival. Thus, if these views are integrated, the actual goals of the organization result from a continuous bargaining-learning process and, therefore organizations have multiple goals. At the same time, the determination of a goal for collective action becomes a standard by which the collective action is judged. This approach is similar to that of Simaon. He notes that when we are interested in the internal structure of an organization, the problem cannot be avoided. Either we must explain organizations in terms of the goals of individual members of the organizations or we must postulate the existence of one or more organizational goals, over and above the goals of the individuals.

Organizational Structure and Laws Governing It

Organization structure is somewhat illusive. However, it is real and affects everyone in the organization. In a simple term, structure is the pattern in which various parts or components are interrelated or interconnected. Thus, organization structure is the established pattern of relationships among components or parts of the organization that prescribes the relationship among various positions and activities. Since these positions are held by individuals, the structure is the relationship among people in the organization.

The organization structure being abstract, is not visible in the same way as a biological or mechanical structure, though it can be inferred from the actual operation and behaviour of the organization. The biological and mechanical systems, such as organisms and machines, can be identified even when they are not working because they have both anatomy and physiology. The study of the anatomy is basically the study of the structure of the organism, whereas the physiology is concerned with the study of the function of living organisms. Thus, biological and mechanical systems can be studied in both these terms of structure as well as function. This is not the case with social systems, which do not have both anatomy and physiology. As such, it is very difficult, if not impossible, to make distinction between structure and process of the origination. In fact, some authors suggest that it is not possible to study the structure of the organization as distinct from its social process. A social system is a structuring of events or happenings rather than of physiological parts and it, therefore, has no structure apart from its functioning.

The need for organization structure arises because large numbers of people are associated in achieving organizational objectives. They perform a number of functions. As such, there must be a plan for the systematic completion of the work of each specialized job, so that the total activities accomplish a single objective. The basic purpose of designing organization structure should be three-fold:

(i) All the necessary activities are performed; no unnecessary activity is done.

(ii) There is no unnecessary duplication in performing necessary activities.

(iii) The various activities are performed in a synchronized and coordinated way.

Any structure fulfilling these requirements is suitable for the organization. However, contingency approach of organizing suggests that there cannot be a particular structure, which can be suitable for all organizations. Rather the appropriateness of the structure is determined by a number of factors, these factors can broadly be classified as: environment, technology, size, and people. An analysis of these factors may show how they might influence an organization's actions in designing an organization structure. The strength of each will, of course, vary from instance to instance, but the management, which is quite sensitive to them, can better assess the problems and decide which mode of organization structure is appropriate for it.

Leadership: Nature and Types

Human beings are the most civilized among living beings. Organization cannot develop without leadership, since it is a confused mass. Leadership is the ability to persuade others to seek defined objectives.

Human factor binds a group together and motivates it towards goals. Leadership changes potential into reality. It is the final act that brings to success all the potential that is in an organization and its people.

Leadership is important for group achievement that people are concerned with from the beginning.

Nature of Leadership

Leadership is the relationship in which one person or leaders influences others to work together willingly on related areas to attain that the leader desires. Leadership form a part of management. It is the duty of the executive to plan and organise. There are two aspects of leadership: the influencing agent and the people who are influenced. Without followers, there can be no leader. A leader is like an engine on a train, if any coach is troublesome, engine cannot proceed, and if the engine is troublesome, it will have to be replaced. Leadership is an interpersonal influence, exercised in situations and directed through the communication process, towards the attainment of a specified goal or goals. It is the knack of getting other people to follow you and to do willingly things you want them to do.

Characteristics

Some of the major characteristics of leadership can be mentioned as follows:

1. There exits mutual behaviour pattern between leader and his followers.
2. It is a two way affair. The followers influences behaviour of leader and leader influences the behaviour of followers.
3. Concept of leadership can be understood in the context of followers.
4. It involves element of willingness and voluntary obedience.
5. It is specific to a specific situation. A person cannot be a leader in all the fields.

Pre-requisite of Effective Leadership

The essential requirements of effective leadership may be mentioned as follows:

1. Ability to develop initiative among group.
2. Ability to take decisions and exercise authority.
3. Personal interests should be secondary.

4. Ability to maintain membership.
5. Ability to resolve internal conflicts.

Role of Leader

A leader is supposed to perform following roles and functions:

1. As a Planner: Planning the strategy.
2. Spokesperson: Speaking for behalf of members.
3. Harmoniser: Who creates harmony among the group members.
4. Educator: The one who educates the group members towards the acceptance of strategy or method to achieve the goal.
5. Decision-maker: Taking right decisions according to the needs of the members.
6. Develop leadership to others: Delegating the responsibilities to subordinates to take up the charge after his/her term.

In order to perform the above-mentioned roles, a leader must possess the quality like: open mind to problems, will power, judgement, flexibility, knowledge, enthusiasm, skill for integrity, intelligence, dynamic thinking, sympathetic approach, courage, impartial, health and physical fitness, etc.

Types of Leadership

According to H.T. Mazumdar, there are three kinds of leadership:

(i) Traditional,
(ii) Bureaucratic, and
(iii) Charismatic.

Traditional leader gets his authority through the traditional status ascribed to him. Thus, the Brahmin is the traditional leader of Hindu society. The bureaucratic leader gets his authority and power through delegation, i.e., from election or from appointment. The charismatic leader creates his own authority. He may be a party leader, a religious leader, social leader or a revolutionary leader.

Bogardus has mentioned the following kinds of leadership:

(i) Direct and indirect leadership.
(ii) Social, executive and mental leadership.
(iii) Partisan and scientific leadership.
(iv) Prophets, saints, experts and boss.
(v) Autocratic, charismatic, paternal and democratic leadership.

None of the above classifications of leadership is completely satisfactory. First, we know far too little about the causal sequences in the life course of leaders; second, we have no adequate criterion for determining types; and third, the divergent historical situations in which leaders operate are hard to classify.

Process of Formation of Organizations

The organization process is the forming of structural inter-personal relationship. This process involves eight steps:

(i) Determination of organizational goals or objectives to be strived for;
(ii) Determination of the task requirements necessary to achieve the goals;
(iii) Division of tasks into different jobs to find out how many personnel will be needed for the complete tasks;
(iv) Integration of jobs into departments or other work groups to take advantage of the specialization and efficiency;
(v) Selection of personnel to fill jobs;
(vi) Assignment of work positions to the individuals;
(vii) Granting the authority to the people to carry out the duties of their jobs; and
(viii) Determination of superior-subordinate relationships for facilitating the performance evaluation.

An organization is a mechanism with which a management directs, coordinates and controls the activities of man.

Partnership with Government

Voluntary action is supplementing government efforts and programmes in the social welfare field instead of competing with it. There has been at times a feeling that some types of voluntary action are of the nature of confrontation or conflict with existing policies and programmes. However, in most instances these have been motivated with a desire to gain social justice for the deprived and disadvantaged groups in society. There has been a growing awareness that voluntary action can be much more effective and successful by establishing better working relationship with the government. The government has also endeavoured to support and strengthen such efforts in different ways. The steps taken by the government in this direction include setting up of the Central Social Welfare Board as early as 1953, to develop and support technically and financially, voluntary effort in the country socially, in relation to the welfare of women and children;

implementing a nation-wide large-scale grants-in-aid programme for supplementing, assisting and strengthening rather than substituting or replacing voluntary endeavour; regulating social welfare services and institutions organized by voluntary agencies through licensing of welfare institutions; ensuring minimum standards of services; preventing exploitation of staff and people; helping in the organization of training programmes to prepare a cadre of paid and voluntary workers; providing a forum for exchange of ideas and sharing of experience to evolve and develop common strategies for action.

Voluntary action itself stands at the crossroads. The nature and inspiration of voluntary action have evolved over decades. Starting from social reform, education and health services, voluntary action after independence has moved to welfare, relief and development. At times, voluntary action has been influenced by political factors. Development implies change, which can affect established interests and this is likely to generate tensions and conflicts. Development and social action can impinge on politics; different ideological positions may be adopted in attaining the goal of development with social justice to the underprivileged and the oppressed. Voluntary action has, until now, ventured by and large in aiding government programmes. Success of voluntary action draws local politicians, bureaucrats and other functionaries, for gaining credit and thereby enhance their own popularity.

Indian public opinion should be mobilized to contribute funds for worthwhile social action programmes and projects through voluntary action as much as for disaster relief. Trusts, temples, waifs, gurudwaras, churches, charities, religious and other endowments, and industry command substantial resources, which could be productively and purposefully used in support of voluntary action. It should be possible over time to raise significantly large funds through a variety of fund raising drives that mobilize and harness contributions though flag days, sale of greeting cards, raffles, jumble sales, sponsored works, charity concerts, film premiers, sporting events, and public appeals. Tax concessions would provide an added incentive to make contributions in amounts that qualify for tax rebates.

In the development of voluntary action, the major problem at the moment is not funds but ideas, and people's organization. Any worthwhile idea generally attracts funds even if this takes times. It is not yet adequately appreciated that the awakening of a community through education and organization marks a vital pre-investment phase.

Planning in Organization

Planning

Meaning of Planning

Planning is necessary for providing effective services, constructing infrastructure, setting up an administrative structure, organizing conferences, raising funds or even arranging meeting with the committee. According to the draft of the First Five-Year Plan, "planning is essentially a way of organizing and utilizing resources to the maximum advantage in terms of defined social end". The two main attributes or constituents of the concepts of planning are:

(a) A system of ends to be pursued; and
(b) Knowledge of available resources and their optimum allocation.

Unplanned administration is haphazard, scattered, disorderly and confusing. Planning is simply the introduction of orderly thinking into the areas of life which have hither to been ruled by unconsidered judgement. Planning is conscious and deliberate guidance of thinking so as to create logical means of achieving desired goals. Planning always and inevitably sets priorities and calls for value judgements. Planning is a basic and fundamental approach or way of dealing with the human problems, which besets us. Planning is a point of view, an attitude, an assumption that says it is possible for us to anticipate, predict, guide and control our own destiny.

Planning is fostering the thinking of a group of people, poised for development, and synchronizing their thoughts with their needs and abilities for an anticipated action, which will result in their welfare.

Planning is the blueprint of action, visualizing and foreseeing inherent bottlenecks in implementation as a result of the various system operation, when physical inputs, will of people and technology are harmonized for human welfare. The planning process brings forth a set of questions namely, the purpose, the methodology, the strategy, the beneficiaries, etc., of planning along with the what, whom, who and why of planning.

Steps of Planning

Planning is introduction of orderly thinking in the area of life which have so far been ruled by unconsidered judgement. It is an intellectual process which sets priorities and calls for value judgement. Planning decides the course of action. It is an assumption to predict and control over destiny. The important steps of planning may be as follows:

(i) Define the problem.
(ii) Gathering of facts.
(iii) Studying implication of problem learned through involvement of experts and research personnel.
(iv) Finding solution of the problem.
(v) Action and maintenance of the programme.
(vi) Evaluation of the programme.

Principles of Planning

There are some basic principles, which must be kept in mind in any planning process.

(i) *Participation*: Planning should not just come from the top, it should be done at all levels. Discussions with concerned departments or a group of people or individuals will be helpful to make effective plans, instead of one man at the top deciding everything on his own thinking. It should ensure participation of all levels in the picture.
(ii) *Continuous Process*: Planning is not an end; but it is a continuous process. Because pitfalls in a plan are corrected and revised periodically, if the plan is not achieving the expected goals.
(iii) *Objectives*: Objectives of planning must be laid down beforehand to make a plan effective. If the objectives are not clear the plans made out for them are definitely out of the mark.
(iv) *Need Basis*: Planning should grow out of the need of the people, so as to make it effective. Adequate factual data may be made in basic planning.
(v) *Requirement*: Planning requires professional skills, leadership and understanding the thinking of layperson. Planning constructed on the basic requirement is definitely effective with no doubts.
(vi) *Method of Evaluation*: Planning requires education of the people on proper thinking. The community needs and resources must be taken into consideration while planning. Effective evaluation methods should be used to make sure the effectiveness of planning.

Therefore, before launching any welfare programme, proper planning with the help of useful data and technical personnel are very necessary. Proper thinking should be given to 'what' 'how' and 'why' of a particular service or performance, so that the pros and cons of a project are well thought out, pitfalls are avoided, effective methods are used and maximum economy is exercised.

Planning is nothing but anticipating and attempting to exercise some influence on the direction of the future event. It is an important human process. Community planning is very much needed to have positive effect in community problem-solving function. For example, poorly planned projects may affect the community as a whole, and this type of planning is more positively oriented. It always has reference to other related or similar projects so as to have enough coordination. Previous survey or researches done on similar issues also will help in planning.

Social Welfare Administration and Voluntary Organizations

A voluntary agency may be defined as: "An organization that is administered by an autonomous board which holds meetings, collects funds for its support, chiefly from private sources, and expends money, whether with or without paid workers, in conducting a programme directed primarily to furthering the public health by providing health services or health education or by advancing research or legislation for health, or by a combination of these activities."

The voluntary organizations are different from the non-official organizations, because non-official organizations are an instance of inducted voluntarism by the state, which may or may not secure popular support.

Voluntary organizations fall in two groups:

(1) *Non-Profit and Non-Partisan Organizations*: Non-profit and non-partisan organizations are those voluntary organizations which have legal entity. It should have broad-based objectives serving the social and economic needs of the community as a whole and mainly the weaker sections. It should not work for profit but on "no profit no loss basis". Its activities should be open to all citizens of India irrespective of religion, caste, creed, sex or race. It should have the necessary flexibility, professional competence and organizational skills to implement programmes. Its office bearers should have organizational skills to implement programmes. Its office bearers should not be elected members of any political party. It should adopt constitutional and non-violent means for development. It should be constituted to secular and democratic concepts and methods of functioning.

(2) *Conventional Voluntary Organizations*: As pointed out earlier, conventional voluntary organizations are those, which have their own constitution, elected office bearers with defined division of responsibility of the office bearers, etc.

In the Seventh Five-Year Plan, greater stress has been laid for the involvement of voluntary organizations in the implementation of development programmes. More specifically, the voluntary organizations are asked to perform the role in the following directions:

(a) To supplement government efforts so as to offer the rural people choices and alternatives;
(b) To be the eyes and ears of the people at village level;
(c) To set an example, it should be possible for the voluntary organizations to adopt simple innovative, flexible and inexpensive means with its limited resources to reach a larger number with less overheads and with greater community participation;
(d) To activate the delivery system and to make it effective at the felt needs of the poorest of the poor;
(e) To show how village support and inadequate resources could be used, as well as how human resources, rural skills and local knowledge grossly unutilized at present could be used for their own development;
(f) To mobilize and organize the poor and generate awareness to demand quality services and impose a community system of accountability on the performance of village level government functionaries.

Voluntary organization in the country have played a pioneering role in the provision of welfare services for the vulnerable sections especially for women, children and the handicapped. The decade that followed India's Independence marked a phenomenal increase in the number of voluntary agencies in the country; they have expanded their activities to cover practically every field of social welfare.

Budget, Voluntary Service in Budget

Meaning of Budget

A budget is a complete financial forecast based on available data about the financial condition of the agency during the coming year. It is a process of determining and distribution of funds for certain welfare services based on an examination of needs and availability and effectiveness of the programmers to deal with them and the relevant importance attached to them by the community. It is an estimate of the proposed expenditure for securing the income required. As one of the tools of financial administration, budget is a basic means of controlling the programmes as well as funds. In other words, it is the programme of the work of the agency expressed in rupees and paise. Through the budget we plan for the future of the origination in terms of income, which must be made available and expenditure, which necessitates income and the services, which will require that expenditure.

Voluntary Service in Budget

Most agencies do not run their entire services only with the help of paid staff, some times it becomes necessary to enlist the cooperation of voluntary workers for running various programmes. An agency might enlist the services of persons who might do the job of a nursery teacher, a craft instructor, a recreation worker, medical man or an accountant. In all these cases the contribution of these persons, is as good as cash, which should always be evaluated in terms of money. This could be done by indicating the cash value of such services both on the income and on the expenditure side of the budget. While evaluating voluntary services, the following factors should be taken into consideration:

(a) Experience and educational background of the volunteers;
(b) Market rate of salaries for the personnel rendering voluntary services; and
(c) The time spent by each of such persons.

Problems of Organization

Generally, as stated before, there is a multiplicity of organizations working in the same areas and in identical and similar fields with the result that there is a considerable duplication and consequent waste of resources, Besides, the quality of services provided by these agencies is rather poor. The reasons are lack of finances, employment of untrained personnel, no clear-cut demarcation of function between the voluntary and paid staff and lack of proper equipment and building. Although the problems of public and private social welfare agencies are almost the same, i.e., of planning, organizing, staffing, directing, coordination, reporting, and budgeting, yet for convenience sake we may discuss the problems of voluntary agencies under the following heads:

Programme Activities

The scope of voluntary organization to organize welfare programmes is very wide. They can cover all types of activities, which are in the nature of palliative, rehabilitative or protective activities for all types of groups discussed in the foregoing pages. As Lord Beveridge points out: "Individual philanthropic agencies differ from one another so widely that they cannot be made the subject of a useful statistical summary. They can be grouped under various heads on the basis of services rendered by them, or the area they serve. These may be agencies for the welfare of children, youth, women, old persons, etc., or for the welfare of the physically, mentally or emotionally handicapped, for family welfare services, or for rural and urban communities."

The voluntary workers can assist the agencies in many ways. Some people may donate money, while others may give their free time for services whether as members of the managing committee, as administrators, or may help in welfare, recreational, cultural, educational or some other activity to supplement the services of the paid staff. Due to the multifariousness of the welfare programmes in the country, volunteers could be made use of for various types of services – administrative, technical, financial, etc., whereas some persons may not be able to contribute on the programme side, or on the business side. They may contribute by helping the agency to prepare budgets, compile accounts, as also in fund-raising campaigns some could also help the agencies in public relations work by producing some material for the press and the radio, others may work as experts by being on various committees.

Financial Resources and Regulation

Charity has always held a high and respected place in the cultural heritage of India. The basis of this charity has been personal salvation and the satisfaction that poor people are helped by the charity given by a donor. However, there are many factors, which have affected this charity. In the past, the voluntary welfare agencies in this country have been depending on the charity raised from a few wealthy people and government assistance has been negligible. But in this case the donors sometimes dictate their own terms for using the money for specific purposes or meeting the needs of a particular community. Moreover, religious forces behind charity are weakening. There are economic motives, which sometimes forces rich people to donate some money or land to the charitable organizations, e.g., ceilings on land, high taxation after a particular level of income. But, at the same time, private resources are drying up due to high taxation and more and more means of production going into the hands of the state. In spite of these difficulties, some funds are to be raised by the voluntary organizations, so that they may keep up their voluntary character and indicate that some good people have concern for others. It cannot be denied that government grants have increased, yet some funds are to be raised through voluntary contributions. Lord Beveridge observes: with the changed distribution of income and of leisure, many philanthropic agencies are faced with difficult problems of finance and of obtaining sufficient voluntary service. But still, the mass of people are prepared to give money. However, there are some programmes for which people would like to give more than for others. People may give money for war victims, for animals and then for children. Similarly, it is much easier to get money for crippled children than to get money for crippled adults. It is particularly difficult to get money for administrative expenditure, yet without such expenditure the voluntary agencies cannot be well managed. These contributions may be in the form of donations, subscriptions, income from fixed assets, sale proceeds, special campaigns, donations in kind, lotteries and shows.

In the raising of funds different agencies use different methods depending upon the circumstances. It is possible that some unscrupulous persons may misuse the funds and, therefore, proper check on the collection and use of money is necessary. On the other hand, it is also necessary that the government should be liberal in granting exemption from entertainment tax to agencies, which collect funds from cultural, or cinema shows.

Personnel

Proper staff is a very important tool of administration. This is particularly true about social work, which has been accepted as a profession. Since the agency needs technically trained personnel for running various welfare programmes on proper basis, it needs to recruit suitably trained staff with aptitude for social work. The staff should be recruited according to a personnel policy already laid down by the agency. Regardless of the previous education and experience, a new recruit requires a designated and a carefully planned orientation period of adjustment to the specific duties for which he is being employed. The agency has to orient its employees to the policies and procedures in the form of in-service training.

The idea is still prevalent that in order to serve one's fellow men, the qualifications necessary are a spirit of dedication, a large measure of goodwill and some leisure. But, it cannot be denied that along with these qualities some training is also essential, as social work is becoming a profession. The social problems are complex and must be studied on a comprehensive scientific basis. While it may not be possible immediately to replace the existing paid and voluntary workers running the programmes of agencies by professionally trained workers, it may be worthwhile to have orientation programmes both for voluntary and paid workers.

Voluntary workers need special training. When charity meant giving money or food or clothes it needed little training. When voluntary service means running a citizens' advice bureau or a training college for the disabled, the best intentions are not enough without skill. The public authorities may have enough money to start such services by recruiting qualified staff, but they are apt to be slow in recognizing the needs for specialized training. Voluntary agencies, being specialist by nature, more easily recognize the need of special qualifications and training in their work. Training courses for voluntary social workers who administer such programme need to be given in institutes or universities for a short-term. In this respect, the Central Institute of Research and Training in Public Cooperation has to take initiative and make necessary financial provision.

The pay scale attached to a job should be decided keeping in view the nature of the assignment, the type of personnel required and training for it. However, generally the employees in the voluntary agencies are low paid as compared to the terms and conditions of employment in other government or commercial establishments. To give security of service to employees of voluntary organizations the state government will have to prescribe certain rules and regulations for these employees by fixing the minimum salaries of employees of various categories, employment of trained staff and certain other conditions of service.

Coordination

Coordination has been defined as "a process of bringing into logical and organic relationship". It means adjustment, harmony and cooperation to achieve certain ends. There has to be coordination not only among the various units within the agency, but also between various agencies – public and private – which are providing social service in a community.

The coordination within the agency means: (a) Coordination between various departments of the agency; (b) Coordination between various staff members of the agency; (c) Coordination between various sub-committees of the board; and (d) Coordination between the board and the staff.

Coordination between agencies working in the community is of two types: functional and geographical. In the first case one agency supervises and coordinates the work of other agencies in the same field like the Indian Council for Child Welfare, the All India Women' s Conference. These agencies coordinate the work of the state branches and state branches in turn coordinate the work of district units in any definite field, say, child welfare or women's welfare.

Coordination is also necessary among the various agencies working in different fields in a community or a geographical area. As it is not possible to earmark a well-defined area to an agency and if there is no effective method of coordination, some overlapping is bound to arise. Therefore, there is a need to have coordination among all the welfare agencies in one community, so that one existence of the agency is helpful to another in making its programme more useful to the community. For instance, a home for children may get the services of a dispensary or a hospital in the neighbourhood instead of organizing medical services for the inmates. Similarly, a home for unmarried mothers could utilize a foundling home in the community for placing children.

Voluntary Action, Organization and Social Work

Organization as a Resource

The functions of the modern entrepreneurial organization whether it be privately or publicly owned and operated, may be categorized as follows:

(1) The undertaking or managing of risk and the handling of economic uncertainty;
(2) Planning and innovation;
(3) Coordination, administration and control; and
(4) Routine supervision.

In the very small enterprise, of course, these functions may all be performed by a single person – the proprietor. In larger establishment, there may be a division of functions among a complex hierarchy of individuals. Ownership may be separated from management and management itself may be subdivided into line and staff management. Obviously, the large organization requires more managerial functionaries and perhaps different types and combinations can be quite simple or very complex, depending upon the nature of the business activity, the size of the firm, and the technology employed.

This concept of organization is perhaps most useful in analysing the prerequisites for economic growth in under-developed countries and the reasons for accelerated or retarded growth in more advanced countries. It provides a framework for tangible comparative studies of the role of entrepreneurship in industrial development. In this connection, let us now consider a few tentative propositions.

These propositions are based upon some acquaintanceship over the past two years with approximately seventy-five business enterprises in the following countries: England, France, Germany, Italy, Belgium, Holland, Egypt, Saudi Arabia, Peru, and the United States. This acquaintanceship consists of a visit of a day or two in about three-fifths of the cases and more intensive studies of the managerial organizations and labour policies, averaging about two weeks per enterprise, in the other two-fifths. Admittedly, the evidence at this stage of the research is more impressionistic than definitive. For this reason, the observations which follow are set forth as tentative propositions worthy of more exhaustive study rather than as final conclusion resulting from systematic research.

Role of Professional Social Worker in Voluntary Action and Voluntary Organization

Not many published research studies in the field of voluntary action are available. A study of voluntary social welfare in India by Chowdhary in based on data collected from 6,000 voluntary agencies, 600 *Mahila Mandals* and 66 national organizations. The basic objective of the study was to determine the concept, scope, extent and forms of voluntary work in India which covered about 400 agencies and 856 volunteers in nine cities. Since a majority of voluntary welfare agencies are clustered in the metropolitan cities, the study sample has been drawn mainly from Delhi, Mumbai, Ahmedabad, Chennai, Bangalore, Hyderabad, Lucknow, Patna, and Amritsar.

In the earlier times most of the workers were unpaid, but now they are gradually being replaced by professionals and paid workers. For the full time given to voluntary work, the workers have to earn a living to maintain themselves and their families. The work, too, demands sustained attention of qualified personnel.

Workers in voluntary agencies in many cases function as multi-purpose functionaries largely due to inadequate personnel and material resources. Consequently, they are often found doing work unrelated to their education and professional competence. Recruitment and selection of workers is done through informal channels, personal contacts, camps or work-projects and advertisements to the different methods; recruitment through advertisements plays the least part in getting volunteers. The second and third of the studies mentioned above confirm that a high proportion of workers have come through personal contacts of the personnel already involved in the agencies in one capacity or another. One of the interesting findings of the second study was that one-fifth of the professionally qualified workers became volunteers on their own initiative by contacting the agencies with an open offer of their services. This had been done to gain experience to enable them to qualify for a paid job. Some give time to social work after attending to some other full-time work. Professionally qualified and married women who had ample leisure time, willingly came forward to gainfully and fruitfully use their talent and time.

The field of voluntary action is expected to attract both men and women. According to the third study, a majority of the workers in voluntary organizations are men whereas findings of the second study indicate that volunteers specially in women welfare agencies, are mostly women. But the same study states that in the field of community welfare and backward class welfare, men predominate. Workers in may cases do not belong to the regions where they work. More than 50 per cent are drawn from urban areas and more of them belong to the middle class.

The leadership, with some exception, is concentrated in the hands of elderly persons. Their style of functioning exhibits a combination of authoritarian and democratic leadership. The younger persons who have just been elevated to the position of leadership are found to be more democratic than their older colleagues.

There is a tendency towards monopolization and interlocking of leadership at the top level of voluntary action groups and organizations. This interlocking of leadership can be advantageous in formulating coordinated policies, programmes and activities, facilitating exchange of technical knowhow and experience, and mobilizing people for a common goal and task. The greatest disadvantage of such leadership is that fresh blood is not allowed to flow into the organizations and leadership becomes routinized and rigid.

7

Human Resource Development

Human Resource Development (HRD) is not only a social pre-condition of economic growth but is a major factor for growth with equity and social justice. The human resource investment is not merely a means to and end, but also an end in itself to enable people to live a good and abundant life. The human resource if it remains idle tends to get obsolete at a faster rate than physical capital. The investment in human resource does not depreciate its value during the period of its use. The decision relating to human investment is not measurable in rate of return concept, but it leads to enhancement of freedom, dignity and worth of man for enabling individuals to lead a healthy progressive and creative life. Human resource adds to value, while all other resources adds to the cost. All the firms buy the same material and the machines but it is the people in the firm who build the organization and make a difference in the final product. A machine's maximum value reaches the day it starts producing, whereas, man never reaches an ultimate value throughout his lifetime at work, but is able to change, grow and enrich his value. Success of an organization mainly depends on the quality of its manpower and its performance. Any forward looking management will be greatly concerned with the problems of developing adequate talent for manning various positions in the organization.

The HRD department was created to identify, develop and implement various systems of developing employees in addition to mere training which was so far done by the Personnel department.

Performance appraisals, feedback, counselling, potential appraisal, organization development, etc., were identified and perceived by this department in addition to training. The expression HRD originated in India quite some time ago.

Our Education ministry has however been strong enough in playing a crucial role in the past, in the formation of HRD ministry and in the renaming of the Personnel department as HRD department. Here, most of the organized sectors have their own HRD mechanism. For the unorganized sector, the education system constitutes the most important HRD mechanism and there is considerable scope. Work would have to be done by the ministry in identifying and preparing a list of HRD needs and how they are to be met. The objective here is not to go into the functions of the HRD ministry but merely to show that even at the topmost levels in India the expressions HRD has gained recognition.

Human Resources in the Organization

Human resource approach assumes that the job or task itself is the primary source of satisfaction and motivation to employees – the emphasis in the human resource approach is on individual involvement in the decisions made in the organizations. Organizations of today are producing products and service, which were unknown in the past and thus giving a new life with more material comforts than ever before. All these comforts are possible through the effective utilization of human resources, which need to be polymerized in an organization to result into a cohesive and enormous force.

HRD Concept

In recent years, there has been recognition of the importance of the valuable asset that human beings are in an organization. This has led to the use of the term 'Human Resource Development' (HRD) and even replacing the words, personnel management.

In the organizational context, human resource development can be defined as – a process in which the employees of an organization are continuously helped in a planned way to:

(i) Acquire or sharpen capabilities required to perform various tasks and functions associated with their present or future expected goals.

(ii) Develop their general capabilities as individuals so that they are able to discover and exploit their own inner potential for their own and for their organizational purposes.

(iii) Develop an organizational culture where superior-subordinate relationship, teamwork and collaboration among different sub-units are strong and to contribute to the organizational health, dynamism and pride of employees.

The human resource development is the process of increasing knowledge, skills and capacities of the people of the organization. It is important not only for an organization but also for the entire nation. A nation cannot develop its economy unless it is able to develop its human resources. Generally included in HRD are all the structures, systems and process which an organization uses to help its employees acquire additional strength with their capabilities. This sometimes is referred to as HRD technology.

System of HRD

The systems approach to organization is really a way of thinking about the HRD problem. It views organization as a group of interrelated parts with a single purpose. Because the actions of one part influence the others, managers cannot deal separately with the individual parts. In solving problems, managers using the systems must view the organization as a dynamic whole and must try to anticipate the intended, as well as, unintended impacts of their decisions. Such as managers do not solve the individual's problems, rather they intervene in a total system of interrelated parts, using the organizational functions of planning, organizing and controlling.

Strategy of HRD

The term 'strategy' has been adapted from war, and is used in business to reflect the broad overall objectives and policies of an enterprise. It refers to the firm's overall plan for dealing with factors existing in its environment. Most often, it denotes a general programme of action and emphasis on deployment of resources to attain comprehensive objectives. A strategy is made in the light of the plans of the competitors. An organization's strategy should match between the organization's resources and skills and the environment opportunities and risk it faces. It reflects, in other words the course of action through which the organization plans to adapt to the threats and opportunities in its environment and thereby maintain its effectiveness.

According to Gluecks and Jauch, "A strategy is a unified, comprehensive and integrated plan designed to ensure that the basic objectives of the enterprises are achieved." According to Schendal and Halter, Strategy refers to the basic goals and objectives of the organization, the major programme of action chosen to reach these goals, and objectives and major pattern of resources allocation used to relate the organization to its environment strategies at different levels: corporate, business and functional level.

(i) *Corporate Level*: At the corporate level, strategic decisions relate to organization's wide policies as in the case of multi-divisional companies having wide ranging business operations. Ideally a corporate strategy should include:
   (a) the basic goals the firm hopes to achieve, for instance, in terms of market share or profit,
   (b) the firm's domain in terms of the project or service it will render and to whom, and
   (c) the basic strategic mores the firms plans to match, for instance, in terms of diversity or overseas trade.

(ii) *Business Level*: At the business level, the aim is to achieve the specific objectives of the strategic business unit (SBU) so as to help achieve the overall corporative objectives. SBU is an operating division of a firm, which serves a distinct product market segment as a well-defined set of customers or a geographic area. SBU is given the authority to make its own strategic decisions within corporate guidelines as long as it meets corporate objectives.

(iii) *Functional Level*: The ultimate success of the SBU level strategy will depend, among other things, on the effectiveness with which it is translated into functional areas like marketing, finance, production, personnel and R&D. Thus, it is obvious that functional level strategies are guided by the SBU level strategy.

Human Resource: The Emerging Trends

In the contemporary business environment, organizations are in a constant state of competition. As the intensity of competition increases annually, the need for the organizations to continuously improve their performance has never been so crucial before (Harrel and Tzafrir, 1999). Though traditional sources of competitive success like natural resources technology and economics of sale, add value to an organization, their significance is decreasing as these are easy to imitate.

Type of HR practices also send a strong message about the desired culture. Therefore, emphasis on development of appropriate HRD climate was equally important - HRD should contribute to management of culture. Pareek (1988) believed that the cultural aspect had been the most neglected part of HRD; it is important that HRD focus on organizational culture that will sustains the kind of effort HRD had developed. HR strategies can also serve as powerful tools for bringing about cultural changes and reinforcing those changes once they are made: maintained Grun (1985).

Nystrom's (1993) study suggests that an organization's prevailing culture also affects important outcomes, such as organizational commitment and performance. Abraham's study shows that it is a good HRD climate rather than HRD practices by themselves that are responsible for organizational performance. This does not indicate that good HRD climate were not important. One can create an appropriate HRD practices only through good HRD practices and process; thus literature suggests that HR practices of an organization contribute to the development of HRD climate. However, empirical evidence to support this view was found to be lacking. Literature focussing on this aspect was very limited and largely theoretical. The reviewed articles emphasized that, competitive pressure, changing social values and need pattern of employees, have encouraged organizations to adapt more innovative HR practices.

The organization also helped to enhance employee satisfaction and motivation, increase employee commitment, involvement and pride by way of adopting more people-sensitive HR practices. An impetus for HRD experimentation also deals with the growing aspirations of the executive. The need was increasingly expressed that HRD should become an integral part of organizational culture, thereby creating a climate that fosters employee potential.

Importance of HRD

The major significance of HRD may be stated as follows:

(i) Provides opportunities for people to function as human beings rather than mere resources in the productive process.

(ii) Gives each member individual opportunities to develop to his full potential.

(iii) Seeks to make the individual more effective in meeting all its goals.
(iv) Tries to create an environment in which exciting and challenging work can be found.
(v) Gives, people in an organization the chance to influence the work in the organization and the work environment.
(vi) Treats each human being as a person with a complex set of needs, all of which are important in his work and life.

Prerequisites for HRD System

Successful development tends to be a total systems effort. It is not a programme with a temporary quality. It is rather aimed at developing the organization's internal resources for effective change.

(i) *Support for HRD programme should begin with top management:* HRD is a system-wise concept requiring at least psychological involvement of all the parts of the system in the organization. All the support for the programme is essential and this support should begin with the top management. To overcome system failure, HRD programmes are designed using a vertical slice of the organization where all the members in the chain of command are exposed to the development process.
(ii) *Organization should communicate the objectives of the programme clearly*: The objectives of the programme must be made crystal-clear to all the participants. The organization in order to be effective must make the employees aware about its objectives and goals for its smooth functioning and willing cooperation of human resources.
(iii) *Enough time must be allowed so that the effects of HRD programme are released*: Things in organization are not expected to change drastically over a brief period of time. Managers who introduce intervention to change will be invariably disappointed if they expect quick results of HRD programme. It is because HRD aims at changing the conditioned behaviour of members, which is rather difficult and a time consuming affair. Conditioned behaviour does not change quickly and instantaneously and at time takes a considerable span of time.
(iv) *The role of outside consultant must be understood*: The OD consultant in his technical bag contains the necessary behavioural knowledge, technical problem solving abilities and clinical skills. He also possesses the personality and interpersonal competency to

use his self as an instrument of change. But his role in the organization must be properly understood to ensure the success of HRD programme from the organizational point of view in order to make it beneficial to the organization.

(v) *Use the appropriate intervention*: For the success of the programme use of appropriate intervention is essential and if it is inappropriate, it will have undesirable consequences. Depending on the target group, the organization must use the intervention appropriate methods of intervention in programme.

Principles of HRD

As a tool, HRD organization is expected to facilitate the achievement of certain objectives. In order to facilitate achievement thinkers have laid down certain statements from time to time from certain generally accepted understanding, which may be called the principles of HRD in an organization.

The important principles of HRD in an organization are as follows:

(1) *Consideration of Objectives*: An enterprise strives to accomplish certain objectives, using organization service as a tool to attain these objectives. The objectives must be stated in clear terms as they play an important role in determining the type of structure, which should be developed.

(2) *Division of Work and Specialization*: The entire work in the organization should be divided into various parts so that every individual is confined to the performance of a single job, as far as possible, according to his abilities and aptitudes. This is also called the principle of specialization. More a person continues on a particular job, the better will be his performance.

(3) *Definition of Jobs*: Every position in the organization should be clearly defined in relation to other positions in the organization. The duties and responsibilities assigned to every position and its relationship with other positions should be clearly defined so that there may not be any overlapping of functions.

(4) *Separation of Line and Staff Functions*: Whenever possible, line functions should be separated from staff activities. Line functions are those, which accomplish the main objectives of the company. In many manufacturing companies, the manufacturing and marketing department are considered to be accomplishing the

main objectives of the business and so are called line functions and other functions like personnel, plant maintenance, financing and legal are considered as staff functions.

(5) *Chain of Command*: There must be clear lines of authority running from the top to the bottom of the organization; clarity is achieved through delegation by steps or levels from the top position to the operating level. From the chief executive, a line of authority may proceed to department managers, to supervisors or foremen and finally to workers.

(6) *Party of Authority and Responsibility*: Responsibility should always be coupled with corresponding authority; each subordinate must have sufficient authority to discharge the responsibility entrusted to him. This principle suggests that if a plant manager in a multi-plant organization is held accountable for all activities in his plant, he should not be subject to orders from company headquarters specifying the quantity of raw materials he should buy or from whom he should purchase.

(7) *Unity of Command*: No one in the organization should report to more than one supervisor – stated simply, everyone should have only one boss. Receiving directions from several supervisors may result in confusion, chaos, conflict and lack of action. Therefore, each members of the organization should receive directions from and report to one superior only. This will avoid conflict of command and help in fixing responsibility.

(8) *Exceptional Matters*: This principle requires that organization structure should be so designed that one individual is required to go through the exceptional matters only. The subordinates should take all the routine decisions whereas problems involving unusual matters and policy decisions should be referred to a higher level.

(9) *Span of Supervision*: The span of supervision means the number of persons a supervisor can direct. If many number of employees report to a supervisor, his time will not be utilized properly. Whereas, on the other hand, there is a limit to the number of subordinates that can be efficiently supervised by an executive.

(10) *Balancing of Various Factors*: There should be proper balance in the formal structure of the organization or in regard to factors having conflicting claims within the organization among personnel.

(11) *Communication*: A good communication network is essential to achieve the objectives of an organization. No doubt the line of

authority provides ready-made channels of communication downward and upward, still some blocks in communication occur in many organizations. The confidence of a superior in his subordinates and two-way communication are the factors that unite an organization into an effectively operating system.

(12) *Flexibility*: The organization structure should be flexible so that it can be easily and economically adapted to the changes in the nature of business as well as technical innovations. Flexibility of organization structure ensures the ability to change with the environment before something serious occurs. Therefore, the organization should be such that it permits expansion and contraction without disrupting the basic activities.

(13) *Continuity*: Change is the law of nature. Many changes take place outside the organization. These changes must be reflected in the organization. For this, the form of organization structure must be organic which would help attain its objectives and ensure its effectiveness over a long period of time.

Functions of HRD

The functions of HRD are interdependent and interrelated, there is also overlapping of the functions, as for example, planning and control, organizing and staffing, directing and control and so on.

Planning

Planning is a mental process requiring the use of intellectual faculties, foresight and sound judgement. It is the determination of a course of action to achieve the desired result. It is the selection and relating of facts and the making and using of assumption or regarding the future in the visualization and formation of proposed activities believed necessary to achieve desired results. It is a must to ensure effective utilization of human and non-human resource to achieve the desired goals.

The following is the planning process:

(a) Determination of goals or objectives of enterprise.
(b) Forecasting.
(c) Search alternative course of action.
(d) Evaluation of various alternatives and formulation of a plan.
(e) Formulation of policies and procedure.
(f) Preparation of schedules, programmes and budgets.

Controlling

The function of controlling deals with the measurement and correction of the performance of persons against the pre-determined standards. E.F.L. Brech defined control as the process of checking actual performance against the agreed standard with view to ensuring satisfactory performance process of control involving the following steps: establishment of standards, measurement of performance, appraisal of performance and taking corrective action.

(a) *Establishment of Standards*: The management must establish standards with which the actual performance of the subordinates will be compared. The standards of performance should be laid down in unambiguous terms and should be understood by everyone in the establishment.

(b) *Measurement of Performance*: After the performance is over, the actual performance has to be measured in terms of quantity, quality, cost and time. It is difficult to 'measure' mental work.

(c) *Appraisal of Performance*: The establishment of standards has no meaning unless they are used in actual practice. The management must provide for comparing the actual performance with the pre-established standards. The deviations from the standards should be recorded and brought to the knowledge of the management.

(d) *Taking Corrective Action*: When the deviations from the standards are reported to the management, it must take corrective action so that such deviations do not occur again. While taking corrective steps, management should also consider the improvement of plans and standards.

Organizing

Organizing involves identification and the grouping of activities to be performed and dividing them among the individuals and creating authority and responsibility relationships among them for the accomplishment of organizational objectives.

Staffing

The staffing function of management pertains to recruitment, selection, training, development and appraisal of personnel. There is a controversy whether staffing is function of every manager in the organization.

Directing/Leading

The term 'directing' or 'direction' is generally used in every walk of life and has got a side interpretation these days; it is not restricted to 'commanding', as viewed by Henry Fayol.

(i) *Communication*: Communication is a process of passing information and understanding from one person to another. This process is necessary for making the subordinates understand what the management expects from them.

(ii) *Leadership*: A manager must perform the function of leadership if he is to guide effectively for the achievement of organizational objectives. Leadership may be defined as the process by which a manager guides and influences the behaviour of his subordinate.

(iii) *Motivation*: Motivation means inspiring the subordinates with zeal to do work for the accomplishment of organizational objectives. It is necessary for getting voluntary cooperation of the subordinates.

(iv) *Supervision*: It means overseeing the functioning of the subordinates. Supervision is necessary to ensure that the subordinates are following the instructions given to them and are using raw materials, machines, etc., properly.

Manpower Planning

Manpower or human resource planning aims at ascertaining the manpower needs of the organization, both in right number and of right kind. It further aims at the continuous supply of right kind of personnel to man various positions in the organization. "Human Resource Planning is a process of determining and assuring that the organization will have an adequate number of qualified persons, available at the proper times, performing jobs which meet the needs of the enterprise and which provide satisfaction for the individuals involved."

Concept of Manpower Planning

Manpower planning is the *sine qua non* for all successful staffing. According to Geisler manpower planning including forecasting, developing and controlling is the process by which a firm ensures that it has the right number of people and the right kind of people at right place at the right time, doing work for which they are economically most useful. From this definition it is clear that manpower planning is a right tool in the hands of management to control labour costs, by avoiding both shortage and surplus of personnel in an organization. In a big organization the personnel department performs this function. As in case of any other function like marketing, production or finance, the personnel department's work has also to be planned. Planning in the personnel area is mainly concerned with crystallizing as to where from the right type of people can be secured for future anticipated vacancies. Vetter has defined manpower planning as: "The process by which management determines how the organization should move from its correct manpower position to its desired manpower position. Through planning, management strives to have the right number and the right kind of people at the right time, doing things, which result in both the organization and the individual receiving maximum long run benefit." According to Golden McBeth "Manpower planning involves two stages. The first stage is concerned with the detailed planning of manpower requirement for all types and levels of employees throughout the period of the plan and the second stage is concerned with planning of manpower supply to provide the organization with the right type of people from all sources to meet the planned requirements."

Need for Manpower Planning

In terms of manpower needs, the staffing function has to be performed by the personnel department. This involves procurement and selection, which may be done from outside sources or could include promotions and transfers from within the organization to jobs for which the existing personnel are more suitable. The providing of an appropriate organization climate is also important from the viewpoint of performance likely to emanate from the personnel concerned. For securing maximum motivation, it is always better to encourage existing employees instead of importing new blood for higher appointments. Therefore, as far as possible, it is more effective to meet the manpower requirements from within the organization itself.

(i) *Manpower Inventory*: This involves taking an inventory of the existing personnel to compare what exists in stock with what can be expected in stock at further dates, Thus, the first step in anticipating vacancies is to take an inventory of the current manpower of the unit to determine its capability. This has to be compared with the future organizational structure, which will influence the total manpower requirement at a future point of time.

(ii) *Expected Loss and Extra Needs*: Whilst planning, for say a period of five years, the expected loss situation can be evaluated in terms of settlement, transfer and other causes such as death and disability. In good organizations, their own expected loss rates are estimated on the basis of their own past experience. Their expected losses are examined in terms of organization levels. In this way the future vacancies are the manpower needs which the organization can anticipate. The manpower forecasts is thus concerned with anticipating the number of replacement required by reasons of: (1) resignations, (2) retirements, (3) deaths, (4) dismissals, (5) transfers, and (6) promotions. In addition to this, there must be a forecast of the number of additions needed to the staff because of the anticipated growth or reorganization.

(iii) *Manpower Planning Method*: The four methods generally used to determine the requirements of personnel are: (1) annual estimate, (2) fixed minimum manpower specification requirements, (3) long range estimates of vacancies, and (4) specific position estimation. Annually, the top management team and the directors must examine their organization structure and its adequacy for assigned functions as well as its adaptability for changes anticipated in the near future. This analysis or audit includes a review of the current vacancies and probable future changes in the organization's personnel.

(iv) *Manpower Planning Steps*: Manpower planning should basically be done by observing the following steps:

(1) Determine the period for forecasting requirements of manpower in the future and forecast the manpower required at the end of such period.

(2) From the number available on the commencement of the period, deduct the expected wastage through deaths, resignation, retirements and discharges. This could give the manpower requirements available from existing staff at the end of the period concerned.

(3) In case of shortage, decide how much shortage are to be met and whether any training or development facilities would be required for this purpose.

Surpluses will be dealt with through early retirements, discharges or lay off, etc.

(v) *Responsibility for Manpower Resource Plan*: In the final analysis the overall responsibility for manpower planning must be squarely on the Board of Directors. This is because Board members are in a position to direct the future course of business, set appropriate goals for concerned management in formulation of personnel policy.

(vi) *Manpower Forecasting*: In this a firm or agency uses the instrument called 'management review' as a method of forecasting. This is prepared every year for the next five years and is very similar to the cash forecasts undertaken in an organization. Its objective is to evaluate "in terms of managers the needs of our business which will arise out of expansion of products, new projects and various organizational changes. There needs are then equated with the company's internal resources likely to be generated through promotions from staff to managements, the losses that are likely to occur through retirements and losses through anticipated and unexpected separations".

(vii) *Manpower Development*: Tied in with manpower planning is obviously manpower development. Management of the company realizes that it takes time to make managers particularly to equip them for higher levels of managerial responsibility. Planned transfer and across postings are also used by the company as part of developmental activities. Thus the job of management of good companies are to develop skills in their employees showing potential. This can be only done through adequate manpower planning which makes it possible to plan the career of employees having the necessary potential.

Forms of Manpower Planning

There are two forms of manpower planning: (i) short-term manpower, planning, and (ii) long-term manpower planning.

Short-term Manpower Planning

This planning is done to find a temporary match between the existing individuals and the existing jobs. It aims at quick removal of anomalies in posting and placements following all the steps involved in this planning.

(i) The first step is to identify the weak and strong incumbents. Weak incumbents are those whose skills fall short of their job requirements; similarly, strong incumbents are those whose skills far exceed their job requirements.

(ii) The second step is to set the above anomalies right. In the case of weak incumbents this can be done by:
   (a) assigning difficult parts of their job to others,
   (b) improving them through short-term training or counselling, and
   (c) replacing them by other individuals.

   In the case of strong incumbents the anomaly may be set right by giving them more skilled and difficult jobs. But in no case should their higher skills become a cause for them.

(iii) The final step is to think of persons who can be given additional charge of posts falling unexpectedly vacant due to sudden death, resignation or transfer of the original incumbent.

Long-term Manpower Planning

This planning is done to find a proper match between the future jobs and their future incumbents. The steps that are involved in this planning are as follows:

(i) The first step is to determine the requirement of manpower for a particular period. This is done by making forecasts. Forecasts of future manpower requirements can be made for a period of two to five years. If the period selected is too long, it would be difficult to have an accurate manpower planning in view of the inability to predict effectively the likely changes in the economic, social and technological spheres.

   For forecasting the number of ranks and file of workers, it is better first to make forecasts of sales. On the basis of the sales forecast, we know the schedule of production for various products and the total quantity required to be produced. During the particular period when the output of various departments is ascertained, the requirement of manpower to enable the various departments to attain the required output can be very easily estimated. To make a forecast of the number of executives needed at the end of a particular period and the number of managerial positions that currently exist should first of all be counted with the help of complete and up-to-date organization chart. In the next step, allowance should be made for (a) foreseeable expansion or contraction in the organization structure on the basis of plans, if any, and (b) estimated deaths, retirements and turnover in managerial personnel on the basis of an annual average calculated, say, for preceding five years.

(ii) The second step is to abstain the existing number of rank and file workers in each section, department and unit, and to compare it with the required number. In case the required number is more than the available number, the next step would be to consider, how such shortages are to be provided for, whether through recruitment or through promotion. In case, the available number is more than the number required, the next step would be to consider, how to get rid of the excess hands, i.e., whether through premature retirement or discharge or lay-off, etc.

In case of managerial personnel, their existing number should be worked out for each of the following four categories:

(a) Promotable.
(b) Not promotable through retainable.
(c) Not retainable (i.e., to be replaced).
(d) About to retire.

(iii) The final step is to determine the need for and the kind of training, which must be given to the existing and new employees.

Process of Manpower Planning

The following are briefly the stages of the planning process:

Job Analysis

Job analysis may be defined as a process of discovering and identifying the pertinent information relating to the nature of a specific job. It is the determination of the tasks, which comprise the job, and of the skills, knowledge, abilities and responsibilities required of the worker for successful performance of the job. The process of job analysis is essentially one of data collection and then analysing that data. It provides the analyst with basic data, pertaining to specific jobs in terms of duties, responsibilities, skills, knowledge, etc. This data may be classified as follows:

(a) Job identification
(b) Nature of the job
(c) Operations involved in doing the job
(d) Materials and equipment to be used in doing the job

(e) Personal attributes required to do the job, e.g., education, training, physical strength, mental capabilities, etc.

(f) Relation with the other jobs.

The requirements of a job are known as Job Description and the qualities demanded from the jobholder are termed as Job Specification. Thus, job description and job specification are the immediate products of job analysis.

Skill Inventory

The scarcity of talent, difficulty of discovering it and the time required to develop it fully have forced big organizations to think about their manpower in a systematic way. They attempt to know the inventory of manpower resources, develop and appraise their executives, draw up management succession plans and calculate the replacements that will be needed because of retirements and other causes. To understand the nature of the recruitment and development problems, it is necessary to determine the inventory of different skills and talents existing in the organization. Systematic steps must be taken in order to ensure that a reservoir of talents within the organization must be continuous.

Personnel (Manpower) Forecasting

In order to forecast the number of personnel required at a particular plant, the workload analysis will have to be done and on the basis of workload of the plant, workforce analysis will have to be carried out.

Workload Analysis

In workload analysis, the manpower planning expert needs to find out sales forecasts, work schedules and thus determines the manpower required per unit of product. The departmental workloads are converted into man-hours in terms of different skills required. Workload analysis is used to determine how many employees of various types are required to achieve total production targets. Similarly, plans are made concerning the amount of work that each other part (marketing department, purchase department, etc.) of the organization is expected to accomplish during the coming year.

Workforce Analysis

It is generally better to keep a margin of 10-20 per cent of the manpower required as per workload analysis, on its payroll to meet the annual production target and overcome the loss of manpower through anticipated and unexpected separations. However, it depends upon the organizational capacity.

Employment Plan

This phase deals with planning how the organization can obtain the required number of right types of personnel as reflected by the personnel forecasting. In other words, there is a need to prepare programme of recruitment, selection, training, transfer and promotion so that personnel needs of various departments of the organization are met.

Training and Development of Personnel

The preparation of skill inventory helps in identifying training and development needs of the organization. Training for learning new skills and for refreshing the memory is necessary not only for new employees but also for old employees. Executive development programmes have to be devised for the development of managerial personnel.

Projecting Manpower through Manpower Planning

The need to anticipate and provide for future manpower requirements has made manpower planning a vital function today at the end of staffing or the personnel function. Management can ensure control of labour costs by avoiding both shortages and surpluses of manpower through proper manpower planning. Underestimation either regarding quality or quantity of manpower requirements would lead to shortfalls of performance, whilst overestimation would result in avoidable costs to the organization. If we agree that it is necessary to project deep into the future for skills which would require longer periods of training, it may be possible that if the periods selected are too long, manpower forecast is likely to be less accurate in view of the inability to predict effectively the likely change in the economic, social and technological spheres.

There are various levels of manpower planning in an industrial enterprise, but each has its own objectives and techniques that may broadly be carried out at corporate, divisional or plant levels. The purpose of carrying out manpower planning at various levels is the systematic projection of manpower requirements for the future. It is done to determine the effects of anticipated changes in technology the effects of anticipated changes in technology, markets and products on manpower requirements.

Manpower planning is similar to long-range planning in general. It is better to start at the lowest organizational level, then move up to highest level. If personnel lower down in the organization start the planning process, the organization shall reap the benefits of thoughts of persons who are more familiar with day-to-day problems and will be more interested in fulfilling the plans when they have had involvement in formulating them. Therefore, manpower planning should begin at the lowest organizational level and be reviewed successively at higher organizational echelons; manpower planning at the plant level can be conducted by an operating committee which will review annually the previous year's manpower experience by comparing actual data with estimates. The next step would be to formulate a manpower plan or projection for the next year, including the number of employees required and the sources, which could be utilized to meet those requirements. It would also determine the number of promotable employees for the annual manpower plan.

Finally, the committee will evaluate these plans in the light of expected changes of all kinds within the next five years with the help of manpower planning experts. In line with principles of functional and administrative management this planning would in turn be submitted to the next organizational level. Each division of the department of the organization will have the divisional committee which would review all the manpower plans submitted in the division and formulate similar plans for the staff departments in the division. The division committee would integrate all the manpower plans as well as those of its divisional staff section into a comprehensive divisional manpower planning report, which in turn would be submitted to the top management.

At the highest level of the organization, there may be an executive committee to integrate the manpower plan of all the divisions. The committee will be assisted by specialists in this field and will review all the plans submitted by the divisional committees and will develop similar plans for the headquarter staff. It will make projection of manpower requirement of various kinds during the next five years. At this level much emphasis will be given to the executive manpower planning because it takes a long time before a person is developed into a better executive. The committee will have at its disposal the following records and statistics regarding the plan during the next 5 to 8 years:

(1) Employee's turnover during the previous years.
(2) Employees going to retire in future and so on.
(3) Employees records regarding employees turnover due to death, retirements, resignations, terminations, as guide for manpower planning for future.

Training and Development

The terms 'training', 'development' and 'education' are sometimes used synonymously. This not correct as these terms have different connotations and scope. The term 'training' is used to indicate the process by which attitudes, skills and abilities of employees to perform specific jobs are increased. Thus, training has a specific purpose. But 'development' means growth of the individual in all respects. In practice, the term 'development' is used in relation to the executives or managers of the enterprise. Management development means the processes by which managers acquire not only skills and competency to do their present jobs, but also capacities for future managerial tasks.

Particularly, where the emphasis is being given to off-the-job training, the objective is to increase the knowledge and understanding of the employees about the business and general environment. Thus, business firms are also involved indirectly in the educational process when they are organizing training for the development of their workforce.

Concept of Training

After the selection of people for various jobs, the next function of management is to arrange for their planning and development. This is because a person, however carefully selected is not moulded to specifications and rarely meets the demands of his job adequately; formerly it was thought that the training of personnel was unnecessary on the grounds that the new employees would gradually pick up all the particular requirements of the job. But as the process of work is becoming more complicated, it is being increasingly realized that formal training is important not only for new recruits but also for existing employees. Training function, in fact, has become the cornerstone of sound management.

Training is different from education, Training is the act of increasing the knowledge and skill of an employee for doing a particular job. It is concerned with imparting specific skills for particular purpose. On the other hand, education is a broader term concerned with increasing the general knowledge and understanding of the employee's total environment. Thus, when we teach a person how to assemble two objects and tighten a nut, we are training him to do a specific job, but when we are giving him a course in engineering, it is education. The distinction between the two is like the distinction between applied and pure sciences. Training is also different from development. Being always work-oriented from development, training carries the narrow implications of imparting to an individual some specific skills only. Training is not something that is given only once to new employees. All employees new and old learn and receive training throughout their stay in the organization. This is so because in the process of directing employee's efforts and administering rewards and punishment to them, the manager continually shapes their behaviour everyday, whether consciously or unconsciously.

Types of Training Programmes

(i) *Induction or Orientation Training*: It is a training programme used to induct a new employee into the new setting of his work. The new employee is introduced to his job situation, and to his co-employees. He is also informed about the rules, working conditions, privileges and activities of the company; what the company does, how it serves the community and other particulars pertaining to the company. If the new employee is as unskilled or a semi-skilled worker, for example, a machine operator, he may be asked to spend some time on the shop floor in order to familiarize himself with the machines, equipment and working conditions. In some companies the complete induction is done by the personnel department, which supplies to the new employee all sorts of information relating to the company. In the second phase, the supervisor does the induction. He has the responsibilities of seeing that both the newcomer and the work team accept each other.

(ii) *Job Training*: The object of job training is to increase the knowledge of workers about the jobs with which they are concerned, so that their efficiency, skill and performance are improved. In job training, workers are enabled to learn correct methods of handling machines and equipments, avoiding accidents, removing bottlenecks, minimizing waste, etc.

(iii) *Promotional Training*: Many concerns follow up a policy of filling some of the vacancies at higher levels by promoting existing employees. This policy increases the morale of workers. They try to put up maximum efficiency so that they may be considered for promotion when the existing employees are promoted to superior position in the organization and are required to shoulder new responsibilities. For this, training has to be given to them so that they may not experience any difficulty to shoulder the responsibilities of the new position to which they have been promoted.

(iv) *Refresher Training*: At the time of initial appointment, employees are formally trained for their job. But with the passage of time, they may forget some of the methods, which were taught to them or they may have become outdated because of technological development and improved techniques of management and production. Hence, refresher training is arranged for existing employees in order to provide them an opportunity to revive and also to improve their knowledge. According to Dale Yoder, refresher training programmes are designed to avoid 'personnel obsolescence.'

(v) *Corrective Training*: When an employee violates company rules policies such as by being absent often or by smoking in a no-smoking area, the manager needs to find a way to deal with the problem. Sometimes he thinks that the solution to the problem is discipline, but the trouble with the word 'discipline' is that it is employee's punishment. His aim should be to reform the employee. In other words, he should handle the problem with treatment that corrects rather then punishes. Whenever an employee commits a mistake, he is to be corrected. The management should criticize the act and not the individual and should explain to the employee why it is important to both the organization and employee that he should change his behaviour.

Training Methods

All training methods can be grouped into two categories: training methods for operatives and training methods for managers.

Training Methods for Operatives

On the job training methods are the most important methods used for training the ranks and file workers in the factory. Under these methods, the new employee is assigned to a specific job at a machine or workshop or laboratory. He is instructed by an experienced employee or by a special supervisor who explains to him the method of handling tools, operating machines, etc. Under this method, the worker not only learns the work under the guidance of a supervisor but also produces goods in that process. As this method does not require any special arrangement, such as having a training school, it is inexpensive and has become a very popular method of training for the employees. Further, it enables the workers to learn in the environment of the job. Another feature of this method is that it takes less time to provide training to the worker and also directly adds to the production. Further, this method has the advantage of simplicity because there is no division of responsibility between a staff training department and line supervision. In words of Better: on the job training, for it success, needs a properly trained instructor, otherwise an inefficient instructor can produce a number of inefficient offsprings. There are several methods in vogue which makes use of the on the job training concept. Some of them are described below:

(i) *Vestibule Training*: This method involves the creation of a separate training centre within the plant itself for the purpose of providing training to the new employee. An experienced instructor is put in charge of this training. Machines and tools are also arranged in the training centre so as to create working conditions similar to those in the workshop. This method has several advantages. As the trainees remains free from the confusion and the pressure of the work situation, he is able to concentrate on learning.

(ii) *Apprenticeship Training*: This method of training is meant to give the trainee sufficient knowledge and skill in those trades and crafts in which a certain period of training is required for gaining complete proficiency. This programme consist of providing education, work experience in the actual working environment and imparted theoretical knowledge through classroom lectures which may be arranged either in the plant or in the institution attached to the concern. This method of training enables the trainees to become trained craftsmen. But this method is very expensive and also there is no guarantee that a trained worker will continue to work in the same concern after the training is completed.

(iii) *Internship Training*: This method of training is generally provided to the new skilled and technical personnel. It involves a joint programme of training in which enterprises and the vocational and the training institutions cooperate. The object of this type of training is to bring about a balance between theoretical and practical knowledge. The employees of business enterprises are sent to technical institutions to gain theoretical knowledge as well.

Training Method for Managers

Executive talent is the most important asset which a company can possess. Although it does not appear on the company's balance sheet, but it produces more important effects on the company's progress, its profit and the price of its stock than any other asset in its possession. Research experimentation, testing and experience have unfolded a great variety of training methods which are used in executing development programmes. Some of these training methods aim at increasing the problems solving skills of managers, still others aim at changing their attitudes. A brief description of these methods is given below:

(i) *Observation Assignment*: Under this method, the newly recruited executive called 'understudy' is made an assistant to the correct jobholder. He learns by experience, observation and imitation. If decisions are discussed with him, he is informed on the policies and theories involved. But if he is neglected by the correct jobholders, the understudy does not learn much by this method.

(ii) *Position Rotation*: Under this method, the trainee executive is rotated among different managerial jobs. This not only broadens and enriches his experience as a manager but also enables him to understand inter-departmental relations and the need for coordination and cooperation among various departments.

(iii) *Serving on Committees*: Another important method for training an executive is to make him serve on a committee. While serving on a committee the executive comes to learn not only the various organization problems and views of several senior and experienced members, but he also learns how a manager should adjust himself to the overall needs of the enterprise.

(iv) *Assignment of Special Project*: Sometimes as a method of training, some special project is assigned to a training executive. For example, he may be asked to develop a system of cost location in the production of certain goods for which the company has received an order. While working on such projects the trainee not only acquires knowledge about them but also learns how to work with and relate to the people holding different views.

(v) *Case Study*: A case is a written account seeking to describe an actual situation. A good case study is the vehicle by which a chunk of reality is brought into the classroom to be discussed over by the class and the instructor. Discussion on a case requires a capable instructor who can evoke and guide intelligent discussion and analysis so that meaningful learning experiences occur. There is no right answer or simple explanation in comprehensive case. The advantages of this method are – more depth of thinking, more perception of a situation, greater respect for and consideration for the opinion of others; what may happen to a business student who has not gone through this method is brought out by the following limerick:

A student of business with fact,
absorbed many answers he lacked.
But acquiring a job he said with a sob,
"How does one fit answer to fact".

The number of published cases is so large that an enormous selection is available.

(vi) *Conference and Seminar*: Often an executive is deputed to attend a conference, seminar or workshop to receive a quick orientation in various areas of management with which he might be unfamiliar. One advantage of this type of training is that all the participants coming from different organizations get an opportunity to pool their ideas and experiences in attempting to solve mutual problems. The attitude is one of joint exploration. This encourages cross-fertilization of ideas.

(vii) *Incident Method*: Developed at the Massachusetts Institute of Technology, this method is an outgrowth of dissatisfaction felt by Paul and Pigors with the case method. In the usual case method, the entire problem is presented to the students, whereas in the incident method only a brief incident is presented to provoke discussion in the class. Then, the group put questions to the instructor to draw out of him the salient facts and additional needed information to arrive at a reasonable solution, or resolution of the case. This method draws participants into discussion with greater emotional involvement.

(viii) *Role Playing*: In this method, the instructor assigns parts taken from case materials to group members. The situation is usually one involving contrast between people. The role players attempt to act the parts, as they would behave in a real life situation, working without a script or memorized lines and improvising as they play the parts. The development of empathy and sensitivity is one of the primary objectives of role-playing.

(ix) *Sensitivity Training or Laboratory Training*: This type of training is designed to increase the manager's understanding of himself and of his own impact on others. The training takes the form of group discussion and through a leader trained in the techniques who is present. The group may decide on the subject of discussion or suggest changes in procedure. The course of the discussion, conflict hostility, stress, frustration, may be purposely generated for they later on become motivations for growth as well as a base for learning. As these experiences are worked through and the learning internalized, participants soon begin to experience a deeper sense of self-awareness and acceptance. These in turn, lead to an increased awareness of the situation. According to Katz this method depends for its success on the following conditions:

(a) The trainee must sincerely want to improve his human relation skill.

(b) He must be willing to face up squarely to his own inadequacies, without rationalizing or minimizing them.

(c) He must be provided with a permissive atmosphere which shield out censure or ridicule when he exposes his weaknesses.

(d) He must be provided with direct experiences in working with others, where he can learn and practice the new skills he acquires.

(x) *Autonomy Training*: One of the latest approaches to management training is called Autonomy Training which is aimed at developing the individual ability to manage his own training. It involves leaving the trainee almost entirely on his own. He has to

Exibit 1

Management Development Programme

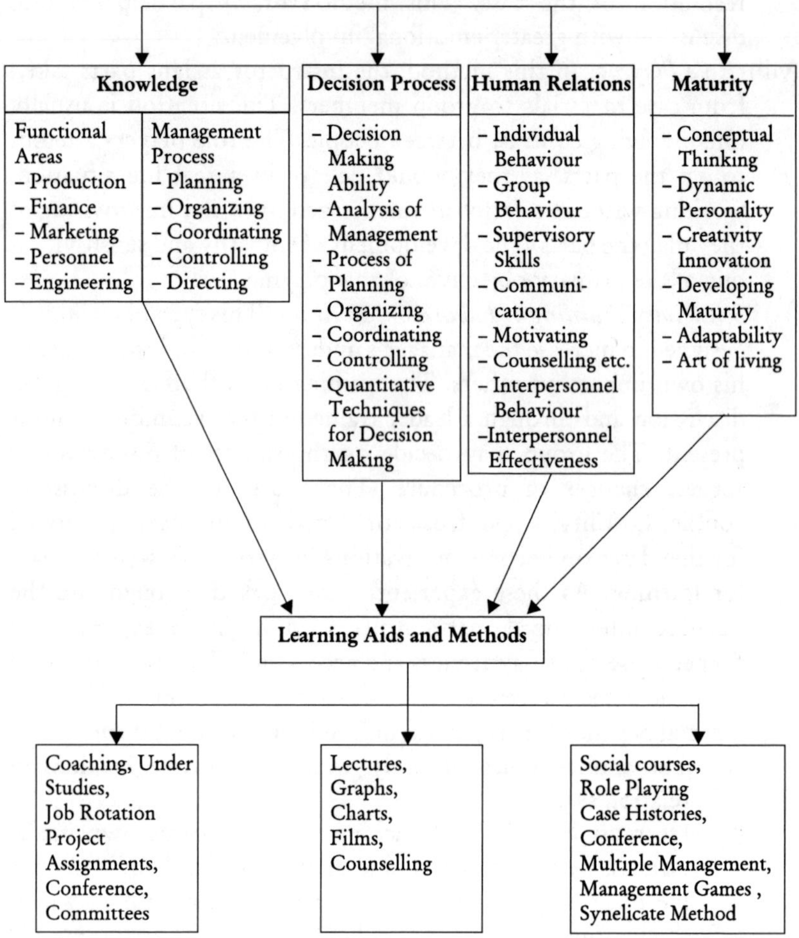

first work out what he would like to learn and then teach himself. The concept on which this method rests, is that with the tremendous speed at which new knowledge is replacing the old, it is impossible for standardized courses to cater to the mass of individual training needs. So, managers must be trained to teach themselves new skills as they go along.

Concept of Development

Development is an evolving process. The general direction of development is towards the actualization of potentialities. Development normally proceeds in an orderly fashion through predictable stages and the quality of development of each stage is limited by what has gone before. The development from birth to maturity is in the direction of increasing differentiation, integration and complexity and includes development from dependence to self-direction, from impulsiveness to self-discipline, from ignorance to knowledge, from incompetence to competence, from defused sexuality to heterosexuality, from immorality to morality and from self-confines to concern for both self and others.

There are certain basic principles of development, which are as follows:

(1) Development should be towards the actualization of growth potentials;
(2) Development should proceed in an orderly fashion;
(3) Development can be viewed in terms of stages having their own characteristic features;
(4) Development should be based on the concept of individual difference; and
(5) Development should be based on previous development stages.

The growth from birth to maturity reveals a sequence from increasing differentiation, integration and complexity. The period of growth to maturity is followed by a period of entropy in which growth processes are reversed, leading to deterioration and death of a system. At each stage of development, there are fairly specific tasks such as skills, attitudes, understanding, which are appropriate to the level of maturity and which society expects the individual to master. Following are the general tasks to be met at each stage:

(a) Achieving a realistic frame of reference about one's self and one's surrounding.
(b) Developing the physical, intellectual, emotional and social competence needs in one's culture.
(c) Learning and preparing for the problems likely to be encountered in life.

There seems to be critical periods, especially in early years, particularly when appropriate stimulation and practice are required if genetic potential are to develop sufficiently. Intellectual development is especially dependent on the quality and type of experience. According to Hurlock, development may be defined as a progressive sense of orderly and coherent changes.

Methods of Developing Strategies and Evaluation

Changing Style

One of the most difficult changes to make is a complete change in the style of a person, and yet industry invests many millions of dollars annually for training and development programmes that concentrate on changing the style of its leaders.

As Fiedler suggests: A person's leadership style reflects the individual's basic motivational and need structure; at best it takes one, two or three years of intensive psychotherapy to effect lasting changes in personality structure. It is difficult to see how we can change in more than a few cases an equally important set of core values in few hours of lectures and role playing or even in the course of a more intensive training. Fielder's point is well taken. It is indeed difficult to effect changes in the style of managers overnight. While not completely hopeless, it is a slow and expensive process that requires creative planning and in fact, it takes from three to seven years, depending on the site and complexity of the organization to implement a new management theory effectively. What generally happens in present training and development programmes is that managers are encouraged to adopt certain normative behaviour style. In our culture, these styles are usually high relationship – low task or high task – low relationship styles; we also recognize that this is not universally the case even in our culture. In fact, it is not often the case with single work group. Most people might respond favourably to the high relationship styles but might react in a negative manner, taking advantage of what they consider a soft touch. As a result, certain individuals will have to be handled in a different way. Consequently, a foreman who has been operating as a task-oriented, authoritarian leader for many years is encouraged to change his style and get in step with the present times, upon returning from the training programme. The foreman will probably try to utilize some of the new relationship-oriented techniques he has been taught. Change in overall management style in an organization should be planned and implemented on a long-term basis so that expectations can be realistic for all those involved.

Changes in Expectations

When a person behaves in a motivating situation, that behaviour becomes a new input to the individual inventory of past experience. The earlier in life that this input occurs the greater its potential effect on future behaviour. At that time, this behaviour represents a larger portion of the individual's total past experience than the same behaviour input would later in life. In addition, the longer a behaviour is reinforced, the more patterned it becomes and the more difficult it is to change. As a person gets older, more time and new experiences are necessary to effect a change in behaviour.

Since changes in expectations in reality are changes in knowledge and attitudes, these can be implemented more rapidly than changes in style. Once they understand their leader's style followers can more easily adjust their expectation to it.

Team Building: Selection of Key Subordinates

It is important to point out that it is not always necessary for superiors and subordinates within an organization to have similar style; people do not have the same personality to be compatible. What is necessary is that they share perceptions of each others roles and have common goals and objectives. It is often more appropriate for a manager to recruit key subordinates who can compensate for areas in which they have shortcomings than to surround themselves with aids who are all alike. And yet, there are large companies today that have created problems for themselves by a testing and selection process that eliminates personalities not congruent with the norm. The usual process is that to measure the values and styles of the top management and then select new people who are compatible with those patterns. The assumption is that if those people got to the top, their values and style must be what is needed to be successful in the organization.

To be effective in the long run, we feel that an organization needs an open dialogue in which there is a certain amount of conflict confrontation and differing points of view to encourage new ideas and patterns of behaviour, so that the organization will not lose its ability to adjust to external competition. Organizations that have had these problems almost have been forced to break their prior policy of promoting only from within, and have had to hire some key people from outside who can encourage open dialogue. What is often needed in an organization is more emphasis on team building, in which people are hired who complement rather than replicate manager's style.

Changing Situational Variables

Recognizing some of the limitations of training and development programmes that concentrate only on changing leadership styles, Fiedler has suggested that "it could seem more promising at this time to teach the individual to recognize the conditions under which he can perform best and modify the situation to suit his leadership style." The philosophy, which he calls 'organizational engineering', is based on the following assumption: "It is almost always easier to change a man's work environment than it is to change his personality or his style of relating to others. In a many cases, the best strategy might be to attempt to make some changes in both the style of leaders and the expectations of the other variables of their situation rather than concentrate on one or the other."

According to Fiedler, there are three major situational variables that seem to determine whether a given situation is favourable or unfavourable:

(a) *Leader Member Relationship*: their personal relations with the members of their group.
(b) *Position Power*: The power and the authority that their position provides.
(c) *Task Structure*: The degree of structure of the task that the group has been assigned to perform.

Evaluation

The implementation of the proposed change has different dimensions, timing and scope. Timing is the selection of the appropriate time to initiate the change; scope is the selection of the appropriate scale of the change. The matter of the timing is strategic and depends on a number of factors, particularly the company's operating cycle and the groundwork preceding the change. Certainly, if a change is of considerable magnitude, it is desirable that it is not completed along with ordinary business operations. On the other hand, if the problem is critical to the survival of the organization, immediate implementation is in order. The scope of the change depends upon the strategy. The change may be implemented throughout the organization and becomes an established fact in a short time. Evaluation is an important and often overlooked step in organizational change programmes. Essentially, evaluation should be made by comparing the results with the objectives of the organizational change programmes. It is difficult to evaluate the effectiveness of most change efforts. But, it is crucial to know what has resulted in terms of attitudes, productivity and behaviour.

Significance of Training and Development

The process of training and development are often confused. Training means learning the basic skills and knowledge necessary for a particular job. To put it in other words, training is the act of increasing the knowledge for doing a particular job. Actually, training is the follow up of selection, which is the first stage in fitting of the individual into a particular job. In training, the main objective is to attain a large degree of uniformity of conduct of different employees. Training is the one of the areas of management where employer and employee have mutual interest.

But development on the other hand, means growth of the individual in all respect. An organization works for the development of its executive or potential executives in order to enable them to be more effective in performing the various functions of management. Executive development programme aims at increasing the capacities of the individuals to achieve the desired objectives. Executive capacities imply his personal abilities and his potentialities. Training occurs as a result of controlled external stimulations but development takes place when the individual is externally motivated to improve. All development is self-development and organization can only provide for the conditions for development or advancement. The initiative for development has to be taken by the individual himself. Unless he has required potentialities for a good manager, an employee cannot be considered fit for development. Executive development programme seeks to develop the overall personality of the executives and not only the skill necessary to do the job efficiently. An executive development programme should be more concerned with the conceptual and human skill of the executives and programme should increase the knowledge, decision-making abilities, skill in dealing with people and maturity of the executives. No doubt, an executive can be given the necessary training to help him to face the problem with the present job or to promote him for the higher job. Training is also necessary to prevent obsolescence of knowledge and skills of individuals. Development towards the actualization of potential is a planned, systematic and continuous process of learning and growth. Development is designed to induce behavioural changes in executives by cultivating their mental abilities and inherent qualities. Development is more akin to education than to training skills.

Career Planning

Meaning of Career Planning

Career planning often means job rotation, successive planning and promotion policy; it is a process which optimizes the inter-dependence of the individuals and also their organizational relationship and is more akin to growth and development of every individual of the organization. Career planning can often be translated into programme and procedures which are designed to give the individual leverage in deciding his personal career within the organizational environment. Career planning helps to facilitate dialogue between the individual and the organization in order to optimize their mutual needs. Career planning programmes should be dynamic, otherwise it will tend to change rapidly because individuals are dynamic and changing entities. Career planning is thus concerned with identifying individuals, who can fill planned future posts. It involves anticipation to enable advance preparation of such individuals so that they are ready in time for such future positions. Career planning process also helps the organization. Recruitment is time consuming and expensive. Career planning reduces turnover and ensures the retention of goods people. In the absence of adequate career planning in terms of the future manpower requirements, dislocations are likely to occur. The objective of career planning and promotion policy is normally to provide and maintain appropriate manpower resources and environment for the effectiveness, efficiency and growth of its employees and motivating them to contribute effectively towards achieving the objectives of the organization. It should be the policy of every organization to provide its employees with appropriate opportunity, encouragement and career growth consistent with their contribution to the growth of their organization.

Responsibility for Career Planning

Assisting individuals with their career development plans can be a powerful tool for integrating the organization. Individuals must know and understand how their goals fit with those of their supervisors and work group. In the absence of such information, individuals cannot find their places in the organization and consequently, will never be able to make optional contribution to it. One R&D organization implemented a career development programme in one of its division. The management of the division initially perceived the programme to be an attempt to get non-supervisory employees to take responsibility for their own career development. Eventually, however, the programme provided not only opportunities for individual growth, but also a way for supervisors to support employee's career goals and to disseminate organizational goals and objectives.

Process of Career Planning

Career planning involves matching an individual's career aspirations with the opportunities available in an organization. The two processes are intertwined. Planning a career requires identifying the activities and experiences needed to accomplish career goals.

Successful practice places equal responsibility on the individual and the organization. Individuals must identify their aspiration and abilities and through personnel counselling recognize training and development required for a particular career path. Organization must identify their needs and opportunities and through personnel planning, provide career information and training to their employees. Career planning cannot proceed unless information about career path, expected vacancies and position requirement is available to employees. Matching individual and organizational needs can be done through a variety of personnel practices.

Informal Counselling

The organization's personnel function often includes counselling services for employees who wish to assess their abilities and interest. The counselling process can also go into personal concerns, and it is proper to do so since these concerns are important factors in determining career effectiveness. In this context, career counselling is reviewed by the organization as counselling is a service to its employees, but not a primary one.

Supervisors often include career counselling during their performance valuation session with employees. The question of the employee's future in the organization quite naturally arises in this setting. In fact, the induction of career information in performance appraisal predates the current interest in career planning.

Formal Counselling

Workshops, assessment centres and career development centres are increasingly being used in organizations. Typically, such formal practices are designed to service specific employee group's management trainers, and 'high potential' or 'fast-track' management candidates are two groups who have received most of the attention to date. All employees cannot be on the fast track and by definition; all employees cannot be members of minority groups. Organization have a vested interest in enabling all employees to continue their progress within the organization. Most employees will reach the limit of their progress within the organization.

Other Human Resource Practices

Organizations can use a variety of personnel practices to facilitate their employees career plan. One of the oldest, most widely used method is some form of the tuition-aid programme. Another practice is job posting: The organization publicizes job openings to employees. This requires more than simply placing a notice on the company's bulletin board.

Development for Career Planning

Career development programmes became a catalyst for managing employee-supervisor relations, because effective career development can succeed only in a workplace that employees believe to be free from arbitrary job and reward assignment. These changes in management's expectations for what a career development programme can accomplish were the result of how a programme for an individual career involves a series of choices from among different opportunities. But from the organization standpoint, a career involves process by which the organization renew itself. Contemporary career development practice recognize the diversity of individual choices and career alternatives. As the emphasis on employee empowerment has gained acceptance in recent years, many organization have undertaken career development programme that acknowledge the realities of the new workplace. These changes in management's expectations for what a career development programme can accomplish were the result of how the programme was designed. Rather than imposing the programme, management designed the programme only after involving managers, supervisors and non-supervisory personnel in a need assessment phase. It was during this phase that it became obvious that an individual's career goals and strategies can be developed only through participation of the individual's supervisor who can represent the organization goals and strategies.

Advantages of Career Planning

Career planning is becoming more widespread in organizations. Individuals who wish to make formal career plans should seek out those organizations that have demonstrated a commitment to career planning. It appears that some individuals gain little from the process. Recent studies, for example, indicate that career planning is most effective for people who have relatively high needs for growth and achievement, the skill to carry-out their career plans, and a past history at career success. But, the findings also indicate that organizations should try to identify people who are most likely to take advantage of career planning programmes.

Performance Appraisal

Concept and Importance of Performance Appraisal

Performance appraisal or merit rating is one of the oldest and most universal practices of management. It refers to all the formal procedures used in working organizations to evaluate the personalities and contributions and potential of group members. Modern management makes somewhat less use of the term 'merit rating' which was common in the earlier periods. In this part, the emphasis used was on the evaluation of merits of an individual and his worth as a person. The approach resulted in an appraisal system in which the employee's merits like initiative, dependability, personality, etc., were compounded with others and ranked or rated. More recently, emphasis has been given to measuring the results of the employee's performance. The trend nowadays is in the direction of attempting to measure what the man does (performance appraisal) rather than what he is (merit rating).

Appraisal can be made by one or more superiors or by subordinates or by peers. They can also be made by two or more of these or by a rating committee or by special appraisers. There may even be a system of self-appraisal in which each employee evaluates his own performance and potential. But appraisals by direct superiors are the most common. Although in day-to-day work, the superior continuously appraises his subordinates, the daily appraisal lacks summation and objectivity. To overcome these deficiencies, most managements turned to periodic appraisal, which may be either annual or semi-annual. In addition, special appraisals may be done at the end of an employee's probationary period or at the time of his promotion.

Purposes of Appraisal

(1) It can serve as a basis for job change or promotion by establishing whether the worker can contribute still more in a different or a higher job; it helps in his suitable promotion and placement.

(2) By identifying the strengths and weaknesses of an employee, it serves as a guide for formulating a suitable training and development programme to improve his quality of performance in his present work.

(3) It serves as a feedback to the employee. By letting the employee know how well he is doing or where he stands with his superiors, it tells him what he can do to improve his present performance and go up in the management hierarchy.

(4) It serves as an important incentive to all the employees who are by the existence of an appraisal system assured of the management's continued interest in them and of their continuous possibility to develop. The employees realize that not only are they being continuously observed but that they have not been forgotten.

(5) The existence of the regular appraisal system tends to make the supervisors and executives more observant of their subordinates, because they will be expected periodically to fill out rating forms and would be called upon to justify their estimates. This knowledge results in improved supervision.

(6) Performance appraisal often provides the rational foundation for the payment of piecework, wages, bonuses, etc. The estimates of the relative contributions of employees or of their characteristics help to determine the reward and privileges.

(7) Performance appraisal serves as a means for evaluating the effectiveness of devices for the selection and classification of workers. Alternatively, knowledge of the characteristics of superiors and inferior workers can be helpful in selection and placement of workers.

(8) Permanent performance appraisal records of employees help the management to give up sole-reliance upon personal knowledge of supervisors who may be shifted.

Methods of Performance Appraisal

Although there is not easy way of classifying all the various kinds of performance appraisal methods that have been devised, we may still classify them into the following types:

Ranking Method

The oldest and simplest method of performance appraisal is to compare one man with all other men and place him in a simple rank order. In this way, ordering is done from best to worst of all individuals comprising the group. The method is simple and natural but its disadvantages are:

(i) It is highly subjective.
(ii) Comparison of the various components of person's performance is not alone. People are compared as a whole.
(iii) The magnitude of difference in ability between ranks is not equal at different positions.
(iv) Its use is difficult in large groups when that rater cannot compare several people simultaneously.

As an answer to the last problem, the paired comparison technique of ranking has been involved. In this method the rater compares each man in his group with every other man, with the final ranking of each worker determined by the number of times he was judged better than others. The number of comparisons involved in this method is thus very large and can be determined by the following formula:

Number of comparison = N (N-1)/2.

N stands for the number of men to be rated.

Rating Scale Method

As the very name implies, this method uses some kind of the scale for measuring absolute differences between individuals. The scales used are generally of two types:

(1) *Discrete*: Where two or more categories are provided, representing discrete amounts of ability of degrees of the characteristics, the rater can tick mark the category which he feels best, describes the

person being rated, for example, the characteristic 'job knowledge', may be divided into five categories on a discrete scale: 'exceptionally good' 'above average' 'average' 'below average' and 'poor'.

(2) *Continuous or (graphic)*: Where just above the category notation, an uninterrupted line is provided, the rater can tick at any point long its length as shown below:

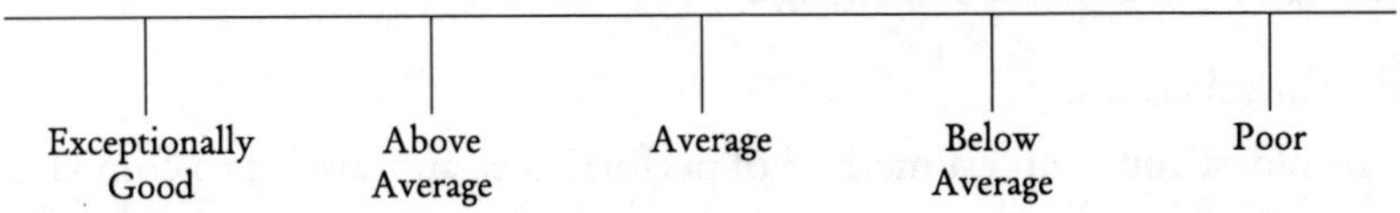

There are four kinds of standards used in rating scales, namely, numerical, or alphabetical, descriptive adjective, man-to-man and behaviour sample. The major difficulty with numerical or alphabetical standard is that the numbers or alphabets, which are used to describe the various categories of a characteristic, do not convey the same meaning to all raters. This difficulty is overcome to some extent in descriptive adjective scale.

In man-to-man rating scale, the standards are very concrete because there are neither numbers nor alphabets nor descriptive adjectives but are of persons of varying ability whom the rater has selected and ranked in the ability under consideration. Thus, a scale of men is created for each trait. In rating other persons, the rater simply looks over this scale and compares them with the persons on the scale.

Checklist Method

Sometimes, the method used for performance appraisal is the list consisting of a number of statements about the worker and his behaviour, and each statement on this list is assigned a value depending upon its importance. Both statements and their values are derived from preliminary research in which the pooled judgement of persons familiar with the job are used. In rating a person, the rater is asked to place a plus sign, a minus sign or question mark in front of each statement, depending, respectively, on whether he feels the description applies, does not apply or there is doubt. No restrictions are put on the rater as to the number of statements he should mark. The worker's final rating is taken as the average of the scale values of all statements that this superior has checked in rating him. The limitations to this method are:

(1) It is difficult to construct a good checklist.

(2) A separate checklist is needed for each job, because statements used in one checklist to evaluate one category of workers cannot be used in another checklist to evaluate other categories of workers.

(3) Since the rater does not know the values given to different statements, he may resent the system as a whole and may not give it his wholehearted support.

Forced Choice Method

A forced choice rating form consists of a number of statements, which describes an individual being rated. These statements are grouped in twos, threes, or fours, sometimes all groups on the rating form are made of favourable statements only, sometimes all have unfavourable statements only and sometimes they have favourable and unfavourable statements in equal number. When all groups on the rating form contain favourable statements only, the rater must check one statement in each group which he believes best characterizes the individual being rated; when all groups are made of unfavourable statements, the rater must check on statements in each group which he believes is the least descriptive of the individual being rated; when each group has two favourable and two unfavourable statement the rater should make two checks in each group, one for the best described and one for the least descriptive. Each statement has a pre-determined weight. As in the case of checklist scales, these weights are unknown to the rater. An individual's rating is determined by adding together the weights of each of the statements that have been checked as describing him.

The limitations to this method are:

(1) It is expensive to install because the statements must be custom-tailored to the demand of the particular job and company.

(2) It is resented by the rater because the implicit assumption behind it is that the rater cannot be trusted to make an impartial evaluation.

Field Review

Under this method, appraisal of workers is done by the personnel officer by collecting oral rating about them from the supervisor at the place of work. The personnel officer later writes his notes and invites the supervisor to make additions or corrections. This method is not widely used because supervisors generally resent what they consider as staff interference.

Critical Incident Technique

In this method, the first step is to draw up for each job a list of critical job requirements, that is, those requirements, which are vital for success or failure on the job. For example, in the job of the salesman the following critical factors may be identified:

(1) Following up complaints, requests and orders.
(2) Planning ahead.
(3) Communicating trade information to managers and customer.
(4) Carrying out promises.
(5) Persisting on tough accounts.
(6) Pointing out uses for the company products, besides the salesman's own line.
(7) Using new sales techniques and methods.
(8) Preventing price-cutting by dealers and customers.
(9) Knowing customer requirements.
(10) Initiating new selling ideas.

A good salesman has to follow all or most of these factors well, in order to succeed as failure on any one account can lead to failure on the entire job. Once all the critical factors of a job are identified, the supervisors may then observe and record instances and events of on-the-job behaviour falling under any of these factors as they take place. In this way, a concrete performance record of a man objectively observed and recorded comes into being for his future evaluation. The supervisor need not depend on recall, which may be incomplete and subject to moods. The limitations to this method are:

(1) It is difficult to identify critical factors.
(2) The recency or severity of incidents may influence the supervisor's opinion.
(3) Supervisors are accused of spying and carrying a 'black book'.

Assessment Centres

So far, we have been talking about assessing past performance. But in several promotion decisions, prediction of future performance becomes necessary, more so, if the selection is to be made for a job from among a group of candidates, none of whom has done the job or one like it, ever before. In these situations, many organizations use assessment centres to predict future performance more accurately.

Typically, individuals from different departments are brought together to spend two or three days working on individual or group assignments, similar to the ones they will be handling if they are promoted. The pooled judgement of observers leads to an order merit ranking for each participant. There is a good deal of research evidence that people chosen by this method prove better than those chosen by other methods. The centres also make it possible for unknown people who are working in competitively less important or low status departments of an organization to compete with people from more well known departments. This has the effect of equalizing opportunity, improving morale, and enlarging the pool of potential promotion candidates.

Limitations of Appraisal Method

All performance appraisal methods suffer from certain limitations. We can divide these limitations into two classes:

(1) Those which are inherent in the particular method.

(2) Those which arise from the way in which the supervisor makes his evaluation.

Limitations of the first type have already been mentioned in the aforesaid description of appraisal methods. A supervisor can hardly be expected to account for these limitations. G.S. Odiorne denounces all appraisal method for their single inherent weakness – that they lay emphasis on conformity. All appraisal methods according to him are like quality control system, which force subordinates to conform to certain standard of physical bearing, mental capacity and social adjustment skills. All those who do not conform to these qualities and skills are rejected. The results often are that we create appraisal system, which merely measure conformity of human performance, ignoring measurement of human values, which though far less tangible are essential ingredients in the whole process. The point here is that the appraisal method now in use would rank both the benevolent and despotic managers equal, if they are found equal on all factors of the rating scale, no matter how different their value system are. Limitations of the second type of manager who makes his evaluations, can be easily be overcome by improving his evaluation technique through increased understanding and training. We can divide these limitations into two classes:

(1) Intrusion of subjective criteria.
(2) Defensiveness of employees.

(1) Intrusion of Subjective Criteria

(a) *Halo Effect*: It is the tendency of the superior to allow his good impression of one or two important work characteristics of an individual to influence over the total evaluation. In such a case, the superior rates all the characteristics of a person much higher than they should be. For example, if the superior is a person who is very fond of punctuality, a punctual worker may get a high rating on practically every factors that have little to do with punctuality. One other example: The man who has done good work in the distant past is assumed to be good in the recent past also.

(b) *Hypercritical of 'Horns' Effect*: It is the tendency of a superior to rate people lower than their performance justify. Following are some examples of this effect:
   (i) The superior is a perfectionist. Because his expectation level is very high, he is more often disappointed and rates his people lower than he should.
   (ii) The maverick or the non-conformists gets a low rating simply because he is different.
   (iii) The man who has recently failed may wipe out the effect of years of good work on his appraisal and be rated low on his recent behaviour.

(c) *Central Tendency and Leniency*: The superior is frequently guilty of averaging too many work characteristics in the middle grades. It may result from the fact that he does not know ratees well enough to express a discriminatory opinion. He may award 'average' on the ground that it will not injure the ratee and at the same time, that it will not expose his lack of more definitive information. The related limitation of leniency reflects a desire to rate on the generous side to avoid controversy by giving each ratee the benefit of doubt.

(d) *Reluctance to 'Play God'*: Some managers are unwilling to 'play god' by judging others. Accepting the responsibility for being a judge for the future of another person causes severe anxiety in some people. The tendency to complete the appraisal forms at the last moment when they are due and to treat the entire process casually may still be necessary to relieve the anxiety of the evaluator the role of 'judge'; further, the aggrieved employee is invariably left with the feeling that the superior is arbitrary in this judgement. This is a very frustrating experience for an honest and impartial superior.

(2) Defensiveness of Employees

The appraisal process frequently creates defensiveness among employees. Since the supervisor's appraisal influences the employees' most vital job concerns – promotions, transfers, and dismissal – the employee's defensiveness during an appraisal interview often makes the procedure unproductive for both supervisor and the subordinate.

Need for Performance Appraisal

A person's performance in any group will be judged in some way by others. Workers and managers have different views and they expect their own differences in performance to be recognized in the managerial view. Performance appraisal is needed for:

(i) Allocating resources in a dynamic environment.
(ii) Rewarding workers.
(iii) Giving workers feedback about their work.
(iv) Maintaining fair relationship within groups.
(v) Coaching and counselling workers.

Hence, appraisal systems are needed for strategic and tactical planning, motivation, communication and equity. Every management opts for day-to-day appraisal but some approaches, which will be systematic, are also needed to make sure that well thought out appraisals are recorded for the organization use, and to justify action to government agencies concerned with good employment. Performance appraisals must be based on mutual trust and confidence between managers and subordinates.

Job Evaluation

Job evaluation objective is to see and gain acceptance for the way in which money wages are divided among workers. It gives equity within the concern by an internal alliance of job values. The alliance is established by a procedure that is sometimes considered to be so objective that most conflicts over wages are removed. Wage relations are seen as automatic functioning of the programmes formula. These individuals know that job evaluation is run by people, and that people are subjective.

Job evaluation is defined by the internal labour office as an attempt to determine and compare the demands which the normal performance of particular jobs makes, on normal workers, without taking account of the individual abilities and performance of the workers concerned.

In fact, we may define job evaluation as the process of comparison, analysis and assessment of one job with other jobs in the organization and using the result as basis for a balanced wage structure.

Thus, job evaluation may be done to find out the demands made by a particular job or as a basis for arriving at a balanced wage structure. Techniques used for job evaluation can be divided into two types, namely:

(1) Non-quantitative, such as ranking and grading.
(2) Quantitative, like factor comparison and point system.

In the ranking method, the job description is first prepared. There are selected raters, who are familiar with all the jobs. These raters then rank the key and other jobs in relation to each other in a single list and similar types of job in relation to each other. From the rating, job classifications are prepared. All jobs within a single group of classification naturally receive the same grade or scale of salary or wage. Thus, under this method, no attempt is made to break down a job. One whole job is compared with another whole job. Whilst this method is the simplest and the least expensive one in terms of time consumed, it provides rough and ready guidelines. It would be unsuitable in large organizations.

Under the grading system, grade levels are established in terms of complexity of the duties and supervisory responsibilities. The grading method is lightly more defined. Jobs requiring the carrying out of simple instructions and close supervision would be graded at the lowest level. Then, depending on the extent of more skill and responsibility required, each higher grade would be fixed. Like the ranking method, this is simple and less time consuming than the other more sophisticated ones.

The factor comparison method consists of evaluation of factors such as skill, experience, mental effort, supervisor's responsibilities, education and safety. Thereafter, to each such factor a value is assigned.

This is based on the relative importance of the factor in the operation. The key jobs are then weighted factor by factor. Finally, monitory values are attached to each factor of such jobs. It will thus be noticed that the factor comparison method is more analytical when compared with the previous two methods.

Finally, the point rating method is still more complicated. As in the last method, the first step consists of selecting the factors for breaking down the jobs. The factors so selected should be common to all the jobs being evaluated. The four major factors generally are skill, effort, responsibility and working condition. Each of these can be divided into minor sub-factors. Thereafter, these factors must be clearly defined, so that the raters would measure the same element of the job. The next step is to identify what factor is needed for the performance of the job.

Human resource development is a process in which the employees of an organization are continuously helped in a planned way. The HRD department was created to identify, develop and implement various systems for the development of the employees in addition to mere training which was so far being done by the personnel department and included performance appraisal, feedback, counselling, organization development and training.

At the end, it is evident that the human resource development is still organized everywhere and human competency development is considered an essential pre-requisite for any growth. Experimentation and research in human resource development experience in the field of HRD have been a growing phenomena in the past decades. Many organizations have set up a new department known as 'HRD Department', which symbolizes the recognition of importance of people's competency development. Indian organizations need their human resources to be developed into a world-class level. It is high time that human resource development gets top most priority in our strategy, putting our economics on a high growth path.

8

Development of Women and Children

Development of women and children hardly needs emphasis. 'Woman' is the mother of the race and is the horizon between generations. "Child is the father of man". Indian culture attaches much importance to this section of the society, therefore India has been symbolized as mother India, keeping in view the exemplary qualities of a woman, i.e., patience, endurance, love, affection, sympathy and generosity. Jawaharlal Nehru once said, "To awaken the people, it is the woman who must be awakened. Once she is on the move the family moves, the village moves, the nation moves."

The title, "Development of Women and Children" means the development of the people of the society. It is not a new idea. The term is new, but the concept is very old. The development of women and children can be in different ways such as economic development, educational development, social welfare, health welfare, recreational and cultural activities, training and employment programmes etc...

The development of women and children is partly due to the social upsurge and change in attitudes, manifesting themselves into various forms, and partly due to the accompanying social, economic and legal measures. The women in independent India have come to acquire a better status in the society. Today's women have better acceptability and responsibility, better status of equality with men, better rights and privileges, better opportunities and avenues in all spheres of national life – social, economic and political.

Situation of Indian Families

The family in India does not consist only of husband, wife and their children, but also of uncles, aunts, cousins and grandsons. This system is called a joint family or extended family system. It is a peculiar characteristic of the Indian social life. A son after marriage does not usually separates himself from the parents but continues to stay with them under the same roof, eating together and holding property in common. The family has joint property and every person has his share in it from the time he is born. The earnings of all the members are put into a common fund out of which family expenses are met. Non-earning members have as much share as the earning members. The Indian family system is thus like a socialistic community in which everyone earns according to his capacity and receives according to his needs.

The family in India is based on patrilineal descent. Children are identified by name and allegiance with the father's family. Property is passed from generation to generation to within the father's family.

Origin of Indian Family System

It may not, however, be presumed that joint family system originated in India. This institution is said to be the outcome of the settling down of the Aryans in different parts of the world. As we have learnt before, in the ancient Roman society, the supreme authority rested in the eldest male member of the family who, in administrating the family affairs was entitled to take all steps. When the pastoral stage was over and people began to live a settled life by tilling the soil, constructing the house and maintaining the patrimony, joint family system came to existence. Difficulties of communication and travel compelled all the members of the family, to live together and carry on jointly the family occupation in agriculture or trade. Over and above, these causes the kinship idea, the religion emphasizing ancestor worship, further made the joint family a complex organization, catering for the spiritual and economic needs of a large family, in the society.

Concept of Indian Family

The family in its earliest origin began as a reproductive or biological association, but gradually it has developed into a primary social unit of the highest importance to the individual and the society.

The family as an institution has many important functions to perform. It has emerged in order to satisfy certain very basic biological, psychological and social needs of man. Even though recent social and economic changes have deeply affected the form and character of the family. Though some of the original functions such as the educational, the economic, the recreational and the religious have been gradually taken away by other social and state agencies, yet its basic functions, which centre round the primary bio-psycho-social needs of man, have not been affected.

The interaction of each of the members with others in the family is of profound significance in determining the individual's mental attitudes and his behaviour in society. The psycho-social influence of the family environment on the child is so swift, that in the view of the psychologists, the child acquires almost all its personality and character traits of later adulthood, before the age of five, and according to some, even earlier. The members of the family often provide the recreational needs of the family, though this has lessened in the urban areas.

The family also provides for the satisfaction of what Thomas regards as the four fundamental wishes or desires, viz., the wish for new experiences, for security, for recognition and for response. The new experiences, the stimuli and the new associations the child meets within the family environment, aids in its mental and social development. The satisfaction of the need for security begins with the physical and emotional security, given to it from birth onwards by embracing, caressing, nursing and other kinds of personal attention. The need for recognition is satisfied through the roles the child plays in the family; the attention he secures, the statuses he occupies and the approvals he gets therein. The need for response is satisfied through the affection and the comradeship he receives in the family.

The traditional family performs and fulfils variety of needs, which may be subsumed as economic, protective, biological, religious, recreational, educational, affectional and status giving. This multi-functional pattern no longer exists, expect on an attenuated form. The changing society has shifted functions from the family, until today it is in many respects a mere shadow of its former self.

Some of the needs fulfilled in Indian families are:

Ensures Economic Progress

It enables economic progress of the country since everyone in the family is granted basic subsistence, a first condition of economic progress. Unless people are assured of food and shelter they would not devote themselves sincerely, to the work of country's progress. It is an essential condition of national progress that the citizens must at least get two meals a day; joint family provides this to its members and thus enables them to devote themselves to nation's progress.

Division of Labour

It secures the advantages of the division of labour. All members including women and children give every member in the family, work according to his abilities without unduly taxing the women. Thus, during the harvest season every member of the family helps in harvesting the crops. No outside labour is required.

Economy

It secures economy of expenditure. Since things are consumed on large quantities they are procured at economic prices. Within small means a large family can be maintained if it lives jointly.

Opportunity for Leisure

It provides opportunities for leisure to the members. The female members divide the household work and finish it within a little time, spending the rest of the while in leisure.

Social Insurance

In the joint family, the orphans find a comfortable asylum instead of being thrown out. Similarly, widows for whom remarriage in India is unthinkable in orthodox culture are assured of their proper livelihood. The joint family acts as a social insurance company for the old, sick and incapacitated.

Social Virtues

It fosters great virtues like sacrifice, affection, cooperation, spirit of selflessness and broad-mindedness among its members and makes the family a cradle of social virtues. Under the care of elders the undesirable and anti-social tendencies of the young are checked and they are prevented from going astray. They learn to exercise self-control. All members learn to obey family rules and respect their elders.

Avoids Fragmentation of Holdings

It avoids fragmentation of holdings and the evils inherent therein. It prevents property from being divided.

Socialism

According to Sir Henry Maine, the joint family is like a corporation where trustee is the father. Everyone in the joint family works according to his capacities but obtains help according to his needs. Thus, it realizes the socialistic ideal from each according to his ability, to each according to his needs.

Position of Women in India

The status of women in India has been a chequered one, as it has seen many ups and downs. There is no denying the fact, that women in India have made some progress. They are doctors, engineers, pilots, journalists, teachers, administrators, judges, etc. In spite of theses achievements, the fact remains that the women's condition is still a grim reality. According to the 1981 census report, there are 933 women per 1,000 men and against nearly 47 per cent literate men only 25 per cent women are literate. Dowry deaths, child marriages, the perpetuation of widowhood and the preference for a son continue to have social sanctions.

The situation on the economic front is no better. The women's work in the house which includes, collection of firewood, bringing of water from long distances, and their helping in the family business or in the fields is not recognized because they are not paid for it. The census report does not take note of this aspect.

The condition in the political arena is no better. Each political party stands up for women's participation in political activities in a big way. But do we see the reflection of their wishes in the Parliament? The percentage of women members of parliament has been on the decrease. Twenty-three women were elected to the Lok Sabha in the first general election while 19 were elected or nominated in the Rajya Sabha.

The overview of the situation generally is distressing. Rape, dowry deaths, misuse of the tests to determine the sex of the child in the womb, and the termination of pregnancy in the event of a female fetus, give an indication of the horrible male behaviour patterns. In recent years, the government has taken a number of steps to correct the wrong that is done to the girl child. The women have yet to go a long way before they can be equated with men.

Role of Education in Development of Women Status

In 1857, when Khurshedji a Parsi gentlemen sought the permission of the syndicate of Bombay University for his daughter to appear in matriculation examination the syndicate categorically refused. Similarly, Miss Chandramukhi Bose was not allowed to appear in the B.A. Examination of Calcutta University. In 1877, however, with the efforts of the Vice Chancellor Hob, women were allowed to appear in the examinations conducted by Calcutta University. It was only in 1882 that two women for the first time received the B.A. degree from Calcutta University. After this, there was such a strong wave of women being educated in India that now it cannot be said that Indian women are anywhere lagging behind men in this respect.

Social Institution and its Impact on Status and the Role of Women

The status of women in any society is the index of the standard of its social organization. The standard of a society rises and falls in correlation with the rise and fall in the status of women. Society is a web of social relationships. Of social relationships, those between male and female are the most intimate and stable. The society has always remained dynamic. The status of women in it has consequently always changed. A study of this change of status will on the one hand show the rights given to women and on the other hand the dynamic nature of social organization.

Status of Women in the Ancient Society

In ancient India, the women were given an equal status along with men in almost every field of life. They received higher education and participated in the discussion of political and philosophical nature with male scholars. The *Vedas*, the *Upanishads*, the *Mahabharata* and *Puranas* mentions the names of lady scholars, philosophers, poets and politicians in ancient India. In *Mahabharata,* the wife has been called the better half of the husband.

In *Aitreya Upanishad*, the wife has been called the companion of the husband. In *Rig Veda,* the wife has been blessed to live as a queen in the house of her husband. The word *Dampati* so often used in the *Vedas* characterizes both wife and husband. According to MacDonnell and Keith, this word signifies the high status of women in ancient India. The wife and husband cooperated in the different functions of the household. They together performed religious duties, enjoyed and carried out other functions.

In *Mahabharata*, the wife has been called the root of Dharma, prosperity and enjoyment. No man was allowed to perform religious duties without a wife. Thus, like the status of the women in contemporary western world, the status of Indian women in ancient India was based on liberty, equality and cooperation. What, however, takes emphasis is on spirituality and religion, duty and cooperation on the family life.

Status of Women in Medieval India

In the medieval India, the status of women was very much lowered. The scriptures prescribed rules for child marriages, which increased the number of widows. The rules of conduct for the widows were even more rigid. The ancient Indian ideal of the equality of male and female was finished and women were considered to be slaves of men. In Buddhist and Muslim periods, the status of women was lowered even further. In the Muslim time, the custom of veil, the *Sati* – the custom of dying on the funeral pyre of the husband was prevalent.

Status of Women in Modern India

About a century ago, the status of women in India was almost the same as it was in the medieval age. Though it cannot be said that the exploitation of women in India has no parallel in any other country, yet it can be safely ascertained that the women had to face much cruelty and exploitation in modern India. Even now, the birth of a daughter is not an occasion of happiness for many families. Ordinarily, the celebrations of the birth of sons are definitely more joyful than those of a birth of a daughter. The daughters are not given equal rights in the matters of food, clothing, education, etc. They are often married even without their consent. In the house of the husband, their status becomes even worse. The husband, the mother-in-law and the father-in-law treat her as a servant of the family whose only duty is to obey everyone; to arise earliest and to sleep late, to eat whatever remains after others have eaten and not to complain on anything or about anyone. If the husband deserts her or remarries or has untimely death, the condition of the woman becomes worst of all, as her family members believe that this calamity has fallen because of her bad luck. The widow gets no share in the property of her husband, nor is anyone prepared to marry her.

Mostly males, who kept the women without equal rights in the social life, formulated the principles of social organization. For centuries, the women tolerated all sorts of cruelties at the hands of males. Some male philosophers even called them as the doors of hell as if male were very much pure and great. The male made her to toil for the satisfaction of his desires and put the entire responsibility over her head. The widows were not permitted to marry and males of the household tried to enjoy with them secretly. She was turned out of the house. The helpless, weak and young widows were forced to adopt the job of prostitutes. This is the story of thousands of prostitutes in India. The women were asked to live as a complete celibate after the death of her husband. She was encouraged to die at the funeral pyre of her husband, as if in an effort to meet him in the heavens. The male could marry several times and the women had no right so to speak against him.

Problems of Women

There has been a constant rise in dowry death, bride burning and other forms of torture against women in the country. Rape, assault, molestation, kidnapping and illegal confinement are also rampant; both in rural and urban areas. In Delhi alone, the number of dowry deaths was 132 from January 1989 to February 1990 as discloses by the union minister in parliament. This apart, in 1987, Delhi led all union territories with 103 registered cases of rape, and in more than half of these cases the victims were minors. And, there were 161 rapes cases and many more such unreported cases, in the year 1989. If the crime situation in the nation's capital is so alarming, it is no better elsewhere.

Apart from heinous crimes, there are other offences too which are committed against women in subtler forms and on a wider scale. These are, for instance, abortions on suspicion that the child to be born may be a female, and denying the daughters the same quantity and quality of food as given to the sons.

Prostitution

Prostitution has been generally defined as being promiscuous; i.e., in-discriminate intercourse for hire whether paid in money or in kind. Elliott and Merrill remark that prostitution has been frequently defined, but all definitions are in essential agreement, namely, that the practice involves illicit sex union on a promiscuous and mercenary basis with accompanying emotional indifference. Prostitution is not to be confused with the illicit sex union of lovers, for there is no affection in prostitution.

Prostitution as a commercialized vice, has existed in the world from time immemorial, though its institution has never been recognized by the society as such. As the world's oldest profession, prostitution has undoubtedly existed in some form as long as society has attempted to regulate and control sex relationships through the institutions of marriage and the family. Society has not recognized it, because it brings in its trail, not only the personal disorganization of the persons concerned, but also affects the life organization of the family and the community at large.

Causes of Prostitution

The causes of prostitution fall under two main heads: biological and socio-economic. The first one is a natural phenomenon, while the second one is the creation of society. The biological course operates through sex urge in human beings. It is only by applied efforts that a man can control his sex desires, but it is not possible to do so in all cases. It is also the reason that man like the anthropoid apes can prostitute his sex by introducing sexual stimuli into intrinsically non-sexual situation, which is not possible in other lower species. Among the socio-economic factors have been included many, the most important being the poverty of the female who in the absence of any other means of support for herself or for her children resorts to prostitution. Davis Kingsley has explained prostitution on the basis of dominance and subordination.

In most of the societies, the male is the dominant factor in sex equation. This dominance is based upon both superior physical strength and certain traditional social norms. The female attempts to equalize this situation by attracting and holding the attention of the male by the use of the only power at her command – sexual stimulation and satisfaction. Among other socio-economic factors may be included: modern industrialization and rapid urbanization which have affected the sex ratio in the cities, control, lack of moral teaching, more contacts between men and women during employment, overcrowding, commercialized recreation including cinemas and dancing halls, drinking and late marriages to maintain high standard of living.

Panekar and Rao, who conducted a study of prostitutes in Mumbai, have mentioned 26 causes, which led females to prostitution. They have grouped these causes under six major heads. In the first are included deaths of parents or husbands, etc. In the second group are included economic causes, such as poverty and destitution. In the third are included domestic causes, such as ill treatment or neglect by the parents, husbands or relatives. In the fourth group are included kidnapping, deception, bad influence, etc. In the fifth group are included cases of psychological significance such as sexual urge, illegitimate pregnancy, etc. And the sixth cause relates to mental disposition or attitude such as ignorance, desire for easy life and moral values.

They further point out that any of these causes may occur as contributory causes, predisposing or direct causes depending upon each case. In other words, these are always more than one cause which lead one to prostitution. For example, the death of parents of a girl may render her vulnerable to prostitution, but the direct cause maybe the exploitation of her by a persecutor. However, we have discussed these causes under the following heads:

(1) Economic factors,
(2) Social values against the chastity,
(3) Mental deficiency or certain temperament traits,
(4) Ignorance,
(5) Unhappy marriage relationship,
(6) Inordinate sex desire,
(7) Desire for new experience,
(8) Restrictions on widow remarriage, and
(9) *Devdasi* system.

Research studies have described widely different motives and characteristics to females who become prostitutes. In general, however, it would appear that the main consideration is the need for money. It is an entry into what appears to a quick and easy way to make a living. There does not appear to be any systematic process of recruitment, at least in the United States, but rather a process of enlistment.

Females who do enlist come from all social classes, although majority appear to come from lower class or lower-middle class homes. However, some come from upper-middle and upper class who have had every advantage in terms of education and material resources. At the other extreme are females from poverty stricken areas that have not been so fortunate and turn to prostitution as the most accessible option for money-making and for maintaining at least a marginal way of life.

In fact, Haggerty has concluded that "prostitution seems to be a natural dumping ground for uneducated and unemployed, in a male dominated society". Often, prostitutes come from unstable families and have histories of frequent episodes during adolescence. Somewhere along the line they may receive money, as well as other presents for their sexual favours and become interested in the possibility of a career in prostitution.

The inclination to become a prostitute must be implemented by a profession. In a minority of cases, this may be achieved by entering a house of prostitution or brothel where training is provided. In some cases, where two females had been friends, sometimes the contact starts with homosexual relationship between the two. Their initial contact usually determine the type or social level of prostitution at which the woman began. These 'social levels' ranged from street walking to serving a select clientele as a high-class call girl.

Once the contact is acquired and the decision made to become a prostitute, the novice typically enters a period of apprenticeship that may last for several months in the case of call girls. After acquiring the necessary skills and a clientele, she has completed her training period and can go into business for herself.

Widow Remarriage

There are many references of widow marriage in ancient Indian literature. In the Vedic period, widow marriages were not prohibited. The word *Punarma* was used for that widow whose marriage was solemnized or performed for the second time. According to Narad Purana, there are three types of widow remarriages, viz., that of a woman who has been married but no cohabitation has taken place with her husband; then there is the woman who after leaving her first husband returns to him after leaving her second husband; and that of a woman who has been given to a spinster. In ancient period, widow remarriage was allowed.

From the beginning of 10th and 11th centuries, widow marriage was rather universally prohibited among the Hindus. There were only two options for the widows, namely, either to live as widows throughout their life or to burn themselves along with their deceased husbands on the funeral pyre. So long as the *Sati* custom remained prevalent, the condition of the widows in Hindu society continued to be very deplorable. They had to face and undergo many types of hardships, social, religious and cultural. Consequently, many efforts were made from time to time to end this custom. Mohammad Tuglug and Akbar tried to abolish this custom. Their efforts proved to be in vain. On December 4, 1829, Lord William Bentick abolished the custom of *Sati*. Thus burning in the pyre stopped, but they continued to lead a hard life.

Causes of Prohibition of Widow Remarriage

It is one of the main restrictions of Hindu marriage that women cannot remarry after her husband's death. In the Vedic period, widow marriages were not prohibited. It is evident from the fact that *Niyoga* custom was allowed by Manu. This custom allowed the practice of younger brother rising up to seed for his deceased elder brother who has left a childless widow. But later on, all Hindus deprecated this marriage custom. Therefore, the problem of widow marriage became a social problem. The following are some of the main causes of prohibition of remarriage of females:

(i) *Idca of Kanyadan*: According to this concept, the girl is denoted to a suitable candidate. One who enacts *Kanyadan* cultivates *punya* for his next birth. As anything can be denoted only one time, therefore the same concept also applies in case of girl.

(ii) *Idea of Sacredness*: All the religious texts of Hindus give a great importance to sacredness. Woman can retain her purity only when she may remain faithful to her husband in all aspects, namely her mind, body and intellect. Therefore, a Hindu widow cannot render her body to another man.

(iii) *Emphasis on Racial Purity*: After the Mohammedans settled in India, Hindus recognized the necessity of maintaining their racial purity. This feeling strengthened the restrictions upon women.

(iv) *Concept of Eternal Relationship*: A Hindu marriage is not only a social contract but it also recognizes that marriage relations are eternal. A husband and wife of their present birth remain husband and wife in their next birth. Therefore, almost all Hindu widows never accept to remarry.

(v) *Economic Dependency*: One of the most important factors on the hindrance of widow marriage lies in economic dependency of women. Their economic dependency is the main factor, which discourages them from taking a step towards this direction.

Divorce

Divorce is something alien or foreign to Hindu viewpoint. Hindus consider marriage as a sacrament, which is regarded as unbreakable throughout life. In spite of having different and opposite views the wife and husband are bound to live together. There is no reference of divorce in the whole of Vedic literature.

However, the reference of divorce is found in Kautilya's *Arthashastra.* According to Kautilya, if there is mutual jealousy between the wife and husband, then they can leave each other. Present age believes in providing equal opportunities to each person – his or her development. Hence, in such circumstances emphasis has been given on the validity of the provisions of divorce. Consequently, many provisions of law have been made in this connection. But some women face problems after divorce. They become prostitutes. They face economic and social problems and there is a chance of losing their life.

Dowry

The practice of giving dowry is very common among the Indian people. Among Hindus, a girl gets all the domestic utensils that are necessary to set up a new family; the practice of dowry was prevalent during Vedic period. During this epic age, dowry was recognized as a woman's property. It included all types of gifts from parents, brothers and relations.

Now, the custom of dowry has undergone a great change. It is considered as the bridegroom's price by which a father buys a husband for her daughter. Development of education has enhanced this practice. Though the dowries are normally proportional to the means of bride's family, yet it is one of the most apparent causes of indebtedness. We will now make a reference to the custom of dowry that was prevalent among Hindus for a long time and because of which many great difficulties were being experienced. In Delhi alone, the number of dowry deaths was 132 between 1989 and 1990.

Cases of Missing Women/Girls

Justice seems to be a dream for a large number of tribals in the state. Largely living under a below poverty line status, these tribals are exposed to exploitation. Their young daughters and women face open threats of sexual abuse and often are forced to remain mum without even filing reports with police. In a large number of cases, professionals who take them to metro cities to work as bonded sex workers abduct young and beautiful tribal girls.

These girls are further sold to agents who take them abroad for the same immoral acts. Parents of these sex models are given petty amounts in order to silence them. The alarming rise in cases of missing tribals and low recovery of such persons has caused considerable worry at police headquarters, but no substantial action has been initiated so far.

Sources informed that most of these women and girls hail from economically weak sections of the society. Officials informed that lower class tribals in rural areas are exposed to such crimes and fall prey to agents who generally camouflage themselves as labour working in metro cities and take the girls along with them to bigger cities. These girls are first forced into immoral activities in the metro cities and then sold through agents. These girls are forced to work as sex workers in other countries as well.

Cases of Missing Women/Girls Registered in MP during 2001

Month	*Women*	*Recovered*	*Girls*	*Recovered*
January	228	109	157	80
February	182	72	154	58
March	247	85	197	80
April	275	96	233	96
May	270	85	211	77
June	288	93	180	71
July	233	96	159	87
August	215	80	146	86
September	186	74	127	57
October	249	146	185	115
November	228	89	170	84
December	226	102	188	98

Source: The Voice, July 31, 2002.

Rape

It is a most atrocious act against women and human rights, which impairs their freedom and fundamental rights. According to *Student News*, February 7, 2002, "a rape occurs every 40 minutes". This happens not only with unmarried women but with married ones too. Today, women have complained about their husbands that they come home drunk and force them to have sex with them. When women stand against it they are beaten and thrashed by the family. These women are generally uneducated who are scared to stand against it. Many are going through unbearable sufferings but very few stand for them.

Rape has increased more rapidly in the last decade than any other type of violent crime; in 1974 the FBI reported over 55,000 cases of forcible rape. The actual incidence is considered to be 3 to 4 times more than what these figures indicate, since most cases go unreported due to the social stigma involved and the additional trauma the victim is likely to undergo if she reports being raped. Most of the time, rape tends to be a repetitive activity rather than an isolated act, and most rapes are planned events. About 80 per cent of rapists commit the act in the neighbourhood in which they reside. Most rapes take place in an urban nocturnal setting.

Exploitation

According to the Constitution of India, everyone has a right to live in the society according to his or her will. But today, the world has changed. There is a big gap between sexes, the poor and the rich. The situation of our country is becoming worst. In this situation, we can divide the exploitation of women in the following manner:

Population Exploitation

If we see the population of our country we find more men than women. There are some reasons, which cause population and sex difference such as abortion, toxaemia, anaemia, bleeding pregnancy, etc. Today having sex illegally and abortion have become common. No one considers it as malice. This case often occurs with educated men and women. They want to have sex but do not want to have children in their laps. Many times, not wanting a child, they do abortion and many times in the process they die.

Reason	*1989 (%)*	*1995 (%)*
Abortion	10.9	17.6
Toxaemia	7.5	7.9
Anaemia	20.3	17.0
Bleeding	23.8	28.9
Other Reasons	20.3	14.1

Source: Register General of Indian Women and Men in 1999.

Educational Exploitation

According to the Constitution, every man and women has a right to have education. It is the eye for people. Arusto says, "The education differs from the uneducated as much as the living from the dead." But today it is tragedy for our country when only 8.86 per cent women are educated. The reason behind this is that she is *paraya dhan* (other's wealth). The parents therefore, feel that educating a girl-child is a luxury. She has to ultimately get married and look after another family. Also it is believed that educating them is like westernization, especially for the middle class women and children. They consider it a mistake to send their children to schools because educating them is also a threat to men over the females. The boys are, there fore, given more care for their studies and the girls are forced to stay at home. When they are above ten or twelve years of age, the girls are settled because some parents see them as burden for the family. Today, women need to be educated because educating them will breed a new generation. If the woman is educated there will be positive effect in health care, cleanliness and education. But the general condition of women today is bad in our country. Only a handful of women are educated which is illustrated in the following table:

Literacy Rate in Different Years

Year	*Percentage of Literacy*	
	Women	*Men*
1951	8.86	27.16
1961	13.34	40.40
1971	21.97	45.95
1981	29.75	56.37
1991	39.29	64.13
2001	53.67	75.26

Source: Census Record of Literacy Level of Population.

Socio-Health Exploitation

It is tragedy for an independent country like ours where lots of health centres are provided but yet there is so many death of mothers and children. About 3 lakh women die annually because they do not get even general medical care.

On the other hand, in rural areas, the health centres are not properly functioning due to inadequate medical professionals and the people generally go for country medical treatment by non-qualified medical practitioners which results in other complications or even death. Today, we can see the situation of women in our society where they have to go through such terrible pain and death because of lack of medical facilities.

Economic Exploitation

It is true that men have made women to be meek and submissive. There are some other reasons of their victimization. It is by tradition that they are deprived of property, as long as they are with their husbands. It is noticed that if a father has only daughters the brother-in-law inherits the property, which does not seem to be appropriate. In such cases a woman is totally abandoned of her right in the family. The lack of employment, poverty and alcohol are also a cause of their exploitation. The root cause, however, is illiteracy and poverty.

Women are paid half to three quarters of the money their male counterparts earn for the same job. This is the case whether it is agricultural or other contractual jobs. They have to do the work for 10 to 16 hours per day. Besides, they have to do cooking, washing, cleaning up the house, etc. In the case of young married women, it is pathetic when they have to carry the burden of early pregnancy and childbirth and feeding.

Current Statistics on Women's Problems

- 28 per cent of India's workforce is women, up from 13 per cent in 1987.
- Women hold 3 per cent of senior management posts in corporate India.
- 1 million women have been elected to Panchayats since 1993.
- 48 women MPs in the 13th Lok Sabha.
- 9 women head state governments.
- 16,496 rapes in 2000, up from 15,468 in 1999. Every 54 minutes a women is raped.
- 374 rapes in 2000 makes Delhi the most unsafe metro followed by Mumbai (124), Kolkata (35) and Chennai (24).
- 1,651 rape cases pending trial in Delhi courts. 350 cases are added every year. All India conviction rate is 29.8 per cent.
- 488 molestation cases in Delhi in 2000. Delhi share 19.9 per cent of all other cities.

- 80 per cent woman say sexual harassment exits in the workplace.
- 53 per cent say women do not get equal opportunity and are treated unfairly by supervisors, employers and co-workers.
- 70 per cent respondents in the survey say women in general face inappropriate behaviour. Verbal abuse is the most commonly reported form of sexual abuse.

Source: Sunday Times of India, New Delhi, December 8, 2002.

Crime Against Women in Delhi

Year	*Dowry Death*	*Rape*	*Kidnapping*	*Abduction*
2001	125	435	998	1269
2001	113	384	1061	1095
2002	130	383	842	1333

Source: The Hindu, December 29, 2002.

General Reasons for Rise in Crimes Against Women and their Remedies

(1) One reason why crimes against women continue to increase is that there is hardly any deterrent and the culprits feel that they can easily get away with anything. Imagine, in all the cases of dowry deaths in Delhi over the past four years, there has been only one conviction.

(2) Dowry Prohibition Act 1961, has been modified. The rape law also, with the cases of cruelty to married women, was modified to remove some of its drawbacks. All these measures, however, could not check the crime from further escalating. The objectives of these laws may not be faulted; but what is of crucial importance is their enforcement. A wide gap exists between laws with high social and economic purposes and their implementation, on account of police inefficiency and widespread corruption. In this climate, the cutting edge of laws, both as instruments of crime prevention and that of social change, is bound to get blunted.

(3) Legal remedies alone cannot cope with a regressive social-economic set-up in the absence of radical structural, social and economic reforms, which can be implemented only by mass protests and mass participation. A struggle even for the implementation of the existing laws that can help to uphold, protect the demands of women can be of much value.

(4) It is also a matter of regret that the courts have of late begun to treat the accused with what might be described as irresponsible leniency. Apart from negating the serious views of custodial rape, the decision also mollifies the guidelines issued by the central government in late eighties to prevent the police misbehaving with women.

(5) Long delays in the law courts are also responsible for a spurt in crimes. The courts will certainly have to ensure speedy justice to victims not otherwise possible under the normal process of law, which are not only time consuming but also humiliating.

(6) Ironically, public response to violence against women is one of indifference. This is evident from the cold-blooded murder of a young school girl, Rinku Patil, by her boy friend and four of his companions in Ulhasnagar, near Mumbai in broad day light. Four young gun totting youngsters walked into the examination hall unmindful of police presence, poured petrol on the girl and set fire to her. Within a minute, the living girl was reduced to lifeless ash in full public view. After performing the cruel deed, the criminals walked out without facing any resistance from the public.

In sum, there can be no two opinions about the need for necessary laws, sensitive judiciary, effective enforcement machinery, and vigilant women's groups to deal with such atrocious crimes against women. But, what is needed more than anything else, is a total evolution in the thinking of society that always blames the women for the crime of which she is victim not the perpetrator.

Constitutional and Legal Safeguards for Women

After independence, all-round efforts have been made to promote the welfare of women. The new Constitution declared India to be sovereign democratic republic based on four pillars of justice, liberty, equality and fraternity. Article 15 of the Constitution confers equal rights for sexes, though the state could make any special provision for women. Article 14, 15 and 16 relating to fundamental rights guarantee to all citizens irrespective of sex, equality before the law, equal protection of the law and equality of opportunities in matters of public employment. It is in the light of these provisions in the Constitution that social legislation has been passed to improve their rights. Special steps are being taken to improve their education, health facilities, economic position and for their proper participation in family and community life.

Policies and Programmes for Women: Review of Present Situation and Its Impact

The policies and programmes for women differ to a great extent in different communities, and therefore, the programmes for their welfare are to be worked out differently to fulfil the needs of each section. For example, the pattern of work in the urban areas is different from the rural areas and the role of women is different in upper and lower classes.

Improvement in Rights and Status

The various Acts passed are the Hindu Marriage Act 1955, Hindu Succession Act 1956, Hindu Minority and Guardianship Act, 1956 and the Hindu Adoption and Maintenance Act 1956. Under the Hindu Succession Act, widows have been conferred full rights over their property. Besides, the mother and daughters have also been given equal rights in property with the sons. Under the Hindu Adoption and Maintenance Act, a woman can adopt a son in her own name. When both male and female are alive, the husband will have to take the consent of his wife for adoption. Thus, in many respects the rights of women have been brought at par with men.

Education Advancement

In 1929, the All India Women's College with expertise in home science was established in New Delhi. With this college, the significance of home science studies received added emphasis in women's educational programmes in all school curricula and the university courses. In spite of all these steps, women's education did not receive the required attention of the state. The Central Social Welfare Board, with the twin objects of providing employment opportunities to deserving and needy women, and to create a band of competent trained workers required to man the various welfare projects, particularly in rural areas, started the scheme of job contents courses of education for adult women in 1958. And, on the whole the programme has been successful.

Health Services

Maternity benefits are granted by Acts passed by state governments. The scope qualifying conditions and the period and rate of maternity benefits vary in different states. Some employers try to avoid complying with the Maternity Benefits Acts, while there are others who go beyond the provision and provide for free medical aid, supervision and treatment when necessary, and the employers provide crèches for babies of women workers in large industries. Under the employee's state insurance against the risk of sickness, maternity also is provided. In the rural areas under the community development programme and welfare extension projects sponsored by the social welfare board, such facilities are being provided. Under this programme, family planning scheme is also provided.

Economic Emancipation

Throughout the ages within the memory of man, women have been engaged in farm jobs and have performed a multiplicity of tasks requiring manual labour. With the advancement of education and the coming of the industrial revolution, women have taken up various types of jobs in the educational, professional or industrial fields. Our Constitution provides equal rights to women in case of employment. At the same time, the states make special legislation for the protection of women due to their certain disabilities.

Programmes for Victimized Women

Among the victimized women may be included those who are in moral danger, criminals, economically dependents or widows and physically or mentally handicapped.

Prostitutes

The Suppression of Immoral Traffic Act has been passed in 1956. Rescue homes are to be set up all over the country to rehabilitate women who are the victims of social vice. The association has undertaken the main work for moral and social hygiene in India. The association has set up a rescue home in Delhi, where abducted women are admitted. There, they are given domestic science and higher education.

After Care Service

Under these schemes, state homes are being set up to provide temporary shelter, organize protection units and give guidance and help to women who come out of the institutional correctional and non-correctional homes. Therapy which helps in the process of their ultimate rehabilitation in the community is also given. It was estimated that by end of Second Plan period, there would be about 80 production units and 330 district shelters providing facilities to nearly 40,900 persons including women.

Destitutes and Physically Handicapped Women

The state social welfare departments and the central social welfare board are now rendering financial aid to deserving organizations and institutions working for the welfare of women. The Planning Commission points out, "The central social board will continue to assist voluntary organizations which implement programme of women welfare, such as condensed courses of education for adult women, urban welfare extension projects, etc. It is proposed to allocate one core group specifically for assisting voluntary organizations for the welfare programmes for destitute women."

Welfare Programme for Women at the Central and State Levels

Women all over the world have been struggling for their rights and privileges and initiating women liberation movements to achieve their rightful place in their respective societies. The United Nations had declared 1975, as International Women's Year and the 1975-85 as the International Women's Decade. March 8 is observed as women's day in our country every year. All these anniversaries and commemorative days are observed to focus the attention and concern of the governments and the society on the needs of women and the efforts required to meet them, and of their fundamental right to equality, the equal rights to nutrition, health education and opportunity to begin with right to survive.

(i) Many states launched the 20-point programmes that lay special emphasis on accelerated programmes for women welfare and nutrition programmes for pregnant women, nursing mothers, especially on tribal hilly and backward areas.
(ii) Set up women and children development corporations.
(iii) Construction of a number of women's hostel buildings by voluntary organizations with the aid given by the central and state governments.
(iv) Provision of crèches in conjunction with working women's hostels as well as in other establishments.
(v) Various concessions, facilities for working women like relaxation on age limit in entering government services, special level benefits, etc.

(vi) The Central Social Welfare Board, State Social Welfare Advisory Boards, Indian Council for Women Welfare, etc., were in existence long before the international women's decade.

The Department of Women and Child Development is charged with the nodal responsibility to implement and coordinate programmes of women's welfare and development. It activates different ministry departments, both at the centre and state levels dealing with women's development. The department besides playing a nodal role also implements the following schemes for the welfare and development of women:

- Hostels for working women.
- Employment and income generating production programmes.
- Women's training centres; institutes for the rehabilitation of women.
- Short-stay homes for women and girls.

Role of Women's Organizations and Voluntary Action on Women's Development

It is the measures taken for the development and welfare of women that was partly due to social upsurge and change in attitudes, manifesting themselves into various forms and ways, and partly due to accompanying social, economic and legal measures, that the women in Independent India have come to acquire a better status in the society. Today's women have better acceptability and respectability, better rights and privileges, better opportunities and avenues in all spheres of national life – social, economic and political.

Indra Mahila Yojana

Mahila Sabhas, would include women from all those areas that would administer the *Indira Mahila Yojanas* in villages and *mohallas*. They would be governed by the Gram Panchayat in rural areas and *nagarpalikas* in urban areas. The *Mahila Sabhas* would choose from among themselves the *saathis* or voluntary lady workers, who would primarily be in charge of informing women of the locality of the schemes that were available. Over the next few years, a women and child development centre would be opened in every village panchayat area or municipal ward of the country.

Women's Development Corporation

Under the scheme, the union government will provide funds to states through equity participation. The authorized capital of each corporation will be decided keeping in view the total programme, which the corporation proposed to undertake. The ministry will participate in the equity in the 49:51 ratios so that the state governments have an incentive and assistance to set up such corporations. In other words, the Department of Women and Child Development will give up to 49 per cent of the paid up capital as financial assistance.

Financial Assistance for Self-Employment to Women

In order to promote entrepreneurship amongst women, corporations release loans from its own funds at highly subsidized rates of interest varying from 3 per cent to 7 per cent. Of late, it had been arranging loans for women mainly through banks and advancing loans on a restricted scale to be able to utilize its funds for other economic and social welfare programmes, where bank assistance is not available. In a case of financial assistance to women through banks, benefit of interest subsidy is allowed from yellow cardholder families up to a loan amount of Rs 10,000.

Training and Employment Programme

In order to prepare women for self-employment by making full use of their financial assistance arranged and made available by it, the corporation organizes training and orientation camps, in rearing of cross-breed cows, raising poultry farms, training in knitting, soap making, fruit preservation and a few other trades independently as well as in collaboration with departments and organizations connected with particular activities. The corporation has also set up handicraft centres where women learn traditional and non-traditional arts, embroidery as well as tailoring and cutting.

Training and Guaranteed Employment Programmes

All women are not able to take up an independent economic activity for various social and economic reasons. The corporation has, therefore, undertaken a number of assured and guaranteed employment programmes. For example, it set up a readymade garments unit at Mohali in July 1983, which has trained more than 200 women workers. It has been declared as an approved source for the supply and stitching of government uniforms and office linen. It also gets quota for export of garments to USA and Canada.

Problems of Women Workers

According to the Directive Principles of our Constitution, state is required to secure equal pay for equal work for both men and women, right to work, education, public assistance in case of unemployment, old age, silences and disablement. It seeks to protect the interest of the weaker section of the society. Weaker sections among the industrial workers are those, who are either unorganized or underprivileged and whose economic and social condition needs special attention. We may include under this category female labourer, child labourer, physically handicapped, contract labourer, inter-state migrant workman, casual labourer, contract and *badli* labourer, bonded labourer and agricultural labourer who form a sizeable segment of the workforce both in the formal and informal sectors.

Women Workers

According to 1981 census, women workers constitute about 18 per cent of the total workforce. Women are employed in large number in plantation, cotton, textile, *bidi*, garment, rice mill, tobacco crushing, cashew nut, matches, construction work, household and small scale industries and in different informal sectors activities. As a result of advancement of education, science and technology in recent years, there is marked increase in the number of women employed in newer seeking employment is increasing from year to year due to several reasons in public undertaking and organized industries. Increased opportunities to women in educational and training institutes have also widened their employment potentials.

Problems

Some of the major hindrances for women in employment are as follows:

1. *Restrictions*: There is certain restrictions for employment of female labour in tea plantation especially in Assam. In industries also, there are some jobs that women's cannot perform as men. Such as working near dangerous machines, cotton openers, etc. The working hours for women is also prohibited from 7 p.m. to 7 a.m. They are also restrained from being employed below ground in any part of mines.

2. *Illiteracy*: Generally, illiteracy is widespread among the women that make them dependent and obstruct them to build up to a status in the society. In need even if they want to seek employment, it becomes difficult.
3. *Early marriage*: Due to early marriage for girls, they are not given a chance to go for education and pressurized by both the sides to follow traditional family customs only and they are not supposed to cross the limit of family norms laid down by the elders. This makes a narrow outlook for women and consequently in time of need employer exploits them if they want to work.
4. *Unequal remuneration*: Generally, women are paid less wages as compared to men even for work of similar nature.
5. *Lack of amenities and facilities*: The facilities like crèches, maternity benefits, hospitals, health benefits, housing, hostels, separate toilets, bathing, washing, etc., generally are not provided by the employers for women hence it becomes very difficult especially for the working expectant mothers. In a safety survey, the working condition of women employed in plantation, cashew and coir industry were also far from satisfactions.
6. *Insecurity*: Due to lack of organization and dependency on others even the Trade Unions have not come forward to look upon the interest of the women employees that further leads to job insecurity.
7. *Lack of freedom*: Women do not have much freedom from home and family to come out better in the society due to *status quo*, or prestige issue or several other reasons.
8. *Overburdened*: To much household responsibilities are endowed upon women which further effects the work efficiency. In addition to this, family problems and misunderstandings may also force them to leave employment.
9. *Lack of welfare provision of farm woman labourers*: In all agriculture communities, women work side by side by men and share equally with men all the work in the field, except ploughing. But such women workers in agriculture do not receive any statutory protection and amenities as their counter parts in industries, such as provision for crèche, separate provision for health, safety, welfare and working hours of female labours in factories, mines, plantations and industrial and commercial establishments.

Government has taken some measures for the welfare and protection of women in the society such as constituting Women Right Commission, setting up of Vocational and Technical Education Center, Urban Female Welfare Scheme, Welfare extension projects, State Women Welfare Department, Family and Child Welfare projects, etc.

In spite of good intention with which our country has adopted beneficial pieces of welfare legislature in practices they leave much to be desired. Not much stress seems to have been laid to the effective implementation of these protective legislative provisions.

State of Girlchild in Indian Milieu

The sex ratio of a population is not purely a biological phenomenon but is a result of biological and social factors that cannot be easily separated. Biological phenomenon does not vary much from one country to another. But the sex ratio in advanced countries is significantly different from that of the less developed countries, i.e., female tend to outnumber men in advanced countries whereas in the less developed world there are more men that women.

The existence of preferences for children of given sex is evident not only from biblical and anthropological literature but also from everyday experience. Relative preferences for different contributions of sons and daughters are heavily conditioned by culture, social customs and general economic mortality and health conditions of the people. They are also dependent on the difference between males and females in their roles at various stages in the life cycle and also on the difference in the nature of their participation in different economic activity and other responsible work. The preference for a son holds much importance in our country. For a Hindu the '*Shraddha*' ceremony after his death is very important since he believes that without this his soul will not complete its transmigration and reincarnation. Only his son can carry out this ceremony fully and properly. In India, traditionally, a married woman possesses a higher position in her husband's household only after the birth of a son and couples with many sons are admired. Further more polygamy is not fully recognized in India, but it is found that childlessness and inability to produce a male child may lead a man establishing a polygynous household. To some extent, the dowry system in India may lead to some dislike for female offspring. This system was officially abolished in 1960 by an Act of parliament proclaiming punishment in fines or imprisonment for giving, taking or demanding dowry. In spite of this prohibitory order by the government, this system in some from or other is still widespread on large scale in India. It is perhaps more prevalent among the educated class.

Some of the important problematic areas of girlchild in India are as follows:

Age at Marriage

In more than one-third of the total districts in India, the age of marriage for girls is less than 15 years. Most of these districts are in the states of MP, Bihar, Rajasthan and UP. It is observed that most of these states are form the heartland of the country. A case of woman remaining unmarried after 30 years is usually unheard of in rural areas. With early marriage, compulsory marriage, childbirth and family responsibility, women have to suffer a large number of handicaps in terms of their health, education and employment opportunity.

The Child Marriage Restraint Act XIX of 1929 in British India was the first legal step to check the custom of child marriages. Undoubtedly, this had some impact and the incidence of marriages at very early ages (even before puberty) tended to decrease. However, the period between the passing of the Act (September 28, 1929) and its enforcement on April 1, 1930, was still utilized by the public to perform child marriage on the large scale. Also the Special Marriage Act of 1954 revised and replaced the Special Marriage Act of 1872 so as to provide a special form of marriage, which can be taken as advantage of by any person in India and by citizens of India in foreign countries irrespective of the faith, which either party to the marriage may profess. This Act provides for the minimum age for females to marry as 18 years and 21 years for the males.

Literacy Rates and Education

Kerala has the highest literacy rate in rural and urban India, while Rajasthan has the lowest rate. A substantial advance in women's education as also in other sphere of education came out only after independence. In spite of this expansion, enrolment of girls at all stages lies behind that of boys. One out of every 3 girls in the age group of 6-11 years is out of school. The rate of school drop-outs is also high at the primary stage where out of every 100 girls enrolled in class I, only about 30 reach class V itself. This has serious consequences for female literacy. On primary education and literacy, the Constitution of India had stipulated by a directive principle that compulsory elementary education of eight years be provided to all children in age group of 6-14 years. Not only does the promise remain unfulfilled today but also it has been found impossible to enrol in schools even the lower elementary age group of 6-11 years (class I to V), in full. Girls' enrolment in school from SC/ST is very low. In fact, in certain backward areas education of girls has hardly made any beginning. It has been noted earlier that one-third of the age group of 6-11 years do not enter the school and those who enter, drop-out in the Ist standard. This means that more than half of the younger generation of girls goes into life without literacy. This along with the slow rise in female literacy, the total number of illiterate women is also increasing from decade to decade.

Female Work Participation

Female workers are generally confronted with discrimination attitude in varying degree on ground of sex in matters of employment opportunity, wages and working condition. Most of the girl children among the lower class families are engaged in work as domestic worker or agricultural labourer. The single largest group of women works as landless labourers. Some of the reasons given for more work participation of women as landless labourers can be explained in terms of:

1. Most agricultural operations are simple and do not require skills.
2. Female employments in agricultural is of seasonal nature and women are not required to be away from homes.
3. Since the wages paid to female workers are low, employers find it economical to employ them.
4. In agriculture, female workers could be made to work for extra hours.

A major difference between productivity of female and male labour begins to develop when men become specialized producers of some non-agricultural goods and services. While females continue to produce goods for family consumption only. As long as this specialized worker in agriculture or craft is trained within the family, the difference in male and female productivity remains small. But the gap in productivity between the two sexes widens considerably at the stage when boys get systematic training in schools or workshops while girls continue to be taught only by their mothers. Labour productivity of women in developing countries is inferior to that of male workers from the same community because women have lower level of education and training. Based on above discussions certain constitutions can be drawn. We may sum up as follows:

- Female population faces risk at every stage of life, as the infant and maternal mortality rates are very high especially in rural India.
- Female population is illiterate and does not posses much skill.
- Most of the females work as landless labourers. They do not posses specialized skills that will bring them better wages.

To overcome this situation, some institutional changes would be necessary while some of the changes are immediate, some would take many years.

Child Development

Each person comes to the formal study of child development with a unique background and a unique set of expectations. Unlike the approach to many academic disciplines, opinions have already been formulated on the points of view of child development. The varied expectations of students influence their ability to profit from the study of specific competencies in preparation for parenthood after the teaching. Others may seek to understand a specific child more adequately. Thus, one recognizes that the students of widely varied experiences, backgrounds, and expectations frequently study child development.

The Role of the Family in Child Development

The family is the major environmental influence and remains throughout life the most pervasive of all influences. It is in the family that the child either learns to trust people or to be fearful and uncertain of others. It is in the home that the child first experiences the meaning of life; it is here that he comes to experience the give and take of family life. The child who cannot get along with other siblings may eventually have difficulty in getting along with other persons. One of the advantages of family life is the opportunity to learn the responsibilities of caring for others. The family has a most significant role to play on the development of personality. The customs and beliefs of our society are first handed down with the family. Here, the child first observes and then internalizes the value of the parents. Social, political, and religious beliefs and customs are transmitted via the family. It is in the family that the child first struggles with developing a feeling of adequacy. It is here that he is put to the test to show what he can produce or achieve. The family gives him his first objects for identification and provides the situation for the eventual development of an ego identity. Kagan indicates that the significant motive for the identification process is the desire to possess desirable characteristics of the model.

The child wishes to posses adult qualities such as power, competence, strength, and receipt of affection. The integrity displayed in family relations also is a model for the child in developing his own sense of integrity. The family usually teaches well, what is punished and what is encouraged, what is valued and what is ignored, and regardless of what parents say, the child is quite astute in observing what is actually adhered to.

Importance of Child Development

Child development is important for the child himself, for the family and for the society. It is important for the child himself in the sense that he will be able to perform his duties well, when he has a good physique, a good mind and a good personality. His development is good for the family as he forms a part of the family, being its member. His betterment is also the betterment of the society. The child on this sense is the most important element of society. As Milton has rightly said, "child shows the man as morning shows the day". The childhood is the best period for physical, mental and spiritual development. Child is the potential force for the nations. He is the future and should be developed on the right lines. He is the present as well as the future. The child is the father of the man. Thus, child development is very important.

Problems of Children

Nowadays children face a lot of problems. For example, child labour, education, food and so on. These problems leads them towards crime. They become more confused and disorganized persons. Environmental factors that affects them very much are: the family condition in a broken home, size of family, unsatisfactory parent-child relationship, etc. Children can be categorized as follows and each group face some problems: normal children, children of unmarried mothers, disabled children, orphans, children of prostitutes, destitutes, street children and deserted children.

Role of Social Worker in Child Development

Social worker plays a very important role in child development, since the children face a lot of problems and the social worker helps him to face the problems strongly. The social worker cannot be with children always but he supports in all the possible ways. He helps the children along with the parents; the parents give them physical growth and the social worker gives the relaxation part and it goes hand in hand. He promotes earning opportunities and social esteem and realizes his potentialities for future growth. He promotes optimism, emotional stability like a secure home, discipline, socialization, and parental acceptability of the child as a personality in his own right. Then he gives a social acceptable value that is acceptable in the behaviour pattern in a community. He promotes individuality, flexibility, self-responsibility and self-understanding that the freedom to explore permissive attitude, democratic approach and encouragement to examine his needs, purpose and potentiality for future growth.

Development of Women and Children in Rural Areas

Government of India has sponsored programmes for development of women and children belonging to families below poverty line in rural areas. It aims at promoting income generation activities amongst women and its main focus is on making and marketing of products, by organizing women in groups to take up economic activities. To begin with, it is proposed to constitute 240 groups in two districts.

The corporation also runs *Anganwadi* training centres under integrated child development scheme of the Government of India. In short, the scope of the corporation is very vast, since it intends catering to women of all social and income groups, of course, with social emphasis on women from weaker sections of the society and socially under privileged women. Almost all activities of the corporation are of promotional nature. Enhanced economic status is a pre-requisite to enhance social prestige and status. Corporation, therefore, plans to go ahead at a faster speed for further increasing its scope of functioning.

It aims at helping the women not only to help themselves, but also to bring prosperity to their families, particularly beneficiaries of mothers' prosperity.

Child Development: Few Essential Traits

"Give me a team of young people of character, and I can change the face of this country," said Swami Vivekanand. Character cannot be attained in a day or two. It is a continuous process. Today's world is personality driven. 'Personality', that is, the behaviour you put up when you are being watched and for 'character' that is the behaviour you put up when you are alone and nobody is watching you.

Children who have been taught 'character' by their parents automatically know 'right' from ' wrong' and have the will to practice what is the right thing to do irrespective of the costs and consequences attached to them.

Some points worth mentioning about development of character are:

- *Accountability*: Making the child accountable for his behaviour teaches him to differentiate right from wrong. It also teaches your kids that we are all allowed to make the right choice. All children who have character make right choice. The child will quickly learn to be accountable for right choice.
- *Forgiveness*: Teaching the child to forgive is the best way to achieve peace of mind and live a stress-free life; children are unique in the sense that they cannot remember the wrong done to them more than a day or two.
- *Humour*: Laughing with your children as often as you can is enjoyable for the parents and the children. Children come out with funny things which are a joy to behold.
- *'No' – Use it and Mean it*: It is difficult to say no to our children at times but it is imperative to say no, when the occasion requires. So let your children not intimidate you.
- *Respect – Show your Children due Respect:* While talking to your children, it is must to talk nicely, to show them that you feel they are worthwhile people. Shouting, screaming or yelling only make matters worse, as parents tend to loose the respect in the eyes of their children. Parents are required to set an example for their children. They should not forget the fact that their little eyes and a tender mind are keeping watch on them and the actions will have an everlasting impression in their minds.

Child Welfare

In this age, the term 'child welfare' has assumed a broader meaning. It is not only concerned with the case of the maladjusted and delinquents, but incorporates the social, economic and health activities of public and private agencies, which secure and protect the well-being of the children, in their physical intellectual and emotional development. Scientific progress in the fields of anthropology, biology, medicine, psychology and social research during the past hundred years has changed the attitude of society towards the child. He no longer is treated as an adult person only smaller in stature, but as a human being with his own different rhythm of life and with his own laws of biological and mental growth. We are aware that the child is following drives, social forces and motivations from those that govern adult behaviour.

Evaluation of Child Welfare on Pre- and Post-Independence Periods

As in many other fields, independence ushered in a new era in the field of child welfare.

Constitutional Provisions

Our constitution made the following provisions in Part III under fundamental rights, Article 15 provisions for women and children. Article 24 provided protection against child labour. In Article 39 is provided protection against exploitation and against moral and material abandonment. Under Article 45 is the provision for free and compulsory education for all children until they compete the age of fourteen years. Article 46 states that the state shall regard the raising of the level of nutrition and the standard of living of its people and the improvement of public health as among its primary duties.

Child Health and Nutrition Services

At the sub-district level, there will be a woman doctor having specialized training in this branch and two health visitors, whose main function would be training of *dais*, supervision of midwives and *dais* and care of maternity cases needing hospitalization. The ultimate aim is to have one unit of maternity centre for a population of 10,000. Health services for school-going children are very meagre. The corporation and municipalities in cities and towns have been making attempts to conduct annual physical examination of children. In order to provide wholesome diet to the people, this programme was started in selected community development blocks in the beginning of the Third Five-Year Plan. The main components of the programmes are production of protective foods like eggs, training of selected villagers engaged in the production of these foods and organization of educational feeding schemes.

Recreational and Cultural Activities

Play is a vital need in the life of the child and his playing activities may be in the home, school or community environments and take the form of playthings, companionship and playground activities. The extra-curricular activities in schools have opened up a new era in the field of child welfare. The children centre is now being equipped with playgrounds, indoor space for a children's library, a dramatics hall, and facilities for developing child arts and hand crafts so that the scope of children's recreations can be extended. Besides this, holiday camps and programmes for children of low-income group were also organized.

Handicapped Children

Among the handicapped children may be involved the physically mentally and socially handicapped.

(i) *Physically Handicapped:* Among the physically handicapped may be included the blind, the deaf, the dumb and suffering from other physical disabilities. The Planning Commission in the First Five-Year Plan recommended that at least one child guidance clinic should be brought into existence in every state, and where possible such clinics should be organized by municipalities. The organization of this service is likely to be handicapped for want of psychiatrists and child psychologists. Necessary training will have to be provided in the schools of social work to train personnel for them.

(ii) *Feeble Minded Children*: The problem of feeble mindedness did not receive due attention till recently and there was not a single institution in the country to look after and treat the feeble minded children. The psychologists and educationists are now gradually giving their attention to this problem and efforts are afoot to start some pilot projects in order to tackle this problem on a comprehensive scale. Sufficient number of trained psychologists and psychiatrists will be needed for this purpose.

(iii) *Socially Handicapped Children*: In an economically underdeveloped country, the number of destitute children must be very large. To this may be added the number of children who are virtually without guardians, such as lone, orphaned, neglected, deserted or destitute children. Several legislations for children have been passed in various states, but they are not very effectively enforced. There are some ashrams, missionary homes, salvation army homes, Ram Krishna Mission homes, etc., for the destitute. Besides, there are a large number of unregistered institutions, which very often exploit the needy boys and girls.

Child Welfare Schemes

Some of the major schemes of child welfare are as follows:

Financial Assistance to Dependent Children

To provide assistance to orphaned and destitute children below the age of 16, of those parents who are unable to maintain them due to some chronic disease or permanent disability, but to not more than two children in a family, preference being given to the school going children.

Maintenance of Orphaned and Destitute Girls

Between the age of 6 to 16 years at *Bal Bhawan*, Jalandhar at free of cost.

Foster Care Services Scheme

It started in 1961 for providing destitute, orphans and unattached children with proper physical, mental and emotional growth and a normal family setting, thus eliminating the ill effects of impersonal treatment of institutions.

State After Care Home for Boys

Ludhiana started this in 1967-68 for orphan and destitute boys between the age group of 16-21 years, discharged from correctional or non-correctional institutes to various crafts.

Special Nutrition Programme

To provide protein diet to the children in the age group of 0-6 years and expectant and nursing mothers for a period of 300 days in a year.

Family and Child Welfare Projects

It caters to the needs of children up to the age of 5 years and women living in rural areas. Children are provided pre-school education and refreshment while in *Balwadis*, camps are arranged for girls and women in rural areas where they are taught home craft, mother craft, poultry and dairy keeping, etc.

Integrated Child Development Services (ICDs) Schemes

It provides free package of services namely supplementary nutrition, immunization, health and nutrition education, health check-up, non-formal pre-school education and referral services to children below six years. It is a centrally sponsored scheme and was first introduced in Nurpur Bedi block of the State in 1975-76. The scheme has brought substantial benefits to the children and mothers, particularly to those belonging to poor socio-economic groups in reducing infant mortality, improving health and nutritional status of children and providing pre-school education for children.

Family-Centred Social Work: Concept and Methods of Intervention

The social worker with sound knowledge of casework has an important role on improving the relationship within the family. The progress in psychology, psychiatry as well as in natural sciences, enables the caseworker to recognize difficulties in family life and find ways of solution. However, social work is not the only source which attempts to help in such difficulties, other professional aid by the psychiatrist, the physician, the priest or the nurse might be effective but social casework remains one of the most important ways of helping to straighten out the family problems.

Primarily the private family service agencies deal with personal family. These caseworks attempts to help on the solution of such problems, by counselling in health, educational and adjustment question, for healthy family living. Counselling may include advice on family budget and house management, and on vocational opportunities by reference to employment services and occupational guidance centres.

Sometimes, family casework includes premarital counselling, when the young couple or the parents consult the social worker. It is often concerned with marital disturbances, helping the couple to better mutual understanding and satisfaction and with the adjustment of difficulties which have arisen between parents and children. Although a majority of the family welfare agencies provide their services on a graduated scale, so that the client pays a fee according to his financial ability. In a few large cities, some individual social workers carry on such activities independently without having any connection with a social agency, sometimes under the title of personal relations counsellor.

Right to Education

The 'Right to Education' has to be one of the central themes of child development to envisage a world where children can have access to quality education. Besides, schools should respect and uphold child rights, especially the rights of the most marginalized child (girls, *dalits, tribals* and disabled) and they should challenge injustices and transform children's lives so that they can play an effective role in achieving a more equitable society.

The above involves commitment from the state and civil societies to be partners in change at two levels:

1. Ensure that all out of school children, especially the *pull-outs*, i.e., the girls who are pulled out for domestic work and the *push-outs*, i.e., children from the marginalized sections who are pushed out due to social disparity and inadequate systems in schools are re-integrated back to school.
2. Work with the state for the rationalization of the education systems. This would mean the following:
   - *Improving accessibility*: In terms of geographical spread of schools and reduction in social inequity.
   - *Making education sector more adequate*: In terms of improving the school infrastructure, ratio of primary and secondary schools, meeting the needs of specific children like the disabled, migrant and children in difficult circumstances, governance and ensuring a correctional mechanism for the defaulters in the system.
   - *Enhancing the appropriateness*: In terms of developing a curriculum to augment the children's cognitive, conative and affective needs and also to critically look at the curriculum from the perspective of gender, globalization and secularism (for example).
   - *Affordability*: In terms of financial aspects of education and the financial gap both at the state as well as household level.

The Indian Council for Child Welfare

The Indian Council for Child Welfare was organized in 1952, whose main functions were to coordinate the work of various child welfare agencies and to serve as information exchange and research centre in the field of child welfare. This council has got branches in all the states and are known as State Council for Child Welfare.

In UP, there is the UP Council for Child Welfare (UPCCW) affiliated to the Indian Council for Child Welfare (ICCW). The aims and objectives of this council are similar to those of the ICCW, i.e., initiation, organization and activation and coordination of action for promoting child welfare services in all its aspects. The main programme of the UPCCW is to give directives and help to organize children's education in pre-primary and primary for the age group up to 6 and 6 to 10, play and recreation with suitable play apparatus, initiation of library and reading rooms, organization of holiday camps for children of low income group, to arrange crèches for children of working women and above all to create public awareness of the problems in relation to the welfare of the children. It has district councils in many districts.

Department of Women and Child Development are the nodal agencies for the development and welfare of women and children, but to pass the buck to them is not fair. It is to be realized that the regulative and primitive measures have to be initiated by several ministries and agencies for the development and welfare of women and every one of them should play its role in the best manner. It is to be understood that more than pious wishes, legal amendments and lofty pronouncements, it requires a strong will and dogged perseverance on the part of both government and women to ensure for the latter a place of pride and respectability in society. With all the concern that is reflected in the policy of the government and the massive programmes undertaken by it for the development and welfare of women and children the future scenario for women and children is indeed bright.

9

Urban Community Development

The rapid growth of urban population and its concentration in a few large cities and metropolitan centres in India have resulted in serious deterioration in environmental conditions particularly in respect of health, housing and civic amenities. Estimates may vary but most studies put the figurative numbers for below the poverty line population in urban areas at around 50 per cent. The Planning Commission has placed the proportion of slum dwellers at one-fifth of the total urban population, and there is evidence to suggest that the figure is higher in the large cities: the percentage being as high as fifty in the case of several class I cites of India. The urban poor live in a squalid chaos of tenements, hovels and shacks, huddled together in narrow congested lanes in areas where the absence of basic amenities is almost total. Anti-social behaviour such as crime, delinquency and prostitution are the natural consequences of such sub-human condition of living. Dissatisfaction and frustration arising out of these conditions have implications for the exiting rural-urban dichotomy and for India's urban future.

Both preventive and curative measures are being contemplated by policy makers to contain the population of urban slums and to foster their organic linkages with the city economy. It is now well accepted that the large cites of India, that are growing at a relatively faster rate than the others, would have an increasing percentage of slum dwelling population, as the movement of dispossessed rural migrants toward these centres is likely to go on unabated for many years to come. It was for this reason that the Third Five-Year Plan drew attention to the social and economic consequence of rapid urban growth and to the need for an Urban Community Development (UCD) programme to bring about social, economic and environmental change; to help particularly the slum dwelling population. The Urban-Rural Relationship Committee which reported in 1966, also highlighted the need for public participation in the urban development programme and suggested a framework for undertaking the UCD programme.

Experience in the field of community development was gained through the rural community development programme, which was begun in 1952. With this experience in the background, a number of pilot community projects were initiated in the urban areas which included the projects in Delhi (1958), Ahmedabad (1962), Baroda (1965) and Calcutta (1966). In 1966, the Government of India decided to launch formally, a national experiment in urban community development (UCD) similar to that of rural community development.

Urbanization

Along with the growth of population in the last few decades, there has been a shift in the population from rural to urban areas. The increasing urbanization has led to problems like crime and juvenile delinquency, alcoholism and drug abuse, housing shortage, over-crowding and slums, unemployment and poverty, population and noise, and communication and traffic control among others. But if cities are place of tension and strain, they are also the centres of civilization and culture. They are active, innovative, and alive. They provide opportunities to achieve one's aspirations. If the future of our country is linked with the development of rural areas, it is equally linked with the growth of cites and metropolitan areas. But before analyzing these problems, let us understand the basic concepts.

Concepts of Urban, Urbanization and Urbanism

Urban

What is an 'urban area' or a city or a town? The term 'urban' is used in two senses – demographically and sociologically. In the former sense, emphasis is given to the size of population, density of population and nature of work of the majority of the adult males while in the latter sense, the focus is on heterogeneity, impersonality, inter-dependence, and the quality of life. The German sociologist, Tonnies (1957), differentiated between rural and urban communities in terms of social relationships and values. The rural community is one in which social bonds are based on close personal ties of kinship and friendship, and the emphasis is on tradition, while the urban gesellschaft society is one in which impersonal and secondary relationship predominate, and the interaction of people is formal, contractual and dependent on the special function or service they perform. The emphasis on gesellschaft society is on utilitarian goals and competitive nature of social relationship. Other sociologists like Max Weber (1961) and Georg Simmel (1950) have stressed on dense living conditions, rapidity of change and impersonal interaction in urban settings. Louis Wirth (1938) a relatively large, dense and permanent settlement of socially heterogeneous individuals. Scholars like Ruth Glass (1956) have defined city in terms of factors like: size of population, density of population, main economic system, type of administration, and some social characteristics.

Urbanization

The term 'urbanization' refers to the process by which a population becomes concentrated in cites or 'urban place'. The process may proceed in either of two distinct ways: (1) through an increase in the number of urban places or (2) through an increase in the size of population resident in each urban place. Although the term is sometimes also used to refer to the consequence of living in urban places, scholars prefer, for the purpose, to use the word 'urbanism', as in "Urbanism as a way of life".

Urbanization is the movement of population from rural to urban areas and that results in increasing proportion of population that resides in urban rather than rural places. Thompson Warren (*Encyclopedia of Social Sciences*) has defined it as "the movement of people from communities concerned chiefly or solely with agriculture to other communities, generally larger whole activities are primarily centred in government, trade, manufacture, or allied interests". According to Anderson (1953), urbanization is not a one way process but it is a two-way process. It involves not only movement from villages to cities, change from agricultural occupation to business, trade, service and profession, but it also involves change in the migrants attitudes, beliefs, values and behaviour patterns. He has given five characteristics of urbanization: money economy, civil administration, cultural changes, written records and innovations.

Urbanism

Urbanism is a way of life. It reflects an organization of society in terms of a complex division of labour, high levels of technology, high mobility, interdependence of its members in fulfilling economic functions and impersonality in social relations (Theodorson, 1969).

Characteristics of Urbanism

Louis Wirth (1938) has given four characteristics of urbanism:

Transience

An urban inhabitant's relation with others last only for a short time; he tends to forget his old acquaintances and develops relations with new people. Since he is not attached to his neighbours, members of the social groups, he does not mind leaving their places.

Superficiality

An urban person has limited number of persons with whom he interacts and his relations with them are impersonal and formal. People meet each other in highly segmental roles. They are dependent on more people for the satisfaction of their life needs.

Anonymity

Urbanites do not know each other intimately. Personal mutual accountantship between the inhabitants which ordinarily is found in a neighbourhood is lacking.

Individualism

People give more importance to their own vested interests.

Causes of Urbanization

The rising trend towards urbanization, as reflected in the larger rise in urban population, and concentration of the major proportion of urban population in larger cities is a phenomenon caused by several factors. These may be studied under the three heads: natural population increase, migrations, and boundary changes.

Natural Population Increase

One important factor in the rising trend towards urbanization is the natural increase in population. This is manifested in the birth rate in urban area, which is probably higher than the rural, and also because of the health and medical facilities the net survival rate tends to be higher as well. The birth rate in the urban areas in 1971 has been estimated at 30.1 (per thousand) with death rate 9.7 (per thousand). In 1991, the birth rate declined to 24.3 and the death rate fell to 7.1. This has caused the growth rate to be high largely because of such reasons as: greater medical and health services, good water supply and sanitation reducing the incidence of water borne diseases, etc. This natural factor must have added a lot to the phenomenal population growth of urban area at 46 per cent in 1971-81 and 36 per cent in 1981-91 decade. This is much higher than the decadal growth of rural population at 19 per cent and 20 per cent in the two respective decades.

Migration

Of the total rise in urban population, while a major contributory factor is the natural growth, a part is also contributed by migrations from rural areas. Their number at the moment is not exactly known. But it can be guessed that it may be something to do with the swelling of urban population. The rural to urban migrations have been caused by several factors in the past since independence. Industrial development has, for example, led to creation of many activities of manufacturing, trading, etc., attracting rural people for seeking jobs or higher incomes. After the Second World War, many moved to the cities or towns in search of work and jobs. Portion of the country in 1947, made many people, uprooted in the rural areas, to settle in towns. Backwardness of the villages in respect of living conditions (such as negligible arrangements of education, medicine, health, entertainment; as also insecurity associated with land disputes, caste conflicts, etc.) is another factor pushing people out of the village. The availability of many opportunities for good education and living in urban areas have also attracted rural people to the urban areas.

When the migrations are viewed at the disaggregated regional state level, one can specify different areas. In the regions with the fastest urbanization, the following cause have been at work: heavy public investments in industry and mining, as for example, in Jharkhand

(Ranchi, Dhanbad, Bokaro), and in Chattisgarh (Durgapur, Bhilai, Raipur), sustained large agricultural development, as for example in Uttranchal. In the comparatively richer states, it is largely industrial development as, for instance, in Maharashtra and Gujarat and largely agricultural development as in Punjab and Haryana that have been responsible for urbanization. All such causes are usually described as demand 'pull factor', i.e., rural population migrating to urban areas in response to demand for labour. However, part of urbanization has been caused by the 'push factor', i.e., when rural population gets pushed out of villages because of bad economic conditions there. This is particularly true of the poor states wherein urban growth has been the fastest in the 1978-81 decade. In these states, there have been small increase in agricultural productivity. As a result, agricultural incomes have not been rising. And there is no land available for extensive cultivation. Hence, rural population has been getting out of villages. This is supported by the fact, that there is a considerable decline in the growth of rural population in these states. Thus, both 'pull factor' and 'push factor' have operated in the recent phenomenon of urbanization.

Boundary Changes

At times, the boundaries of the towns have been extended. As cities expanded, the outlying rural areas have been included in the urban areas. It is not that these rural areas suddenly become urban areas. They may even continue to retain most of the characteristics of villages. But their inclusion in the expanding cities put them under the area classification of towns. Of course, at the time of reclassification these areas held rural population, but they are counted as urban population by virtue of being classified as urban areas. In future, these are bound to acquire the features of urban life. However, rural population falling in these areas swell the number of urban population.

Process of Urbanization

More and more people in most countries are becoming city or town dwellers. This flow of population from the landbound occupations to other types of work is something new in human history. Such an urban trend could not have happened prior to the industrial revolution, and since the industrial revolution the trend has gone forward even though there have been efforts here and there, to curb or guide it.

In a document on the causes and implications of urbanization prepared by the Economic Commission for Asia and the Far East (ECAFE), the term was defined in these words: "In its most simple and demographic sense, urbanization can be defined as the process whereby population tends to agglomerate in clusters of more than a designated size." This definition reflects the definition of the demographer Warren S. Thompson writing in the *Encyclopedia of Social Science* who called urbanization the "Movement of people from communities concerned chiefly or solely with agriculture to other communities, generally large, whose activities are primarily centred in government, trade, manufacture or allied interests."

This definition cannot be accepted without reservations. Assuming for the moment that urbanization is simply a one-way process, it need only be added that the rate of the process varies from time to time, as well as from place to place. During the pioneering settlement in the United States, for example, it was necessary for governments to encourage the location and building of towns. Before a half century had passed, town building was moving at a rapid rate and by 1900, many Americans feared that their country was becoming too urban, too fast. Yet within a decade since 1900, the United States has become increasingly urban. This trend has been frequently described in terms of the relative percentages of rural or urban. Moreover, the rate of urbanization, as a one-way process, has been more rapid in all countries since the industrial revolution. It would, in fact, be difficult for some countries to survive, were most of the people not living in urban agglomerations.

Such a definition of urbanization, however, tends to exclude too much. It is more than a shifting of people from country to city and from landbound work to urban types of work. Merely moving a man to the city does not necessarily urbanize him (although it helps), while another rural man may be very much urbanized and never leave his rural work of habitat. Urbanization involves basic changes in the thinking and behaviour of people and changes in their social values. It is not merely a matter of an individual or group changing from one kind of work to another, but involves changes in attitudes towards work, and means entering a new and ever changing division of labour. Thus, Karl Mannheim used the term urbanization and its ramifications.

Urbanization may assume the form of 'idea migration' from the most urban to the less urban places. In the case of the American dairy industry, we find an example of a rural occupation which has become quite urbanized. Most of the dairy farms are located in United States. The fact that this type of rural work is often called an industry is seen in the timing of the dairy man's work with the tempo of the city. Raper notes that as cities have grown, farm people have been "brought into closer and closer contact with urban centres". He then names some characteristic influences, that of urbanism on dairy farming and mentions as a second form of urbanization, the "continued growth of part-time farming rural residences of urban or other non-farm employment".

Thus, it would be a mistake in our study of modern community life to think of urbanization as merely a one way process; the urban way of life also moves into the non-urban and less urban. Urbanization also means a changeover from one way of life to another. It corresponds in the variety of its application to 'detribalization', a term used by students of social change in Africa. Some Africans move from the tribal village to industrial places and there enter the struggle of becoming adjusted to the urban way of life. But the ways of doing and thinking and the characteristic of the urban way of life also invade the tribal villages, and there the struggle for adjustment may take another form. However, the term is used, the end product of urbanization is urbanism as a way of life.

Significance of Industrialization

Industry is an important economic activity and to some economists industrialization is synonymous with economic development. Most of the developed countries of the world particularly the UK and USA have achieved high stage of economic development and growth due to industrialization. Prior to industrial revolution in England and America, real income and level of employment were not so high. Industrialization is of vital importance for underdeveloped countries: (i) for removing stagnation in the economy, (ii) for eradicating mass poverty which has become chronic, and (iii) to improve the method of production and organization. The following advantages of industrialization bring out the full significance of industrialization:

Acceleration of Real Income

Industrialization accelerates real income of a nation, hence raises the standard of living of the people. High standard of labour leads to a rise in labour productivity. Thus, industrialization increased the productivity of all sectors of the economy and increases in productivity accelerates real output income.

Benefit of Higher Productivity

Compared to industries, agriculture has a lower level of productivity. Industries offer the much required benefit of higher productivity on account of the use of large volume of capital, use of extensive machinery, and greater specialization of all the factors of production. The productivity of agricultural is very low, whereas labour productivity in industries is quite high.

A Pointer to the Stage of Development

The share of industries in the total national income provides a pointer to the stage of development of economy of a country. In the developed countries of the West, this share is quite large, for instance, for the year 1967-68, the share of industries in national income was about 47 per cent in USA, 36 per cent in Japan and 37 per cent in Canada. In India, the industries account for 19 per cent of the national income for the same year.

The Advantages of Technological Progress

Industrialization leads to establishment of new industries in the country. Different industries are interdependent, hence the result is the network of all types of industries in the economy. Planned establishment of new industries leads to balanced regional development.

Provision of Employment

Underdeveloped countries are over-populated. Agriculture being the main sector, there is prevalence of open unemployment and disguised unemployment in the rural sector. Industrialization may siphon off surplus labour force from agriculture and is gainfully absorbed in industrial sector. Thus, industrialization brings about a change in occupational distribution of population.

Diversification of International Trade

Growth of domestic industries changes the magnitude, direction and composition of international trade. In the absence of industrialization, a country's exports consist of primary products and natural resources, and imports are of manufactured goods – both consumption goods and capital goods. Industrialization leads to exports of manufactured goods and reduction in imports as import substitutes are produced in home industries.

Generation of External Economies

Planned investment in infrastructure creates external economies in the country. The generation of external economies accelerates the process of industrialization and a country achieves take off in the process of economic development.

Increase in Income

Industrialization increases the ratio of industrial population to total population. It means two things: (1) pressure on agricultural sector is reduced and secondary and tertiary sectors expand; and (2) the number of wage-earners increases. This leads to increase in incomes of not only highly paid wage-earners, but also of industrialists. Government taxation can progressively shift from indirect to direct taxes.

Facilitates Modernization of Agriculture

Agricultural sector is a feeding sector in any economy. It not only feeds population but also the industries. Industrialization facilitates mechanization in agriculture. There is not only improvement in techniques of production in agriculture, but also mechanization in the agricultural sector. Both the sectors of the economy should be simultaneously developed; agrarian revolution goes together. Industrial development provides machinery, fertilizers, new techniques and agricultural sector provides the needed raw materials to industrial sector and food to the population.

Characteristics of Urban Community

A sociological analysis of the urban life and community reveals the following salient features in it:

Social Heterogeneity

If villages are the symbol of cultural homogeneity, in cities we find a variety of groups, each representing a typical culture. The villages are natural carriers of culture and they preserve its integrity intact and unbroken. On the other hand, in cities we find a confluence of many cultures, each reacting with the other and thus all cultures participate in this interplay and interaction, and are changed or modified to some extent at least. Thus, whereas unity and uniformity are characteristics of villages, in cities we find multiplicity of cultures and viewpoints.

Secondary Control

In villages, there is strict control over individual's behaviour which is exercised by family, caste or class. But, however, in cities none of these groups exercises effective control over behaviour. In cities, the individual's behaviour is controlled by such agencies as police, law courts, etc., this is known as secondary control.

Social Mobility

The most important feature of urban industrial society is its social mobility. In urban society, the social status of an individual is determined not by heredity or circumstances of his birth but by his work and economic status. In cities, men are not born good but made good. Thus, in urban life a man can achieve as much progress as he wishes according to his intelligence and efforts. By the dint of hard work and sharp intelligence an individual can go a long way in achieving great things. In cities, the caste barriers are breaking down. The incidence of intercaste marriages is growing. The women's education is encouraged and the educated men and women are not orthodox in their ways and habits. In colleges and universities men and women belonging to Brahmin, Kshatriya, Vaishya and Shudra mix up without consideration of caste or class. New social changes and reforms are accepted much better by city dwellers than by rural people.

Voluntary Association

Owing to a variety of professions, castes, groups and cultures in cities, there are numerous voluntary groups and associations. The primary groups like family lose there orthodox character and have a tendency towards liberalism.

Individuality

On account of voluntary association and secondary control, the city dwellers develop a personality of their own. The ideals, the viewpoints and the conduct and behaviour which a city dweller encounters are also varied and contrary to the traditional moral codes, and cease to have much meaning for him. A city dweller feels compelled to fashion out his own conduct of life according to his own reason and choice. On account of this, whereas his behaviour tends to be arbitrary, it also bears the indelible stamp of this own personality.

Lack of Community Feeling

Not only is there lack of community feeling in the cities, there is also lack of unity and harmony in the family. In cities, people are not bothered by social obligations or ridicule. They can pursue their individual ends, unmindful of what others think about them.

Lack of Unity in Family

In cities, we find not only the lack of community feeling but there is also lack of unity, homogeneity and harmony in the family. Each member of the family: father, mother, sisters and brothers are so busy with their own programmes that they do not interfere with each other's independence. Each member has his own society and pursues his individual ends. Generally, the unity and cohesiveness among family members is no better than among the people staying in a hotel.

Moral Laxity

On account of the lack of community feeling, lack of homogeneous family, western influence and an atmosphere of luxury and comfort prevailing in the cities, moral laxity results. In the hustle-bustle of the city, there is no control over individual's behaviour and the incidence of pre-marital and extramarital sex is fairly high. In Western cities, polygamous tendencies are clearly accepted and people freely enjoy themselves.

Unbalanced Personality

A combination and mixture of such facts, as looseness of character and morals, artificial environs and atmosphere, the deleterious influence of cinema and other means of entertainment, high ambition and lustful desires and general mentality of materialism, have resulted in producing unbalanced personality of city dwellers; specialization has also contributed in a big way. People are mad after false facade and artificial glitter of the city. In cities, the element of humanity seems to have gone out of the dwellers. We find highly literate and skilled professionals like professors, doctors, lawyers, etc., in the cities but we rarely come across human beings. People in city work at a fast pace but the growth of their personalities is usually one-sided.

High Incidence of Crime

As a consequence of the above mentioned features the rate of crime is very high in cities. All kinds of crimes: infanticide, abortion, theft, promiscuity occur in great number and with high frequency.

Social Disorganization

Again, owing to above mentioned features, we find social disorganization in the cities; people are dissatisfied and discontented. Many conflicts, both direct and indirect, constantly ravage the mental and physical health of city dwellers. The class and status feeling are very acute. The strikes and class conflicts are frequent. The viles of communalism and factionalism are quite rampant. The interpersonal relations and inter-familial relations are also uneasy. Thus, urban society is a divided society and urban life a divided life shot with conflicts and tensions.

Peculiarities of Marital Life

In urban societies, marriages take place rather late in life. There is no prohibitive or strict control over pre-marital and extra-marital relations. Many boys and girls prefer to live single and are averse to marriages; to them sex need is of the same class and nature as food need. Both can be met in the same manner. Love marriages are common practice. Due to the use of contraceptives, fewer children are born. The pursuit of comfort, luxury and sensual pleasures is common. In cities, we also come across prostitutes and society girls. Generally, men outnumber women in cities.

Heterogeneity

In cities, all over the world, we find great disparity in the living conditions of rich and poor. Where some persons live in grand air conditioned mansions, their needs, attended to by an army of servants, there are many who have no shelter overhead and do not have enough victuals to appease their hunger. In cities we also find great disparity with regard to food habits, living condition, language, religious beliefs, cultural outlook, customs and traditions and social norms of city dwellers; there is great variety and contradiction in this regards. In cities, people of different religious persuasions, holding different ideals, inspired by different cultural customs and traditions live; there thinking and outlook differs widely from each other. The city dwellers, as a rule are ambitious, individualistic, rationalists, materialists, secular and alert to their personal interests.

Consequences of Rapid Urbanization

The rapid urbanization has its healthy aspects as also unhealthy ones.

Healthy Aspects

The urbanization associated with development is something normal as has been the experience of the present developed countries. In the process of development, many industrial cities came into existence in these countries. Alongside manufacture, service sector also developed. As a result commercial, financial and other activities like repair, maintenance, etc., got expanded, with some cities specializing in them. The same can be said about the industrial towns that have come into existence in India. These produce and service manufacture which symbolize the developing character of the economy. This has raised the proportion of the value of manufacturing and service sectors in the national product of the country, although the increase has been small.

Another desirable aspect is related to the new and expanded employment opportunities that are created in the urban areas. These benefit urban population, as also the migrants from rural areas. The benefits to the rural labour from the agriculturally advanced state or regions of the country have been particularly marked. With the increase in the demand for labour in the urban areas for non-food consumer industries producing radios, TVs, cycles, etc., as also for capital goods industries producing machines, tools, equipment, etc., and service industries, there has been a drawing of labour from agriculture which has surplus labour. This has raised the product per head for the remaining labour in agriculture. In these rural areas, modernization of agriculture (i.e., mechanization, use, of chemical fertilizers, etc.) has at the same time freed labour for urban areas where the industrial activities have been located. This is a familiar scenario of 'industrialization-urbanization'. This has been observed all over the world since the Industrial Revolution. This consequence is inevitable and universal too, as also desirable. Besides employment in the modern sectors, quite a few may in the urban areas get work in the small establishments largely producing traditional goods and goods or services for the large industries. Domestic service in the wealthy as also in the middle class families is also a source of considerable employment, particularly for women.

There is also gain arising out of the external economies that cities give rise to. Growth in the city-size to some point, for example, makes it possible to reap further gains in the provision of various services. It is cheaper, for instance, to provide infrastructure like transport, communication, etc. It is also possible to meet the needs for education, water, drainage and medical facilities at lower costs. Many a cultural activities, as also entertainment can be organized without much expenditure of resources for large number of people.

A very important result of urbanization pertains to changes in attitudes that accompany it. This process is furthered also because of the large reduction in the costs of organizing and disseminating information. The many contacts among people from different backgrounds, as also the variety of jokes and existence of cultural activities, tend to promote modernization of behaviour and motivation. The changed attitudes, which replace the traditional ones, further promote the development of economic activities in the urban areas. Together with the other facilities mentioned above, it is rightly said that urbanization itself, becomes the powerful factor in further urbanization.

Unhealthy Aspects

While there are a number of benefits associated with urbanization, there are some serious problems that it gives rise to. One problem is that of congestion. It exhibits itself in various forms. The traffic jams and, therefore, slowing down of movements, results from too many automobiles, in particular privately owned because of high income elasticity of demand for them. While the number of vehicles increase, there is little that the government with limited resources can do in respect of widening streets, or roads, installation of electronic devices, enforcement of parking regulations, etc. Other causes of congestion are heavy concentration of population due to the centralization of employment in urban areas, the creation of dense business areas, etc., requiring more transportation to these places as also within these areas.

Another unhealthy aspect of the urbanization is the excess of population which can find no jobs, houses, education, proper medical facilities, etc. Since population is too much for the urban areas, it has led to the emergence of large unemployment, slums, restlessness in educational institutions, violence, etc. The over-crowding has led to many evils and vices, diseases and degradation, crime and cruelties and the like. In other words, the quality of human life deteriorates.

Apart from the serious problems that congestion and over-crowding create in the urban areas, the rural areas suffer from migrations. In quite many areas, rural people with strong physique and good brains leave for urban areas. They cause loss of productivity in the villages. Those who get jobs may be able to earn more in the cities, but the net earning will be less because of the loss of production in the rural areas. Quite many of them do not get work in urban areas, thereby causing only loss. The people left behind in villages are mostly women, old people and children. This causes many family and social problems. The village economy, already much backward and uncared for, is further neglected by the people and the authorities. In sum, urbanization is beset with many undesirable consequences.

It is thus obvious that urbanization is not an unmixed blessing. It is no doubt an essential part of development. But, beyond a certain point, it is, in fact, a highly unhealthy phenomenon which negates the very progress itself.

Cities as a Centre of Power

City is a community where thousands or even millions of people live and work. Cities are the world's most crowded places. New York city, for example, has an average of about 7,490 people per square kilometre. The United States as a whole, however, averages only 20 people per square kilometre. Similarly, other large cities of the world have population densities hundreds or thousands of times as large as the average national population densities.

Many people choose to live in or near a city simply because they like the rapid pace of city life. Perhaps these very people also complain bitterly about the crowds, dirt, and noise in a city. But, they like the bustling activity that makes city life so different from rural life.

Characteristics of City

Broadly, following are the main characteristics of a city:

Community of Communities

According to the noted sociologists Mackenzie, a city is not a mere community but is a super community that is, it comprised of several communities. We find a diversity of cultures, religions and professions in a city.

Absence of Community Feeling

In as much as a village is, as a rule, a homogeneous community, there is a feeling of oneness and fellowship in the village. But, in a city where therein live heterogeneous communities, there is no feeling of oneness and fellowship among the city dwellers. In short, a city lacks the feeling of communal fellowship which is an important characteristic of a village.

Lack of Family Unity

Not only does a city lack the community feeling, but there is absence of the feeling of oneness and harmony among family members. The father, the mother, the son and the daughter usually are members of their separate clubs and societies and have more kinship with their club members than among themselves.

Moral Laxity

The lack of the community feeling and family unity and kinship coupled with the impact of Western civilization have resulted in the fall of moral standards. Due to multitudes of people everywhere it is easy to lead a life of anonymity in the city. Therefore, there is considerable increase in the incidence of pre-marital sexual relations. The easy availability of vulgar entertainment and sex-oriented literature in the cities contribute towards moral laxity.

Unstable Personality

The moral laxity, unnatural environment, stimulating entertainment coupled with rising expectations among people are helping to generate neuroses. The people have lost firm grip over life and have become aimless. Their moral indifference to the kind and quality of their lives is an ideal ground for the production of simple schizophrenia.

Increase in Crime

In cities, every variety of crime flourishes; smuggling, defrauding, kidnapping, sexual abuse, abortion, murder, rape, etc., are common occurrences in the cities.

Social Disorganization

As a consequence of the above-mentioned features, social disorganization starts in the cities. There is general discontent and unrest among city dwellers. There is rise in the expectations of people and this leads to a continuous class struggle. All sorts of agitations take place. Communal violence erupts from time to time. The people do not feel secure in spite of the presence of large police force.

Marital Problem

In cities, the average age of marriage is quite advanced as compared to rural areas. There is no strict institutional control or restraint on pre-marital and extra-marital sex. Many young men and women prefer to stay single as this affords greater freedom and scope to their aims and activities. In cities, the incidence of both love marriage and divorce is more than in villages; there is commercial sex-oriented entertainment and professional men and women are available to cater for specialized sex needs of people. This obviously contributes to and complicates marital problems.

Shortage of Houses

In almost every city, the problem of housing accommodation is acute. Lakhs of people are forced to live in sub-human conditions.

Diversity

In every big city, there is a great variety. People of different faiths, rich and poor, professional and non-professional live in the same city. Thus, in a city we have diversity of religion, culture and people.

Artificial and Dependent Existence

The life in cities becomes mechanical, and is cut off from natural environment. People drink powdered or bottled milk, eat canned food and go to overcrowded parks to find a stimulant of nature. Though cities produce many variety of goods, they are dependent on villages for the essential foods and vegetables, milk and ghee, etc.

Stimulating Atmosphere

The atmosphere of the cities is highly stimulating. The streets are crowded with people wearing bewildering variety of dress, moving in gay carefree manner. The hotels and restaurants are busy and cater not only for a bewildering variety of food but also bewildering variety of sex. They are busy with the lascivious dances of cabaret girls and there are joints where you can buy sex to order. There are gambling points, painting and photographic exhibitions, lectures and discussions on miscellaneous things are a feature of every big town.

Types of Cities

The geographical conditions, population make-up and differentiation and other features of each city are unique. Thus, whereas Delhi is the central capital, Kanpur is an industrial city, and whereas Mumbai is an important harbour, and a summer resort. In spite of the unique character of every city there are also some common features among various cities. For example, Agra, Kanpur, Kolkata, Ahmedabad, Mumbai are all industrial cities. Therefore, the feature of industrialization is common to scores of Indian cities. We can thus classify the cities on the basis of some fundamental features shared by all cities of a class. All the cities mentioned above are industrial cities and therefore are production centres. In these cities, a variety of goods is produced and manufactured. However, it must be clearly borne in mind that though many cities share some fundamental features, each city is unique and there are features which are peculiar to it alone. For example, both Kanpur and Mumbai are big industrial cities. Both are centres of cloth production having numerous textile mills; both are important rail junctions. But, Mumbai is a major port which Kanpur is not. Whereas, Kanpur is a centre of leather technology, Mumbai is an important centre of film production. Thus, the cities of one class also have numerous diverse features as well.

On the basis of broad common features of the cities, we can classify them into following types:

1. Production centres
2. Centres of trade and commerce
3. Capitals
4. Health and recreation centres
5. Cultural centres
6. Diversified cities

As we have mentioned earlier, there can be no absolute classification of cities; all classification are relative. May cities fit into more than one category mentioned above. For example, Delhi fits in with the first three categories. It is an important production centre, an equally important centre of trade and commerce and is, of course, a capital city. Mumbai, on the other hand, satisfied the necessary condition of first five categories listed above. It is an important production centre, an important centre of trade and commerce, capital of Maharashtra, a centre of health and recreation and also a cultural centre. Besides these Mumbai also has may other specialties. Being on the sea coast, its climate is temperate and it is also the most important film-making centre. It is also the world's renowned centre of entertainment and amusement. Mumbai's importance, therefore, lies not only in the fact that it is a famous city. Not without reason it is called Gateway of India. Again, the importance of Mumbai does not lie in its being a big centre of culture and entertainment but from the fact that it is a port through which import and export worth millions of rupees is made. Though Mumbai is the centre of cloth production, it is more important as a centre of trade and commerce. Therefore, after taking into consideration everything, we find that Mumbai fits in with the second category most, that it is a centre of trade and commerce. Thus, while classifying a city we have to see as to which of its features is most prominent. Therefore, though Delhi is an important production centre as well as the centre of trade and commerce its most important feature is that it is a capital city.

Types are not Pure

It must be borne in mind that the above classification of types of cities has been on the basis of the most fundamental or prominent features of a city. If a city is a capital as well as big trade and commercial centre, our classification will be determined by the fact whether the fact of being capital or being a commercial centre is more fundamental or prominent. To illustrate, Chandigarh is the capital of Punjab and it is also a commercial centre. But the fact of capital is more fundamental and important than the fact of being the commercial centre. On the contrary, of Mumbai the fact of being the commercial centre is far more important than that of its being the capital of Maharashtra. It is generally observed that once a city is made the capital of a state its importance and stature grows. Owing to official patronage, greater security and availability of easy loans, etc., such cities become important production centres or centres of trade and commerce. On the other hand, some cities are big production centre naturally. In modern times it is difficult to find examples of pure types of cities.

Some of these are purely centres of health and recreation. Below we shall discuss the types of cities in detail.

(i) *Production Centres:* Generally, the more important cities of the world are industrial towns. The main reason for increasing urbanization in modern times is increased industrialization. Consequent upon industrial revolution, the urban population all over the world has increased considerably. In India, the majority of cities having population of one lakh or more are industrial towns. According to the kind of population, the production centres can be classified in two following categories:

(a) *Primary Production Centres:* The primary production centres are those places where any materials for industrial use are produced. For example, mining centres where oil, coal, iron, etc., are produced are primary production centres. The population of such places is usually not very large. Generally, only those persons live at these centres that are connected with places at which raw materials are further refined. Among such towns in India are: Nellore, Mauslipatnam, Ranchi, Gauhati, Mysore, Kolar, Dehradun, Bareilly, etc. In Bareilly, the wood obtained from forest is sawed and packed on to secondary production centres. Bareilly is also known for its bamboo production. In Gauhati, we have oil wells, in Ranchi, we have coal mines, and in Kolar, there are gold mines.

(b) *Secondary Production Centres:* Most of the centres of production are included in this category. In secondary production centres, the raw materials obtained from primary production centres are used for manufacture of a variety of goods. At such places, population is large and keeps growing; secondary production centres usually produce scores of items but are famous for one or two items. For example, Ferozabad is famous for its glass bangles, Kanpur for leather goods, Moradabad for brass-work, Gwalior for earthen wares, Aligarh for locks and scissors, Jamshedpur for steel and iron, Rampur for knives and scissors, Bareilly for furniture, Banaras for sarees and brocade work and Bangalore for silk sarees. In these towns, a major portion of population is involved in the production of goods specific to it. The industrial activity obviously affects greatly the economic and social life of the industrial town. In some cities, some goods are produced. For example, Meerut and Aligarh both are famous for scissors. In some cities, one type of goods is primarily produced. For example, Moradabad brass works industry is not only major but virtually the only industry. In some cities, numerous things are produced. In Mumbai, not only there is cloth production but there is also production of electrical and engineering goods in a big way. If there are more than one industry in any city the chances of unemployment due to economic recession in one industry are less. This is because if one industry faces recession and there is retrenchment, the retrenched men may find jobs in the other industry. Whereas, if the labour force of a place is employed only in one industry retrenchment would result in whole sale unemployment and the labour would be compelled to migrate.

(ii) *The Centres of Trade and Commerce:* Generally, the cities are production centres and centres of trade and commerce; but in some cities the trade and commerce is the dominant feature and production is secondary. For example, though Mumbai is a major production centre, it is far bigger centre of trade and commerce. Therefore, Mumbai must be regarded primarily to be a centre of trade and commerce. Generally, the cities situated on the sea coast and those which are ports are centres of trade and commerce. Naturally through these ports large quantity of goods are sent to and received from foreign lands. More than 95 per cent of trade and commerce transacted with foreign land is made through sea. The major Indian ports are: Porbandar, Surat, Kandla, Mumbai, Marmiegao, Mangalore, Kozikode, Kochi, Allapuza, Quilon, Tuticorin, Dhanushkodi, Neggapattam, Karikal, Cuddlore, Pondicherry, Chennai, Masulipatnam, Kakinad, Vishakhapatnam, and Kolkata. With the exception of Kolkata, Chennai and Mumbai all other ports are known exclusively for trade and commerce. Though Chennai is primarily a centre of trade and commerce but it is also the capital of Tamil Nadu. Mumbai and Kolkata, however, are so diverse and vast that these virtually fit in every category mentioned above. While it is true that ports are usually the centres, indeed there are many inland towns which satisfy the condition of being centres of trade and commerce. For example, Meerut is a big *mandi* for *gur*, so is Muzaffarnagar. Dehradun is a *mandi* for rice. In *mandi*, goods from far and wide are collected and from there distributed to retailers. Kolkata, Delhi, Kanpur, Chennai are *mandis* where goods from great distance are collected.

(iii) *Capitals:* All cities, world over, which happen to be capitals of states have shot into prominence. Their importance and eminence is not due to their industry or *mandis* but due to their being the capitals. Indeed, once a place is made the capital, business and industry are but sequel to the main fact of its being the capital. Prior to Industrial Revolution, capital cities generally were the most eminent cities of the world. The example of Rome, Paris, London and Moscow amply bear this out. However, as mentioned before, on account of official policy and patronage, the capitals tend to become centres of trade, commerce and production. London, New York, Delhi, Moscow, Berlin and Peking can be cited as examples. However, the chief importance of capitals is political, rather than industrial or commercial. In the field of industry and commerce, Kanpur is the foremost town of UP. But, the city of pride in UP is Lucknow and not Kanpur. This is because it is the capital of UP. Some cities' importance lies only in the fact of their being capitals: Shillong, Bhubaneshwar, Chandigarh, Jaipur, Hyderabad, Tiruvanandapuram, Patna are few such examples. Mumbai, Kolkata, Chennai, Bangalore, Ahmedabad and Srinagar are capitals respectively of Maharashtra, Bengal, Tamil Nadu, Mysore, Gujarat and Jammu and Kashmir. But the importance of these cities lies not mainly in the fact of their being capitals but on other facts. Srinagar, for example, is a summer resort and health centre. Ahmedabad is an industrial city. Bangalore is famous for its aeronautic industry. Mumbai, Kolkata and Chennai are centres of trade and commerce.

(iv) *Health Recreation Centres:* Many towns have very salubrious and healthy climate owing to their peculiar geographic location and conditions. Generally, the town situation on the seacoast have temperate climate throughout the year and, therefore, people go there to escape the extreme heat of summer and extreme cold of winter. Similarly, hill towns are cool and people from plains flock in great numbers to such towns in summer months and also go there to watch snowfall in winter. In order to attract more tourists to such places, municipal and state authorities do everything possible to beautify such places, and make available all amenities. Many cultural shows are arranged, and health clubs are opened. Similarly, a number of amusement centres, dance clubs are opened and beauty shows are arranged. In almost every state of India, there are one or more important hill resorts. In British days, these towns were made the summer capitals in India. Now this practice has been discontinued, but much official work, particularly conferences during summer days, are arranged in these hill towns. The important summer resorts in India in Uttar Pradesh are: Almora, Bhovali, Chakrauta, Lansdown, Mussoorie, Nainital and Ranikhet; Mysore and Bangalore in Karnataka; Cherrapoonji and Shillong in Assam; Conoor, Kodaikanal, and Octacommand in Tamil Nadu; Dalhousie, Kulu and Shimla in Himachal Pradesh; Darjeeling and Kalimpung in Bengal; Mahabaleshwar in Maharashtra; Mount Abu in Rajasthan; Panchmani in Madhya Pradesh and Ranchi in Jharkhand. At these places, few people live permanently but most come in season. The livelihood of permanent residents of these places depends upon tourist traffic. At these places, diverse type of entertainment is available. There are big hotels where wine flows freely and cabarets and western dances are staged for the entertainment of the audience. Most of the tourists coming here hail from the rich affluent class and they spent lavishly. These places get their distinctive colour and personality as a result of the kind of tourists reaching these places. Some hill resorts are patronized by government and officialdom whereas others are patronized by rich industrialists. There are some, where middle class tourists also go. The personality of a hill resort is determined by the kind of tourists. Some health resorts have sanatorium and health clinics and these are visited mostly by the sick. In Bhovali, there is sanatorium for tuberculosis and Ranchi has a hospital for the mentally sick. In Kasauli, there is a Pasteur Institute.

(v) *Cultural Centres*: In India, where sentiment dominates, many towns have become famous and developed into big cities on account of their religious value and importance. All the towns situated on the riverbank have an aura of holiness attached to them. Besides, India is a multi-religious country and each religion has one or two places regarded holy by the followers of each religion. For example, Amritsar has a place of pilgrimage known as Golden Temple. Ajmer is a place pilgrimage for the Muslims. Ayodhya, Haridwar, Rameshwaram, Prayag, Puri, Mathura, etc., are holy cities of Hindus. Both Gaya and Sarnath are holy places of Buddhists. Pilgrims from far and near come to these places to obtain spiritual solace and earn the religious merit. There are a number of historic cities in India renowned for some monument, mausoleum on some other structure celebrating some historic event. Agra, for example, is well-known world over for its historic monument, Taj Mahal, in particular; Bijapur is known for its circulate tower and Chittorgarh for its victory tower. Delhi is famous for its Red Fort, Sanchi is famous for its *Stupas*; Nalanda and Taxila for their ancient universities now in ruins; Fatehpur Sikri for its *Buland Darwaza*. Many cities are famous for being centres of higher learning. Allahabad, Mumbai, Kolkata, Delhi, Lucknow, Meerut, Chennai, Nagpur, Roorkee, Kurukshetra, Sagar, Tirupati, Cuttak, Dharwar, Ujjain, Shantiniketan, Jadavpur, Burdwan and many other towns are famous for their universities. Pondicherry is famous world over for its Aurobindo Ashram.

(vi) *Diversified Cities:* Besides the cities which fit into one or the other of the above-mentioned category, there are some towns which fit into none of the categories. They may be holy but holiness is not the fundamental reason for their growth; they may have a university but this, too may be incidental. There are places which may equally be important cultural centres, production centres and as capitals. Thus, it would be unjustified to put them in any one category. Such towns are accordingly referred to as diversified towns. For example, Varanasi is a holy city of Hindus, it has a famous university also in which students and teachers of all nations get together. It is a commercial centre famous for its gold work on saris. Thus, in Varanasi, we find intellectuals, merchants, mendicants, beggars and prostitutes. A man may go to Varanasi for business, pleasure, study or for learning merit or reaping spiritual solace. All these things add colour and charm to the town. It is a most appropriate example of a diversified town.

Role of City

Urban Roles for Emerging Nations

The city tends to become the new country's major point of contact with the 'outside' world. The new nations attracts political representatives from other countries and, eventually, travellers and tradesmen who are interested in coming in contact with the new country and its officials. Correspondingly, the city that stands at the head of the emerging country plays a very important role in providing a proper image of the new country to the outsider. This sometimes encourages new countries, to erect imposing public structures for prestige purposes as well as for symbols of new government to the native population.

(i) *Locus of Power:* The city also becomes extremely important as the major locus of power in the new country. This power is not just what is represented by the national government headquarters, which are invariably located in an urban context. In the city, are established the policies and programmes that determine the dominance or influence this urban political organization is likely to have over the remainder of the country.

The city also becomes the locus of economic power. This derives partly from the fact that it tends to become the headquarters of industrial, commercial, and other enterprises developing within the country or having contacts with countries outsides. Supporting this locus of power is the expenditure pattern of the national government, which tends whether or not by plan, to be concentrated rather intensively in the national capital first among the various cities, if there is more than one major city. The ramifications of this focusing of economic power in the major city of newly developing countries are related to certain factors of inertia. For economic and other reasons, once a headquarters is established in a particular city it is unlikely that it will move elsewhere. The national capital is relocated very rarely as in the case of Pakistan and a few other countries. The implications of this centring in a particular city for a city's dominance over the remainder of the country are indeed significant. Once this locus has been established "and all roads lead to Rome" orientation will rapidly tend to develop.

(ii) *Agency and Diffusion Point of Social Change*: Another significance of the city in newly developing countries is that it serves as the primary agency and diffusion point of social change for the new nation. It is likely, that here new ideas of national policy will emerge, new leaders will be discovered, new national programmes will be evolved, and the administrative centres for the diffusion, propagation, and implementation of the programmes will be centred. It is from here that the bureaucracy, at least until it develops to the point where it can establish effective branch offices, is likely to exercise supreme extensive control over the life of the city and, correspondingly, of the countryside and thus of the nation.

(iii) *Place of Investment:* Equally important is the fact that the city or cities become a receptacle for the major investment funds available internally to the country and from outside via foreign aid and industrial and commercial enterprises. The crucial question here is whether this precludes, or may be likely to preclude, the distribution of these national investment funds over the countryside as a whole. In a country that has only one or a primate type of city, the answer assumes great importance since the newly developing country is not likely to have unlimited resources.

Much of what has been discussed above in connection with the developing role of urban areas in the countries with which we are concerned has become evident over a long period of time, and development of different aspects has proceeded at different rates. This development has been held in check under some circumstances either by controls of colonial powers or, subsequently by controls introduced by new national governments. In other cases, some of aspects of development have been accelerated through time by the same sources of authority; some have been left to work out their own fates irrespective of much colonial or national intervention. From an examination of a number of these cities in newly developing countries, however, it would appear that a relatively uniform sequence of events or at least a relatively uniform result can be observed leading from the processes to which we have referred.

Contemporary Roles of Urban Areas

(i) *Continuing Functions:* Urban areas have three major characteristics resulting from what has happened in these urban areas over a long period. In the first place, the city has had to be responsible for retaining and improving its earlier colonial functions. In addition, it has had to face the responsibilities of a considerable extension of its work and its role. For example, the coming of nationhood has inevitably required the creation of new administrative units and the reorganization of business and industry, not to mention political matters, personnel and practices have had to be developed for controls over communications, police, new national armies, and similar extensions of administration by the new country.

(ii) *Centre for Domestic and Foreign Activities:* A second role of primate cities at present, and likely for some time into the future, is as locus of commercial, foreign, and international activities. We are not suggesting that if foreign or national investment takes place in certain rural types of activities, such as rubber plantations or various kinds of mining operations, there will not be major administrative units located outside the central city. On the other hand, it still is true that, at the minimum, a small office for administrative purposes and maintaining contact with the national heads is likely to be retained in the national capital.

(iii) *Magnet for Rural Population:* A third existing function or role of urban centres in newly developing countries is as magnets for the national population, so much so, as to induce migration in numbers generally far above the capacity of the city to employ, and for providing house, food, service, and education. Nevertheless, there continues to be a kind of undiminishable 'tropism' affecting the population of newly developing countries, the net result being the undiminished swelling of urban population.

(iv) *Policy Implications:* Not all of the implications of these urban roles can be considered here, but some attention will be directed to four of them.

The first policy implication should be obvious, and yet it is sometimes only reluctantly admitted even by those who are mostly in a position to understand why it should be taken into account. We refer to the crucial importance indeed, necessity of an urban locus for carrying forward those activities that are indispensable to nationhood in modern times. Administrators and politicians of newly developing countries rather wistfully wish that they did not have to cope up with the problems of such urban areas in addition to all the other problems which confront them, for there is no question that urbanization is an extremely important component, yet these same persons readily admit that no modern nation can hope to exist without at least one urban area. The reasons are apparent and have been suggested in the lists of factors to be taken into account in assessing the role of urban areas in newly developing countries. The second major policy implication of urbanization concerns the enormous pressure for differential investment of national funds into urban areas. In the case of countries having only one such city, this results in pressure to make the heaviest investments there; where there are more cities, the allocation problem is much more complex.

Because of the exigencies of other responsibilities faced by new nations there is a tendency to 'live with' what appear to be inevitable differentials in allocation of funds favouring cities. The urgent requirements of national defense, organizing new agencies of government, maintaining a level of living, tolerable to the new country's population, providing increased educational opportunities and, above all, providing employment, are so great and so complex that it cannot be expected or hoped that much attention will be given to the question of exactly where the solutions to problems will be applied. It is obviously much easier to apply the solutions available in the area closest at hand, namely, the urban area.

The third major policy implication of urbanization is one which inevitably follows from an influx of population to urban areas, and the recurrent and inevitable problems that arise in this connection. This is the policy question of how to cope with short-term urban problems. As we have noted elsewhere, the numbers of these problems is great and their dimensions are not to be underestimated. An illustration worth noting is the provision of housing and related facilities for the new and swelling population. The problem is universal; its dimensions are almost unmeasurable; its ramifications for the development of the urban population are inestimable. For example, the possible political repercussions of shortcomings in the provision of housing and amenities are at least frightening, if not discouraging, especially since national resources are extremely limited.

The fourth and final policy implication is the long-term versus the short-term view as to where a nation's resources shall be invested most beneficially. This does not apply particularly to the large new countries, but is applicable to the more numerous small new countries, and especially to those with only a primate city. Although the pressure to allocate resources to one existing urban area of most newly developing countries is almost irresistible, a question which continually lurks in the minds of many persons responsible for these decisions is whether it is preferable and possible to risk the short-term consequences of what would appear to be a better alternative in the long run, namely, the development of a group of cities rather than one or two. There would be difficulties in attempting to diversify the investments of time, money, energy, and staff in endeavouring to develop concurrently several urban centres rather than one or two. Nevertheless, it is apparent in large countries although it is only slightly less true of smaller ones. There is a sound logic involved in the long-term considerations to attempt to develop more than one or a very small number of urban centres. If as assumed will be the case, the small, newly developing nation survives and prospers, it is extremely likely that it will require additional urban centres to service the growth of the new economy and to carry forward the programmes of the new government. These additional centres are always more difficult to develop once heavy investments have been made in only one urban area.

Various cultural stresses and strains are associated with the development of urbanization in newly developing countries; an urbanization which more often than not is both discordant to the predominantly rural culture and typical to the limited urban culture which exists before the formation of a new nation. Exceptions occur in those cases where some urbanization is developed under colonial auspices, or in the rare instances where urbanization, such as among the Yoruba, develops indigenously.

An observer ordinarily thinks of the impact of an urban area upon the countryside's rural and village customs. There is also an obverse to this relationship which should not be overlooked.

Urban Development

In India, the concept of planned urban development is of recent origin. Although development schemes for urban areas were drawn up and implemented from the beginning of the Five-Year Plans, the need for planned urban development was recognized only in the Third Plan when an allocation of Rs. 3 crores was made by the Central government for giving grants to state governments for this purpose. Till March 1969, the scheme for urban development continued as a centrally sponsored programme. From 1, April 1969, the preparation of master and regional plans was transferred to state governments with the central government acting only in an advisory capacity. In the Fourth Plan, an allocation of Rs. 73.47 crores was made for the urban development programme. An outlay of Rs. 90 crores has been made in the Fifth Plan for the Housing and Urban Development Corporation under the central sector. The Sixth Plan provided Rs. 997.53 crores for urban development.

The Town and Country Planning Organization is a technical advisory body on all matters pertaining to urban and regional development. It provides technical guidance and assistance to all state governments and union territories. It also undertakes project work for development on consultancy basis from public undertaking and local bodies.

The Urban Land Ceiling and Regulation Act came into force on 17, February 1976. It seeks to curb speculation and to implement the policy of socialization of urban land. The Act puts a ceiling on the ownership of urban vacant land on a graded basis. It also empowers the concerned state governments to acquire vacant land in excess of the ceiling limits, prescribes compensation payable therefrom, grants exemption from the ceiling provisions to certain specific categories of vacant land and restricts the plinth area of future construction of dwelling units.

While the responsibility for administering the Act vests in the State government, with a view to facilitating expeditious implementation of the objectives of the Act, the Government of India has set up a Central Coordination Committee, with the representatives of the state and union territories, serving on it. This Committee reviews the progress in the implementation of the Act and suggests measures for resolving the difficulties, if any, that may be encountered by the states. A series of guidelines clarifying the intent and purport of the provisions of the Act have been issued to the state governments, who in turn, have laid down further guidelines.

Statements submitted by the holders of excess vacant land have been taken up for scrutiny. In the states of Gujarat, Karnataka, Maharashtra and Uttar Pradesh, excess of vacant land has been vested in the State. Land held for industrial purposes, is being exempted; also land held in excess of the ceiling limit is exempted on grounds of undue hardship and in public interest. The notices on application of permission to transfer vacant land or urban property are being processed by the competent authorities expeditiously.

Some states have taken complementary measures, e.g., the West Bengal government has enacted the West Bengal Urban Land Taxation Act, 1976.

Importance of Urban Development

Economic development accelerates urbanization. This raises a variety of problems of spatial implication such as land use, location of industries, laying out of transport, communication and power facilities and provision of housing, water supply, sanitation and other social services. It becomes necessary to harmonize all activities inscribed on land – industrial and agricultural, commercial and residential, cultural and social. The objective of urban community development and planning is to achieve this.

Urban Political Life

Some of the peculiarities of social life in an urban society are seen reflected in its political life. Like the social life in a city, the urban political life is also dynamic, conflict ridden and full of intricacies. Broadly the urban political life has two aspects: on the one hand, there is an administrator appointed by the state government and, on the other, there is a municipal committee or corporation consisting of the elected representatives of the people.

City Administration

Every district headquarters has a district magistrate (DM) who is the top-most government official. The DM is responsible for the law and order in the district. Besides the district magistrate, city magistrate, additional district magistrate, and a number of top police officials are responsible for the law and order situation in their respective wards. There are many circles in a city and each circle has a circle inspector and some sub-inspectors. Under a sub-inspector, there are numerous head-constables and constables, etc. Besides, station officers who are chief police officials or Kotwals, there are deputy superintendents and superintendents of police. A commissionary is under a DIG. In most cities, there is a probation officer and officers of Criminal Investigation Department. Besides all these officials, there is a municipal board in each city. In municipal boards or corporations, there elected representatives who are elected on the basis of adult franchise. These elected representatives fight elections on behalf of their respective political parties. There are also some independent members who are not affiliated to any particular political party. These elected representatives look after hygiene, education, water, electricity, medical and cultural departments. For each department, there is committee of municipal members. Nowadays municipal boards are assisted by one town planning officer.

People's Representatives

From the above description, it is clear that city administration is under the control of dual authority. On the one hand, there are government officials and on the other hand, there are elected representatives of people. Sometimes, this dual authority comes into conflict. The municipal elections are fought on the basis of political parties and each political party wishes to control the municipal board. If the control of a municipal board goes into the hands of the opposition party the chances of conflict are high. Moreover, nowadays elections have become very costly. Each candidate has to invest a lot of money for his election. It is natural that he should try to make good the money spent by him on elections. This means that as a member of municipality he must take recourse to corrupt practices.

City Government

City government is a minor form of national administration and it aims at bringing decency and order into the urban social life. It plans the structure of the city and favourable location of its functions. It looks after the executive administration of the city. It fixes land values and the norms governing zoning and construction of different varieties of buildings. It lays down and enforces the norms of city culture and traffic regulation. It is usually a body of elected representatives who represent different areas in a city proportionate to the city population. It derives its main income from federal grants and local taxes. It maintains its own police force and is supposed to keep control over the spread of vices and social disorganization within the city. Today, city governments are playing a prominent part in slum clearance and urban renewal.

Although a common problem of all contemporary societies, rapid urbanization becomes more acute in a relatively less planned and unorganized country like India. Beyond a certain limit, it becomes a problem since the city at that stage becomes incapable of providing for the minimal products and services essential for a healthy and happy life of the urban dweller. Thus, the problem of rapid urban growth is in reality a problem of improper planning and unbalanced development of the city. The problems created by rapid urban growth are immediate and are of the nature that affect the day-to-day life of the urban community. Hence, they require immediate attention and handy solutions. Some of the problems which are increasingly experienced by many of our cities specially the metropolises like Mumbai, Chennai, Bangalore, etc., include congestion, shortfall in the provision of essential services like water supply, housing, educational and medical facilities, public transportation, etc., noise pollution and to some extent air and water pollution, growth of slums and consequent vices. It is a patent fact that services will not grow in proportion to population, since they are products of man's creation.

The concept of a city government and city planning are novel to India. The city government in contemporary India are modeled on the federal government structure and consists of a mayor and elected councilors representing different areas of a city. A bureaucratic structure with technical experts looks after the day-to-day administration. The city government has upon it, the task of city planning as well as provisions of essential services. City planning in relation to many of our cities refers to the amelioration of existing anomalies of urban growth.

Role of NGOs

Success of any programme depends on its acceptance by the people. Unless the community is fully involved in the programme and it considers it to be its own programme, it may not be possible to achieve the desired results. This can be achieved in a better way by the non-government organizations as these have very intimate relations with the people. Their role in removing deep-rooted beliefs favouring large families and male children, improving female literacy, raising the age of marriage of girls, essential newborn care, birth spacing, etc., can be very significant. Such organizations, not only have the capacity to reach the remote areas, but also their activities are cost-effective. The Department of Family Welfare has launched several schemes in the last five to six years to ensure better participation of the NGOs in the family welfare programmes. Some of these schemes are: (i) helping NGOs to the extent of 90 per cent of the cost of the project on promotion of small family norm and population control schemes, (ii) wide publicity of the government for informing voluntary organizations to come forward to undertake these schemes, (iii) holding of a number of regional conferences to increase the involvement of the NGOs, (iv) recognizing six larger organizations (in Delhi, Mumbai, Kolkata, Chennai and Lucknow) as mother units for identifying small NGOs in their areas and giving them grants for approval schemes, (v) setting up State Standing Committees on Voluntary Action under the chairmanship of the Family Welfare secretary with power to sanction up to Rs.10 lakh per project, (vi) asking states to identify one institution in the NGO sector for the purpose of providing training to health workers, and (vii) arranging study tours for NGOs from states with poor community participation to better performing states.

Urban Planning

Urban land use and town planning legislation fall within the province of state governments. The Acts under which the Town Improvement Trusts were created from the start of the present century are the precursors of the town planning legislation existing in most of the states at present. The earlier Town Improvement Trusts did not have power to prepare master plans. Subsequently, many states passed legislations under which Town Planning Trusts were invested with this power. Thanks to the urbanization policies of the Five-Year Plans from the Third Plan onwards, now there are full-fledged town planning departments in almost all the states, which have generated a large number of master plans although most of them have not yet been implemented.

Most cities in India as elsewhere have grown from small beginnings with gradual accretion of economic activities, without any initial attempt being made to plan and direct their growth. In some cases, master plans are now imbalanced to direct their future growth. But, sometimes the scale of new economic activities is so large that the existing settlement cannot easily accommodate them or the nature of the activities itself may demand an altogether a new location. In their case, there is a need to build a new town which provides an opportunity to the planners of planning the community from the start.

Before independence, with a few notable exceptions such as Jamshedpur and New Delhi, the new towns were mostly planned as railway colonies or military cantonments. Since independence, however, more than 100 new towns have been built, but most of them have been planned to serve specific industrial projects and a few for administrative purposes. Some of the new towns such as Sindri near Dhanbad and Gandhinagar near Ahmedabad have been designed as satellites to the existing cities nearby, on whom they are dependent for the satisfaction of many of their needs. Some other new town have been planned as autonomous and self-contained communities not depending upon any nearby old cities for the satisfaction of their day-to-day needs. Chandigarh is a good example of a self-contained new town.

However, in planning new towns, in most cases, it is mainly the physical aspects which have received attention on the part of the planners. By and by the new towns have also become heirs to the same kinds of growing problems which plague the older cities.

Regional Planning

Regional planning in the context of urban and regional development is based on the idea that urban and rural development are complementary to each other and that regional planning contributes to the development of both the types of areas. This kind of regional planning is organized around the nodal aspect of the urban settlements, which brings about the exchange and integration of activities in the region; in the development process the urban settlements are regarded as the growth poles.

The need for integrated rural urban development in Indian planning was stressed for the first time in the Third Five-Year Plan, which recognized the economic interdependence between the town and the surrounding rural areas. Ever since, a number of urban and regional development projects have been formulated. Some of these projects deal with regional plans centred on metropolitan cities and some others on small and medium-sized towns. But most of these schemes are yet to be implemented.

Urban and regional planning, more than any other approach to planning, leans heavily on a national urbanization policy, but such a policy has not yet crystallized in India. Secondly, it is also based on the assumption that urbanization is an independent variable in economic growth and rural development; but this is a problematic assumption and the conditions under which urbanization plays such a role have yet to be thoroughly investigated. These and other related issues need to be resolved before the regional planning approach can become effective.

The Rule of Law

The Rule of Law: The Soul of Democracy

The rule of law is the soul of a democratic system of government, whether parliamentary or presidential. It means three things: (i) It means the supremacy of law or absence of arbitrariness in dealing with or determining the rights of individuals in the state. Arbitrary and capricious exercise of power by government authorities in the state is the very negation of democracy. (ii) The rule of law also means and includes equality before the law, passed by the legislative assembly, popularly elected on universal adult franchise, after following a prescribed legislative process as discussed above. The rule of law in a democracy therefore, means that the country is governed not by men, but by laws and only by laws of the land. (iii) Finally, the rule of law demands that law must be administered fairly. The standard of 'fairness' must be applied to all executive actions. Thus, for example, if rights of an individual are taken away, the court invariably insists that the party concerned must be given notice and should be heard. In the words of Justice M.C. Chagla, "Legal technicalities must take a second place before the paramount consideration of fairness." It is, therefore, submitted that every judge, while deciding a case suggesting the rights of citizens, should ask himself: "Is it fair and just?"

Dicey's Doctrine of the Rule of Law

The concept of the rule of law was first developed in England in 1887 by A.V. Dicey. According to him, the rule of law has three different faces, or it may be regarded from three different points of view, as discussed below:

(i) *Absolute Supremacy of Regular Law (i.e., Absence of Arbitrary Power on Part of the Government):* The expression "rule of law" means that no man is punishable, or can be lawfully made to suffer in body, or goods, except for a distinct breach of law, established in the ordinary legal manner before the ordinary courts of law" (A.V. Dicey, *Introduction to the Study of Law of the Constitution*, Tenth Edition, (1959), p. 188).

The 'rule of law', as conceived by Dicey, stands for (a) the absolute supremacy of regular law, as opposed to influence of arbitrary powers, and (b) excludes the existence of wide discretionary authority on the part of the executive (government) in the matters of arrest, of temporary imprisonment, of fine, of seizure of property, etc.

(ii) *Equality Before the Law.* The expression 'rule of law' means and includes "not only that no man is above the law, but that every man, whatever be his rank or condition, is subjected to the ordinary law of the realm and amenable to the jurisdiction of the ordinary tribunals" (A.V. Dicey, *Introduction to the Study of the Law of the Constitution*, Tenth Edition, (1959), p.193).

According to Dicey, the concept of legal equality, or of the universal subjection of all classes of people to one law administered by the ordinary courts of law in England, has been pushed to its maximum limit. To quote him, "with us every official from the prime minister down to a constable or a collector of taxes, is under the same responsibility for every act, done without legal justification, as any other citizen" (Ibid.). Thus, all people's highland law is subject to one and the same law.

The rule of law, accordingly requires that the officials must be brought before the ordinary courts of law and made, in their personal capacity, (a) liable to punishment, or (b) to the payment of damages, for acts done in their official capacity but in excess of their lawful authority. Thus, no man is above the law.

In France, there is administrative law and administrative tribunals, under which, all disputes in which the government or its servants are involved must be dealt with by special and more or less official bodies. This idea is completely unknown to the law of England and indeed is basically opposed to the English custom and traditions.

(iii) *General Rules of Constitutional Law are the Result of Ordinary Law of the Land (i.e., Constitution is the Consequence of the Rights of Individuals)*: Finally, the English Constitution is said to pervade by the rule of law on the ground that the general principles of the Constitution, especially those relating to fundamental rights, as for example, the right to personal liberty on the right of public meeting, etc., are the result of judicial decision, determining the rights of private persons in particular cases before the courts. This in contrast to constitution, under which, the guarantee or the security, given to the rights of individual flows from or appears to result from the general principles of the constitution.

In the English Constitution, there is an absence of any declaration of fundamental rights, as is found in the constitutions of the United States, or Belgium, or India. This is so because, in England, there is greater concentration on remedies than of abstract declarations or definitions of rights, "So dear to foreign constitutionalists."

Dicey, thus suggests that the ordinary law of land may prove a more effective protection to fundamental rights (as for example the right to individual freedom, etc.) than constitutional guarantees embodied in written constitution, because the latter can be suspended or taken away in times of emergency.

It may here be noted that when Dicey suggests that guarantees contained in a written constitution, are capable of being suspended or taken away, he ignores the obvious fact that those contained in the ordinary law of the land, can be suspended or taken away still more easily. There is almost no chance of this happening in England, not because of their legal system, but because of the spirit, in which the whole system is worked, which is the spirit of intense veneration for individual rights by the citizens, by the executive, and finally by the legislature. Thus, the English always assumes that the rights have always been there, and they always proceed to enforce them in practice.

Thus viewed, the 'rule of law' means and includes: (a) supremacy of the regular law and complete absence of arbitrary power on the part of public officials; (b) equality before the law or the equal subjection of all classes of people to the ordinary law of the land administered by the ordinary law courts; and (c) a formula for expressing the fact that the law of the Constitution is not the source but the consequence of the rights of individuals, as defined and enforced by the courts.

Criticism on Decey's Concept of Rule of Law

Dicey's doctrine of the rule of law, as discussed above, has been subjected to criticism in the light of the growth of the concept of the modern welfare state. "Under the philosophy of the welfare state", writes Justice P.B. Gajendragadkar, "Laissez faire becomes irrelevant and the rule of the market and absolute freedom of contract cease to govern the socio-economic affairs of the community."

The government, therefore, has entered several fields, such as education, industry, trade, transport, and communication, etc., and regulates almost all socio-economic relations and attempts to bring about balance in the socio-economic structure of the community at large. In achieving the above goal, law becomes a dynamic weapon in the hands of a democratic government. Wherever social inequality exists, or economic injustice is discovered a democratic government enters the area, and with the help of law restores social equality and economic justice; this is a continuous process. Thus viewed, the doctrine of the rule of law is more dynamic, and constructive than what was developed by Dicey.

Urban Growth in India

During the last century and a quarter, there has been a far-reaching redistribution of population in the world from rural to urban settlements. In some of the industrially developed countries over three-quarter of the population is urban and the population of the world as whole is well on the way to becoming preponderantly urban. India too is set on the same course, but its population is still overwhelmingly rural; barely 20 per cent of its population was urban in 1971. It is proposed to discuss in this paper some of the important trends and problems of urbanization and urban development in this country.

Although the emergence of urban settlements in India dates back to the Indus Valley civilization more than 4,000 years ago, the proportion of the urban population remained quite modest for a long time with minor fluctuations; its steady rise has been taking place only during the last half a century or so. However, factual information or rural and urban distribution of population of India systematically collected and presented is available only from the 1901 census onwards. Information on the subject, in a processed form, is also readily available in several sources. Accordingly, the period covered for viewing urban development in India is roughly the first three quarters of the 20th century.

Causes of Growth of Cities

It is very difficult to say where did the first city from where or when did it originate. As Gist and Halbert have very aptly observed, "Like the origin of civilization itself the origin of the city is lost in the obscurity of the past." The growth and development of cities is linked with two factors: on the one hand, it is dependent upon the growth of population, and on the other, it is linked with the growth and development of industrialization. Industrialization results in increased production and the increased production, in turn, leads to division of labour. The produce has to be transported from one place to the other and put on the market. This requires means of transport, markets, godowns, shops, etc. With industrialization, there is not only increase in production but also in the growth of population. This is due to the fact that wherever there is industrialization a big labour force is needed; besides, we need enough supervisory staff. Moreover, in as much as industrialization involves new construction, creation of markets, shops and business premises, thousands of men would be absorbed in these works. Naturally, therefore, the population of an industrial centre would grow immensely in response to various needs of the newly grown population and educational, cultural and other institutions and associations come into being. If the population of a place is large, it is bound to be heterogeneous; and heterogeneous people require large police; contingents and other law enforcing agencies in order to maintain law and order. All these factor are instrumental in the development of cities. If a university, high court or medical college is established anywhere, there is great influx of population to that area. With the substantial increase in the population of a place, many shops, markets, hotels, restaurants, clubs and cinemas come into existence and thus the foundation of a city is well laid. The towns situated on sea coast easily turn into big cities as a result of industrialization. Industrialization implies increase both in import and export. Most of the goods entering a country or going out of it are carried by ships. If a coastal town has good harbour facilities, traffic through it is bound to increase with industrialization. The greater the traffic through a harbour, greater will be its population and greater would be the turnover and handling of goods. All these things naturally help the rapid development of cities. Similarly, the hill resorts or towns situated on coasts are liable to become cities if these command good views and the climate is salubrious. In short, wherever there is industrialization or good climate or government offices or scenic beauty with good climate or education with cultural institutions, such places are liable to develop into cities.

Causes of Development of New Cities

The above discussion makes it plain that there is no single factor or cause which can be held responsible for the development or origin of cities. It is not possible to define or enumerate the causes of the development of various towns. This is because, besides general causes of origin and development of cities, every city has its personal history and certain causes of its origin and development are peculiar to it. For example, if and when a certain place is declared to be the capital of some state or country it is bound to become a city overnight. Broadly, following may be enumerated as the main causes of the development and origin of cities.

Industrial Revolution

The cities are business centres. The increase in business stimulates industrial activity. When large industrial complexes come into existence big markets, housing and shopping complexes are a natural sequel to industrial activity. The places situated in the vicinity of large industries automatically become important business centres, and at a business centre there is a collection of a large number of people and when population of a place is big enough it naturally turns into a city. There has been one per cent per annum increase in the urban population in Indian towns.

Business Revolution

Wherever there is large turnover of trade and business that place must, in due course, turn into a city. As N.L. Sims observes, "Trade is a necessary cause for the life of an organism. A large business centre must naturally have big markets, shopping complexes, housing colonies, educational and cultural associations, clubs, restaurants and hotels. All these things are *sine qua non* of a city and if some place has these it must be a city."

Agricultural Revolution

During this revolution in the 20th century, science has completely metamorphosed the centre, structure and quality of agriculture. Today, we possess highly sophisticated agricultural tools and implements and these help us get far higher yield of crops than before using very few hands. The revolution in agriculture has relieved a big labour force who now hunt for jobs. Being available, they are cheap and the capitalist is induced to invest money into new factories in order to utilize this cheap labour. When large labour force migrates to any place, that place grows and tends to develop into a city. In the West, agricultural revolution is an important factor in the development of cities.

Increase in the Means of Transportation

In the development of cities, means of transport plays a crucial role. Without the facilities of transportation and the easy availability of such means as trains, trucks, buses, taxis, scooters, etc., no place can become a business centre. Previously, the chief means of transport available was the bullock cart and this means is expensive as well as time consuming. Today, by means of rail, road or air we can transport goods from one place to another very quickly and inexpensively. In big towns or metropolises, therefore, goods are brought from great distances by air, rail or road transport and they become business centres for national as well as international goods. One of the reasons for the quick growth of metropolises like Kolkata and Mumbai is the easy availability of the various means of transport.

Development of Communication

With the development of means of communication like postal, telegraph and wireless services, it has now become possible for the businessmen away from each other by great distance to establish contacts with each other. This in turn stimulates business and trade activity. The trade becomes intra- and inter-national. The facilities of communication have helped greatly in the growth and development of cities.

Political Factors

Owing to political reasons certain places assume great importance; and consequently, become great cities. In almost all states, the capitals have developed greatly and fast. For example, Chandigarh was an obscure village but when it was metamorphosed it became a modern city. Similarly, the growth of London, Tokyo and Delhi can be traced to the fact that these are capitals of Great Britain, Japan and India respectively. Besides the reason of being capitals, many towns develop, in fact, into metropolises if some strategic importance is attacked to these.

Education Centres

The places which are centres of higher learning, soon become big cities. This is because students and teachers from far and wide assemble at such places, and in order to cater to their needs shops, markets, hotels, restaurants and clubs come into existence. Thus, all the prerequisites of a city materialize and wherever there are big markets, shopping and housing complexes a city is bound to come into existence.

Growth of Population

It is an evident fact that whenever and wherever there is increase in the population all prerequisites of cities are bound to come into existence. Subsequent to independence of India and consequent blood bath of communal frenzy and rioting there was great influx of population from Pakistan to India due to which many a small towns in India grew into cities. Thus, increase in the population is an important factor in the growth of cities.

Security

A place which is vulnerable to external attack or which is subject to attack by some marauding tribes cannot grow into a city because nobody would like to invest any money at such a place. People would invest money and do business only at those places which are safe and secure and where life and property are not consequently threatened.

Municipal Facilities and Means of Entertainment

In good cities there are schools, colleges, universities, music institutes, dance centres, medical colleges and industrial training institutes. People can avail of these facilities and enhance their abilities. In villages, in spite of plenty of money with people, they are no means of enjoyment and entertainment. On the other hand, in cities there are cinemas, music and dance clubs, theatres, nightclubs, hotels and restaurants. In cities people can buy comfort and enjoyment by spending money. On account of easy availability of means of improving one's abilities and self-culture and also easy availability of means of entertainment, people are attracted from villages to cities.

Slums

Nearly 30 per cent of population in the metropolitan cities in India live in slums and the number is increasing. In Kolkata alone, the number of slum dwellers was 11.64 lakhs a decade back. Today, this number is 38.83 lakhs.

Definition of Slum

There is no general agreement on the definition of 'slum'. Some writers regard it as a special type of disorganized area, others treat the terms 'slum' and 'blighted area' as synonyms. Still others believed that slums can also be found in rural areas, which is however a debatable proposition.

Slums may be characterized as areas of sub-standard housing within a city. A slum is an inhabited uninhabitable habitation. A slum is an area of dilapidated houses which are, in fact, worthly of distraction. Slums exist either in the zone in transition or around factories or in congested districts. Poverty constitutes the main characteristic of slum dwellers. Multi-family dwellings are a typical feature of slums and sometimes two or more families live in a single room. Self-subsistence and struggle for survival are the main features of slum life. Basic facilities like adequate air, water, lighting and other sanitary facilities are wanting. Slums are usually full of filth and marsh which are the breeding places of diseases carrying germs. Slums act as cover for hideouts for all sorts of crimes and vices like gambling which prevail and live upon the city population. Slums are an area of constant family conflict, desertion and evictions. A person is left on his own to look after himself. Educational and recreational facilities are conspicuous by their absence. Thus, a slum knocks down all forms of settled life. Juvenile delinquency and mal-socialization or more or less orphan juveniles of the slum society are the curses of the slum upon city life. Thus, a slum is a highly destructed area of worn out buildings, which provides housing facilities to the city's poor and needy. Congestion and lack of privacy are the concomitants of a slum culture.

Kinds of Slums

There are three main types of slums in our cities. These are:

(i) *Original Slum:* This is an area which from the very beginning consisted of unsuitable buildings. These are usually areas around an old factory or mining site which is now given up or in the zones which are in transition. These sections are beyond recovery as they consist of age old structures and they need to be razed in order to be eradicated, e.g., the Mexican Slum in USA.

(ii) *Transitional Zone Slum*: The second type consists of slum created by the departure of middle and upper class families to other sections. Or it may be due to the starting of a new industry or due to congestion and subsequent deterioration of the living area. These types of slums are to be found in the transition zone of the developing cities such as South End Slum in Boston (USA). These are the areas which house vice and crime and where all sorts and shades of people live. In rehabilitation of this type of slums there is no need for wholesale demolition. Only dilapidated structures must be replaced by housing project. The remaining rehabilitation is mainly a matter of administration and community organization. But vested interests act as hindrances in the clearance of these slums.

(iii) *Blighted Slum*: The third and most unpleasant type of slum is mainly a phenomenon of transition once the area around a main business district has become blighted. Physical and social deterioration spreads rapidly. This type of slum looms with flop houses, one night accommodations for the destitute, houses of prostitution and street-lassies. It is populated by transients, tramps, vagrants, chronic alcoholics, beggars, homeless men and habitual criminals. Its economic activities are carried out by proprietors of saloons and porn rooms, fences, pawnbrokers, dope peddlers, etc. This type of slum clearly defies rehabilitation. The proper remedy is better administration and stricter zoning laws.

Slums differ physically. Thus, there are rooming house slums, tenement slums and slums of one family homes. Rooming house slums consist of structures where different rooms are let out to different persons and families. Tenement slums consist of multistoried structures which house two or more families in a single dwelling. Rooming houses are let out on a temporary basis. Slums of one family house, which consists of a typical small family structure are very rare.

Slum Improvement Programmes

Evils of Slums

Slums are a constant menace to healthy urban social life. Slums are usually dirty areas of congested housing with overpopulation and lack of basic amenities like light and water. Slums develop due to poverty.

Life under slum conditions results in several physical and mental diseases like contagious diseases, depression, etc., and social evils like broken families, lack of healthy social life, development of all sorts of vices like juvenile delinquency, prostitution, etc. Further, slums affect the morals and peace of the surrounding urban community. Slums develop due to lack of proper housing.

Needs of Slum Improvement

Hence, slum improvement programmes form one of the vital factors of urban housing and reconstruction. The basic aim of slum improvement programme is to provide to the slum dwellers decent housing with provisions of minimal necessities of life. Slum improvement programmes bear an obligatory duty of every city government today. Slum improvement programmes while removing many physical and social evils of city life add to city beautification.

Factors of Slum Improvement

(i) *Housing*: The basic factor of a slum improvement programme is housing. This requires the total destruction of a slum area and its replacement with a colony for low income housing. Herein are constructed small tenements and multi-storied independent dwellings which contain the basic minimum of a living room, kitchen, bath, etc. These houses are compactly constructed along well laid out streets. These are then given to the poor dwellers, more often, on a scheme of hire purchase.

(ii) *Water Sanitation and Light*: The next factor for slum improvement is provision of water and light which can be made good by laying out pipelines and poles and by putting up public taps at equal distances and street lights. If possible, the houses should also be provided with lights and taps. Provision of proper sanitation facilities also form a part of slum improvement programme. Next comes the question of setting up of a fair price shop, amidst a slum colony where the government provides foodstuffs, clothing, etc., to the dwellers under subsidized rates.

(iii) *Medical Care and Education*: Next comes the question of setting up of hospital or health centre, wherein the facilities for average medical care are available. The provision of a school with proper teachers solves much of the problems of juveniles in a slum area. The removal of vices to a far off place forms the crucial issue of a slum improvement programme. More than all this, lies the factor of inducing and interesting the slum dwellers into the concept of a healthy and responsible social life through proper social education.

Problems of Slum Improvement

However, much of the slum improvement programmes in our cities are falling short of achieving their results due to the shortage of funds, overpopulation, non-cooperation of slum dwellers, absence of ambitious administrators, political influence of the bosses on vice, and apathy and attitude of aversion towards slum dwellers of our general society. The number of slums in our cities baffles the comprehension of any social reformer. However, in the formulation and effective implementation of slum improvement programmes, lie the solution of many of our urban ills and also it is a social obligation upon the more fortunate to improve the living conditions of their less fortunate brethren.

Growth of Slums

Industrialization has resulted in shortage of accommodation and this, in turn, has given rise to slums with overcrowded shabby living quarters. These slums are populated by workers and other indigent people. The persons living in these slums are constantly exposed to all kinds of diseases and are liable to become social deviates and criminals; the loss of morals is an inevitable consequence of living in slums. The Ahatas of Kanpur, Bastis of Delhi, Chawls of Chennai are stigmas on the face of India. These shabby quarters are worse than stables of horses and pens of cattles. There is no ventilation, no drainage, no drinking water. A besmirched draggled piece of jute hanging in front of home is an eloquent testimony of their pitiable condition. The glaring contrasts in the palatial lives of industrialists and the dirt laden existence of workers testify to the hollowness of our socialism and democratic life. Pandit Jawaharlal Nehru was so moved emotionally on seeing slums that he wanted them to be burnt down and the persons responsible for them to be hanged. They symbolize extreme moral and physical decline, the nadir of all that is bad in life. According to Radhakamal Mukherjee, "In the thousand slums of India's industrial centres manhood is, unquestionably brutalized, women dishonoured and childhood is poisoned at its very source."

Urban Development and Urban Community Development

The Community Development Programme, both in rural and in urban areas, is based on the sound economic principle that in an economy characterized by striking underemployment and disguised unemployment, there is considerable scope for development through the organization of its surplus labour or surplus labour time. The programme stresses the need to provide organizational inputs no less than capital inputs. Urban Community Development (UCD) envisages a process of social transformation in urban areas through which the people could organize themselves in communities, understand their local situation, and work for its improvement with limited assistance from the government. The programme was seen as a catalyst in the development process wherein the community would be the most important actor, with the local authorities and government playing, at best, sponsoring and supervising role. The objectives of the programme were stated thus: (i) creating a climate of social coherence by promoting a sense of belonging to the community and of natural integration through activities requiring popular participation; (ii) creating civic consciousness in the community and improving its problem-solving capacity through investment in human resources; (iii) encouraging local initiative and getting voluntary agencies involved in the developmental efforts; and (iv) ensuring fuller utilization of the technical and welfare services available in the area and creating suitable facilities and the environment.

Organizational Structure of UCD Programme

The programme was started in the central sector with fifty per cent expenditure being met by the Central Government, the rest being shared equally by the state and the local authority. In 1969, three years after the initiation of the project, it was transferred to the state sector and as a result the expenditure was to be borne by the state government and the local authority.

In most cases, the municipalities and municipal corporations have been identified as the agency responsible for implementing urban community projects. An attempt is often made to establish a separate department as an integral part of the municipality or municipal corporation to take care of the programme. The relationship of this department with other concerned departments at different levels of hierarchy is established to ensure their cooperation and coordination.

Some states have established an urban community development department at the state level (e.g., Andhra Pradesh) to supervise the programme and to coordinate the activities of all governmental agencies operating within the project area. In others some existing state department or any other agency, e.g., the metropolitan development authority in Chennai, has been assigned this responsibility. The personnel associated with the programmes fall into following categories: (i) Part-time community volunteers (e.g. slum helpers in Hyderabad) chosen from different localities whose basic responsibility is to educate and prepare the people and to ensure community participation in the formulation and implementation of different components of the programme. They are given simple training to be able to act as a connecting link between the community and the official agencies concerned. The volunteers may receive small monthly honorarium. (ii) Trained paraprofessionals (e.g., community organizers) who support the community volunteers and help give formal shape to the project at the local level. They try to strengthen the existing local organizations and start new ones like Basti-Welfare Committees, *Mahila Mandals*, etc., that can take up major responsibilities in the implementation of the project. (iii) Technicians and professionals located with the local authority or the concerned state departments whose expertise can be made available to the project staff. (iv) Personnel responsible for administration and coordination at the city and state levels. They would include functionaries such as project officer, deputy project officer, etc., and administrative staffs working in the urban community development and other departments concerned with the programme at the state level.

UCD Programme: Success and Failures

The UCD programme was initially intended to cover fairly quickly all class I cities with population of one lakh or more, having problems of deteriorating urban environment. However, in the first phase, only twenty experimental projects were identified by the Central government to cover the major states and union territories. Fourteen projects got started in 1966, and remaining materialized in subsequent years.

Projects were generally delayed by the executing agencies, in view of financial constraints and administrative and other problems. After the transfer of the programme to the state sector in 1969, some states (e.g., Goa, Daman and Diu, West Bengal and Rajasthan) decided to close the projects. However, a few projects were even started after central assistance ceased to flow into the programme, e.g., Jamnagar, Surat and Barata (Gujarat), Quilon (Kerala) and Gauhati (Assam). In the beginning of the Fifth Plan, only five UCD projects in Gujarat (Baroda, Rajkot, Surat, Bhavnagar and Jamnagar) and one in Andhra Pradesh (Hyderabad) were functioning effectively.

The ninth conference of municipal corporations (September, 1973) considered urban community development in the context of the Minimum Needs Programme for slum improvement and strongly urged the Government of India and State governments to expedite implementation of the recommendations of the conference. The conference also suggested that programme should be taken up by municipal authorities on their own, in cities where public response is encouraging. State governments were requested to ensure adequate follow-up action.

The conference of Ministers of Housing and Urban Development held in 1978 recommended the setting up of a committee to report, among other things, on the need for an integrated approach to the problems of slums and to consider the amalgamation of the UCD programme with the Sixth Plan Scheme of Environmental Improvement in Slum Areas. This suggestion was reiterated in a letter addressed by the Government of India to all State governments in May 1980.

It is being increasingly realized that mere physical improvements undertaken under the scheme for environmental improvement of slum areas and provision of indirect benefits such as education maternal and child health and nutrition cannot yield substantial results, unless these are supplemented by schemes giving immediate economic gains. Also, it is now recognized that the programme to help individuals cannot be totally ignored in the enthusiasm to pursue community projects and that "economic development was essential", without which social programmes would be of less lasting significance. These considerations led to appropriate modifications being made in the detailed project design of the UCD programme.

Urban Community Development Project

The Delhi Municipal Cooperation created a Department of Urban Community Development in September, 1958 with financial assistance from the Ford Foundation. The need for such a department arose as: (i) it was felt that a continuous trend towards urbanization unless properly planned brought deterioration in the quality of community life and extension of slum conditions, and (ii) the problem of rural community development could not be viewed in isolation and an integrated approach to rural and urban problems would be helpful. The pilot project started under the department, involved six types of improvements: (a) the organization of citizens' development councils or *vikas mandals* (a *vikas mandal* comprises of 250 families); (b) the establishment of neighbourhood councils (a neighbourhood would be a loose confederation of 10-15 vikas mandals); (c) an attempt to improve the work of the local voluntary group, called *mohalla* committees; (d) the development of health and welfare council and community chest, and (e) various civic campaigns and contests to improve the physical appearance and to arouse citizens' cooperation.

The object of the project is to promote the growth of community life and to encourage the development of citizens' participation in programmes of self-help and civic improvement. In 1962, there were 32 *vikas mandals* in various stages of development, 20 of them being formed into two large neighbourhood councils, with a total of approximately 45,000 persons. In addition, there were projects involving a *bazaar*, *mohalla* committees, a health and welfare council, community chest and civic campaigns.

The programme had a special evaluation unit. It evaluated the impact of activities in relation to social integration; fall in anti-social activities; acceptance of new practices; better use of civic services, recreation, health education, self-help, fund raising for community works, change in outlook, attitudes to health and patterns of living, etc. "Caste, religious, professional, cultural and residents' welfare associations were found helpful, but the political organizations did not appear to have a positive attitude towards the programme. Preoccupation with major problems of life giving employment, better employment and better standard of life stood in the way of citizens' full appreciation of the urban community development programme." Less coordinated activities of the municipal departments, procedural delays in the municipal administration, groupism among people and their leaders; and transfer of community workers from one area to another affected the urban community development work adversely. However, it was found that even in depressed localities, in spite of differences that divided people, they could respond to self-help programmes with enthusiasm.

Jamshedpur Experiment

As against Delhi project, in Jamshedpur town the volunteers were enlisted from the communities themselves. The initiative came from the Tata Iron and Steel Company, whose employees live in this town. They were given a four-month orientation course, which was available in the morning or evening according to the convenience of volunteers. They were paid an allowance of Rs. 15 per month. In the year 1958, when the project was started, some 58 volunteers were involved in orientation. With the help of volunteers, communities took up activities like running cooperatives, dispensaries, reading rooms, adult night school, recreational programmes for children and youth, etc. Jamshedpur being a company town, the company provided the initiative and acted as the catalytic project. A similar project was taken up in Ahmedabad by the Textile Labour Association in 1962, with the help of 200 volunteers, who were given orientation before taking up their work.

The Government of India appointed the Rural-Urban Relationship Committee in 1963 which was requested to submit an interim report on Urban Community Development projects which could be taken up during the Third Five-Year Plan. The Committee having examined the working of existing projects continuing in Delhi, Jamshedpur, Ahmedabad, Kolkata, etc., recommended that different items should be taken up in different projects depending upon their needs. In the initial stages, it is neither desirable nor even possible to undertake a large number of activities. These should be gradually increased with the progress of work. However, three conditions must be fulfilled before any activities are taken up: (i) The people must be motivated with a desire for change and be involved from the start in planning and execution of programmes. (ii) Priorities in the selection of the programmes should be determined with reference to the urgency of the needs. (iii) Cooperation of the departmental agencies concerned must be fully ensured in advance. They should generally be carried out though the voluntary workers, though they may be guided by paid community organizers. Even if the work is entrusted to voluntary agencies, the corporation or the municipality should be the agency for the implementation of the scheme, and the assistance from the

Government of India should be channelized through the state government and the local body concerned.

The Ministry of Health drew up a detailed scheme for setting up 40 projects in urban community development in the various cities having a population of one lakh or over during the Third Five-Year Plan. On the basis of the above report, it was decided to undertake 20 pilot projects in 1965-66, with 50 per cent contribution. The centre was to pay Rs. 15,000 per annum for three years for staff and other expenses for each centre covering a population of 50,000 to 60,000. There were to be *mohalla* units of 6,000 to 7,000 each. In its final report, it was recommended that the programme should be primarily people-centred aiming at organizing the people for corporate community action. "The emphasis is primarily on the change in the attitudes and motivations of the people and community rather then social welfare. This object is not so much to take social service to the underprivileged as it is to evoke in them a desire for self-reliance." A coordination committee was set up under the chairmanship of the Union Deputy Minister of Health, Family Planning and Urban Development to review and guide the programme from time to time and also to formulate schemes on research, training and evolution.

Urban Growth Patterns

Cities are always changing. As business expands, industries move in. There is growth in area and population, changes in spatial arrangements and the social conditions which alters the city as a result. The changes take place, in a definite order. For instance, there is a tendency towards centralization as well as decentralization with increasing economic activity. Land values go up, taxes increase, marginal businessman in the loop, no longer able to compete, move out to cheaper outlying localities. Similarly, as the loop becomes unable to satisfy the needs of an increased population, sub-centres and convenience stores spring up in outlying residential areas. In some cases, business replaces residences and the residential areas are pushed to the periphery.

The fringe of the business area is the most affected during expansions or contraction. An expanding business section causes flight from hitherto well-organized residential areas. Land values adjacent to the new business area begin to decline and the whole border district deteriorates. Poor people may move into buildings hastily remodelled into cheap living quarters and a new slum arises. In a similar way, population growth or decline changes the spatial pattern of a city. As residential areas become overcrowded, land values, taxes and rents rise. The result is a mass concentration and centralization of residential sections. But this process is accompanied by a process of decentralization. The upper classes who find the area inconvenient to live in migrate. The poorest who could not pay the high rents and the mixed group of all those who could not find adequate accommodation move out. Different types of new residential areas develop, such as high class sections with spacious homes, middle class settlements and aggregations of hastily erected shabby houses for the lowest income group. Apartment houses predominate in the original section and one family units move towards the outskirts of the city and beyond and the suburb is created. As this process is repeated, the spatial feature of the city changes. Fashionable suburbs become middle class sections and the upper classes build on vacant land.

Thus, in an expanding city the business centres tend to grow in size thereby dislocating residential areas. At the same time residential areas show a centrifugal tendency by moving more and more toward the outskirts and beyond the city limits. Urban settlements form into distinct and regular ecological patterns. A city is a clearly distinguishable spatial order to urban activities. The sentinel differences within a city arise out of social consideration which create for each part of a city a different evaluation and different functions. The ecological patterns of a city exhibit: (i) differentiations of function, (ii) class separation, and (iii) cultural segregation.

However, this explanation does not conform to the actual growth of cities. It is rarely that we notice a deteriorated neighbourhood surrounding a business district although there may be slums. Further, the growth of suburban shopping complexes have immensely reduced the prominence of central business district. Contrary to the explanation, housing districts are generally found in the midst of a city. Apartment houses sometimes exist amidst one family houses. However, the notion of congestion and relative land values is understandable. The explanation serves as an ideal construct which may provide a guideline to future city planners.

A number of pilot projects were initiated in the urban areas which included the projects in Delhi, Ahmedabad, Baroda and Kolkata. In 1966, the Government of India had decided to launch formally a national experiment in urban community development (UCD), similar to rural community development. The most successful UCD project by far has been considered to be the one in Hyderabad which started in December 1967, following a month's training of the project staffs at the Baroda University. Many UCD programmes and plans were initiated in big cities. They were very successful.

To sum up, UCD is not a comprehensive plan for the development of cities and their hinterland. It is basically intended to secure the welfare of certain sections of the population and, in this sense, has limited development objectives. To be meaningful, it must be integrated with the overall development plan for the city or the region.

10

Rural Community Development

Any talk of rural development is generally construed as unfashionable, unprofitable and unholistic. The common refrain is that it is prudent to talk of development of the entire country and its people. No doubt, this mindset has prevented the discourse on rural development from coming to the centre stage, and many people from putting their stakes in it. It is not an irony that the development discourse has left 73 per cent (latest census) of India's rural population uncovered? Is it not inconceivable that Indian economy ranking 5th in the world has failed to touch majority of its population living in rural areas? Is it not odd that India has nuclear bombs and rockets along side hand-pulled rickshaws, hyper consumerism in the cities, with starvation deaths in places like infamous Kalahandi district of Orissa. Today, in our country, less than half of the rural population come in the middle class or lower middle class category. Millions of people live under poverty line and they suffer from the dregs of poverty. The disparities are divesting, in spite of the poverty line having considerably gone down. The inflation rate of our country has come down but the prices of essential commodities which are the bread and butter of the common man are still high and even soaring.

The overarching need for rural India is alleviation of its chronic and rampant poverty, compounded by growing unemployment and dwindling income opportunities. The village industries, which provide income and self-employment for numerous artisans across the country, are gradually disappearing. The highest number of employment in

India is really household manufacturing employment. Massive urban drift is taking place with women migrating to cities in masses, which is depleting villages and burdening cities. Having seen this, the old methods of generating growth of employment in traditional sectors are no more effective to support the ever-growing rural population. New ways, technologies, institutions have to be put in place.

India is predominantly a rural country with 75 per cent of its population still living in the villages of various sizes ranging from small hamlets to large village settlements. They continue to suffer from underdevelopment, poverty and social backwardness. Rural environments are much cleaner and greener than urban environments, but their degradations are the combination of the problems that have risen from low levels of development. In fact, environment degradation is a form of environmental change, which leads to lower level of production, degradation of agricultural land, shortage of fuel wood and fodder, biological diversity, change in microenvironment, etc. A two-approach strategy is required, first to solve the rural problems through development process and second to protect environment through community participation by creating awareness among rural people.

Development thinking has a perceptible shift towards people-centred programmes. Without information or communication, no development can take its firm root. New opportunities need to be provided and all the information needs of the community ought to be met to stimulate their awareness and better their capabilities.

Communication technology and media, which are steadily improving and expanding, are to be treated only as tools and means and not an end in themselves. Development also means change, and the change involves attitudinal and behavioural changes besides material and environmental changes.

The founders of planning in India considered cooperation as an instrument of economic development of the disadvantaged, particularly in the rural areas. Rural development helps to liberate the energies of the rural people, especially the poor, so that they can realize their full potential and thus improve their capacity as well as commitments to development, organize and govern themselves towards the attainment of a higher quality of life for the individual and for the entire community,

There are many voluntary organizations and NGOs which have not only grown in size but have also developed infrastructures for research, training and demonstration on alternative methods suitable for rural usage, development and life. Further, few NGOs have also achieved quality skills in specialized field of primary education, micro financing, health related issues, marketing of rural produce, etc.

Democratic decentralization is the key to the planning process in the country. Efforts have been on to activate the system of panchayat raj institution, so that these bodies could facilitate the participatory process at the grass-roots level to meet local needs and aspirations of the rural people.

Rural Community Development

Rural people, accounting for about three-fourths of the total population, have for long, lagged much behind the overall progress of the economy. To overcome this undesirable trend, special programmes for rural development began to be designed since the seventies as supplement to the provisions of the Five-Year Plans of the country. People living in the rural areas are up against three problems of great magnitude. These are: utter backwardness of the rural economy; widespread unemployment; and massive poverty.

Meaning of Community

MacIver defines community as "an area of social living marked by some degree of social coherence". He further says, "whenever the members of any group, small or large, live together in such a way that they share not this or that particular interest, but the basic conditions of a common life, we call that group a community". We know that a person rarely exists alone. He is linked in many ways to his fellows who form a group. We cannot however, expect a man to become the member of all the groups existing in the world. He can establish his relations only with the people who reside near him in a definite part of the territory; it is inevitable that people who over any length of time reside in a particular locality should develop social likeness, should have common social ideas, common traditions and the sense of belonging together. This fact of social living and common specified area gives birth to community.

Rural Communities

The earliest human communities were perhaps the loosely organized aggregations of a few families who carried on mutually interdependent activities in gathering food and defending themselves against their enemies. Gradually, man acquired skill and knowledge in agriculture and with the consequent stabilization of the source of food, the people began to lead a settled life and human communities became more stationary. The village emerged which signified that man has passed from nomadic mode of collective life to the settled one. Bogardus says "human society has been cradled in the rural group". In spite of modernization and urbanization, it is a fact that even at the present time a large proportion of population lives in villages.

Features of Rural Community

The rural community is marked by several features. The important ones are the following:

Community Consciousness

The village dwellers have a sense of unity. The relations between the village people are intimate. They personally know each other. Their customs, conventions and culture are common. Structurally and functionally the village is a unit.

Role of Neighbourhood

In a village, neighbourhood is of great importance. There is not enough of individuality and speed in the life of the village which disables one from paying attention to his neighbours, his sorrow, and joys. In the village, people assist each other and thus they have closest neighbourhood relations.

Faith in Religion

The people in the villages have deep faith in religion and deities. Their main occupation is agriculture, which largely depends upon the vagaries of nature. The farmer acquires an attitude of fear and awe towards natural forces and starts worshipping them.

Simplicity

The rural people lead a simple life. It is not ostentatious. They are far away from the evils of modern civilization. They are simple and plain people believing in God. They do not show pretensions. Their behaviour is natural and not artificial. They live a peaceful life. They are free from mental conflicts. They are sincere, hospitable and hardworking. The level of morality is high, social crimes are very rare. Their life is governed by norms.

Joint Family

Though in the cities the joint family system is breaking down, yet in the villages it still retains its hold. The agricultural occupation requires the cooperation of all the family members. The men plough the field, the women harvest the crops and the children graze the cattle.

Growth of Village Community

The growth of village community depends upon the following factors:

Topographical Factors

Among the topographical factors are included land, water and climate. It is obvious that these factors influence the growth of rural community. People would like to settle at a place where land is fertile and plain. The villagers settled on fertile lands are more developed and prosperous.

The facility of water also contributes to the growth and prosperity of villages. Water is required not only for drinking, bathing, cooking, etc., but also for irrigating the lands. The villages situated on the banks of canals or having tube wells are in a much prosperous condition than those which are seeking out a miserable existence in the deserts and hills.

A temperate climate is most favourable to the growth of village community. Man cannot lead a natural and prosperous life in areas of extreme climate.

Economic Factors

Among the economic factors we may include the condition of agriculture, rural economy and cottage industries. Agriculture is the main stay of the village community. As such, the growth of village communities depend upon the condition of agriculture. If farming yields a good crop, the economic condition of the village people will be better.

The village economy is also an important factor in the growth of the village community. The farmer must be in a position to procure animals of good breed, good seeds, good manure and scientific implements. There should be cooperative societies for supplying capital, good seeds, implements and to a arrange the sale of agricultural produce at reasonable prices.

Social Factors

Among the social factors, we include peace, security, cooperation and intelligence. For the development of the village community it is essential that there must be peace in the village. Besides peace, the village people must be guaranteed security from disease, and in agriculture. They also need security against natural calamities. Agriculture insurance can give them this sense of security.

Community development is not possible without cooperation. In the village there are many activities, which depend upon cooperation of the whole community. Such activities, for example, are public health, sanitation, peace and order, proper use of public amenities, education and recreation, etc. Through cooperation the village people can bring about this development and put the village community on the way to prosperity.

An Approach to Integrated Rural Development

Rural development has been talked about since our independence in 1947. Pandit Jawaharlal Nehru strongly supported the community development programme started in 1952. Since then, a plethora of different rural development programmes and projects running into hundreds have been taken up by the Central and State governments, non-government organizations, foreign aid agencies, World Bank, UN agencies, and the like, but the fact still remains, that we have more persons illiterate and those living below poverty line than when we had before.

A large number of rural development programmes have been taken up during the last 15 years, but they have suffered from basic deficiencies like inadequate inputs of education and relevant technology and absence of an efficient, honest and all inclusive delivery system. It is strongly recommended, that the know-how and expertise available with the scientific and technological institutions in the country should be fully exploited in an integrated manner, for micro-level planning and execution of both short-term and long-term projects in a selected region within the framework of a Social Cybernetic model. This would avoid adhocism and inconsistency in programmes and projects and would ensure a well conditioned and integrated scientific approach with adequate technological input for overall development of the people in all the spheres of activity.

Benefits

(i) Integrated rural development programme will ensure integrated planning, programmes and projects for overall development of the entire population.
(ii) It will ensure participation of people in programmes of their own welfare through available scientific and technological knowledge and personal.
(iii) Generate gainful employment for all categories of educated, skilled and unskilled, through employment and partially employed people of the district.
(iv) Inculcate the spirit and practice of sustainable consumption.
(v) Build self-reliance and advance the development of society through "self-help groups and *Gram Swarozgar Yojana*".

Nature and Characteristics of Rural Society

Real rural development is poor-people initiated, poor-people centred and poor-people led. The rural people should realize that it is their right and duty to participate in development activities in order to develop all the sectors of rural economy, all regions of rural areas and all sections of rural society. The essence of rural development is to prepare the rural people to take sustained interest and initiative and assume the responsibility for improving their socio-economic and cultural life through locally available means.

Rural society is a comprehensive mix of activities, which include agricultural growth, putting up of economic and social infrastructure, village planning, public health, education and functional literacy, communication, etc. In this multi-pronged effort involving development and conservation of resources – land, water and human – the objective is to raise the standard of living and quality of life of the rural masses. Rural development thus encompasses both spatial and functional integration of all relevant programmes bearing on increased agricultural production and provision and reduction of unemployment and provision of gainful employment among the rural people.

To rejuvenate and regenerate India's rural life, community development programme was launched on October 2, 1952, the birthday of Mahatma Gandhi. Three-tier system of Panchayati Raj followed later.

A viable infrastructure for all round development was created. The specialist services were provided through the extension agency. Once the definite infrastructure was put on the ground, special intensive programmes were undertaken, specially directed towards the welfare of the weaker sections. Selected programmes, like drought-prone area programme, small and marginal farmers development agencies, agricultural credit, etc., have all been brought within the ambit of activities under rural development. Rural development helps to liberate the energies of the rural people, especially the poor, so that they can realize their full potential and thus improve their capacity as well as commitments to development; organize and govern themselves towards the attainment of a higher quality of life for the individual and for the entire community.

Social Factors of Rural Society

Rural people suffer from conservatism, superstition and social evils because of which they are not able to make progress either in the social or economic fields. People from outside cannot go and teach these people that they need to change their faith and beliefs. It is the village people who can make them do all this. Gram Panchayats that have representatives of the people in them can play their role very effectively. So far these institutions have not played their vital role in this field, but they can certainly play their part in future.

Social Reform

Village people are a prey to various social evils like child marriage, opposition to widow remarriage, casteism, spending a lot at the time of marriage and other social and ceremonial occasions.

Making Provisions for Education

In village, illiteracy is the biggest problem. It can be removed only with the help of the Gram Panchayats. Once illiteracy is removed, many of the problems of the rural society shall automatically disappear.

Programmes for Child and Women Welfare

A large number of programmes for child and women welfare can be carried out through panchayats. They can carry out programmes of educating men about the importance of women in the family. They can also undertake the responsibility of providing nutritive diet to children, pregnant and feeding women, etc.

Programmes for Recreation

Healthy recreation is very much needed in rural society. Village people have a good deal of leisure, which they employ in so many evil things. In villages, factionalism grows only because they have a lot of time. It means that if healthy recreation is available the leisure shall be gainfully utilized. Panchayats can have radio sets, they can arrange for occasional show of films, can arrange reading of news papers, organize games and plays, etc.

Economic Empowerment of Society

The basic objectives of the policies, laws and institutions of the Indian welfare system is to bring the target group into the main stream of development by making them self-reliant. In this direction, the state embarked upon strategies of planned development for minimizing inequalities of income, status and opportunities for its people. The efforts directed at securing distributive justice and distributing economic resources to support educational and economic interests of disadvantaged and marginalized sections of society, viz., Scheduled Castes and Scheduled Tribes, minorities, backward classes, disabled and women need further strengthening. Most of these sections of society live below poverty line and are much larger than those in the rest of the society. They still possess poor assets and are engaged in low-income activities. There is a continuing wide gap in the socio-economic development of disadvantaged and marginalized section of population, compared to our national average. The strategies of the government are, therefore, reinvigorated and intensified to create a better and effective impact on the quality of life of these sections. There is an increase in efforts and speed for bridging the gap in respect of those sections who live below poverty line and others who belong to better off sections of society.

Government has taken up necessary initiatives to extend economic development, parallel to social empowerment by establishing viable financial institutions for extending credit at low interest especially to the families under the poverty line. Among various ministries and departments at the centre, the Ministry of Social Justice and Empowerment entrusted with the welfare, social justice and empowerment of weaker sections, in general, and those of Scheduled Castes, Scheduled Tribes, Backward Classes, and minorities in particular, and the development of women and child entrusted with the welfare, development and empowerment of weaker sections have set up financial corporations/institutions for making these sections of population self-dependent and independent.

Gender Inequalities

A technology may be appropriate for women if it reduces their drudgery, improves their environment, their skill and enhances their comforts. A lack of sensitivity, total blissful ignorance and a general apathy to the general problems of rural women, basically underlie all attempts to formulate even a simple technology package for rural women. While urban women have been vociferously vocal in expressing their needs – mental, social, physical and also emotional – there lies a great lack of a sensitive and human approach in even identifying the problems faced by rural women, for example, 'paddy thrashing' is carried out manually by women with their own feet. This manual labour spread over several hours for several days caused the feet of the women to form blisters and bleed. But for long and even today this has not been identified as a problem either by the women themselves or by the others.

Bound in their traditional die-hard styles, rural women do not consider many of their back breaking chores as 'labourious or unjust'; this in primarily because for centuries now, the male gender has been ruling as the family need. To date, it has been only the male gender who served as leaders in problem identification and technology generation and dissemination for the rural women. While enacting his role of women benefactor, the male gender overlooked many issues, basically important to women – especially rural women. This can be witnessed by a mere scanning of the daily routine activities of rural women and the status of appropriate technology assistance/backing available to them, for example, agricultural tools for harvesting, weeding, etc. These were invented several hundred years ago as per the requirement of the male gender and there has been no technical change or improvization done to them for easy use by women, who today, form the major bulk of labour force involved in agricultural activities.

Integration

Society is a constellation of groups, organizations, institutional agencies, collectives and ecological entities so interrelated that it operates as an interconnected system. In society, persons are bound together and dependent upon each other in systems of interrelationships that combine to constitute a total functional structure. But despite the fact, that the structural units of society are interconnected and interdependent so that they constitute a continuing entity, we find in every society, what Matron called "a strain towards income". This refers to condition where the continuity of the society has broken down to some degree. The degree of anomie may range from slight contradiction and confusion to serious deterioration and disintegration. Integration is the harmonizing or unifying process whereby the various structural components of society are properly organized. Integration does not involve similarity of various structural parts. Thus, the family system may not be similar in the different communities or all the people may not believe in the same religion or carry on the same occupation. What is essential for integration is that certain values must be accepted as common, and the different institutional agencies should preserve and promote these values. When basic changes occur in a society as when a new technology is introduced in the economy, and the old values become inadequate and the structures serving these values cease to function effectively, then new altered values may be developed and new social forms created or old ones readjusted to serve the altered values. This process serves to maintain integration.

Caste System in Society

The British rule in India gave a serious blow to the caste system in the villages. The economic policy and the law of British rule, induced the different caste to adopt occupations other than the traditional ones. The hold of caste panchayat was loosened. The status of a village man was determined on the basis of his economic position and personal attainments. The restrictions on food, dress, mode of living and other matters imposed under caste system were removed. Even untouchability was weakened. Thus, caste system has now lost its traditional hold in the villages; however, caste system is now getting strengthened on account of selfish political interests.

Characteristics of Rural Society

Isolation and Self-sufficiency

Almost till the middle of the 19th century, the villages in India were more or less self-contained, isolated and self-sufficient units. The inhabitants of the village had very little to do with the people outside. All of their essential needs were satisfied in the village itself.

However, changing political and economic conditions are putting an end to the isolation and self-sufficiency of the Indian village. The rapid development of the means of transport and communication has broken the barriers between the village and city. The former is now socially and even economically connected with the neighbouring city or town. Political parties have made village the centre of their activities as much as the city.

Peace and Simplicity

The second feature of an Indian village is the atmosphere of simplicity, calmness, and peace prevailing therein. In the village there is no noise and very little sophistication. The villagers lead a simple life, eat frugally, dress simply and are without the trappings of modern civilization.

But here also, the old order is yielding its place to a new one. The muddy walled houses are giving a place to well designed buildings. Fashion is making its inroads in the life of young men and women of the village. Here and there, notes of music issue from dry cell radio. However, this is gradual and slow.

Poverty and Illiteracy

Probably the most glaring and also depressing features of Indian villages are the poverty and illiteracy of the village people. They are generally poor with a very low income. They take coarse food and put on rough clothes. The pressure on land is high, resulting in fragmentation of holdings and poor productivity. Besides poverty, the village people are steeped in ignorance and illiteracy. The village school is generally in a dilapidated condition. Facilities for higher education are practically nil. Due to poverty, the villagers cannot send their children to the city for education. Due to illiteracy they cannot improve upon their agriculture or supplement their income by other means. Poverty is thus the cause and effect of illiteracy and the backwardness of the villagers.

However, recently the need has been realized for rural reconstruction. An all India organization under the name of 'All India Kissan Sammelan' has been formed to focus the attention of the government to the problems of the peasantry class. There is greater realization now that the country can march ahead only if its villages are prosperous. The governments, both at the centre and states, have launched schemes for liquidating illiteracy and removing poverty of the people living in the villages.

Local Self-Government

The villages in ancient India enjoyed a considerable measure of autonomy or self-government. The villagers managed their own affairs through the traditional institution of panchayat. The central government had neither the inclination nor the means for interfering with the self-government of villages. With the advent of Britishers in India and their introduction of a highly centralized system of administration, the importance of Panchayats began to decline. Their judicial powers were taken over, after the British courts and the officers were appointed to look after the administrative affairs of the villages. This change produced unpleasant results. Since the times of Lord Ripon, attempts were made to revive the old system of village local self-government, but the progress was very slow in this direction. With the attainment of freedom, now fresh efforts are being made to revive the old panchayat system and make Panchayats play a better part in the work of reconstruction.

Concept of Democratic Decentralization

Since times immemorial, India has been committed to democratic decentralization. Self-governing village communities characterized by agricultural economics had existed in India since the Vedic times. Gram Samitis are mentioned in the Rig Veda; these village bodies were the lines of contact with higher authorities on matters affecting village welfare. In the course of time, these village Panchayats were endowed with judicial and police powers as well. They enjoyed sacred position of authority. Even during the medieval and Mughal times, Panchayats enjoyed privileged position in village affairs. Though under the Mughals, the judicial powers of Panchayats were drastically reduced and cut down, local affairs still remained under their jurisdiction. A change came with the arrival of the British. They did not believe in decentralization of powers; they centralized all judicial and police powers in their own hands. As a result, in the pre-independence period, Panchayats lost much of their clout.

Present Change in the Panchayati Raj System in India

Despite India's traditional commitment to decentralization of power and despite the commitment of our freedom fighters, including Mahatma Gandhi to this ideal, the framers of the Indian Constitution did practically nothing to re-establish Panchayats which could play an important role in social transformation and implementation of development programmes. This fact, however, could not be so easily ignored. Gandhi's ideal of Gram Swaraj was there to help visionaries in Indian politics to implement the system of community development. Under this system each state was divided into a number of blocks. The Panchayati Raj Institutions were conceived as local bodies meant to ensure people's participation in development programmes. This system, however, did not produce the desired results.

In 1977, the Government of India appointed the Ashok Mehta Committee to review the working of the community development programmes in the whole country. The Committee's report suggested measures to strengthen the Panchayati Raj Institutions so that the decentralized system of planning and development could become effective. The Committee suggested that the whole of system be so organized that village folk participate in their own affairs and develop a capacity to take decisions. The Committee also recommended that there should be elected bodies at village, block and district levels. However, because of the lack of constitutional support, state governments did not take up the task of creation of the panchayat seriously, and in a big way.

It was in the last decade of the previous century, that serious efforts were made to implement the idea of democratic decentralization in right earnest. The 73rd and 74th Constitutional Amendment Acts were introduced in the parliament in 1992. These amendments brought about a fundamental change, not only in the realm of local self-government but also in India's federal character.

These constitutional amendments widened the base of the earlier Indian polity, wherein, elected representatives was restricted to parliament and the state assemblies. The new amendments provided for elections to panchayats as well. Now, there are hundreds of district panchayats, thousands of block panchayats, and more than two lakh Gram Panchayats. These amendments also have brought about a significant change in the federal structure, with elected local bodies at the districts level and below.

Generic Role of Panchayats in the New Millennium

The role of panchayats in the new millennium need not be dramatized into something fabulously exotic. Panchayats have to work within the broad framework of good governance doing what is basically right. In this perspective, local governments or panchayats should be: (i) small enough to be accessible, (ii) large enough to be effective and efficient, (iii) adaptable enough to be accountable, and (iv) serve all sections of the community. There is a need for a fundamental redefinition of the role of government at the local level given its financial base and demand overload.

Agency of Poverty Removal

Poor people live under multiple deprivations. Fundamental freedom of action and choice are alien to them. Lack of food, shelter, extreme vulnerability to ill health, economic dislocation and natural disasters and inability to influence key decisions affecting their lives are the dimensions of poverty they are exposed to. The community along with the panchayat and its leaders has to provide jobs, roads, electricity, markets for their produce and schools, water sanitation, and health services which form the canvas of material opportunities that would enable the poor to leapfrog over poverty.

Panchayats themselves have to ensure that their administration and function are accountable to the people to facilitate empowerment. Panchayats have to create networks with state governments to reduce vulnerability to economic shocks, natural disasters, ill-health, disabilities and personal violence.

Agency of Monitoring Education and Health

Getting educated in rural India is nothing short of a miracle. Endless accounts of the shocking state of rural schools are the bane of rural India today. The staggering 95 per cent drop-out rate from class I to class X effectively renders rural schooling a colossal waste, not only of financial but human resources as well, as most of these students lapse back into illiteracy.

In the area of health, quacks nonchalantly dish out saline drips to pregnant women or malaria patients, at times leading to deaths. Government hospitals are without doctors as doctors practice privately, and medical health centres are pilfered of large quantities of medicines. The rural medical infrastructure and staff has to come under the jurisdiction of the PRIS. Greater literacy and health achievements of disadvantaged groups can increase the ability of these groups to resist oppression, to organize political activities and get a fair deal.

Agency of Participative Planning and Development

The panchayat has to energize the Gram Sabha as the fulcrum of participative planning for development. Four standards of work on participation is formulated: social or community participation, political participation, the use of participatory methodologies and new understandings of citizenship or citizen participation. Social participation is the process by which social group or communities excluded from control over resources, take in decision-making in order to gain control.

Agency Promoting Associationalism

Finally, it must be admitted that social change and rural development, which go beyond the process of decentralization and gram panchayats, cannot be effectively engineered without the group system. Although there may be gaps in group representation, they are steadily closed over a period of time. The group system is dynamic, shifting and relatively open, be it community group, gender groupings such as *Mahila Mandals*, non-profit collaborations within the village. To whatever extent groups may be perceived as mischievous, there is still a threshold point of entry for other groups to challenge or counteract them.

We are living in a world of gross uncertainties, positive and negative. The forces of globalization that are shaping the economic, social and even political heuristics of our world seem to have a proclivity against the local. The integration of world's economics has aggravated the situation of poverty and led to deprivation amid plenty. Fighting poverty is our second greatest challenge, after population. The demand for decentralization reflects the desire of the people for a greater say in their government. Institutions of governance at the local level, therefore, have a clinching role in promoting a new equilibrium in rural India. The tasks before the panchayat in the new millennium are indeed overpowering. But as far as the Panchayati Raj Institution System (PRIS) is embedded as people's institution, there is no cause for despair.

Voluntary Organizations in Rural Development

Nature and Functions

Voluntary organizations have a long history of active involvement in the promotion of human welfare and well-being. Lord Beveridge called them "a private enterprise for social progress". Voluntary organizations came into existence spontaneously, voluntarily and without any compulsion or contract to fulfil the particular needs of some groups of people. These agencies are flexible and possess the virtues of human services with dedication. Their programme covers a diverse range of functions embracing human welfare. The programmes of voluntary organizations include the strictly professional, specialized and technical organizations, broadly based associations, of persons or group organized for a particular purpose; for example, information and service activities, educational institutions and associations, social welfare organizations, religious groups, women's organizations, youth groups, children councils, trade unions, family planning associations, etc.

Meaning and Definition of Voluntary Organizations

"An organizations that is administered by an autonomous board which holds meetings, collects funds for its support, chiefly from private sources, and expends money, whether with or without paid workers, in conducting a programme directed primarily to furthering the public health by providing health services or health education or by advancing research or legislation for health, or by a combination of these activities."

The voluntary organizations are different from the non-official organizations, because non-official organizations are an instance of inducted volunteerism by the state which may or may not secure popular support.

Types of Voluntary Organizations

Non-Profit and Non-Partisan Organizations

These are those voluntary organizations which have legal entity. It should have broad-based objectives, serving the social and economic needs of the community as a whole and mainly the weaker sections. It should not work for profit but on "no profit and no loss bases". Its activities should be open to all citizens of India irrespective of caste, creed, religion, sex and race. It should have necessary flexibility, professional competence and organizational skills to implement programmes. It declares that it adopts constitutional and non-violent means for development. Its office bearers should not be elected members of any political party. It is constituted of secular and democratic concepts and methods of functioning.

Conventional Voluntary Organizations

As pointed out earlier conventional voluntary organizations are those which have their own constitutions, elected office bearers with defined divisions of responsibility for the office bearers. In Seventh Five-Year Plan, greater stress has been laid for the involvement of voluntary organization in the implementation of development programmes.

Roles of Conventional Voluntary Organizations

(i) To supplement government efforts so as to offer the rural people choice and alternatives.
(ii) To be eyes and ears of the people at village level.
(iii) To set an example; it should be possible for the voluntary organizations to adopt simple innovation, using flexible and inexpensive means with less overheads and with greater community participation.
(iv) To activate the delivery system and to make it effective at the village level to respond to the felt needs of the poorest of the poor.
(v) To disseminate information.
(vi) To make communities as self-reliant as possible.
(vii) To show how village support and inadequate resources could be used, as well as, how human resources, rural skills and local knowledge grossly unutilized at present could be used for their own development.
(viii) To demystify technology and bring it in simpler forms.
(ix) To mobilize and organize the poor and generate awareness to demand quality services and impose a community system of accountability on the performance of village level government functionaries.

Ministry of Rural Development

As a result of reorganization of the ministries of agriculture, irrigation and power in October 1974, the work of the then department of community development and work relating to agricultural credit and indebtedness was allocated to the department of rural development.

Functions

The ministry is mainly responsible for the following functions:

(i) All matters relating to Panchayati Raj and public cooperation.

(ii) Land reforms, desert development programmes, warehousing, godowns, etc., in rural areas.

(iii) Programmes for tackling rural unemployment; all matters relating to the minimum needs programme, food for work programme and elementary and adult education.

(iv) Integrated rural development, including small farmers development agency, marginal farmers and agricultural labourers drought prone area programme.

(v) Setting up of agricultural markets in rural areas and agricultural produce.

Organizational Structure

The ministry is headed by a secretary, assisted by an additional secretary, five joint secretaries and other supporting staff of directors, deputy secretaries, under secretaries, etc. Broadly, the ministry is divided into five wings: rural unemployment, integrated rural development, land reforms, finance and administration, each headed by a joint secretary.

Activities

The five wings of the ministry and the three subordinate organizations coordinate their efforts in uplifting the lot of the poorest among the poor in the rural sector. Various programmes, like the small farmers development agency (SFDA), special livestock production, and training of rural youth in self-employment have been merged and substituted by one single Integrated Rural Development Programme (IRDP). This programme now dealt with by a single agency, at the district level called the rural development agency, has been extended to all 5,011 blocks in the country since October, 1980.

The IRDP seeks to improve the economic conditions of the weaker sections with marginal income, including grants of loans and subsidies and training for self-employment to women. To help the farmers, particularly the small and the marginal ones, the ministry, through the directorate of marketing and inspection and its regional, sub-regional offices spread all over the country has been implementing various schemes for the development and regulation of agricultural produce.

National Institute of Rural Development

The National Institute of Rural Development was established in November, 1965 to meet the training needs of personnel engaged in rural development and also to conduct research studies on various aspects connected with rural transformation. The institute's research, training and consultancy services are available to different departments of the state and the central governments, public sector undertakings, international agencies and voluntary organizations concerned with rural development.

Functions

(i) Improving social and economic well-being, increasing employment opportunities for women and all disadvantaged sections of the rural community.
(ii) Assisting in improvement of Panchayati Raj and other institutions for better implementation of development programme and delivery systems of rural development administration.
(iii) Formulating area plans, appraisal and monitoring of development projects in rural areas.
(iv) Promoting coordinated approaches among rural organizations, cooperative bodies and voluntary agencies for rural development.
(v) Human resource development training, social institutions, social actions.
(vi) Assisting in policy formulation and choice of options in rural development.

Activities

The main activities of the institute include conducting research, organizing training programme, and handling consultancy assignments. Its research studies are action-oriented and are fed into the training programmes. The focus is on problems of implementation.

Between April, 1966 and March, 1979, the institute conducted 188 training programmes for 5,360, participants and completed 100 research studies, of which 46 were consultancy assignments. It disseminates the results of its research studies and the recommendation of various seminars and workshops conducted by it during the period through 64 publications. The institute brings out two periodicals namely, behavioural sciences and rural development.

Association of Voluntary Agencies for Rural Development

The Association of Voluntary Agencies for Rural Development (AVARD) was established in 1958, to meet the need for a federation to solve problems faced by voluntary agencies within the country. It was registered in the same year under the Societies Registration Act of 1860. It acts as an All India Federation of Voluntary Agencies having member agencies in almost all states and union territories.

Aims and Objectives

The objective of the association is to strengthen voluntary agencies involved in rural development. It aims:

(i) To develop areas of mutual cooperation and understanding among the voluntary agencies, institutions and individuals for the welfare of the rural community.

(ii) To strengthen existing agencies and foster development of new agencies.

(iii) To act as a clearing house for disseminating information and knowledge through arranging seminars, conferences, etc., and by publishing literature like monographs, periodicals, journals, etc., in furtherance of the objects of the association.

(iv) To arrange training of personnel and assist in understanding research and evaluation in the area of rural development.

International Voluntary Organization

Any review of international voluntary organizations runs into a basic terminological difficulty. Since these organizations first appeared on the international scene, a plethora of agencies has grown, each with its own structural and operational peculiarities. "Any international organization which is not established by intergovernmental agreement shall be considered as a non-governmental organization including organizations which accepts members designed by government authorities, provided that such membership does not interfere with the free expression of views of the organizations."

An organization to be considered international, certain things are required:

(i) The agreement by which it is established must include three or more states as parties.

(ii) Its aims must be genuinely international in character with the intention to cover operations in at least three countries.

(iii) Voting power must be such that no one rational group can control the organization.

(iv) There must be a permanent headquarters with provision made for continuity of operation.

(v) Substantial budgetary contributions must come from at least three countries.

Origin and Development

International cooperation in the area of social welfare began in the mid-nineteenth century. The earliest initiatives were motivated by a desire on the part of private charities and public welfare and correctional agencies to confer with each other, and by sharing this experiences to improve their methods of providing charitable and relief services, preventing delinquency, and rehabilitating criminals.

Role of International Voluntary Organization

The role of international voluntary organizations in India has been a matter of some debates. Essentially it can be viewed in three ways:

(a) as a method of religious and ideological instruction and conversion.

(b) as instrument of international charity.

(c) as a catalyst of professional thinking and mode of transfer of development, technology and experience.

The last role, namely, that of a catalyst, has been more palatable, but even this interpretation of the role of an international voluntary organization needs to be recast in order to have greater credibility with the decision-making authorities in the country. So long as the international voluntary organization is not interested in operating purely for the sake of charity or as a medium for disseminating a religious or ideological message, but as a tool for generating understanding between communities and countries at various stages of developments, it is recognized that the international voluntary organization has a bonafide role to play in the country.

Fields of Operation

The yearbook of the union of international organizations lists over a thousand international voluntary organizations. These are classified into 19 categories according to their objectives: The three largest groups are concerned with (i) labour, employers, trade unions, and professionals; (ii) commerce and industry; and (iii) science.

The major fields of operation of international voluntary organizations are: (i) prevention of crime and delinquency; (ii) treatment of offenders and juvenile delinquents; (iii) migration and rehabilitation; (iv) mental health; (v) physically handicapped and other groups of handicapped people; (vi) welfare of vulnerable and weaker groups (such as, women, children, socio-economically handicapped, etc.); and (vii) emergency relief.

Cooperation

India is pledged to the establishment of a new social order, free from all exploitation. The objective before us is to establish a society based on the principles of welfare and democracy; under the prevailing circumstances cooperation is the only alternative for the achievement of this common goal. It is against this background that cooperative has assumed a supreme role in many branches of economic activity especially in rural reconstruction, agriculture, small industry, marketing and processing and supplies.

Meaning of Cooperation

There is nothing complicated about the doctrine of cooperatives. In fact, cooperation is the very basis of human civilization. Mutual help and inter-dependence are the essential ingredients of social life.

"Cooperation is a form of organization in which person voluntarily associate together on the basis of equality for the promotion of their economic interests. Those who come together, have a common economic aim which they cannot achieve by individual and isolated action because of the weakness of the economic position of a large majority of them. This element of individual's weakness is overcome by pooling up their resource, by making self-help effective through mutual aid and by strengthening the bond of moral solidarity between them."

Essential Elements of Cooperation

Cooperation is based on self-help and mutual aid. Its essential elements are as follows:

(1) Cooperation is a voluntary organization.
(2) The members have a common economic aim.
(3) It is a democratic organization based on the principles of "one person, one vote, and decisions by majority".
(4) The profits are distributed among the members in proportion to their respective shares.
(5) The slogan of cooperation is "each for all and all for each".

Principles of Cooperation

Universality

Cooperation makes no distinction of caste or creed, sex or colour, religions or political affiliation. The only distinction which it makes is between good and bad, honest and dishonest, between moral and immoral. Thus, admission to a cooperative society is open to all whether rich or poor, high or low.

Voluntariness

Admission to a cooperative society is absolutely voluntary. Any person who feels the need of joining a cooperative society and enjoying its benefits become its member whenever he likes. He can also leave it at his will, subject to the regulations of the society in the making of which he himself as a member had a hand.

Democratic Spirit

The cooperative society is managed by the members themselves either directly or through their own elected representatives.

Equality

The cooperative society is guided by the principle of equality.

The Basis of Cooperation is Self-Help

It is based on the recognition that man can develop only through his own efforts and therefore, must stand on his own leg.

Mutual Aids

Mutual aid is another basis of cooperation.

Equality and Justice for All

While cooperation stands for the benefits of its members it believes in justice to all in equitable relationship between various sections of the society. It does not believe in exploitation or benefits at the cost of others. In other words, cooperation believes in the general good of the people against the good of any particular society,

Service above Profit

The primary aim of cooperation is to give service to its members. It, therefore, aims at profit only to the extent that is necessary as a business organization and extra profit is distributed to its members in the form of dividend, bonus or rebate.

Meet the Economic Requirements of its Members

Cooperation is also a form of business organization. A cooperative society is a business institution with the object of meeting the economic requirements of its members. It is thus neither a charitable organization nor mere service institution.

Obtain the Material Advantages

Cooperation is the base of social progress where people act together and obtain and share the material benefits.

History of Cooperation in India

Although the cooperative movements in its present shape began in India since 1904, its history in our country is very old. Shelvankar has said that by the end of the 18th century, the ownership of agricultural land centralized in the village community under which the farmers solved the problems of agriculture through mutual cooperation. The tendency of collective efforts and cooperation were clearly visible in such works as construction of wells and tanks.

During the last decade of 19th century, the country was over-taken by poverty, exploitation and political insecurity. The aim of the cooperative was to promote social services and economy and provide credit facilities to the farmers, craftsmen and persons of limited means.

The liability in rural societies was unlimited, while in urban societies it might be limited or unlimited as the members choose.

Cooperative Movement Under the Five-Year Plans

The Five-Year Plans have given an important place to cooperatives as a major form of organization in many branches of economic activity. The main schemes of cooperative development in the Five-Year Plan, therefore, relate to the rebuilding and strengthening of the cooperative credit structure in regard to resource, personnel and procedure. Greater emphasis has been placed on consolidation, eliminating the existing weakness and working for the creation of viable cooperative credit structures.

Classification of Cooperative Societies

The cooperative societies may broadly be classified into the following categories:

(1) Primary societies.
(2) Central societies.

The primary societies have only individuals as members, while the central cooperative societies have both individuals and cooperative societies as members. The smaller units are usually primary in character while larger units specially those at the district or the state level are usually central in character.

Classification According to Functions

Cooperative society may also be classified according to their functions or membership. Classifications on the basis of functions are as follows:

(1) Credit societies.
(2) Non-credit societies.

Credit societies are those whose main function is to advance loans for their members. On the other hand, non-credit societies are those whose main function is other than advancing loans to their members. Non-credit societies may further be classified as follows:

(i) Marketing cooperatives.
(ii) Consumer cooperatives.
(iii) Milk cooperatives.
(v) Housing cooperatives.
(v) Labour cooperatives and so on.

It is thus evident, that cooperative movement in India has been extended to all the important fields of economic activities. About 90 per cent of the villages in India are covered by the cooperative societies.

Commendable progress has been achieved in the field of cooperative credit, cooperative marketing, cooperative processing, storage and cooperative farming.

Micro-Level Planning in Rural Development

After independence, India has adopted the process of planned development with the objective of raising living standards and opening up to the people new opportunities for a richer and more varied life. A specific aim of our planning is to make social services available to the people. Therefore, efforts have been made towards the development of rural people. It is the people who, in the final analysis, are the architects of the progress, even as they are the beneficiaries of this necessity. Investment in the building up of this social capital has to be on a massive scale in a country of the size of India.

Substantial ground has been covered in the Five-Year Plans in providing schools for general education and technical training, medical and public health and family planning facilities, welfare of backward classes and tribes, houses for industrial workers, etc.

Planned Educational Services

Marked progress has been achieved in the extension of educational services through the constitutional directive regarding free and compulsory education up to the age of 14. A number of steps have been taken to fulfil this obligation.

Basic Education

It is this accepted pattern that guides and shapes the educational system at all levels. The National Institute of Basic Education is engaged in carrying out research and offering training and guidance to teachers and administrators of basic education.

Vocational and Technical School Education

A major task in the field of post elementary education is to provide large variety of vocational courses for children who do not intend to continue their general education beyond the elementary stage.

Rural Higher Education

On the recommendations of the Rural Higher Education Committee, a National Council for Higher Education in rural areas was established in 1956 to advise the government on all matters relating to the development of rural higher education.

The post-graduate diploma in rural economics and cooperation, and rural sociology and community development programme were also started.

Adult Education

Adult education aims at providing education to the adult population for the betterment of their lives and for creating in them an urge for change from traditional to progressive society, with faith in themselves and the future of the country.

Planned Health Services

There has been steady improvement in the general health services. Health is the primary need of the community in mountain areas. In 1977, the WHO declared that all governments should aim at attainment of a level of health by all citizens of the world by the year 2000, that will promote rural people to lead a socially and economically productive life, that is, health for all by the year 2000. The WHO has defined health as a state of complete physical, mental, social well-being and not merely absence of desires or infirmity.

Rural women are generally living in extreme poverty with arduous workload. They suffer from economic deprivation and health problems. Poor nutritional status, social cultural customs, high altitude, paucity of safe drinking water, food habits become the cause of chronic respiratory diseases, worm infections, communicable diseases and many more. To tackle such kind of health problems and diseases, rural development ministry has taken several steps and planned innumerable programmes.

Family Planning and Welfare

Overpopulation is the biggest problem of today in our country. Family planning was adopted in 1952, as an official programme. In the Five-Year Plans steps were taken to tackle this overpopulation. "The objective of stabilizing the growth of population over a reasonable period must be at the very centre of planned development."

The programme aims at a substantial levelling down of the population growth rate as soon as possible and for that purpose to reduce the annual birth rate from 40 to 25 per thousand of population within the next decade. The operational goals are: adoption of family planning by the people as a ways of life, through group planning of the small family norm, personal knowledge of family planning methods and ready availability of supplies and services.

Planned Employment Services

The employment services, started in 1945, consists of a network of employment exchanges, each staffed by trained personnel. The employment exchanges provide placement facilities to all categories of employment seekers and discharge certain special responsibilities, such as providing employment assistance to physically handicapped, ex-servicemen, Scheduled Castes, tribes, professional and executive offices. In addition to this placement activity, the employment service also carried on other functions such as collection and dissemination of employment market information and conducting surveys and studies in the field of employment and occupational research. In order to divert the educated youth to channels of gainful employment, the service renders vocational guidance and career advice to such work seekers.

Appropriate Technology

The supply of right kind of technology to different segments of society, particularly those living in vast rural areas is critical for mitigating the inequities and promote growth. Any technology strategy should concentrate on preserving the rural bio-diversity, and any technology prescription should in principle be pro-poor, pro-nature and pro-employment. Rural India cannot be a market for technology propelled forces and market generation of employment; simpler handling of tools is relevant for rural India. Development of technologies which contribute to improvement in farming, food, transport and energy will be imperative for rural development.

Schumacher, a German development economist said "I know of no better way of changing the 'system' than by putting into the world a new type of technology by which small people can make themselves productive and relatively independent." The choice of technology is important as we are living in a world whose character has been defined by increasing domination of technology. It is the growth of technology that led to war between nations and then the decision was to convert the war technology to peace technology; this is often political and value-loaded. Under the current circumstances, technology should promote sustainable development, which requires primarily an ethical shift in favour of the poor and nature. The choice of technology must be participatory. It is traditional, indigenous and appropriate technology that is relevant for rural India. The modern technology, born out of the concept of modernism, breeds competition, selfishness and greed. Technology should contribute to improvement in farming, food, transport, energy and local economic life.

The information and communication technology which is the latest fashion in modern technology, is necessary for rural India. Rural India can live peacefully and grow comfortably with traditional wisdom and technology.

Communication in Rural Development

The communication or media have to bring a change in rural people's approach and instil in them the importance of various issues concerning rural development like water harvesting, rural housing and industries. The media have to reorient their programmes for the rural community and generate new approaches to discuss the problems of the rural areas in broader perspective.

It is true, that what we mean by a technology for the rural areas is its application to the farming sector, and this has to be recognized on all hands. For many years now, the radio in the form of the national network of All India Radio, and ever since the TV medium began to penetrate the rural areas the national network of Doordarshan have been putting programmes for the benefits of farmers. We must recognize that media have succeeded to great extent and wherever they have gone deep into the problems of the farming community, and fully identified themselves with the farmers, this success has been more marked.

Watershed Management in Rural Development

Agriculture in Indian contributes nearly 30 per cent of net domestic product and employs 70 per cent of the people. Undoubtedly, agriculture is the backbone for the development of our economy. Out of 323 million hectares of the geographical area in India, 123.6 million is cultivated. Out of this 123.6 million, only 40 per cent of the land has fully or partially assured irrigation. The other 60 per cent is either rain-fed or non-cultivable.

There is a general perception that lack of water resources is the main barrier to improved productivity. However, studies confirm that it is the effective utilization of water and not the quantum of rainfall which is needed for productivity. So, it can be rightly said that the enhancement of productivity and bringing more lands under irrigation is the need of the hour, given the phenomenal growth in the demand for agricultural commodities.

Watershed committees comprising villagers both the farmers and the landless poor undertake participatory watershed development plans in the demarcated areas. Under the plan, water harvesting is adopted as the main strategy to improve agricultural productivity. The 'ridge to valley' treatment of water is generally taken up. The treatment includes the interception of run off water with water harvesting structures, soil and moisture consumption works (like contour bounding, rock filled dams, gully control structures) and water harvesting structures (check dams, percolation tanks, farm ponds, etc).

Objectives of Watershed Projects

(i) To develop and adopt a sustainable and profitable agricultural system through farmers' active participation.
(ii) To give a boost for large scale farming involving high value crops for meeting domestic and export requirements.
(iii) Deep ploughing for improved infiltration of rainwater, thereby increasing water storage capacity of soil.
(iv) Drip irrigation system for ensuring optimal irrigation.
(v) Sprinkler irrigation system for timely and effective land preparation.

Participatory Rural Development

When the goal of development is overall improvement in the quality of life, people have to participate in all stages of the development process. The job of Panchayati Raj Institutions is to ensure people's participation at different stages of rural development.

So far the stress has been on details of the programmes taken up for rural development. Basic approach to rural development and deeper behavioural and attitudinal issues have already been deeply analyzed. There is an impression that development means just creation of infrastructure. As a result of this, development could not become need based and relevant to local rural circumstances. The development of human resources have been neglected.

The United Nations Development Programme (UNDP) report 1993, has observed that people's participation is becoming central issue of our times. In India, the importance of people's participation in development has been recognized. The community development programme was initiated in 1952, to ensure widespread participation by the people in all developmental programmes. The Panchayati Raj Institutions ensure people's participation in local planning in implementation of programmes. Even the cooperative system aims at popular participation.

Meaning and Scope

People's participation implies participation at all stages of the programmes, viz., planning, formulation, implementation, decision-making, sharing the benefits of development, monitoring and evaluation. There is a strong case for people's participation in the process of need identification and their prioritization, planning and implementation.

Participation is broadly of three types:

(i) where people come forward on their own to participate without any external support and force.

(ii) where people participate because of some mandate and official endorsements and where people participate because it has been made compulsory and its violation may invite coercion.

(iii) popular participation may be either wide or narrow; we can visualize four situations.

- a small portion participation in limited context.
- a small portion of popular participating in diverse context.
- a substantial portion of population participating in limited context.
- a major portion of population participating in a wide variety of contexts.

Benefits

The major objectives of rural development programmes are: accelerated economic growth, wider participation and most equitable distribution of its gains. Many agricultural and rural development programmes leads to a fall in the incidence of leakages, an increase in the political awareness of the people, easier mobilization of local resources and empowerment of the socially and economically disadvantaged people.

People's involvement ensures strict supervision at the cutting edge level of the administration. Participation also enables implementing meaningful and predictive programmes and not softer projects. People's participation should be encouraged owing to the fact that people in the villages know their needs better than government officials working at block, district and state levels.

The main objectives of people's participation include:

(i) better planning and implementation of rural development programmes.

(ii) mobilization of additional resources required for rural development programmes.

(iii) empowering the people, particularly the poor to play an effective role in rural development.

Some Problems

Ensuring people's participation in the development process is no easy task. There are some problems which includes the following:

(1) Rural people generally suffer from low level of awareness about the various development programmes.

(2) Participation is handicapped by village factionalism, adverse rural power structure and vested interests.

(3) Non-involvement of the local leadership in various stages of planning.

(4) The unhelpful attitude of the bureaucracy.

(5) Inadequate use of the mass media.

If communities are called upon to perform tasks while the control and decision-making remains with development workers from outside, then people's active participation may not be possible. Indian villages lack community character. They consist of heterogeneous groups with conflicting interests. The situation worsened because of the social factors like religion, caste, unscientific values and low status of women. The oppressive and hierarchical nature of the social factors have divided rural India to such a point that common interest of community are unthinkable. Of course, the problems can be easily overcome, if grass-root institutions are strengthened and the cooperation of voluntary agencies is sought.

Measures Needed

The extent of people's participation in rural development programmes largely depends on the extent of decentralization in planning. The production relations in rural India are also not favourable for the poor. The majority of the poor do not have any assets like land; social relations naturally suffers. Therefore, relative 'equity' is a pre-requisite for the involvement of people in the process of developing. Absence of this renders participation of weaker sections almost impossible. Some measures to secure people's participation in rural development should include:

(1) The programmes should be based on the felt needs of the people.
(2) The change-agent or extension worker should enthuse and motivate people to participate.
(3) Democratic leadership is highly essential to ensure people's participation.
(4) Extension worker should play a positive role in ensuring peoples participation.
(5) Voluntary organizations which are close to local people and situations should be encouraged to ensure people's participation.

Popular participation would be effective when the programmes follow bottom-up approach. People are provided correct, clear and complete information regarding the programme. People are educated about their rights. A sense of ownership and responsibility are promoted.

Unless the poor can build up an adequate institutional framework to support and protect their activities, they will again be dominated by the more powerful in the villages.

Participatory Rural Appraisal

In recent years, importance has been given to Participatory Rural Appraisal (PRA). The term 'PRA' probably was first introduced in Kenya to describe the village level investigations, analysis, and planning undertaken by the national environment secretariat in association with Clark University. The PRA is a family of approaches and methods to enable rural people to share, enhance and analyse their knowledge of life conditions to plan and to act. It can be viewed as a process of involving local people in the analysis and interpretation of a rural situation. The PRA is not a new idea. It evolved from an old methodology that mobilizes communities. It enables multi-disciplinary teams to join with village leaders to gather data, assess village needs and priorities, and on the basis of this, draw up a village resources management and enable local institutions like panchayats to cooperate.

The principles of PRA are:

(1) A reversal of learning, i.e., learning from people.
(2) Learning rapidly and progressively with flexible use of methods, improvization and cross-checking.
(3) Triangulating, meaning using a range of methods, types of information, etc.
(4) Seeking diversity, i.e., seeking variability rather than averages.
(5) Self-critical awareness and responsibility.
(6) Sharing of informations and ideas.

Participation and Rural Development

The ultimate goal of development is integrated and balanced sector, spatial and societal development; but in spite of four decades of rural development efforts, the lot of the vast majority of the rural poor has not improved very much. The major reason for this state of affairs is the lack of personal and direct participation of village folk in the process of accelerated and sustained development. We need to generate resources for rural development, through a self-help development process with equity and justice in order to achieve decentralized, bottom up process with wide participation. A majority of rural people do not know the 'what', the 'why' and the 'how' of the people's participation in development activities in order to drive maximum benefits from accelerated socio-economic growth and development efforts. However, it is imperative to evolve a precise and comprehensive definition of the concept of participation in rural development of those who are supposed to benefit, and design a methodology for enlisting personnel and direct participation of the rural people.

Popular participation generally means people sharing power at an individual and collective level in making decisions over matters that effect their lives. Inherent in this meaning is respect for the capacity of people to develop their own awareness of their needs and to act in their own interest.

As a contemporary ideology and practice, people's participation, therefore, must involve empowerment of the masses and have as one of its goal the reduction of inequality of power and also the growth of personal power. People are not seen as objects to be acted upon, but as objects who act on their own behalf, and what changes in this process is not the system but also the people.

No programme can be a success without the involvement of the people. The main reason for the failure of various programmes for rural uplift like the community development programme, national extension service, etc., was the non-participation of people and their representative at the planning and execution stages. At the same time, it has been seen that non-involvement of people in the development programmes also has a great concern and challenge to rural development.

People's participation implies participation in decision-making, process, viz., planning, formulation, implementation, decision-making, monitoring, evaluation and sharing, the benefits of development. According to Benninger (1991), "people's participation may be described as taking part in the events taking place in the community or large area". People's participation plays a vital role in achieving comprehensive rural development. It is the need of the hour to involve people from grass-roots level for sustainable rural development. Power with greater choice and voice is essential.

Rural community development has been talked about since our independence in 1947. A large number of rural development programmes have been taken up during the last many years, but they have suffered from basic deficiencies like inadequate inputs of education and relevant technology and absence of an efficient, honest and all-inclusive delivery system. It is strongly recommended that the know-how and expertise available with the scientific and technological institutions in the country should be fully exploited in an integrated manner for micro-level planning and execution of both short-term and long-term projects in a selected region within the framework of a social cybernetic model. To avoid adhocism and inconsistency in programmes and projects and to ensure a well coordinated and integrated scientific approach with adequate technological input for overall development of the people in all the spheres of activity, a 'task force' approach is being advocated which also possesses a sound delivery system.

The ultimate goal of development is integrated and balanced sectoral, and societal development, but in spite of four decades of rural development efforts, the lot of the vast majority of the rural poor has not improved very much. The major reason for this state of affairs is the lack of personal and direct participation of village folk in the process of accelerated and sustained development. We need to generate resources for rural development, through a self-help development process with equity and justice in order to achieve a decentralized, bottom up process with wide participation. A major contributing factor for this state of affair is that majority of rural people, do not know 'the what' 'the why' and 'the how' of people's participation in development activities in order to derive maximum benefits from accelerated socio-economic growth and development effort.

The media have to play a great role to bring change in the approach of rural people and instil in them the importance of various issues concerning rural development like water harvesting, rural housing and industries. The media have to re-orient their programmes for the rural community and generate new approaches to discuss the problems of the rural areas in broader perspective. Communication technology and media which are steadily improving and expanding are to be treated only as tools and means and not an end in themselves. Development also means change and the involves attitudinal and behavioural changes, besides material and environmental changes.

Rural development is a comprehensive mix of activities which include agricultural growth, putting up of economic and social infrastructure, village planning, public health, education and functional literacy, communication, etc. In this multi-pronged effort involving development thus encompasses both spatial and functional integration of all relevant programmes bearing on increased agricultural production and reduction of unemployment and provision of gainful employment among the rural people.

Bibliography

Agrawal, A.N., *Indian Economy, Problems of Development and Planning*, New Delhi: Wishwa Prakashan, 2002.

Ahuja, Ram, *Crime Against Women*, Jaipur: Rawat Publications, 1987.

—, *Social Problems in India*, Jaipur and New Delhi: Rawat Publications, 1999.

Alfred, J. Kahn, *Theory and Practice of Social Planning*, New York: Russel Sage Foundation, 1969.

Anderson, Nels, *The Urban Community*, New York: Holt, Rinehart and Winston, 1959.

ARC Reports of the Study Team, Financial Administration, May 1967, Chapter III.

Arnold and Feldman, *Organizational Behaviour*, New Delhi: McGraw Hill, 1987.

Avasthi, Amresh W., *Public Administration*, Agra: Lakshmi Narain Agrawal, 1995.

Barnard, Chester I., *The Functions of the Executive*, Cambridge: Harvard University Press, 1968.

Beverage, S.W.H., *Voluntary Action: A Report on Methods of Social Advances*, London, 1946.

Bhambhri, C.P., *Public Administration*, Meerut City: Jai Prakash and Public Education, 1993.

Bhatia, S.K., *Personnel Management and Industrial Relations*, New Delhi: Deep & Deep Publications, 1988.

Bhattacharya, Amit Madhab, *Industrial Labour in Economic Development*, New Delhi: Criterion Publication, 1986.

Bhushan, Vidya, *An Introduction to Sociology*, Allahabad: Kitab Mahal Publication, 2001.

Biddle W. William, *Encouraging Community Development*, New Delhi: Light and Life Publisher, 1968.

Blood, David E. and Joyce, V. Lyons, *Economic Implication of AIDS in Asia*, UNDP, 1993.

Bose, A.B., *Urbanization in India*, Mumbai: Academic Press, 1970.

Bottomore, T.B., *Society: A Guide to Problems and Literature*, London: Routledge and Kegan Paul, 1966.

Brech, E.F.L., *Principles and Practice of Management*, London: Longmans, Green & Co., 1965.

Breese, Gerald, *Urbanization in Newly Developing Countries*, New Delhi: Prentice Hall of India, 1969.

Chaudhary, D.P., *Profits of Voluntary Action in Social Welfare and Development*, New Delhi: Sidhartha Press, 1981.

—, *Social Welfare Administration through Voluntary Agencies*, New Delhi: Atma Ram and Sons, 1962.

Clinard, Marshal B., *Slums and Community Development*, New York: The Free Press, 1957.

Coleman, James C., *Abnormal Psychology and Modern Life*, Mumbai: Taraporevala Sons & Co, 1982.

Dahama, O.P., *Social Organisation and Planning*, Jabalpur, 1973.

Dahama, O.P., *Social Organization and Planned Social Change*, Agra: Association of Schools of Social Work in India, 1973.

Datt, R., *Indian Economy*, New Delhi: S. Chand and Company Ltd., 1965.

Davis, James, *Society and Law*, The Free Press, 1962.

Davis, Keith and Scott, William G., *Human Relations and Organisational Behaviour*, New Delhi: Tata McGraw Hill Publication, 1975.

De'Souza, Alfred, *Urban Growth and Urban Planning*, New Delhi: Indian Social Institute, 1983.

Desai, Neera, *A Decade of Women's Movement in India*, Mumbai: Himalaya Publishing House, 1988.

Desai, V., *Rural Development*, Vol. I-IV, Bombay: Himalaya Publishing House, 1988.

Dessler, Garg, *Human Resource Management*, New Delhi: Prentice Hall, 1997.

Dhillon, D.S. and Hansra, B.S., *Development Not Welfare*, Social Welfare, Vol. XI, No. 5, August, 1993.

Dinkmeyer, Don C., *Child Development*, New Delhi: Prentice Hall, 1967.

Dubey, S.N., *Administration of Social Welfare Programmes in India*, Bombay: Somaiya Publications, 1973.

Dubin, Robert, *Human Relations in Administration*, New Delhi: Prentice Hall of India, 1970.

Encyclopaedia of Social Work in India, Vol. I, New Delhi: Ministry of Welfare, Government of India, 1987.

Encyclopaedia of Social Work in India, Vol. II, New Delhi: Ministry of Welfare, Government of India, 1987.

Encyclopaedia of Social Work in India, Vol. III, New Delhi: Ministry of Welfare, Government of India, 1987.

Encyclopaedia of Social Work in India, Vol. IV, New Delhi: Ministry of Welfare, Government of India, 1987.

Fayol, Henri, *General and Industrial Management*, London: Sir Issac Pitman & Sons Ltd., 1949.

Ferguson, A., Elizabeth, *Social Work*, New York: Toronto, 1975.

Fernando, S., Emmanuel, M.S.W., *Project from Problems*, Mumbai, 1999.

Flippo, E.B., *Personnel Management*, New York: McGraw Hill, 1984.

—, *Principles of Personnel Management*, New York: McGraw Hill, 1966.

Forder, Anthony, *Concept of Social Administration: A Framework for Analysis*, London: Routledge and Kegan Paul, 1972.

Ghosh, S.K., *Indian Women through the Ages*, New Delhi: Ashish Publishing House, 1989.

Goel, S.L. and Jain, R.K., *Social Welfare Administration*, Vol. I & II, New Delhi: Deep & Deep Publications, 1988.

Gomes, James, *Project from Problems*, Mumbai: April, 1999.

Goode, William J., *The Family*, New Delhi: Prentice Hall of India, 1965.

Gore, M.S., *Social Work and Social Work Education*, Mumbai: Asia Publishing House, 1965.

—, *Some Aspects of Social Development*, Hong Kong: Department of Social Work University, 1973.

Gulick, Luther, *Science, Values and Public Administration*, New York: Institute of Public Administration, 1937.

Gupta, Rajan, *Implementing Human Resources Development*, Jaipur: Rawat Publications, 1990.

Hall, R.M., *Organisations: Structure and Process*, Englewood Cliffs: Prentice Hall, 1972.

Handy, Charles, *Understanding Voluntary Organizations*, London: Penguin Books, 1990.

Hardiman, Margaret and James Midgley, *The Social Dimensions of Development*, London: John Willey and Sons, 1982.

Haripad R., Subramania Iyer, *Development and People's Participation*, Kurukshetra, No. 4, January 1995.

Harrel, Thomas W., *Industrial Psychology*, London: Oxford and IBH Publishing Co., 1964.

Jacob, K.K., *Social Policy in India*, Udaipur: Himanshu Publications, 1989.

Jain, S.C., *Community Development and Panchayati Raj in India*, Bombay: Allied Publications, 1967.

Jain, S.P. and Krishnamurty, Reddy, *Rural Organisations*, Hyderabad: National Institute of Rural Development, 1980.

Johnson, Harry M., *Sociology*, New Delhi: Allied Publication, 1995.

Joysuriya, D.C., *HIV, Law, Ethics and Human Rights*, New Delhi: UNDP, 1995.

Koontz, H. and Weihrich, *Essentials of Management*, New Delhi: Tata McGraw Hill Publication, 1998.

—, *Management*, Tokyo: McGraw Hill, 1993.

Krech, David, Richard and Ballachey, *Individual in Society*, Berkeley: University of California Press, 1962.

Kulkarni, P.D., *Social Policy and Social Development in India*, Chennai: Association of Schools of Social Work in India, 1979.

Kumar, D.R., *Indian Society and Social Institution*, Agra: Lakshmi Narayan Agrawal, 1995.

Kumar, R., *Child Development in India*, Vol. I & II, New Delhi: Lok Sabha Secretariat, 1990.

Kumari Bajpai, Rajendra, *Encyclopaedia of Social Work in India*, Vol. II, New Delhi Press, 1987.

Kurukshetra, Vol. 46, November, 2002.

Likert, Rensis, *The Human Organisation*, New York: McGraw Hill, 1967.

MacIver, R.M. and Page, H.C., *Society: An Introductory Analysis*, London: Macmillan, 1955.

Madan, G.R., *India's Development Villages*, Lucknow: Print House India, 1983.

—, *India's Social Transformation*, Vol. II, New Delhi: Allied Publication, 1984.

—, *Indian Social Problems*, Vol. 1 & 2, New Delhi: Allied Publication, 1994.

Maheshwari, A., *Public Administration*, Agra: Lakshmi Narain Agrawal Publication, 1995.

Mandelbaum, D.G., *Society in India*, Vol. I, Mumbai: Popular Prakashan, 1970.

Marge, Berer and Sunada, Rai, *Women and HIV/AIDS: An International Resource Book*, Pandora, 1993.

Merton, R.K., *Social Theory and Social Structure*, New York: The Free Press, 1957.

Misra, K.K., *Political Theory*, New Delhi: S. Chand and Company Ltd., 1936.

Misra, S.K., *Development and Planning*, Mumbai: Himalaya Publishing House, 1986.

Mittal, A.K., *Personnel Management and Industrial Relations*, UP: Sanjeeva Prakashan, 1998.

Mohapatra, M.K., *Indian Constitution and Government*, Cuttack, 1983.

Mooney, James, *The Principles of Organisation*, New York: Harper and Brothers, 1947.

Mukerjee, K.K. and Mukherjee Sutapa, *Guide Book for Strengthening Voluntary Organisations*, Ghaziabad: Gram Niyojan Kendra, 1989.

Mydral, G., *Challenge of World Poverty*, London: Allen Lane, 1970.

Northwood, L.K., *Social Welfare and Urban Development*, USA: National Association of Social Workers, 1966.

Odiorne, George S., *Personnel Management by Objectives*, New York: Righard DI, 1971.

Ogburn, W.F., *Social Change*, New York, 1922.

Pareek, Udai, *Managing Transitions: The HRD Response*, New Delhi: Tata McGraw Hill, 1992.

Parvi, Khorshed M., *Challenge of AIDS*, National Book Trust, 1992.

Pfiffner, John M. and Shrewood Frank P., *Administrative Organisation*, New Delhi: Prentice Hall of India, 1968.

Raj, D. Sunder, *Rural Development Need of People's Participation*, Third Concept, Vol. 14, No. 158.

Rao, M.R., *The Development of Indian Policy, Light and Life*, New Delhi: Allied Publishers, 1978.

Reddy, Narayana G. and Reddy, Narayana S., *Women and Child Development*, Allahabad: Chugh Publication, 1984.

Reddy, O'Chinnappa, *Problems and Concerns of Indian Women*, New Delhi: ABC Publishing House, 1987.

Robins, Stephen P., *Organizational Behaviour*, New Delhi: Prentice Hall, 1996.

Ross, Murray G., *Community Organization*, London: Harper and Row, 1967.

Sachdeva, D.R., *Indian Social Welfare Administration in India*, Allahabad: Kitab Mahal Publication, 2000.

Sachdeva, D.R., *An Introduction to Sociology*, Allahabad: Kitab Mahal, 1999.

Saksena, C.S., *Business Administration and Management*, Agra: Sahitya Bhawan Publication, 1983.

Sapru, R.K., *Development Administrations*, New Delhi: Deep & Deep Publications, 1986.

Seth, M.L., *Principles of Economics*, New Delhi, 1995.

Sharma, R.D., *Organizational Management*, New Delhi: Light and Light Publishers, 1978.

Sharma, R.N., *Urban Sociology*, Delhi: Surjeet Publications, 1993.

Singh, K., *Indian Social System*, Lucknow: Prakashan Kendra, 1996.

—, *Social Work Theory and Practice*, Lucknow: Prakashan Kendra, 1996.

Srinivas, M.N., *Social Change in Modern India*, Berkeley: University of California Press, 1966.

Stahl, C. Gleen, *Public Personnel Administration*, New Delhi: IBH Publishing Co., 1975.

Streeten and Lipton, *The Crisis of Indian Planning*, London: Oxford University Press.

Stroup, H.H., *Social Work: An Introduction to the Field*, New Delhi: Eurasia Publishing House, 1965.

Sunday Times of India, December 8, 2002.

The Hindu, December 29, 2002.

The Voice, July 31, 2002.

The World Book Encyclopaedia, London: World Book International, Vol. 4, 1997.

Thudipara, Jacob Z., *Urban Community Development*, Jaipur and New Delhi: Rawat Publications, 1993.

Tiffn, Joseph and McCorarich, Ernest., *Industrial Psychology*, Mumbai: Asia Publishing House, 1973.

Timbergen, Jan, *Development Planning*, London.

Titmus, Richard M., *Commitment to Welfare*, London: George Allen and Unwin, 1968.

Tiwa Ramesh, C. Shrivastava, NGOs Securing People's Participation for Progress, Social Welfare, February, 2000.

Toppo, Amritlal, *Women in Our Society*, Patna, 2002.

Tripathi, P.C. and Reddy, P.N., *Principles of Management*, New Delhi: Tata McGraw Hill, 1983.

Turner, Roy, *India's Urban Future*, Bombay: Oxford University Press, 1982.

Vashist, Purshotam D., *Raj to the Indian Raj*, New Delhi: RNC Print and Publishing Co., 1989.

Visvanathan, S.S., *Performance Budgeting in Government: An Illustrative Guide*, New Delhi: IIPA, September 1972, pp. 1-2.

Voluntary Action Network India: State Panchayat Act, New Delhi: VANI, 1995.

Wadhwani, M.R., *Elements of Social and Economic Life in India*, Mumbai: Shri H.A. Sheth.

White, Leonard D., *Introduction to the Study of Public Administration*, New Delhi: Eurasia Publishing House, 1965.

Yoder, Dale, *Personnel Management and Industrial Relations*, New Delhi: Prentice Hall of India, 1974.

Yojana, October, 2002.

Index